Colonels in Blue —
Michigan, Ohio
and West Virginia

Colonels in Blue — Michigan, Ohio and West Virginia

A Civil War Biographical Dictionary

ROGER D. HUNT

McFarland & Company, Inc., Publishers
Jefferson, North Carolina, and London

LIBRARY OF CONGRESS CATALOGUING-IN-PUBLICATION DATA

Hunt, Roger D.
Colonels in blue — Michigan, Ohio and West Virginia : a Civil War biographical dictionary / Roger D. Hunt.
p.   cm.
Includes bibliographical references and index.

ISBN 978-0-7864-6155-4
softcover : 50# alkaline paper ∞

1. United States — History — Civil War, 1861–1865 — Biography — Dictionaries.
2. Michigan — History — Civil War, 1861–1865 — Biography — Dictionaries.
3. Ohio — History — Civil War, 1861–1865 — Biography — Dictionaries. 4. West Virginia — History — Civil War, 1861–1865 — Biography — Dictionaries. 5. United States. Army — Officers — History — Civil War, 1861–1865 — Dictionaries. I. Title.
E467.H893   2011   355.0092'2 — dc22 [B]   2011005373

BRITISH LIBRARY CATALOGUING DATA ARE AVAILABLE

© 2011 Roger D. Hunt. All rights reserved

No part of this book may be reproduced or transmitted in any form or by any means, electronic or mechanical, including photocopying or recording, or by any information storage and retrieval system, without permission in writing from the publisher.

On the cover: (*counterclockwise from top*) Horace Park, Norval E. Welch (courtesy of Steve Meadow) and James H. Dayton (L. M. Strayer Collection, copied by Richard A. Baumgartner); background image and eagle insignia © 2011 Shutterstock.

Manufactured in the United States of America

McFarland & Company, Inc., Publishers
Box 611, Jefferson, North Carolina 28640
www.mcfarlandpub.com

In memory of
Benedict R. Maryniak
(aka the Rev. Philos G. Cook)
(1947–2009)

Table of Contents

Acknowledgments
ix

Introduction
1

Ohio
Regiments 3
Biographies 19

Michigan
Regiments 137
Biographies 141

West Virginia
Regiments 182
Biographies 184

Bibliography
197

Index of Names
213

Acknowledgments

Although I appreciate the contributions of all of the individuals in the following list, I want to mention a few whose contributions to this volume have been especially noteworthy. The energy and expertise of Larry Strayer has been a major factor in the successful search for images of Ohio colonels. Dale Niesen, Mike Waskul, and Bob Coch have taken the lead in locating images in Michigan. Richard Wolfe has performed a similar role in West Virginia. Richard Baumgartner, Rick Carlile, Henry Deeks, Perry Frohne, Thomas Harris, Steve Meadow, and Brad Pruden have been especially helpful in providing elusive photographs and valuable information. Mike Winey, Randy Hackenburg, and Dr. Richard Sommers have provided ready access to the unparalleled photo archives of the U.S. Army Military History Institute during the past 30 years. Alan Aimone has been equally hospitable in providing access to the outstanding collections at the U.S. Military Academy Library.

Jill M. Abraham, National Archives, Washington, DC
Alan C. Aimone, U.S. Military Academy Library, West Point, NY
Michael Albanese, Kendall, NY
Gil Barrett, New Bern, NC
Richard A. Baumgartner, Huntington, WV
Martin Bertera, Southgate, MI
Everitt Bowles, Woodstock, GA
Mike Brackin, Manchester, CT
Timothy R. Brookes, East Liverpool, OH
Rick Brown, Leesburg, VA
Paul J. Brzozowski, Fairfield, CT
Matt Burr, Bellevue, OH
David L. Callihan, Dryden, NY
Robert Cammaroto, Alexandria, VA
Nan J. Card, Rutherford B. Hayes Presidential Center, Fremont, OH
Richard F. Carlile, Dayton, OH
William H. Carr, Mason, MI
Michael A. Cavanaugh, Bethlehem, PA
Robert M. Coch, Brownstown, MI
Henry Deeks, Ashburnham, MA
John E. Ellzey, Yazoo City, MS
Jacqueline T. Eubanks, Stuart, FL
Jerry Everts, Lambertville, MI
David D. Finney, Howell, MI
Linda Cunningham Fluharty, Baton Rouge, LA
Perry M. Frohne, Oshkosh, WI
John Fuller, Columbia, MD
William A. Gladstone, West Palm Beach, FL
Gilbert Gonzalez, Rutherford B. Hayes Presidential Center, Fremont, OH
Peter Good, Athens, OH
John P. Gurnish, Mogadore, OH
Randy Hackenburg, Boiling Springs, PA
Thomas Harris, New York, NY
Lisa Hess, Ross County Historical Society, Chillicothe, OH
Scott N. Hilts, Arcade, NY
Michael A. Hogle, Okemos, MI
Craig T. Johnson, Towson, MD
Alan Jutzi, The Huntington Library, San Marino, CA
Dennis M. Keesee, Westerville, OH
Jeff Kowalis, Orland Park, IL
Michael Kraus, Pittsburgh, PA
John W. Kuhl, Pittstown, NJ
Kenneth L. Lawrence, Orwell, OH
John Cass Lenahan, Sr., Tonganoxie, KS
Mary Beth Linne', National Archives, Washington, DC
Robert F. MacAvoy, Clark, NJ
Michael J. McAfee, Newburgh, NY
Edward McGuire, New York State Library, Albany, NY
Marcus S. McLemore, Poland, OH
Steven J. Meadow, Midland, MI

Acknowledgments

Mike Medhurst, Kansas City, MO
Marie Melchiori, Vienna, VA
Julie K. Meyerle, Archives of Michigan, Lansing
Tom Molocea, North Lima, OH
Malgosia Myc, Bentley Historical Library, Ann Arbor, MI
David A. Neuhardt, Dayton, OH
David M. Neville, Export, PA
Dale R. Niesen, South Rockwood, MI
Howard L. Norton, Vilonia, AR
John E. Norvell, Canandaigua, NY
Olaf, Berkeley, CA
Ronn Palm, Kittanning, PA
David K. Parks, Utica, MI
Nicholas P. Picerno, Bridgewater, VA
Rev. Linda C. Pope, Hartshorne, OK
James Quinlan, Alexandria, VA
Edmund J. Raus, Jr., Manassas, VA
David L. Richards, Gettysburg, PA
Jeffrey I. Richman, Brooklyn, NY
Stephen B. Rogers, Ithaca, NY
Paul Russinoff, Baltimore, MD
John C. Rutherford, Springfield, MO
Donald K. Ryberg, Westfield, NY
Patrick A. Schroeder, Daleville, VA
Alan J. Sessarego, Gettysburg, PA
Linda Showalter, Marietta College Library, Marietta, OH
John Sickles, Merrillville, IN
Ann K. Sindelar, Western Reserve Historical Society, Cleveland, OH
Sam Small, Gettysburg, PA
Wes Small, Gettysburg, PA
Timothy H. Smith, Gettysburg, PA
Dr. Richard J. Sommers, U.S. Army Military History Institute, Carlisle, PA
Philip W. Stichter, Columbus, OH
Larry M. Strayer, Dayton, OH
Karl E. Sundstrom, North Riverside, IL
David W. Taylor, Sylvania, OH
Noel W. Tenney, Upshur County Historical Society, Buckhannon, WV
Henry R. Timman, Firelands Historical Society, Norwalk, OH
Daniel C. Toomey, Linthicum, MD
Ken C. Turner, Ellwood City, PA
Robert J. Van Dorn, Findlay, OH
Michael W. Waskul, Ypsilanti, MI
George Wilkinson, Dexter, MI
Michael J. Winey, Mechanicsburg, PA
Richard A. Wolfe, Bridgeport, WV
Buck Zaidel, Cromwell, CT
Dave Zullo, Lake Monticello, VA

I am also indebted to the staffs of the following libraries for their capable assistance:

Akron-Summit County Public Library, Akron, OH
Archives of Michigan, Lansing
Bentley Historical Library, University of Michigan, Ann Arbor, MI
Burton Public Library, Burton, OH
Cadiz Public Library, Cadiz, OH
Center for Archival Collections, Bowling Green State University, Bowling Green, OH
Charles W. Gibson Public Library, Buckhannon, WV
Chillicothe & Ross County Public Library, Chillicothe, OH
Cincinnati Historical Society, Cincinnati, OH
Civil War Library & Museum, Philadelphia, PA
Clark County Public Library, Springfield, OH
Colorado Historical Society, Denver, CO
Connecticut State Library, Hartford, CT
Coshocton Public Library, Coshocton, OH
Dearborn Historical Museum, Dearborn, MI
East Liverpool Historical Society, East Liverpool, OH
E. P. Foster Library, Ventura, CA
Family History Library, Salt Lake City, UT
Firelands Historical Society, Norwalk, OH
Grand Rapids Public Library, Grand Rapids, MI
The Huntington Library, San Marino, CA
Jordaan Memorial Library, Larned, KS
Kalamazoo Public Library, Kalamazoo, MI
Library of Congress, Washington, DC
Mansfield/Richland County Public Library, Mansfield, OH
Marietta College Library, Marietta, OH
Meigs County Public Library, Pomeroy, OH
Middletown Public Library, Middletown, OH
Minnesota Historical Society, St. Paul, MN
Morrison County Historical Society, Little Falls, MN
Napoleon Public Library, Napoleon, OH
National Archives, Washington, DC
National Society Daughters of the American Revolution, Washington, DC
New England Historic Genealogical Society, Boston, MA
New Hampton Public Library, New Hampton, IA
New Jersey State Archives, Trenton, NJ
New York Genealogical and Biographical Society, New York, NY
The New-York Historical Society, New York, NY
New York State Library, Albany, NY
Norwalk Public Library, Norwalk, OH
Oakland County Pioneer and Historical Society, Pontiac, MI
Ohio Genealogical Society, Mansfield, OH
Ohio Historical Society, Columbus, OH
Ottawa Public Library, Ottawa, KS
Public Library of Steubenville and Jefferson County, Steubenville, OH
Reed Memorial Library, Ravenna, OH
Rodman Public Library, Alliance, OH
Ross County Historical Society, Chillicothe, OH
Rutherford B. Hayes Presidential Center, Fremont, OH

Acknowledgments

Rutland Free Library, Rutland, VT
San Diego Public Library, San Diego, CA
Santa Cruz Public Library, Santa Cruz, CA
Schaffer Library, Union College, Schenectady, NY
State Library of Michigan, Lansing, MI
Tacoma Public Library, Tacoma, WA
Three Rivers Public Library, Three Rivers, MI
Toledo–Lucas County Public Library, Toledo, OH
Upshur County Historical Society, Buckhannon, WV
U.S. Army Military History Institute, Carlisle, PA
U.S. Military Academy Library, West Point, NY
Wabash Carnegie Public Library, Wabash, IN
Washington County Public Library, Marietta, OH
Way Public Library, Perrysburg, OH
West Virginia State Library, Charleston, WV
West Virginia University Library, Morgantown, WV
Western Reserve Historical Society, Cleveland, OH
Wisconsin Historical Society, Madison, WI
Yazoo Library Association, Yazoo City, MS

Introduction

At the beginning of the Civil War the Regular Army of the United States numbered only 1,098 officers and 15,304 enlisted men. Faced with this shortage of manpower in suppressing the escalating rebellion, President Abraham Lincoln issued a call for 75,000 militia for three months service on April 15, 1861, and then a call for 500,000 volunteers for three years service on July 22, 1861. These calls for troops and others issued later in the war specified that the various state governors would appoint the commanding officers of the regiments raised in their states.

Patriotic fervor throughout the Northern states resulted in spirited competition to complete the organization of regiments to meet the state quotas. In most cases the prospective commanders of these regiments were prominent citizens whose military background (if any) consisted of service in a local militia organization. In general the early war Union army colonels were known more for their patriotic enthusiasm than for their military competence. Many of them were more successful in convincing their fellow townsmen to enlist than they were in actually leading them into battle. Fortunately for the Union cause, the colonels who stayed in the service eventually acquired the necessary military skills or were replaced by subordinates who proved their capabilities on the field of battle.

This book is the fourth in a series of books containing photographs and biographical sketches of that diverse group of motivated citizens who attained the rank of colonel in the Union army, but failed to win promotion to brigadier general or brevet brigadier general. This volume presents the colonels who commanded regiments from Ohio, Michigan, and West Virginia. Preceding the photographs and biographical sketches for each state is a breakdown by regiment of all the colonels who commanded regiments from that state, with the name of each colonel being followed by the dates of his service. Included in this breakdown are the colonels who were promoted beyond the rank of colonel, with their final rank indicated in bold letters. Those indicated as attaining the rank of brigadier general are covered in the book *Generals in Blue,* by Ezra J. Warner, while those attaining the rank of brevet brigadier general are covered in the book *Brevet Brigadier Generals in Blue,* by Roger D. Hunt and Jack R. Brown.

Some explanatory notes are necessary concerning the content of the biographical sketches:

1. The date associated with each rank may be the date when the colonel was commissioned or appointed or the date when he was mustered at that rank. Generally, the date of muster was used whenever available. The reader should be aware that these dates were often adjusted or corrected by the War Department during and after the war, so that any hope of providing totally consistent dates is virtually impossible.

2. When the word "Colonel" is italicized, this indicates that the colonel was commissioned as colonel but never mustered as such.

3. Images not identified as to source are from the author's collection.

4. The following abbreviations are used in the text:

AAG	Assistant Adjutant General
ACM	Assistant Commissary of Musters
ACP	Appointment, Commission, and Personal
ADC	Aide-de-Camp
AIG	Assistant Inspector General
AQM	Assistant Quartermaster
Brig.	Brigadier
Bvt.	Brevet
Capt.	Captain
CB	Commission Branch
Co.	County or Company
Col.	Colonel
CSA	Confederate States Army
DOW	Died of Wounds
GAR	Grand Army of the Republic
Gen.	General
GSW	Gun Shot Wound
KIA	Killed in Action
Lt.	Lieutenant
MOLLUS	Military Order of the Loyal Legion of the United States
NHDVS	National Home for Disabled Volunteer Soldiers
RQM	Regimental Quartermaster
Twp.	Township
U.S.	United States
USA	United States Army
USAMHI	United States Army Military History Institute
USCT	United States Colored Troops
USMA	United States Military Academy
USMC	United States Marine Corps
USV	United States Volunteers
VRC	Veteran Reserve Corps
Vol.	Volume
VS	Volunteer Service

OHIO

Regiments

2nd Volunteer Militia
John Fox Wiltsee   Sept. 4, 1862   Musteres out Oct. 4, 1862

6th Volunteer Militia
Theodore Haffner   Sept. 2, 1862   Resigned Sept. 14, 1862
Frederick John Mayer   Sept. 14, 1862   Mustered out Oct. 2, 1862

8th Volunteer Militia
Bernhard Eith   Sept. 3, 1862   Mustered out Oct. 3, 1862

11th Volunteer Militia
William Floto   Sept. 3, 1862   Mustered out Oct. 2, 1862

1st Cavalry
Owen P. Ransom   Aug. 17, 1861   Resigned Dec. 16, 1861
Minor Millikin   Jan. 11, 1862   KIA Dec. 31, 1862
Thomas C. H. Smith   Dec. 31, 1862   Promoted **Brig. Gen., USV,** March 16, 1863
Beroth B. Eggleston   April 1, 1863   Mustered out Sept. 13, 1865, **Bvt. Brig. Gen.**

2nd Cavalry
Charles W. Doubleday   Sept. 5, 1861   Resigned June 16, 1862
August V. Kautz   Sept. 2, 1862   Promoted **Brig. Gen., USV,** May 7, 1864
George A. Purington   May 9, 1864   Mustered out Nov. 1, 1864
Alvred B. Nettleton   April 22, 1865   Resigned June 13, 1865, **Bvt. Brig. Gen.**
Dudley Seward   June 20, 1865   Mustered out Sept. 11, 1865

3rd Cavalry
Lewis Zahm   Sept. 27, 1861   Resigned Jan. 5, 1863, **Bvt. Brig. Gen.**
James W. Paramore   Jan. 6, 1863   Dismissed July 1, 1863
Charles B. Seidel   Sept. 24, 1863   Mustered out Jan. 18, 1865
Horace N. Howland   May 17, 1865   Mustered out Aug. 4, 1865, **Bvt. Brig. Gen.**

4th Cavalry
John Kennett   Aug. 30, 1861   Resigned Jan. 23, 1863
Eli Long   Feb. 23, 1863   Promoted **Brig. Gen., USV,** Aug. 18, 1864
Oliver P. Robie   Nov. 3, 1864   Mustered out Nov. 30, 1864

5th Cavalry
William H. H. Taylor   Aug. 26, 1861   Resigned Aug. 11, 1863
Thomas T. Heath   Aug. 11, 1863   Mustered out Oct. 30, 1865, **Bvt. Brig. Gen.**

6th Cavalry

William R. Lloyd	Dec. 19, 1861	Resigned April 2, 1863
William Stedman	March 26, 1864	Mustered out Oct. 6, 1864, **Bvt. Brig. Gen.**
Frank C. Loveland	July 30, 1865	Mustered out Aug. 7, 1865

7th Cavalry (1861)

William O. Collins	Oct. 1, 1861	To 6 OH Cavalry, Dec. 19, 1861

7th Cavalry

Israel Garrard	Sept. 18, 1862	Mustered out July 4, 1865, **Bvt. Brig. Gen.**

8th Cavalry (Designation changed from 44th Infantry, Jan. 8, 1864)

Alpheus S. Moore	May 9, 1864	Resigned Jan. 4, 1865
Wesley Owens	May 12, 1865	Mustered out July 30, 1865

9th Cavalry

William D. Hamilton	Dec. 16, 1863	Mustered out July 20, 1865, **Bvt. Brig. Gen.**

10th Cavalry

Charles C. Smith	Feb. 23, 1863	Discharged Jan. 13, 1865
Thomas W. Sanderson	April 9, 1865	Mustered out July 24, 1865, **Bvt. Brig. Gen.**

11th Cavalry

Regiment not entitled to a colonel since it never attained full strength

12th Cavalry

Robert W. Ratliff	Nov. 24, 1863	Mustered out Nov. 14, 1865, **Bvt. Brig. Gen.**

13th Cavalry

Stephen R. Clark	June 6, 1865	Mustered out Aug. 10, 1865

1st Light Artillery

James Barnett	Oct. 16, 1861	Mustered out Oct. 15, 1864, **Bvt. Brig. Gen.**
Charles S. Cotter	Nov. 27, 1864	Mustered out Aug. 9, 1865

1st Heavy Artillery
(Designation changed from 117th Infantry, May 2, 1863)

Chauncey G. Hawley	Aug. 1, 1863	Mustered out July 25, 1865

2nd Heavy Artillery

Horatio G. Gibson	Aug. 15, 1863	Mustered out Aug. 23, 1865, **Bvt. Brig. Gen.**

1st Infantry (3 months)

Alexander McD. McCook	April 16, 1861	Mustered out Aug. 16, 1861, Later **Major Gen., USV**

1st Infantry (3 years)

Benjamin F. Smith	Oct. 12, 1861	Discharged June 2, 1862, **Bvt. Brig. Gen.**
Edwin A. Parrott	June 1, 1862	Resigned Feb. 15, 1864

2nd Infantry (3 months)

Lewis Wilson	April 17, 1861	Resigned June 20, 1861

2nd Infantry (3 years)

Leonard A. Harris	Aug. 8, 1861	Resigned Dec. 24, 1862

John Kell	Dec. 24, 1862	KIA Dec. 31, 1862
Anson G. McCook	Jan. 20, 1863	Mustered out Oct. 10, 1864, **Bvt. Brig. Gen.**

3rd Infantry (3 months)

Isaac H. Marrow	April 27, 1861	To 3 OH Infantry (3 years)

3rd Infantry (3 years)

Isaac H. Marrow	June 12, 1861	Resigned Feb. 4, 1862
John Beatty	Feb. 12, 1862	Promoted **Brig. Gen., USV,** Nov. 29, 1862
Orris A. Lawson	Nov. 29, 1862	Mustered out June 21, 1864

4th Infantry (3 months)

Lorin Andrews	April 26, 1861	To 4 OH Infantry (3 years)

4th Infantry (3 years)

Lorin Andrews	June 5, 1861	Died Sept. 18, 1861
John S. Mason	Oct. 3, 1861	Promoted **Brig. Gen., USV,** Nov. 29, 1862
James H. Godman	May 22, 1863	Resigned July 28, 1863, **Bvt. Brig. Gen.**
Leonard W. Carpenter	Nov. 1, 1863	Mustered out June 21, 1864

5th Infantry (3 months)

Samuel H. Dunning	April 25, 1861	To 5 OH Infantry (3 years)

5th Infantry (3 years)

Samuel H. Dunning	June 11, 1861	Resigned Aug. 13, 1862
John H. Patrick	Aug. 2, 1862	KIA May 25, 1864
Robert Kirkup	July 20, 1865	Mustered out July 26, 1865

6th Infantry (3 months)

William K. Bosley	April 20, 1861	To 6 OH Infantry (3 years)

6th Infantry (3 years)

William K. Bosley	June 12, 1861	Discharged Aug. 19, 1862
Nicholas L. Anderson	Nov. 9, 1862	Mustered out June 23, 1864, **Bvt. Major Gen.**

7th Infantry (3 months)

Erastus B. Tyler	April 25, 1861	To 7 OH Infantry (3 years), Later **Brig. Gen., USV**

7th Infantry (3 years)

Erastus B. Tyler	June 19, 1861	Promoted **Brig. Gen., USV,** May 14, 1862
William R. Creighton	May 20, 1862	DOW Nov. 27, 1863

8th Infantry (3 months)

Hermin G. DePuy	May 4, 1861	To 8 OH Infantry (3 years)

8th Infantry (3 years)

Hermin G. DePuy	July 9, 1861	Resigned Nov. 9, 1861
Samuel S. Carroll	Dec. 7, 1861	Promoted **Brig. Gen., USV,** May 12, 1864

9th Infantry (3 months)

Robert L. McCook	April 23, 1861	To 9 OH Infantry (3 years), Later **Brig. Gen., USV**

9th Infantry (3 years)

Robert L. McCook	May 28, 1861	Promoted **Brig. Gen., USV,** March 21, 1862
Gustav Kaemmerling	May 6, 1862	Mustered out June 7, 1864

10th Infantry (3 months)

William H. Lytle	May 3, 1861	To 10 OH Infantry (3 years), Later **Brig. Gen., USV**

10th Infantry (3 years)

William H. Lytle	June 4, 1861	Promoted **Brig. Gen., USV,** Nov. 29, 1862
Joseph W. Burke	Jan. 20, 1863	Mustered out June 17, 1864, **Bvt. Brig. Gen.**

11th Infantry (3 months)

James F. Harrison	April 25, 1861	Resigned May 29, 1861

11th Infantry (3 years)

Charles A. DeVilliers	July 7, 1861	Dismissed April 23, 1862
Augustus H. Coleman	April 23, 1862	KIA Sept. 17, 1862
Philander P. Lane	Sept. 17, 1862	Resigned Oct. 26, 1863
Ogden Street	Oct. 26, 1863	Mustered out June 21, 1864

12th Infantry (3 months)

John W. Lowe	May 2, 1861	To 12 OH Infantry (3 years)

12th Infantry (3 years)

John W. Lowe	June 28, 1861	KIA Sept. 10, 1861
Carr B. White	Oct. 1, 1861	Mustered out July 11, 1864, **Bvt. Brig. Gen.**

13th Infantry (3 months)

Abram S. Piatt	April 20, 1861	Mustered out Aug. 25, 1861, Later **Brig. Gen., USV**

13th Infantry (3 years)

William Sooy Smith	June 26, 1861	Promoted **Brig. Gen., USV,** April 15, 1862
Joseph G. Hawkins	May 13, 1862	KIA Dec. 31, 1862
Dwight Jarvis	Jan. 1, 1863	Mustered out June 26, 1864, **Bvt. Brig. Gen.**

14th Infantry (3 months)

James B. Steedman	April 27, 1861	Mustered out Aug. 13, 1861, Later **Major Gen., USV**

14th Infantry (3 years)

James B. Steedman	Sept. 1, 1861	Promoted **Brig. Gen., USV,** July 17, 1862
George P. Este	Nov. 20, 1862	Promoted **Brig. Gen., USV,** June 26, 1865

15th Infantry (3 months)

George W. Andrews	May 4, 1861	Mustered out Aug. 30, 1861

15th Infantry (3 years)

Moses R. Dickey	Aug. 7, 1861	Resigned Oct. 24, 1862
William Wallace	Oct. 25, 1862	Discharged July 19, 1864
Frank Askew	July 28, 1864	Mustered out Nov. 21, 1865, **Bvt. Brig. Gen.**

16th Infantry (3 months)

James Irvine	May 3, 1861	Mustered out Aug. 18, 1861

16th Infantry (3 years)

John F. DeCourcy	Sept. 22, 1861	Discharged March 3, 1864

17th Infantry (3 months)
John M. Connell	May 13, 1861	Mustered out Aug. 15, 1861

17th Infantry (3 years)
John M. Connell	Aug. 16, 1861	Resigned Nov. 12, 1863
Durbin Ward	March 1, 1864	Resigned Nov. 8, 1864, **Bvt. Brig. Gen.**

18th Infantry (3 months)
Timothy R. Stanley	May 29, 1861	To 18 OH Infantry (3 years), **Bvt. Brig. Gen.**

18th Infantry (3 years)
Timothy R. Stanley	Aug. 6, 1861	Mustered out Nov. 9, 1864, **Bvt. Brig. Gen.**
Charles H. Grosvenor	April 19, 1865	Mustered out Oct. 9, 1865, **Bvt. Brig. Gen.**

19th Infantry (3 months)
Samuel Beatty	May 29, 1861	To 19 OH Infantry (3 years), Later **Brig. Gen., USV**

19th Infantry (3 years)
Samuel Beatty	Aug. 10, 1861	Promoted **Brig. Gen., USV,** Nov. 29, 1862
Charles F. Manderson	April 14, 1863	Resigned March 17, 1865, **Bvt. Brig. Gen.**
James M. Nash	May 31, 1865	Mustered out Oct. 24, 1865

20th Infantry (3 months)
Thomas Morton	May 23, 1861	Mustered out Aug. 18, 1861

20th Infantry (3 years)
Charles Whittlesey	Aug. 21, 1861	Resigned April 19, 1862
Manning F. Force	May 1, 1862	Promoted **Brig. Gen., USV,** Aug. 11, 1863
John C. Fry	Jan. 8, 1864	Discharged Sept. 18, 1864
Harrison Wilson	June 21, 1865	Mustered out July 15, 1865

21st Infantry (3 months)
Jesse S. Norton	April 27, 1861	Mustered out Aug. 12, 1861

21st Infantry (3 years)
Jesse S. Norton	Sept. 19, 1861	Resigned Dec. 20, 1862
James M. Neibling	Dec. 20, 1862	Resigned Dec. 6, 1864
Arnold McMahan	July 12, 1865	Mustered out July 25, 1865

22nd Infantry (3 months)
William E. Gilmore	May 23, 1861	Mustered out Aug. 19, 1861

22nd Infantry (3 years)
(Designation changed from 13th MO Infantry, July 7, 1862)
Crafts J. Wright	Aug. 3, 1861	Resigned Sept. 9, 1862
Oliver Wood	Sept. 16, 1862	Mustered out Nov. 18, 1864, **Bvt. Brig. Gen.**

23rd Infantry
William S. Rosecrans	June 7, 1861	Promoted **Brig. Gen., USA,** June 14, 1861
Eliakim P. Scammon	June 27, 1861	Promoted **Brig. Gen., USV,** Oct. 15, 1862
Rutherford B. Hayes	Oct. 24, 1862	Promoted **Brig. Gen., USV,** Oct. 19, 1864
James M. S. Comly	Jan. 11, 1865	Mustered out July 26, 1865, **Bvt. Brig. Gen.**

24th Infantry
Jacob Ammen	June 22, 1861	Promoted **Brig. Gen., USV,** July 16, 1862
Frederick C. Jones	May 14, 1862	KIA Dec. 31, 1862

Ohio Regiments

David J. Higgins	Jan. 1, 1863	Resigned Oct. 23, 1863
Armstead T. M. Cockerill	Oct. 23, 1863	Mustered out June 24, 1864

25th Infantry

James A. Jones	June 26, 1861	Resigned May 16, 1862
William P. Richardson	May 16, 1862	Discharged May 9, 1866, **Bvt. Brig. Gen.**
Nathaniel Haughton	May 25, 1866	Mustered out June 18, 1866, **Bvt. Brig. Gen.**

26th Infantry

Edward P. Fyffe	June 18, 1861	Discharged Dec. 18, 1863, **Bvt. Brig. Gen.**

27th Infantry

John W. Fuller	Aug. 18, 1861	Promoted **Brig. Gen., USV,** Jan. 5, 1864
Mendal Churchill	June 27, 1864	Resigned Sept. 15, 1864, **Bvt. Brig. Gen.**
Isaac N. Gilruth	May 31, 1865	Mustered out July 11, 1865

28th Infantry

August Moor	July 16, 1861	Dismissed Nov. 27, 1863
Godfried Becker	Nov. 27, 1863	Colonel Moor dismissal revoked
August Moor	Feb. 16, 1864	Mustered out July 23, 1864, **Bvt. Brig. Gen.**

29th Infantry

Lewis P. Buckley	Aug. 27, 1861	Resigned Jan. 26, 1863
William T. Fitch	June 18, 1863	Discharged Oct. 13, 1864
Jonas Schoonover	July 12, 1865	Mustered out July 13, 1865

30th Infantry

Hugh Ewing	Aug. 20, 1861	Promoted **Brig. Gen., USV,** Nov. 29, 1862
Theodore Jones	April 18, 1863	Mustered out Aug. 13, 1865, **Bvt. Brig. Gen.**

31st Infantry

Moses B. Walker	Sept. 23, 1861	Mustered out July 20, 1865, **Bvt. Brig. Gen.**

32nd Infantry

Thomas H. Ford	July 26, 1861	Resigned Nov. 8, 1862
Benjamin F. Potts	Dec. 28, 1862	Promoted **Brig. Gen., USV,** Jan. 12, 1865
Jefferson J. Hibbets	May 18, 1865	Mustered out July 20, 1865

33rd Infantry

Joshua W. Sill	Aug. 27, 1861	Promoted **Brig. Gen., USV,** July 16, 1862
Oscar F. Moore	July 16, 1862	Resigned July 20, 1864
Joseph Hinson	June 26, 1865	Mustered out July 12, 1865

34th Infantry

Abram S. Piatt	Sept. 2, 1861	Promoted **Brig. Gen., USV,** April 28, 1862
John T. Toland	May 14, 1862	KIA July 18, 1863
Freeman E. Franklin	July 18, 1863	Dismissed Aug. 1, 1864

35th Infantry

Ferdinand Van Derveer	Sept. 24, 1861	Mustered out Aug. 26, 1864, Later **Brig. Gen., USV**

36th Infantry

George Crook	Sept. 13, 1861	Promoted **Brig. Gen., USV,** Sept. 7, 1862
Melvin Clarke	Sept. 7, 1862	KIA Sept. 17, 1862
Ebenezer B. Andrews	Sept. 18, 1862	Resigned April 9, 1863
William G. Jones	April 18, 1863	KIA Sept. 19, 1863
Hiram F. Devol	March 19, 1864	Mustered out July 27, 1865, **Bvt. Brig. Gen.**

37th Infantry
Edward Siber	Sept. 12, 1861	Resigned March 23, 1864

38th Infantry
Edwin D. Bradley	Sept. 10, 1861	Resigned Feb. 8, 1862
Edward H. Phelps	Feb. 9, 1862	KIA Nov. 25, 1863
William A. Choate	Nov. 25, 1863	DOW Sept. 12, 1864

39th Infantry
John B. Groesbeck	Aug. 16, 1861	Resigned July 8, 1862
Alfred W. Gilbert	July 9, 1862	Resigned Oct. 1, 1862
Edward F. Noyes	Nov. 1, 1862	Resigned April 22, 1865, **Bvt. Brig. Gen.**
Daniel Weber	May 18, 1865	Mustered out July 9, 1865

40th Infantry
Jonathan Cranor	Sept. 11, 1861	Resigned Feb. 5, 1863, **Bvt. Brig. Gen.**
Jacob E. Taylor	March 5, 1863	Mustered out Oct. 7, 1864, **Bvt. Brig. Gen.**

41st Infantry
William B. Hazen	Oct. 29, 1861	Promoted **Brig. Gen., USV,** Nov. 29, 1862
Aquila Wiley	April 15, 1863	Discharged June 7, 1864, **Bvt. Brig. Gen.**
Ephraim S. Holloway	May 31, 1865	Mustered out Nov. 27, 1865, **Bvt. Brig. Gen.**

42nd Infantry
James A. Garfield	Nov. 27, 1861	Promoted **Brig. Gen., USV,** Jan. 11, 1862
Lionel A. Sheldon	March 14, 1862	Mustered out Dec. 2, 1864, **Bvt. Brig. Gen.**

43rd Infantry
Joseph L. Kirby Smith	Sept. 28, 1861	DOW Oct. 12, 1862
Wager Swayne	Oct. 18, 1862	Promoted **Brig. Gen., USV,** March 8, 1865
Horace Park	April 26, 1865	Mustered out July 13, 1865

44th Infantry
(Designation changed to 8th Cavalry, Jan. 8, 1864)
Samuel A. Gilbert	Oct. 15, 1861	Resigned April 20, 1864, **Bvt. Brig. Gen.**

45th Infantry
Benjamin P. Runkle	Aug. 19, 1862	Discharged July 21, 1864, **Bvt. Brig. Gen.**
John H. Humphrey	June 16, 1865	Mustered out June 12, 1865

46th Infantry
Thomas Worthington	Jan. 28, 1862	Resigned Nov. 21, 1862
Charles C. Walcutt	Oct. 16, 1862	Promoted **Brig. Gen., USV,** July 30, 1864
Edward N. Upton	July 16, 1865	Mustered out July 22, 1865

47th Infantry
Frederick A. Poschner	Aug. 15, 1861	Resigned July 17, 1862
Lyman S. Elliott	July 18, 1862	Resigned Jan. 13, 1863
Augustus C. Parry	March 12, 1863	Mustered out June 19, 1865, **Bvt. Brig. Gen.**
Thomas T. Taylor	Aug. 10, 1865	Mustered out Aug. 11, 1865, **Bvt. Brig. Gen.**

48th Infantry
Peter J. Sullivan	Jan. 23, 1862	Resigned Aug. 7, 1863, **Bvt. Brig. Gen.**
Job R. Parker	April 12, 1864	Mustered out Jan. 17, 1865

49th Infantry
William H. Gibson	Aug. 20, 1861	Mustered out Sept. 5, 1864, **Bvt. Brig. Gen.**
Joseph R. Bartlett	June 26, 1865	Mustered out Nov. 30, 1865

50th Infantry

Jonah R. Taylor	Aug. 23, 1862	Resigned Oct. 16, 1862
Silas A. Strickland	Oct. 27, 1862	Mustered out June 26, 1865, **Bvt. Brig. Gen.**

51st Infantry

William P. N. Fitzgerald	Oct. 14, 1861	Resigned Oct. 23, 1861
Stanley Matthews	Oct. 23, 1861	Resigned April 11, 1863
Richard W. McClain	April 14, 1863	Resigned Sept. 30, 1864
Charles H. Wood	Jan. 20, 1865	Mustered out Oct. 3, 1865

52nd Infantry

Daniel McCook	July 15, 1862	Promoted **Brig. Gen., USV**, July 16, 1864
Charles W. Clancy	May 31, 1865	Mustered out June 3, 1865

53rd Infantry

Jesse J. Appler	Feb. 8, 1862	Mustered out April 29, 1862
Wells S. Jones	May 21, 1862	Mustered out Aug. 11, 1865, **Bvt. Brig. Gen.**

54th Infantry

Thomas Kilby Smith	Oct. 31, 1861	Promoted **Brig. Gen., USV,** Aug. 11, 1863

55th Infantry

John C. Lee	Nov. 28, 1861	Resigned May 8, 1863, **Bvt. Brig. Gen.**
Charles B. Gambee	May 8, 1863	KIA May 15, 1864
Edwin H. Powers	June 6, 1865	Mustered out July 11, 1865

56th Infantry

Peter Kinney	Sept. 11, 1861	Resigned April 2, 1863
William H. Raynor	April 2, 1863	Discharged Oct. 27, 1864, **Bvt. Brig. Gen.**
Henry E. Jones	April 20, 1866	Mustered out April 25, 1866

57th Infantry

William Mungen	Dec. 16, 1861	Resigned April 16, 1863
Americus V. Rice	May 24, 1863	Promoted **Brig. Gen., USV,** May 31, 1865
Samuel R. Mott	Aug. 10, 1865	Mustered out Aug. 14, 1865, **Bvt. Brig. Gen.**

58th Infantry

Valentine Bausenwein	Oct. 1, 1861	Dismissed Aug. 11, 1862

59th Infantry

James P. Fyffe	Sept. 26, 1861	Resigned Oct. 6, 1863

60th Infantry (1 year)

William H. Trimble	Feb. 25, 1862	Mustered out Nov. 13, 1862

60th Infantry (3 years)

Regiment not entitled to a colonel since it never attained full strength

61st Infantry

Newton Schleich	April 1, 1862	Resigned Sept. 23, 1862
Stephen J. McGroarty	Sept. 23, 1862	To 82nd Infantry, March 31, 1865, **Bvt. Brig. Gen.**

62nd Infantry

Francis B. Pond	Oct. 31, 1861	Resigned Nov. 5, 1864

Henry R. West	June 16, 1865	To 67th Infantry, Sept. 1, 1865, **Bvt. Brig. Gen.**

63rd Infantry

John W. Sprague	Jan. 23, 1862	Promoted **Brig. Gen., USV,** July 30, 1864
Charles E. Brown	June 6, 1865	Mustered out July 8, 1865, **Bvt. Brig. Gen.**

64th Infantry

James W. Forsyth	Nov. 11, 1861	Discharged Jan. 1, 1862, Later **Brig. Gen., USV**
John Ferguson	Jan. 21, 1862	Dismissed March 11, 1863
Alexander McIlvain	March 12, 1863	KIA May 9, 1864
Robert C. Brown	June 24, 1864	Mustered out Feb. 23, 1865
Samuel M. Wolff	Dec. 15, 1865	Mustered out Dec. 3, 1865

65th Infantry

Charles G. Harker	Nov. 11, 1861	Promoted **Brig. Gen., USV,** Sept. 20, 1863
Orlow Smith	Nov. 24, 1865	Mustered out Nov. 30, 1865, **Bvt. Brig. Gen.**

66th Infantry

Charles Candy	Dec. 17, 1861	Mustered out Jan. 14, 1865, **Bvt. Brig. Gen.**
John T. Mitchell	July 13, 1865	Mustered out July 15, 1865

67th Infantry

Otto Burstenbinder	Oct. 17, 1861	Dismissed July 29, 1862
Alvin C. Voris	Sept. 1, 1865	Mustered out Dec. 7, 1865, **Bvt. Brig. Gen.**

68th Infantry

Samuel H. Steedman	Nov. 29, 1861	Mustered out July 5, 1862
Robert K. Scott	July 12, 1862	Promoted **Brig. Gen., USV,** Jan. 12, 1865
George E. Welles	Jan. 16, 1865	Mustered out July 10, 1865, **Bvt. Brig. Gen.**

69th Infantry

Lewis D. Campbell	Oct. 2, 1861	Resigned Aug. 9, 1862
William B. Cassilly	Aug. 10, 1862	Dismissed Dec. 31, 1862
Marshall F. Moore	Feb. 23, 1863	Resigned Nov. 7, 1864, **Bvt. Brig. Gen.**
Joseph H. Brigham	July 10, 1865	Mustered out July 17, 1865

70th Infantry

Joseph R. Cockerill	Dec. 20, 1861	Resigned April 13, 1864, **Bvt. Brig. Gen.**
DeWitt C. Loudon	April 26, 1864	Discharged Aug. 9, 1864

71st Infantry

Rodney Mason	Oct. 15, 1861	Mustered out Aug. 22, 1862
Henry K. McConnell	June 7, 1863	Mustered out Nov. 30, 1865, **Bvt. Brig. Gen.**
James H. Hart	Nov. 29, 1865	Mustered out Nov. 30, 1865, **Bvt. Brig. Gen.**

72nd Infantry

Ralph P. Buckland	Jan. 10, 1862	Promoted **Brig. Gen., USV,** Nov. 29, 1862
Le Roy Crockett	Nov. 29, 1862	Died Dec. 10, 1863
Charles G. Eaton	April 9, 1864	Mustered out Sept. 11, 1865, **Bvt. Brig. Gen.**

73rd Infantry

Orland Smith	Nov. 26, 1861	Resigned Feb. 17, 1864, **Bvt. Brig. Gen.**
Richard Long, Jr.	Feb. 17, 1864	Resigned June 27, 1864
Samuel H. Hurst	July 10, 1864	Mustered out July 21, 1865, **Bvt. Brig. Gen.**

74th Infantry

Granville Moody	Feb. 28, 1862	Resigned May 16, 1863, **Bvt. Brig. Gen.**
Alexander Von Schrader	May 16, 1863	Declined, **Bvt. Brig. Gen.**
Josiah Given	June 5, 1863	Resigned Sept. 29, 1864, **Bvt. Brig. Gen.**
Robert P. Findley	July 12, 1865	Mustered out July 10, 1865

75th Infantry

Nathaniel C. McLean	Sept. 18, 1861	Promoted **Brig. Gen., USV,** Nov. 29, 1862
Robert A. Constable	Dec. 3, 1862	Resigned Jan. 12, 1863
Robert Reily	March 1, 1863	DOW May 3, 1863
Andrew L. Harris	May 22, 1863	Mustered out Jan. 17, 1865, **Bvt. Brig. Gen.**

76th Infantry

Charles R. Woods	Oct. 13, 1861	Promoted **Brig. Gen., USV,** Aug. 4, 1863
William B. Woods	Sept. 10, 1863	Promoted **Brig. Gen., USV,** May 31, 1865
Edward Briggs	July 13, 1865	Mustered out July 15, 1865

77th Infantry

Jesse Hildebrand	Oct. 5, 1861	Died April 18, 1863
William B. Mason	April 18, 1863	Mustered out Dec. 31, 1864
William E. Stevens	March 7, 1866	Mustered out March 8, 1866

78th Infantry

Mortimer D. Leggett	Jan. 21, 1862	Promoted **Brig. Gen., USV,** Nov. 29, 1862
Zachariah M. Chandler	Nov. 29, 1862	Discharged July 23, 1863
Greenberry F. Wiles	Nov. 8, 1864	Mustered out July 11, 1865, **Bvt. Brig. Gen.**

79th Infantry

Henry G. Kennett	Nov. 1, 1862	Resigned Aug. 1, 1864, **Bvt. Brig. Gen.**
Azariah W. Doan	June 8, 1865	Mustered out June 9, 1865, **Bvt. Brig. Gen.**

80th Infantry

Ephraim R. Eckley	Dec. 29, 1861	Resigned Feb. 24, 1863
Mathias H. Bartilson	Feb. 14, 1863	Died Aug. 15, 1863
James E. Philpott	Aug. 15, 1863	Commission revoked
Pren Metham	Jan. 4, 1864	Mustered out April 7, 1865
Thomas C. Morris	June 16, 1865	Mustered out Aug. 13, 1865

81st Infantry

Thomas Morton	Sept. 24, 1861	Resigned July 30, 1864
Robert N. Adams	Aug. 12, 1864	Mustered out July 13, 1865, **Bvt. Brig. Gen.**

82nd Infantry

James Cantwell	Dec. 31, 1861	KIA Aug. 29, 1862
James S. Robinson	Aug. 29, 1862	Promoted **Brig. Gen., USV,** Jan. 12, 1865
Stephen J. McGroarty	March 31, 1865	Mustered out July 24, 1865, **Bvt. Brig. Gen.**

83rd Infantry

Frederick W. Moore	Sept. 13, 1862	Mustered out July 24, 1865, **Bvt. Brig. Gen.**

84th Infantry

William Lawrence	June 7, 1862	Mustered out Sept. 20, 1862

85th Infantry

Charles W. B. Allison	June 10, 1862	Mustered out Sept. 23, 1862

86th Infantry (3 months)
Barnabas Burns | June 10, 1862 | Mustered out Sept. 25, 1862

86th Infantry (6 months)
Wilson C. Lemert | July 13, 1863 | Mustered out Feb. 10, 1864

87th Infantry
Henry B. Banning | June 25, 1862 | Mustered out Oct. 4, 1862, **Bvt. Brig. Gen.**

88th Infantry
George W. Neff | July 31, 1863 | Mustered out July 3, 1865, **Bvt. Brig. Gen.**

89th Infantry
John G. Marshall | Aug. 26, 1862 | Discharged Oct. 2, 1862
Joseph D. Hatfield | Oct. 2, 1862 | Dismissed June 6, 1863
Caleb H. Carlton | July 7, 1863 | Mustered out June 23, 1865

90th Infantry
Isaac N. Ross | July 16, 1862 | Resigned April 14, 1863
Charles H. Rippey | April 14, 1863 | Resigned Oct. 20, 1863
Samuel N. Yeoman | Oct. 20, 1863 | Mustered out June 13, 1865

91st Infantry
John A. Turley | Aug. 22, 1862 | Discharged Nov. 4, 1864, **Bvt. Brig. Gen.**
Benjamin F. Coates | Dec. 9, 1864 | Mustered out June 24, 1865, **Bvt. Brig. Gen.**

92nd Infantry
Nelson H. Van Vorhes | Sept. 2, 1862 | Resigned March 22, 1863
Benjamin D. Fearing | April 14, 1863 | Mustered out May 19, 1865, **Bvt. Brig. Gen.**

93rd Infantry
Charles Anderson | Aug. 9, 1862 | Resigned Feb. 21, 1863
Hiram Strong | Feb. 22, 1863 | DOW Oct. 7, 1863
Daniel Bowman | March 5, 1865 | Mustered out June 8, 1865

94th Infantry
Joseph W. Frizell | Aug. 23, 1862 | Resigned Feb. 22, 1863, **Bvt. Brig. Gen.**
Stephen A. Bassford | Feb. 22, 1863 | Resigned April 16, 1864

95th Infantry
William L. McMillen | Aug. 16, 1862 | Mustered out Aug. 14, 1865, **Bvt. Brig. Gen.**

96th Infantry
Joseph W. Vance | Aug. 19, 1862 | KIA April 8, 1864

97th Infantry
John Q. Lane | Sept. 2, 1862 | Mustered out June 10, 1865, **Bvt. Brig. Gen.**

98th Infantry
George P. Webster | Aug. 8, 1862 | DOW Oct. 9, 1862
Christian L. Poorman | Oct. 8, 1862 | Resigned June 12, 1863
John S. Pearce | Nov. 5, 1863 | Mustered out June 1, 1865, **Bvt. Brig. Gen.**

99th Infantry
Albert Langworthy | Aug. 11, 1862 | Discharged Sept. 4, 1862
Peter T. Swaine | Sept. 4, 1862 | Mustered out Dec. 31, 1864

100th Infantry

John C. Groom	Aug. 28, 1862	Resigned May 13, 1863
Patrick S. Slevin	May 13, 1863	Discharged Nov. 30, 1864, **Bvt. Brig. Gen.**
Edwin L. Hayes	Jan. 2, 1865	Resigned May 12, 1865, **Bvt. Brig. Gen.**

101st Infantry

Leander Stem	Aug. 30, 1862	DOW Jan. 5, 1863
Isaac M. Kirby	Feb. 14, 1863	Mustered out June 12, 1865, **Bvt. Brig. Gen.**

102nd Infantry

William Given	Aug. 18, 1862	Mustered out June 30, 1865, **Bvt. Brig. Gen.**

103rd Infantry

John S. Casement	Sept. 8, 1862	Resigned April 30, 1865, **Bvt. Brig. Gen.**
Philip C. Hayes	June 6, 1865	Mustered out June 12, 1865, **Bvt. Brig. Gen.**

104th Infantry

James W. Reilly	Aug. 30, 1862	Promoted **Brig. Gen., USV,** July 30, 1864
Oscar W. Sterl	Aug. 24, 1864	Mustered out June 17, 1865

105th Infantry

Albert S. Hall	Aug. 11, 1862	Died July 10, 1863
William R. Tolles	July 10, 1863	Resigned Jan. 29, 1864
George T. Perkins	Feb. 18, 1864	Mustered out June 3, 1865

106th Infantry

George B. Wright	Jan. 9, 1864	Resigned March 5, 1864

107th Infantry

Seraphim Meyer	Sept. 6, 1862	Resigned Feb. 17, 1864

108th Infantry

George T. Limberg	Nov. 24, 1863	Discharged May 16, 1864
Joseph Good	May 18, 1865	Mustered out June 9, 1865

109th Infantry (Did not complete organization)

Michael P. Nolan	Sept. 6, 1862

110th Infantry

Joseph W. Keifer	Sept. 30, 1862	Mustered out June 12, 1865, **Bvt. Brig. Gen.**

111th Infantry

John R. Bond	Aug. 28, 1862	Discharged Oct. 18, 1864, **Bvt. Brig. Gen.**
Isaac R. Sherwood	Sept. 8, 1864	Mustered out June 27, 1865, **Bvt. Brig. Gen.**

112th Infantry (Did not complete organization)

113th Infantry

James A. Wilcox	Dec. 28, 1862	Resigned April 29, 1863, **Bvt. Brig. Gen.**
John G. Mitchell	May 6, 1863	Promoted **Brig. Gen., USV,** Jan. 12, 1865
Darius B. Warner	Feb. 23, 1865	Resigned June 6, 1865, **Bvt. Brig. Gen.**
Toland Jones	June 8, 1865	Mustered out July 6, 1865
James A. Wilcox	July 1, 1865	Mustered out July 6, 1865, **Bvt. Brig. Gen.**

114th Infantry

John Cradlebaugh	Aug. 22, 1862	Resigned Oct. 20, 1863
John H. Kelly	Nov. 27, 1863	Mustered out July 31, 1865, **Bvt. Brig. Gen.**

115th Infantry

Jackson A. Lucy	Sept. 12, 1862	Discharged July 6, 1864
Thomas C. Boone	July 20, 1864	Mustered out June 22, 1865

116th Infantry

James Washburn	Aug. 22, 1862	Mustered out July 5, 1865

117th Infantry (Designation changed to 1st Heavy Artillery, May 2, 1863)

118th Infantry

Samuel R. Mott	Sept. 17, 1862	Resigned Feb. 10, 1864
Thomas L. Young	April 11, 1864	Resigned Sept. 14, 1864, **Bvt. Brig. Gen.**
Edgar Sowers	June 20, 1865	Mustered out June 24, 1865, **Bvt. Brig. Gen.**

119th Infantry (Did not complete organization)

120th Infantry

Daniel French	Sept. 10, 1862	Resigned Feb. 18, 1863
Marcus M. Spiegel	Feb. 18, 1863	DOW May 4, 1864

121st Infantry

William P. Reid	Sept. 11, 1862	Resigned Nov. 4, 1863
Henry B. Banning	Nov. 10, 1863	Resigned Jan. 21, 1865, **Bvt. Brig. Gen.**
Aaron B. Robinson	May 18, 1865	Mustered out June 8, 1865

122nd Infantry

William H. Ball	Oct. 8, 1862	Resigned Feb. 3, 1865, **Bvt. Brig. Gen.**

123rd Infantry

William T. Wilson	Sept. 26, 1862	Mustered out June 12, 1865, **Bvt. Brig. Gen.**

124th Infantry

Oliver H. Payne	Jan. 1, 1863	Resigned Nov. 2, 1864, **Bvt. Brig. Gen.**
James Pickands	June 20, 1865	Mustered out July 9, 1865

125th Infantry

Emerson Opdycke	Jan. 14, 1863	Promoted **Brig. Gen., USV,** July 26, 1865
Joseph Bruff	Oct. 16, 1865	Mustered out Sept. 25, 1865

126th Infantry

Benjamin F. Smith	Sept. 10, 1862	Mustered out June 25, 1865, **Bvt. Brig. Gen.**

127th Infantry (Designation changed to 5th U.S. Colored Infantry)

128th Infantry

Charles W. Hill	Dec. 25, 1863	Mustered out July 13, 1865, **Bvt. Brig. Gen.**

129th Infantry

Howard D. John	Aug. 10, 1863	Mustered out March 10, 1864

130th Infantry

Charles B. Phillips	May 3, 1864	Mustered out Sept. 22, 1864

131st Infantry
John G. Lowe | May 14, 1864 | Mustered out Aug. 25, 1864

132nd Infantry
Joel Haines | May 15, 1864 | Mustered out Sept. 10, 1864

133rd Infantry
Gustavus S. Innis | May 6, 1864 | Mustered out Aug. 20, 1864

134th Infantry
James B. Armstrong | May 2, 1864 | Mustered out Aug. 22, 1864

135th Infantry
Andrew Legg | May 11, 1864 | Mustered out Sept. 1, 1864

136th Infantry
William Smith Irwin | May 2, 1864 | Mustered out Aug. 31, 1864

137th Infantry
Leonard A. Harris | May 10, 1864 | Mustered out Aug. 19, 1864

138th Infantry
Samuel S. Fisher | May 14, 1864 | Mustered out Sept. 1, 1864

139th Infantry
Regiment not entitled to a colonel since it never attained full strength

140th Infantry
Robert B. Wilson | May 10, 1864 | Mustered out Sept. 3, 1864

141st Infantry
Anderson D. Jaynes | May 12, 1864 | Mustered out Sept. 3, 1864

142nd Infantry
William C. Cooper | May 13, 1864 | Mustered out Sept. 2, 1864

143rd Infantry
William H. Vodrey | May 13, 1864 | Mustered out Sept. 13, 1864

144th Infantry
Samuel H. Hunt | May 2, 1864 | Mustered out Aug. 31, 1864

145th Infantry
Henry C. Ashwill | May 12, 1864 | Mustered out Aug. 24, 1864

146th Infantry
Harvey Crampton | May 12, 1864 | Mustered out Sept. 7, 1864

147th Infantry
Benjamin F. Rosson | May 16, 1864 | Mustered out Aug. 30, 1864

148th Infantry
Thomas W. Moore | May 18, 1864 | Mustered out Sept. 14, 1864

149th Infantry
Allison L. Brown | May 11, 1864 | Mustered out Aug. 30, 1864

150th Infantry
William H. Hayward	May 5, 1864	Mustered out Aug. 23, 1864

151st Infantry
John M. C. Marble	May 13, 1864	Mustered out Aug. 27, 1864

152nd Infantry
David Putman	May 11, 1864	Mustered out Sept. 2, 1864

153rd Infantry
Israel Stough	May 10, 1864	Mustered out Sept. 9, 1864

154th Infantry
Robert Stevenson	May 9, 1864	Mustered out Sept. 1, 1864

155th Infantry
Harley H. Sage	May 8, 1864	Mustered out Aug. 27, 1864

156th Infantry
Caleb Marker	May 17, 1864	Mustered out Sept. 1, 1864

157th Infantry
George W. McCook	May 15, 1864	Mustered out Sept. 2, 1864

158th Infantry (Did not complete organization)

159th Infantry
Lyman J. Jackson	May 10, 1864	Mustered out Aug. 24, 1864

160th Infantry
Cyrus Reasoner	May 17, 1864	Mustered out Sept. 7, 1864

161st Infantry
Oliver P. Taylor	May 9, 1864	Mustered out Sept. 2, 1864

162nd Infantry
Ephraim Ball	May 20, 1864	Mustered out Sept. 4, 1864

163rd Infantry
Hiram Miller	May 13, 1864	Mustered out Sept. 10, 1864

164th Infantry
John C. Lee	May 3, 1864	Mustered out Aug. 27, 1864, **Bvt. Brig. Gen.**

165th Infantry
Regiment not entitled to a colonel since it never attained full strength

166th Infantry
Harrison G. O. Blake	May 15, 1864	Mustered out Sept. 9, 1864

167th Infantry
Thomas Moore	May 16, 1864	Mustered out Sept. 8, 1864

168th Infantry
Conrad Garis	May 2, 1864	Mustered out Sept. 8, 1864

169th Infantry

Nathaniel Haynes	May 15, 1864	Mustered out Sept. 4, 1864

170th Infantry

Miles J. Saunders	May 14, 1864	Resigned July 1, 1864
Lewis L. Lewton	Aug. 15, 1864	Mustered out Sept. 10, 1864

171st Infantry

Joel F. Asper	May 7, 1864	Mustered out Aug. 20, 1864

172nd Infantry

John Ferguson	May 1, 1864	Mustered out Sept. 3, 1864

173rd Infantry

John R. Hurd	Sept. 21, 1864	Mustered out June 26, 1865, **Bvt. Brig. Gen.**

174th Infantry

John S. Jones	Sept. 21, 1864	Mustered out June 28, 1865, **Bvt. Brig. Gen.**

175th Infantry

Wesley R. Adams	Oct. 11, 1864	Commission returned
Daniel W. McCoy	June 6, 1865	Mustered out June 27, 1865, **Bvt. Brig. Gen.**

176th Infantry

Edwin C. Mason	Sept. 23, 1864	Mustered out June 14, 1865, **Bvt. Brig. Gen.**

177th Infantry

Arthur T. Wilcox	Sept. 23, 1864	Mustered out June 24, 1865

178th Infantry

Joab A. Stafford	Oct. 6, 1864	Mustered out June 29, 1865, **Bvt. Brig. Gen.**

179th Infantry

Harley H. Sage	Sept. 28, 1864	Mustered out June 17, 1865

180th Infantry

Willard Warner	Oct. 27, 1864	Mustered out July 12, 1865, **Bvt. Brig. Gen.**

181st Infantry

John O'Dowd	Oct. 17, 1864	Resigned May 27, 1865, **Bvt. Brig. Gen.**
John E. Hudson	June 16, 1865	Mustered out July 14, 1865

182nd Infantry

Lewis Butler	Oct. 26, 1864	Mustered out July 7, 1865

183rd Infantry

George W. Hoge	Nov. 18, 1864	Mustered out July 17, 1865, **Bvt. Brig. Gen.**

184th Infantry

Henry S. Commager	Feb. 22, 1865	Mustered out Sept. 21, 1865, **Bvt. Brig. Gen.**

185th Infantry

John E. Cummins	Feb. 27, 1865	Mustered out Sept. 26, 1865, **Bvt. Brig. Gen.**

186th Infantry

Thomas F. Wildes	Feb. 28, 1865	Mustered out Sept. 18, 1865, **Bvt. Brig. Gen.**

187th Infantry
Andrew R. Z. Dawson	March 2, 1865	Mustered out Jan. 20, 1866, **Bvt. Brig. Gen.**

188th Infantry
Jacob E. Taylor	March 5, 1865	Mustered out Sept. 21, 1865, **Bvt. Brig. Gen.**

189th Infantry
Henry D. Kingsbury	March 7, 1865	Mustered out Sept. 28, 1865, **Bvt. Brig. Gen.**

190th Infantry (Did not complete organization)

191st Infantry
Robert L. Kimberly	March 10, 1865	Mustered out Aug. 27, 1865, **Bvt. Brig. Gen.**

192nd Infantry
Francis W. Butterfield	March 10, 1865	Mustered out Sept. 1, 1865

193rd Infantry
Eugene Powell	April 13, 1865	Mustered out Aug. 4, 1865, **Bvt. Brig. Gen.**

194th Infantry
Anson G. McCook	March 14, 1865	Discharged Oct. 21, 1865, **Bvt. Brig. Gen.**
Obadiah C. Maxwell	Oct. 22, 1865	Mustered out Oct. 24, 1865, **Bvt. Brig. Gen.**

195th Infantry
Henry B. Banning	March 20, 1865	Mustered out Dec. 18, 1865, **Bvt. Brig. Gen.**

196th Infantry
Robert P. Kennedy	April 14, 1865	Mustered out Sept. 11, 1865, **Bvt. Brig. Gen.**

197th Infantry
Benton Halstead	May 29, 1865	Mustered out July 31, 1865

198th Infantry
Regiment not entitled to a colonel since it never attained full strength

---

Biographies

Wesley Rowe Adams
Private, Co. A, 27 OH Infantry, Aug. 1, 1861. Corporal, Co. A, 27 OH Infantry, April 1, 1862. Sergeant, Co. A, 27 OH Infantry, July 15, 1862. Captain, Co. K, 89 OH Infantry, Aug. 26, 1862. Taken prisoner Chickamauga, GA, Sept. 20, 1863. Confined Libby Prison, Richmond, VA. Escaped Feb. 9, 1864. *Colonel,* 175 OH Infantry, Oct. 11, 1864. Resigned captaincy, Nov. 16, 1864, to accept commission as colonel. Not mustered as colonel (and commission returned) due to reduced strength of the regiment.

Born: Aug. 12, 1838 near Clarksburg, Ross Co., OH

Died: Sept. 7, 1923 Larned, KS

Education: Attended Ohio Wesleyan University, Delaware, OH

Occupation: Farmer and real estate agent

Miscellaneous: Resided Clarksburg, Ross Co., OH, to 1865; Independence, Jackson Co., MO, 1865–68; Olathe, Johnson Co., KS, 1868–73; and Larned, Pawnee Co., KS, after 1873

Buried: Larned Cemetery, Larned, KS (Northeast Section, Lot 96)

References: *The United States Biographical Dictionary.* Kansas volume. Chicago, 1879. Obituary, *Larned Tiller and Toiler,* Sept. 13, 1923. Pension File and Military Service File, National Archives. Obituary, *Larned Chronoscope,* Sept. 13, 1923. Margaret B. Corbet. *Larned Cemetery.* Larned, KS, 1990. Bryan P. Weaver with H. Lee Fenner. *Sacrifice* *at Chickamauga: A History of the 89th Ohio Volunteer Infantry Regiment.* Palos Verdes Peninsula, CA, 2003.

Charles William Brandon Allison

Private, Co. D, 85 OH Infantry, June 1, 1862. Colonel, 85 OH Infantry, June 10, 1862. Commanded Post of Camp Chase, Columbus, OH, June 24–Sept. 23, 1862. Honorably mustered out, Sept. 23, 1862.

Born: Dec. 12, 1820 Middletown, Dauphin Co., PA

Died: Dec. 5, 1876 Wheeling, WV

Occupation: Lawyer

Offices/Honors: Ohio House of Representatives, 1864–66

Miscellaneous: Resided Bellefontaine, Logan Co., OH, to 1867; and Wheeling, Ohio Co, WV, 1867–76

Buried: Greenwood Cemetery, Wheeling, WV (Section G, Lot 24)

References: *Biographical Cyclopedia and Portrait Gallery with an Historical Sketch of the State of Ohio.* Vol. 6. Cincinnati, OH, 1895. Leonard A. Morrison. *History of the Alison or Allison Family in Europe and America.* Boston, MA, 1893. Obituary, *Wheeling Daily Register,* Dec. 6, 1876. Military Service File, National Archives.

Charles Anderson

Colonel, 93 OH Infantry, Aug. 9, 1862. GSW slight, Stone's River, TN, Dec. 31, 1862. Resigned Feb. 21, 1863, on account of ill health due to "an affection of the throat and hemorrhage from the bowels."

Born: June 1, 1814 Soldier's Retreat, Jefferson Co., KY

Died: Sept. 2, 1895 Kuttawa, KY

Education: Graduated Miami University, Oxford, OH, 1833

Occupation: Lawyer and agriculturist

Offices/Honors: Ohio Senate, 1844–46. Lieutenant Governor of Ohio, 1864–65. Acting Governor of Ohio, 1865–66.

Miscellaneous: Resided Cincinnati, OH, 1845–58; San Antonio, TX, 1858–61; Dayton, Montgomery Co., OH, 1861–67; Eddyville, Lyon Co., KY, 1867–77; Kuttawa, Lyon Co., KY, 1877–95. Brother of Brig. Gen. Robert Anderson. Father of Bvt. Brig. Gen. Allen L. Anderson. Uncle of Bvt. Brig. Gen. Nicholas L. Anderson.

Buried: Kuttawa Cemetery, Kuttawa, KY

References: *Memorial Record of Western Kentucky.* Chicago and New York, 1904. J. Fletcher Brennan, editor. *Biographical Cyclopedia and Portrait Gallery with an Historical Sketch of the State of Ohio.* Cincinnati, OH, 1879. William P. Anderson.

Charles William Brandon Allison (Ohio House of Representatives, 1864) (Dennis M. Keesee Collection. Copied by L. M. Strayer).

Charles Anderson (Acting Governor of Ohio, 1865) (photograph by J. W. Winder & Co., National Art Palace, 142 Fourth Street, bet. Race and Elm, Cincinnati, Ohio; courtesy Steve Meadow).

Anderson Family Records. Cincinnati, OH, 1936. Obituary Circular, Whole No. 348, Ohio MOLLUS. Military Service File, National Archives. Walter Havighurst. *Men of Old Miami, 1809–1873.* New York City, NY, 1974. *The Alumni and Former Student Catalogue of Miami University, 1809–1892.* Oxford, OH, 1892. *History of Montgomery County, OH.* Chicago, IL, 1882.

Ebenezer Baldwin Andrews

Major, 36 OH Infantry, Aug. 27, 1861. Lieutenant Colonel, 36 OH Infantry, Sept. 7, 1862. Colonel, 36 OH Infantry, Sept. 18, 1862. Commanded 2 Brigade, Kanawha Division, District of West Virginia, Department of the Ohio, Oct. 1862. Under pressure from a group of mutinous officers who filed unsubstantiated charges of cowardice and disobedience of orders, he resigned April 9, 1863, "since my health has not been good of late, and I fear that it would prove inadequate to a summer and fall campaign in the far South."

Born: April 29, 1821 Danbury, CT
Died: Aug. 14, 1880 Lancaster, OH
Education: Attended Williams College, Williamstown, MA. Graduated Marietta (OH) College, 1842. Attended Princeton (NJ) Theological Seminary.
Occupation: Congregational clergyman, 1846–51. Professor of Geology, Marietta College, 1851–70. An expert on the geology of the coal and oil producing regions of Ohio and West Virginia, he wrote many papers for scientific journals and served as Assistant State Geologist, Ohio Geological Survey, 1869–77.
Miscellaneous: Resided Marietta, Washington Co., OH; and Lancaster, Fairfield Co., OH
Buried: Oak Grove Cemetery, Marietta, OH (Section 23, Lot 3)
References: *History of Washington County, OH.* Cleveland, OH, 1881. Obituary, *Marietta Register,* Aug. 19, 1880. Military Service File, National Archives. George J. Blazier. *Marietta College: Biographical Record of the Officers and Alumni.* N.p., 1928.

George W. Andrews

Colonel, 15 OH Infantry, May 4, 1861. Honorably mustered out, Aug. 30, 1861. Major, 71 OH Infantry, Oct. 29, 1861. Lieutenant Colonel, 71 OH

Ebenezer Baldwin Andrews (Professor of Geology) (Slack Research Collections, Marietta College Library).

George W. Andrews (Ohio House of Representatives, 1860) (The Western Reserve Historical Society, Cleveland, Ohio).

Infantry, April 6, 1862. Taken prisoner Clarksville, TN, Aug. 18, 1862. Paroled Sept. 17, 1862. Resigned June 17, 1863, since "my business and my family require my personal attention."
   Born: Sept. 1, 1825 Medina, Orleans Co., NY
   Died: Nov. 21, 1887 Wapakoneta, OH
   Education: Attended Oberlin (OH) College
   Occupation: Lawyer
   Offices/Honors: Ohio House of Representatives, 1856–62. Ohio Senate, 1874–78.
   Miscellaneous: Resided Lima, Allen Co., OH, 1845–48; and Wapakoneta, Auglaize Co., OH, 1848–87
   Buried: Greenlawn Cemetery, Wapakoneta, OH
   References: *Biographical Encyclopedia of Ohio of the Nineteenth Century.* Cincinnati and Philadelphia, 1876. Pension File and Military Service File, National Archives. Letters Received, Volunteer Service Branch, Adjutant General's Office, File A401(VS)1862, National Archives. C. W. Williamson. *History of Western Ohio and Auglaize County.* Columbus, OH, 1905. W. Cooper. *Sketches of the Senators and Representatives in the Fifty-fourth General Assembly of the State of Ohio.* Columbus, OH, 1861.

Lorin Andrews

Colonel, 4 OH Infantry (3 months), April 26, 1861. Colonel, 4 OH Infantry (3 years), June 5, 1861.
   Born: April 1, 1819 Ashland, OH
   Died: Sept. 18, 1861 Gambier, OH (typhoid pneumonia)
   Education: Attended Kenyon College, Gambier, OH
   Occupation: President, Kenyon College, Gambier, OH, 1854–61
   Miscellaneous: Resided Ashland, Ashland Co., OH; Massillon, Stark Co., OH; and Gambier, Knox Co., OH
   Buried: Kenyon College Cemetery, Gambier, OH
   References: Norman N. Hill, compiler. *History of Knox County, OH, Its Past and Present.* Mount Vernon, OH, 1881. Whitelaw Reid. *Ohio in the War: Her Statesmen Generals and Soldiers.* Cincinnati, OH, 1868. Alfred Andrews. *Genealogical History of John and Mary Andrews.* Chicago, IL, 1872. William Kepler. *History of the Three Months' and Three Years' Service of the 4th Regiment Ohio Volunteer Infantry in the War for the Union.* Cleveland, OH, 1886. *Biographical Encyclopedia of Ohio of the Nineteenth Century.* Cincinnati and Philadelphia, 1876.

Lorin Andrews (N. E. Lewis, Photographer, Corner Main & Gambier Streets, Mt. Vernon, Ohio; courtesy Scott Hilts).

Jesse Josiah Appler

Captain, Co. D, 22 OH Infantry, April 17, 1861. Resigned July 28, 1861. Colonel, 53 OH Infantry, Feb. 8, 1862. He was mustered out April 29, 1862, pursuant to an order of Major Gen. Henry W. Halleck, having been identified by Brig. Gen. William T. Sherman as not conducting himself "with military propriety" at the battle of Shiloh, April 6, 1862.
   Born: Feb. 8, 1814 Washington, DC
   Died: Nov. 2, 1887 Portsmouth, OH
   Occupation: Brick mason
   Miscellaneous: Resided Portsmouth, Scioto Co., OH
   Buried: Greenlawn Cemetery, Portsmouth, OH (Section 9, Lot 43)
   References: Charles Ross Appler. *The Appler Family History.* N.p., 1976. Pension File and Military Service File, National Archives. Obituary, *Portsmouth Times,* Nov. 5, 1887. John K. Duke. *History of the 53rd Regiment Ohio Volunteer Infantry During the War of the Rebellion.* Portsmouth, OH, 1900.

James Boydston Armstrong

Lieutenant Colonel, 95 OH Infantry, Aug. 8, 1862. Taken prisoner and paroled Richmond, KY, Aug. 30, 1862. Dismissed to date Oct. 2, 1862, for absence without leave. Never having been mustered

James Boydston Armstrong (The National Archives [BA-45]).

into service, he could not be dismissed, so his dismissal was revoked, Dec. 23, 1862. Colonel, 134 OH Infantry, May 2, 1864. Commanded 2 Brigade, 3 Division, 10 Army Corps, Army of the James, June 19, 1864–Aug. 25, 1864. Dismissed Aug. 22, 1864, for "having grossly misrepresented the condition of his command in a communication to the President and having falsified his own report in a subsequent statement." Dismissal revoked July 29, 1865, and he was honorably discharged to date Aug. 22, 1864.

Born: Aug. 20, 1824 Wayne Co., OH
Died: Oct. 15, 1900 Cloverdale, CA
Occupation: Civil engineer and banker before 1874. Lumber mill operator, newspaper editor, and extensive land owner after 1874.
Miscellaneous: Resided Urbana, Champaign Co., OH, to 1874; and Cloverdale, Sonoma Co., CA, after 1874
Buried: Rural Cemetery, Santa Rosa, CA (Western Half Circle, Lot 219)
References: Obituary, *Santa Rosa Republican*, Oct. 16, 1900. Pension File and Military Service File, National Archives. Letters Received, Volunteer Service Branch, Adjutant General's Office, File W990(VS)1862, National Archives. Whitelaw Reid. *Ohio in the War: Her Statesmen Generals and Soldiers*. Cincinnati, OH, 1868. D. Warren Lambert. *When the Ripe Pears Fell: The Battle of Richmond, Kentucky*. Richmond, KY, 1995. *History of Champaign County, OH*. Chicago, IL, 1881.

Henry C. Ashwill

Sergeant, Co. I, 3 OH Infantry, April 25, 1861. Honorably mustered out, Aug. 22, 1861. 2 Lieutenant, Co. F, 96 OH Infantry, Aug. 19, 1862. *1 Lieutenant,* Co. F, 96 OH Infantry, March 1, 1863. Discharged for disability, March 17, 1863, due to phthisis pulmonalis. Colonel, 145 OH Infantry, May 12, 1864. Honorably mustered out, Aug. 24, 1864.

Born: Oct. 27, 1839 Marion Co., OH
Died: June 21, 1924 Ottawa, KS
Occupation: Farmer
Miscellaneous: Resided Delaware, Delaware Co., OH; Sumpter Twp., Cumberland Co., IL, 1864–73; Pomona, Franklin Co., KS; and Ottawa, Franklin Co., KS
Buried: Highland Cemetery, Ottawa, KS (Block 50, Lot 33)
References: Pension File, National Archives. Obituary, *Ottawa Herald,* June 23, 1924. Joseph T. Woods. *Services of the 96th Ohio Volunteers.* Toledo, OH, 1874. Robert F. Bartlett, compiler. *Roster of the 96th Regiment, Ohio Volunteer Infantry.* Columbus, OH, 1895.

Joel Funk Asper

Captain, Co. H, 7 OH Infantry (3 months), April 24, 1861. Captain, Co. H, 7 OH Infantry (3 years), June 3, 1861. GSW left thigh, Winchester,

Joel Funk Asper (U.S. House of Representatives, 1869) (Brady-Handy Collection, Library of Congress [LC-DIG-cwpbh-00195]).

VA, March 23, 1862. Lieutenant Colonel, 7 OH Infantry, May 20, 1862. Discharged for disability, March 13, 1863, due to effects of his wound. Colonel, 171 OH Infantry, May 7, 1864. Taken prisoner Keller's Bridge, KY, June 11, 1864. Released on special parole. Honorably mustered out, Aug. 20, 1864.

Born: April 20, 1822 Huntington Twp., Adams Co., PA

Died: Oct. 1, 1872 Chillicothe, MO

Occupation: Lawyer and newspaper editor

Offices/Honors: U.S. House of Representatives, 1869–71

Miscellaneous: Resided Warren, Trumbull Co., OH, to 1864; and Chillicothe, Livingston Co., MO, 1864–72

Buried: Edgewood Cemetery, Chillicothe, MO

References: *History of Caldwell and Livingston Counties, MO.* St. Louis, MO, 1886. William H. Barnes. *The Forty-First Congress of the United States, 1869–71.* New York and Washington, 1872. Lawrence Wilson, editor. *Itinerary of the 7th Ohio Volunteer Infantry, 1861–64.* New York and Washington, 1907. George L. Wood. *The Seventh Regiment: A Record.* New York City, NY, 1865. Pension File and Military Service File, National Archives. Letters Received, Volunteer Service Branch, Adjutant General's Office, File C222(VS)1863, National Archives. Jim Leeke, editor. *A Hundred Days to Richmond.* Bloomington, IN, 1999.

Ephraim Ball

Colonel, 162 OH Infantry, May 20, 1864. Honorably mustered out, Sept. 4, 1864.

Born: Nov. 25, 1812 near Greentown, Stark Co., OH

Died: Jan. 1, 1873 Canton, OH

Occupation: Inventor and manufacturer of harvesting machines

Miscellaneous: Resided Canton, Stark Co., OH

Buried: Westlawn Cemetery, Canton, OH (Section G, Lot 77)

References: John Danner, editor. *Old Landmarks of Canton and Stark County, OH.* Logansport, IN, 1904. Obituary, *Canton Repository,* Jan. 3 and Jan. 10, 1873. Military Service File, National Archives.

Mathias H. Bartilson

Captain, Co. A, 51 OH Infantry, Sept. 17, 1861. Major, 80 OH Infantry, Oct. 28, 1861. Lieutenant Colonel, 80 OH Infantry, Dec. 23, 1861. GSW right thigh, Iuka, MS, Sept. 19, 1862. Colonel, 80 OH Infantry, Feb. 14, 1863.

Born: 1827 Washington Co., PA

Died: Aug. 15, 1863 New Philadelphia, OH (typhoid fever)

Mathias H. Bartilson.

Education: Attended Franklin College, New Athens, OH

Occupation: Lawyer

Offices/Honors: Prosecuting Attorney, Tuscarawas Co., OH, 1854–58

Miscellaneous: Resided New Philadelphia, Tuscarawas Co., OH

Buried: Fair Street Cemetery, New Philadelphia, OH (Section A, Lot 28)

References: Edwin S. Rhodes. *The First Centennial Atlas of Tuscarawas County, OH.* New Philadelphia, OH, 1908. Obituary, *Tuscarawas Advocate,* Aug. 21, 1863. David F. Fryer. *History of the 80th Ohio Veteran Volunteer Infantry.* Newcomerstown, OH, 1904. Military Service File, National Archives.

Joseph Ridgeway Bartlett

Captain, Co. F, 49 OH Infantry, Aug. 26, 1861. Acting AIG, Staff of Brig. Gen. Richard W. Johnson, 2 Division, Right Wing, 14 Army Corps, Army of the Cumberland, Nov. 15, 1862–Jan. 9, 1863. Acting AIG, Staff of Brig. Gen. Richard W. Johnson, 2 Division, 20 Army Corps, Army of the Cumberland, Jan. 9, 1863–Oct. 9, 1863. Acting AIG, Staff of Brig. Gen. Thomas J. Wood, 3 Division, 4 Army Corps, Army of the Cumberland, Oct. 20, 1863–Dec. 17, 1864. Major, 49 OH Infantry, Dec. 5, 1864. Lieutenant Colonel, 49 OH

Joseph Ridgeway Bartlett (Sandusky County Kin Hunters Collection, USAMHI [RG98S-CWP144.12]).

Infantry, March 29, 1865. *Colonel,* 49 OH Infantry, June 26, 1865. Honorably mustered out, Nov. 30, 1865.
  Born: July 16, 1830 Seneca Co., OH
  Died: March 7, 1911 Fremont, OH
  Occupation: Lawyer
  Miscellaneous: Resided Fremont, Sandusky Co., OH
  Buried: Oakwood Cemetery, Fremont, OH (Section 7, Lot 71)
  References: Obituary, *Fremont Daily News,* March 8, 1911. Pension File and Military Service File, National Archives. Letters Received, Volunteer Service Branch, Adjutant General's Office, File B2300(VS)1864, National Archives. John Fitch. *Annals of the Army of the Cumberland.* Philadelphia, PA, 1864. Richard L. Manion and Nan Card. *Sandusky County, Ohio, Civil War Soldiers.* Fremont, OH, 1992.

Stephen Allen Bassford

2 Lieutenant, Co. B, 74 Ohio Infantry, Oct. 3, 1861. Captain, Co. B, 74 OH Infantry, Dec. 5, 1861. Lieutenant Colonel, 94 OH Infantry, Aug. 11, 1862. Colonel, 94 OH Infantry, Feb. 22, 1863. Resigned April 16, 1864, since "my wife has been afflicted with heart disease for several years," and "the only chance to save her life is to be relieved from the care of her children, and to have me return."

Stephen Allen Bassford (U.S. Military Academy Library).

  Born: 1827 New York City, NY
  Died: Dec. 19, 1904 New York City, NY
  Occupation: Tobacconist
  Miscellaneous: Resided New York City, NY
  Buried: Green-Wood Cemetery, Brooklyn, NY (Section 92, Lot 3026, unmarked)
  References: Pension File and Military Service File, National Archives. Obituary, *New York Times,* Dec. 21, 1904. Theodore W. Blackburn. *Letters from the Front: A Union "Preacher" Regiment (74th Ohio) in the Civil War.* Dayton, OH, 1981. *Record of the 94th Regiment Ohio Volunteer Infantry in the War of the Rebellion.* Cincinnati, OH, N.d.

Valentine Bausenwein

Major, 58 OH Infantry, Sept. 21, 1861. Colonel, 58 OH Infantry, Oct. 1, 1861. Dismissed to date April 2, 1862, by order of Major Gen. Halleck, for allegedly requisitioning three horses for regimental officers without giving the necessary receipt. Reinstated. Acting AIG, Staff of Brig. Gen. Peter J. Osterhaus, commanding 3 Division, Army of Southwest Missouri, Aug. 1862. Dismissed to date Aug. 11, 1862, a board of inquiry having concluded that he ordered a regimental party to be sent to Columbus, OH, on purely personal business and allowed captured rebel arms to be converted to personal use.

Valentine Bausenwein (as officer in pre-war Italian army).

Born: 1829? Germany
Died: March 25, 1906 Queens, NY
Education: Graduated Military Academy of the Kingdom of Bavaria, 1848
Occupation: Officer of engineers in Bavarian, Austrian and Italian armies before war. Railroad construction engineer after war.
Miscellaneous: Resided Columbus, OH; St. Joseph, MO; Des Moines, IA; Milwaukee, WI; St. Paul, MN; Stevens Point, WI; and Brooklyn, NY
Buried: Kings County Farm Cemetery, Brooklyn, NY
References: Pension File and Military Service File, National Archives. Letters Received, Volunteer Service Branch, Adjutant General's Office, File A296(VS)1862, National Archives. Jean Fyler Arnold. *The Fyler-Filer Family.* Franklin, NC, 1991. "Carl F. Bausenwein. Former Stevens Point Boy Passes Away at His Home in Denver," *Stevens Point Daily Journal,* June 2, 1905.

Godfried Becker

Lieutenant Colonel, 28 OH Infantry, June 10, 1861. Injured by horse falling on him, Carnifex Ferry, WV, Sept. 10, 1861. Resigned Sept. 24, 1862 due to acute orchitis. Lieutenant Colonel, 28 OH Infantry, Aug. 7, 1863. *Colonel,* 28 OH Infantry, Nov. 27, 1863, to succeed Colonel August Moor, dismissed. Resumed position as lieutenant colonel when Moor's dismissal was revoked, Feb. 16, 1864. Honorably mustered out, July 23, 1864.
Born: Oct. 13, 1827 Frankenthal, Palatinate, Germany
Died: April 11, 1865 Cincinnati, OH (injuries received at Carnifex Ferry, WV)
Occupation: Newspaper editor
Miscellaneous: Resided Cincinnati, OH
Buried: Vine Street Hill Cemetery, Cincinnati, OH (Section 5, Lot 304)
References: Pension File and Military Service File, National Archives. Adolf E. Zucker, editor. *The Forty-Eighters: Political Refugees of the German Revolution of 1848.* New York City, NY, 1950. Letters Received, Volunteer Service Branch, Adjutant General's Office, File O446(VS)1863, National Archives.

Harrison Gray Otis Blake

Colonel, 166 OH Infantry, May 15, 1864. Honorably mustered out, Sept. 9, 1864.
Born: March 17, 1818 Newfane, VT
Died: April 16, 1876 Medina, OH
Occupation: Lawyer
Offices/Honors: Ohio House of Representatives, 1846–48. Ohio Senate, 1848–50. U.S. House of Representatives, 1859–63.
Miscellaneous: Resided Medina, Medina Co., OH
Buried: Spring Grove Cemetery, Medina, OH (Section 5)
References: James L. Harrison, compiler. *Biographical Directory of the American Congress, 1774–1949.* Washington, DC, 1950. Francis E. Blake, compiler. *Increase Blake of Boston: His Ancestors and Descendants.* Boston, MA, 1898. Sharon L. D. Kraynek. *Medina County Gazette Newspaper Abstracts, 1854–1898.* Apollo, PA, 1997. Military Service File, National Archives.

Thomas Chalkley Boone

Lieutenant Colonel, 115 OH Infantry, Aug. 15, 1862. Colonel, 115 OH Infantry, July 20, 1864. Honorably mustered out, June 22, 1865.
Born: May 14, 1823 Gettysburg, PA
Died: Dec. 20, 1893 Salem, OH
Occupation: Saddler and carriage trimmer before war. Banker and engine manufacturer (Buckeye Engine Co.) after war.
Miscellaneous: Resided Salem, Columbiana Co., OH
Buried: Hope Cemetery, Salem, OH
References: Obituary Circular, Whole No. 258,

Harrison Gray Otis Blake (U.S. House of Representatives, 1862).

Thomas Chalkley Boone (J. F. Ryder, Photographist, 171 Superior Street, Cleveland, Ohio; Minnesota Historical Society).

Ohio MOLLUS. Pension File and Military Service File, National Archives. Obituary, *Salem Daily Herald,* Dec. 20, 1893. *Society of the Army of the Cumberland. Twenty-fifth Reunion, Chattanooga, TN, 1895.* Cincinnati, OH, 1896. Letters Received, Volunteer Service Branch, Adjutant General's Office, File M1786(VS)1864, National Archives.

William K. Bosley

Colonel, 6 OH Infantry (3 months), April 20, 1861. Colonel, 6 OH Infantry (3 years), June 12, 1861. Discharged for disability, Aug. 19, 1862, on account of "continuous ill health, ... due to chronic disease of the lungs."

Born: Jan. 1, 1825 Baltimore, MD
Died: Dec. 1, 1866 Cincinnati, OH
Occupation: Wall paper merchant and postal clerk
Miscellaneous: Resided Cincinnati, OH
Buried: Spring Grove Cemetery, Cincinnati, OH (Section 23, Lot 72, unmarked)
References: Ebenezer Hannaford. *The Story of a Regiment.* Cincinnati, OH, 1868. Letters Received, Volunteer Service Branch, Adjutant General's Office, File M2485(VS)1862, National Archives. Military Service File, National Archives.

Daniel Bowman

Captain, Co. D, 93 OH Infantry, July 21, 1862. GSW slight, Missionary Ridge, TN, Nov. 25, 1863. Lieutenant Colonel, 93 OH Infantry, March 15, 1864. *Colonel,* 93 OH Infantry, March 5, 1865. Honorably mustered out, June 8, 1865.

Born: Nov. 15, 1828 OH
Died: May 23, 1892 Middletown, OH
Occupation: Millwright and bridge builder
Offices/Honors: Mayor of Middletown, OH, 1892
Miscellaneous: Resided Middletown, Butler Co., OH
Buried: Middletown Historical Cemetery, Middletown, OH (Square 4, Lot 5)
References: Military Service File, National Archives. Obituary, *Hamilton Daily Democrat,* May 24, 1892.

Edwin D. Bradley

Captain, Co. E, 14 OH Infantry, April 24, 1861. 1 Lieutenant, Adjutant, 14 OH Infantry, April 29, 1861. Honorably mustered out, Aug. 13, 1861. Colonel, 38 OH Infantry, Sept. 10, 1861. Resigned Feb. 8, 1862, due to "continued ill health which has rendered me unfit properly to discharge my official duty."

Born: Aug. 28, 1804 Litchfield, CT
Died: Nov. 1, 1890 Stryker, OH
Education: Attended Litchfield (CT) Academy

Edwin D. Bradley (Weston A. Goodspeed and Charles Blanchard, editors. *County of Williams, Ohio, Historical and Biographical.* Chicago, Illinois, 1882).

Other Wars: Mexican War (Captain, Co. F, 1 OH Infantry)
Occupation: Merchant and farmer
Miscellaneous: Resided Stryker, Williams Co., OH
Buried: Oakwood Cemetery, Stryker, OH (Section A-3, Lot 350)
References: Weston A. Goodspeed and Charles Blanchard, editors. *County of Williams, Ohio, Historical and Biographical.* Chicago, IL, 1882. Obituary, *Bryan Press,* Nov. 6, 1890. Pension File and Military Service File, National Archives.

Edward Briggs

2 Lieutenant, Co. I, 76 OH Infantry, Oct. 3, 1861. Captain, Co. I, 76 OH Infantry, Nov. 27, 1861. Major, 76 OH Infantry, March 12, 1864. Lieutenant Colonel, 76 OH Infantry, Oct. 12, 1864. Commanded 1 Brigade, 1 Division, 15 Army Corps, Army of the Tennessee, June 16–July 15, 1865. *Colonel,* 76 OH Infantry, July 13, 1865. Honorably mustered out, July 15, 1865. Bvt. Colonel, USV, March 13, 1865, for gallant and meritorious services during the war.
Born: 1825? Medina Co., OH
Died: Aug. 5, 1872 Little Falls, MN
Occupation: Wood turner and machinist
Miscellaneous: Resided Massillon, Stark Co., OH; Meriden, LaSalle Co., IL; and Little Falls, Morrison Co., MN

Edward Briggs (Bob Coch Collection).

Buried: Place of burial unknown
References: Pension File and Military Service File, National Archives. Edna A. Hannibal, compiler. *Clement Briggs of Plymouth Colony and His Descendants, 1621–1965.* N.p., 1969. Charles A. Willison. *A Boy's Service with the 76th Ohio.* Huntington, WV, 1995.

Joseph Henry Brigham

Private, Co. F, 12 OH Infantry, April 19, 1861. Honorably mustered out, Aug. 18, 1861. 2 Lieutenant, Co. A, 69 OH Infantry, Oct. 7, 1861. Captain, Co. A, 69 OH Infantry, Oct. 17, 1861. Lieutenant Colonel, 69 OH Infantry, Feb. 10, 1863. Commanded 2 Brigade, 1 Division, 14 Army Corps, Army of the Cumberland, Nov. 16, 1864–Jan. 17, 1865. *Colonel,* 69 OH Infantry, July 10, 1865. Honorably mustered out, July 17, 1865. Bvt. Colonel, USV, March 13, 1865, for meritorious services.
Born: Dec. 12, 1838 Lodi, OH
Died: June 29, 1904 Delta, OH
Occupation: Farmer
Offices/Honors: Sheriff of Fulton Co., OH, 1868–72. Ohio Senate, 1882–84. U.S. Assistant Secretary of Agriculture, 1897–1904.
Miscellaneous: Resided Delta, Fulton Co., OH; and Washington, DC

Joseph Henry Brigham (The Center for Archival Collections, Bowling Green State University).

Buried: Greenlawn Cemetery, Delta, OH (Section D)

References: W. I. Tyler Brigham. *The History of the Brigham Family.* New York City, NY, 1907. Obituary, *Fulton County Tribune,* July 1 and July 8, 1904. Obituary, *Washington Post,* June 30, 1904. Military Service File, National Archives. *Society of the Army of the Cumberland. Thirty-second Reunion, Indianapolis, IN, Sept. 20, 21, 1904.* Cincinnati, OH, 1905. Brigham Family Papers, Center for Archival Collections, Bowling Green (OH) State University.

Allison L. Brown

Sergeant, Co. C, 73 OH Infantry, Oct. 19, 1861. Captain, Co. D, 89 OH Infantry, July 23, 1862. Resigned May 2, 1863, due to chronic diarrhea ... and "general debility following typhoid fever." Colonel, 149 OH Infantry, May 11, 1864. Honorably mustered out, Aug. 30, 1864.

Born: Feb. 20, 1835 Ross Co., OH
Died: Oct. 26, 1879 Hillsboro, OH
Occupation: Farmer
Offices/Honors: Ohio Senate, 1876–78
Miscellaneous: Resided Deerfield Twp., Ross Co., OH; and Chillicothe, Ross Co., OH
Buried: Browns Chapel Cemetery, near Clarksburg, Ross Co., OH
References: Lyle S. Evans, editor. *A Standard*

Allison L. Brown (George Perkins. *A Summer in Maryland and Virginia.* Chillicothe, Ohio, 1911).

History of Ross County, Ohio. Chicago, IL, 1917. Obituary, *Scioto Gazette,* Chillicothe, OH, Oct. 29, 1879. Obituary, *Hillsboro Gazette,* Oct. 30, 1879. George Perkins. *A Summer in Maryland and Virginia; or Campaigning with the 149th Ohio Volunteer Infantry.* Chillicothe, OH, 1911. Military Service File, National Archives. Bryan P. Weaver with H. Lee Fenner. *Sacrifice at Chickamauga: A History of the 89th Ohio Volunteer Infantry Regiment.* Palos Verdes Peninsula, CA, 2003. Jim Leeke, editor. *A Hundred Days to Richmond.* Bloomington, IN, 1999.

Robert Carson Brown

Private, Co. H, 15 OH Infantry (3 months), April 23, 1861. Honorably mustered out, Aug. 29, 1861. Private, Co. C, 64 OH Infantry, Oct. 4, 1861. 1 Lieutenant, Co. C, 64 OH Infantry, Oct. 31, 1861. Captain, Co. C, 64 OH Infantry, Nov. 27, 1861. Lieutenant Colonel, 64 OH Infantry, March 12, 1863. *Colonel,* 64 OH Infantry, June 24, 1864. Honorably mustered out, Feb. 23, 1865.

Born: Nov. 13, 1834 near Fairview, Hancock Co., WV
Died: June 15, 1898 Mansfield, OH
Education: Graduated Franklin College, New Athens, OH, 1860
Occupation: Farmer, insurance agent, pension agent, and Deputy Internal Revenue Collector

Robert Carson Brown (Wilbur F. Hinman. *The Story of the Sherman Brigade*. Alliance, Ohio, 1897).

Miscellaneous: Resided Lexington, Richland Co., OH, to 1891; and Mansfield, Richland Co., OH, 1891–98
Buried: Lexington Cemetery, Lexington, OH
References: Obituary, *Mansfield Daily Shield*, June 15, 1898. Charles G. Brown, editor. *The Sherman Brigade Marches South: The Civil War Memoirs of Colonel Robert Carson Brown*. N.p., 1995. Albert A. Graham, compiler. *History of Richland County, OH: Its Past and Present*. Mansfield, OH, 1880. *Franklin College Register: Biographical and Historical*. Wheeling, WV, 1908. Military Service File, National Archives. Wilbur F. Hinman. *The Story of the Sherman Brigade*. Alliance, OH, 1897.

Joseph Bruff

Captain, Co. A, 125 OH Infantry, Aug. 13, 1862. GSW right side, Missionary Ridge, TN, Nov. 25, 1863. Major, 125 OH Infantry, Feb. 18, 1864. Facing charges of "Conduct to the Prejudice of Good Order and Military Discipline" for having discussed with his junior officers the comments of Colonel (later Brig. Gen.) Emerson Opdycke accusing him of being "deceitful and unscrupulous" and "incompetent to the position," he went before a Board of Examination which found on Nov. 10, 1864, that although his actions were "injudicious," his capacity, qualifications, and efficiency were adequate to his position. Lieutenant Colonel, 125 OH Infantry, Jan. 2, 1865. Honorably mustered out, Sept. 25, 1865. *Colonel,* 125 OH Infantry, Oct. 16, 1865. Bvt. Colonel, USV, March 13, 1865, for gallant and meritorious services during the war.
Born: March 6, 1827 Damascus, OH
Died: Nov. 14, 1885 Damascus, OH (committed suicide on his son's grave)
Occupation: Farmer and lawyer
Offices/Honors: Ohio House of Representatives, 1860–62 and 1866–68
Miscellaneous: Resided Damascus, Mahoning Co., OH
Buried: Damascus Cemetery, Damascus, OH
References: Martha F. McCourt. *Descendants of Thomas Bruff.* N.p, 1973. Obituary, *Salem Era*, Nov. 20, 1885. Military Service File, National Archives. Letters Received, Volunteer Service Branch, Adjutant General's Office, File S3213(VS)1864, National Archives. Charles T. Clark. *Opdycke Tigers, 125th O. V. I., A History of the Regiment.* Columbus, OH, 1895. Robert C. Moon. *The Morris Family of*

Joseph Bruff (photograph by Decker's Cartes de Visite, Camp Cleveland, Ohio).

Philadelphia. Philadelphia, PA, 1898. W. Cooper. *Sketches of the Senators and Representatives in the Fifty-fourth General Assembly of the State of Ohio.* Columbus, OH, 1861.

Lewis P. Buckley

Captain, Co. G, 19 OH Infantry, April 27, 1861. Major, 19 OH Infantry, May 29, 1861. Honorably mustered out, Aug. 31, 1861. Colonel, 29 OH Infantry, Aug. 27, 1861. Resigned Jan. 26, 1863, on account of "my age and poor health" due to tuberculosis of both lungs.

Born: 1804 Cayuga Lake, NY
Died: June 25, 1868 Akron, OH
Education: Attended U.S. Military Academy, West Point, NY (Class of 1826)
Occupation: Foundry and plow works operator, stove and tin merchant, canal toll collector, and justice of the peace
Offices/Honors: Assistant Doorkeeper, U.S. House of Representatives, 1865–67
Miscellaneous: Resided Akron, Summit Co., OH
Buried: Glendale Cemetery, Akron, OH (Section 3, Lot 69)
References: *Our Memorial Chapel Dedicated Tuesday, May 30th, 1876 with the Life and Services of Col. Lewis P. Buckley and a History of Buckley Post No. 12, GAR.* Akron, OH, 1876. Samuel A. Lane. *Fifty Years and Over of Akron and Summit County.* Akron, OH, 1892. Pension File and Military Service File, National Archives. Obituary, *Summit County Beacon,* July 2, 1868. John H. SeCheverell. *Journal History of the 29th Ohio Veteran Volunteers, 1861–65. Its Victories and its Reverses.* Cleveland, OH, 1883.

Barnabas Burns

Colonel, 86 OH Infantry (3 months), June 10, 1862. Honorably mustered out, Sept. 25, 1862.

Born: June 29, 1817 Fayette Co., PA
Died: Oct. 13, 1883 Mansfield, OH
Occupation: Lawyer
Offices/Honors: Ohio Senate, 1847–51
Miscellaneous: Resided Mansfield, Richland Co., OH
Buried: Mansfield Cemetery, Mansfield, OH (Section OS2, Lot 43)
References: *Biographical Cyclopedia and Portrait Gallery with an Historical Sketch of the State of Ohio.* Vol. 1. Cincinnati, OH, 1883. Abraham J. Baughman, editor. *Centennial Biographical History of Richland and Ashland Counties, OH.* Chicago, IL, 1901. Albert A. Graham, compiler. *History of Richland County, OH: Its Past and Present.* Mansfield, OH, 1880. *Biographical Encyclopedia of Ohio of the Nineteenth Century.* Cincinnati and Philadelphia, 1876. Obituary, *Richland Shield and Banner,* Oct. 20, 1883. Virgil A. Stanfield, "Barnabas Burns Had Many Talents," *Mansfield News Journal,* May 23, 1976. Military Service File, National Archives.

Lewis P. Buckley (*Our Memorial Chapel Dedicated Tuesday, May 30th, 1876 with the Life and Services of Col. Lewis P. Buckley, and a History of Buckley Post No. 12, GAR.* Akron, Ohio, 1876).

Barnabas Burns and wife Urath (Gore) Burns (1855).

Otto Burstenbinder

Colonel, 67 OH Infantry, Oct. 17, 1861. Facing charges of "habitual neglect of duty" (due to drunkenness), "tyrannical and capricious conduct, willingly directing and allowing the signing of false muster rolls, and conduct to the prejudice of good order and military discipline," he was dismissed July 29, 1862.

Born: 1830? Hamburg, Germany
Died: Date and place of death unknown
Occupation: Associated with United States Blasting Oil Co. after war
Miscellaneous: Resided Toledo, Lucas Co., OH; and New York City, NY
Buried: Place of burial unknown
References: Military Service File, National Archives. Letters Received, Volunteer Service Branch, Adjutant General's Office, File B1205(VS)1862, National Archives. Jerome Mushkat, editor. *A Citizen-Soldier's Civil War: The Letters of Brevet Major General Alvin C. Voris.* DeKalb, IL, 2002. Frank L. Byrne and Jean Powers Soman, editors. *Your True Marcus: The Civil War Letters of a Jewish Colonel.* Kent, OH, 1985. "Law Reports: The Nitro-Glycerine Case," *New York Times,* April 24, 1866.

Lewis Butler

Private, Co. H, 14 OH Infantry (3 months), April 22, 1861. Honorably mustered out, Aug. 13, 1861. 2 Lieutenant, Co. I, 67 OH Infantry, Oct. 4, 1861. Captain, Co. I, 67 OH Infantry, Dec. 18, 1861. Accidental bayonet wound left foot, Harrison's Landing, VA, July 4, 1862. Major, 67 OH Infantry, Jan. 14, 1863. Colonel, 182 OH Infantry, Oct. 26, 1864. Honorably mustered out, July 7, 1865.

Born: Dec. 2, 1825 Augusta Twp., Carroll Co., OH
Died: Nov. 12, 1916 Petersburg, VA
Occupation: Carpenter and farmer before war. Farmer, contractor and architect after war.
Miscellaneous: Resided Toledo, Lucas Co., OH; Tidioute, Warren Co., PA; Delta, Fulton Co., OH; Runnelsburg, Hall Co., NE; Houston, TX; and Petersburg, Dinwiddie Co., VA
Buried: Blandford Cemetery, Petersburg, VA (Ward T, Section 3, Square 8)
References: Pension File and Military Service File, National Archives. Obituary, *Petersburg Daily Index-Appeal,* Nov. 14, 1916. Jerome Mushkat, editor. *A Citizen-Soldier's Civil War: The Letters of Brevet Major General Alvin C. Voris.* DeKalb, IL, 2002. Letters Received, Volunteer Service Branch, Adjutant General's Office, File O1464(VS)1864, National Archives.

Francis W. Butterfield

Captain, Co. C, 8 OH Infantry (3 months), April 23, 1861. Captain, Co. C, 8 OH Infantry (3 years), June 22, 1861. Accidental GSW right hand,

Lewis Butler (L. M. Strayer Collection).

Francis W. Butterfield (courtesy Brad & Donna Pruden).

Cumberland, MD, Aug. 15, 1861. Acting AIG, Staff of Colonel (later Brig. Gen.) Samuel S. Carroll, Jan.14–May 13, 1864. Acting AIG, 3 Brigade, 2 Division, 2 Army Corps, Army of the Potomac, May 13–July 13, 1864. Honorably mustered out, July 13, 1864. Colonel, 192 OH Infantry, March 10, 1865. Honorably mustered out, Sept. 1, 1865.
Born: 1831? VT
Died: June 18, 1894 Excelsior Springs, MO
Occupation: Produce merchant before war. Insurance agent, newspaper publisher, and real estate agent after war.
Miscellaneous: Resided Bucyrus, Crawford Co., OH, to 1871; and Kansas City, MO, after 1871
Buried: Forest Hill Cemetery, Kansas City, MO (Block 35, Lot 65)
References: Obituary, *Kansas City Star,* June 18, 1894. Pension File and Military Service File, National Archives. Letters Received, Volunteer Service Branch, Adjutant General's Office, File B2059(VS)1862, National Archives. Franklin Sawyer. *A Military History of the 8th Regiment Ohio Volunteer Infantry.* Cleveland, OH, 1881.

Lewis Davis Campbell

Colonel, 69 OH Infantry, Oct. 2, 1861. Appointed Provost Marshal, Nashville, TN, June 29, 1862. Facing unproven charges of "Drunkenness and Conduct Unbecoming an Officer and a Gentleman While on Duty," he resigned Aug. 9, 1862, citing "the unfriendly relations and incompatibility of feeling which subsist between some of the officers of the regiment and myself" ... and "the constant strain on my physical and intellectual energies for the last nine months in recruiting the regiment and in endeavoring to make it effective."
Born: Aug. 9, 1811 Franklin, OH
Died: Nov. 26, 1882 Hamilton, OH
Occupation: Lawyer
Offices/Honors: U.S. House of Representatives, 1849–58, 1871–73. U.S. Minister to Mexico, 1866–67.
Miscellaneous: Resided Hamilton, Butler Co., OH. Brother-in-law of Colonel Robert Reily (75 OH Infantry).
Buried: Greenwood Cemetery, Hamilton, OH (Hill Section, Lot 468)
References: *Dictionary of American Biography. National Cyclopedia of American Biography.* Obituary, *Butler County Democrat,* Nov. 30, 1882. James McBride. *Pioneer Biography: Sketches of the Lives of Some of the Early Settlers of Butler County, Ohio.* Cincinnati, OH, 1869. William E. Van Horne, "Lewis D. Campbell and the Know-Nothing Party in Ohio," *Ohio History,* Vol. 76, No. 4 (Autumn 1967). Military Service File, National Archives. J. Morrow. *History of Warren County, OH.* Chicago,

Lewis Davis Campbell (Richard F. Carlile Collection).

IL, 1882. James E. Campbell. *Military Record of Samuel Campbell and His Descendants.* N.p., 1919.

James Cantwell

Lieutenant Colonel, 4 OH Infantry (3 months), April 26, 1861. Lieutenant Colonel, 4 OH Infantry (3 years), June 5, 1861. Colonel, 82 OH Infantry, Dec. 31, 1861. GSW head, Groveton, VA, Aug. 29, 1862.
Born: Dec. 8, 1810 near Steubenville, OH
Died: Aug. 29, 1862 KIA Groveton, VA
Other Wars: Mexican War (1 Lieutenant, 3 OH Infantry)
Occupation: Farmer
Offices/Honors: Ohio House of Representatives, 1854–56
Miscellaneous: Resided Mansfield, Richland Co., OH, to 1859; and Kenton, Hardin Co., OH, 1859–62
Buried: Mansfield Cemetery, Mansfield, OH (Section OS11, Lot 504)
References: Edward N. Cantwell, compiler. *The Generation of the Upright.* Lyons, IA, 1911. Albert

Caleb Henry Carlton

1 Lieutenant, 4 U.S. Infantry, May 14, 1861. Captain, 4 U.S. Infantry, June 30, 1862. Colonel, 89 OH Infantry, July 7, 1863. Taken prisoner Chickamauga, GA, Sept. 20, 1863. Confined Libby Prison, Richmond, VA. Paroled March 7, 1864. Returned to regiment, June 1, 1864. Commanded Post of Chattanooga, TN, Oct. 17, 1864–May 13, 1865. Commanded 2 Brigade, 1 Separate Division, District of the Etowah, Army of the Cumberland, Nov.–Dec. 1864. Commanded District of Western Kentucky, Department of Kentucky, May 13–June 15, 1865. Honorably mustered out of Volunteer Service, June 23, 1865.

Born: Sept. 1, 1836 Cleveland, OH
Died: March 21, 1923 Atlantic City, NJ
Education: Attended Brown University, Providence, RI. Graduated U.S. Military Academy, West Point, NY, 1859.
Occupation: Regular army (Brig. Gen., USA, retired June 30, 1897)
Miscellaneous: Resided Cleveland, OH; Washington, DC; Hampton, VA; and Rye, NY
Buried: Lake View Cemetery, Cleveland, OH (Section 22, Lot 289)
References: *Annual Reunion,* Association of the Graduates of the USMA, 1924. William H. Powell and Edward Shippen, editors. *Officers of the Army*

Lewis Davis Campbell (courtesy Henry Deeks).

James Cantwell (Massachusetts MOLLUS Collection, USAMHI [Vol. 69, p. 3412]).

A. Graham, compiler. *History of Richland County, OH: Its Past and Present.* Mansfield, OH, 1880. Military Service File, National Archives. William Kepler. *History of the Three Months' and Three Years' Service of the 4th Regiment Ohio Volunteer Infantry in the War for the Union.* Cleveland, OH, 1886.

Caleb Henry Carlton (Roger D. Hunt Collection, USAMHI [RG98S-CWP21.76]).

Caleb Henry Carlton (Archibald Gracie. *The Truth About Chickamauga*. Boston and New York, 1911).

Leonard Willard Carpenter (Roger D. Hunt Collection, USAMHI [RG98S-CWP21.56]).

and Navy (Regular) Who Served in the Civil War. Philadelphia, PA, 1892. Bryan P. Weaver with H. Lee Fenner. *Sacrifice at Chickamauga: A History of the 89th Ohio Volunteer Infantry Regiment.* Palos Verdes Peninsula, CA, 2003. Military Service File, National Archives. Letters Received, Appointment, Commission and Personal Branch, Adjutant General's Office, File 5667(ACP)1882, National Archives. George W. Cullum. *Biographical Register of the Officers and Graduates of the U.S. Military Academy.* Third Edition. Boston and New York, 1891. Obituary, *Cleveland Plain Dealer,* March 23, 1923. Archibald Gracie. *The Truth About Chickamauga.* Boston and New York, 1911.

Leonard Willard Carpenter

1 Lieutenant, Co. A, 4 OH Infantry (3 months), April 27, 1861. Captain, Co. A, 4 OH Infantry (3 years), June 4, 1861. Major, 4 OH Infantry, Dec. 1, 1862. Lieutenant Colonel, 4 OH Infantry, Dec. 13, 1862. Colonel, 4 OH Infantry, Nov. 1, 1863. Muster as colonel revoked since "the regiment was below the minimum number and therefore not entitled to an officer of the grade of colonel." Honorably mustered out, June 21, 1864.

Born: Jan. 26, 1834 Indiana, PA
Died: Feb. 18, 1908 Seattle, WA
Education: Graduated Cleveland (OH) Homeopathic Medical College, 1876
Occupation: Physician

Offices/Honors: Washington State Legislature, 1896
Miscellaneous: Resided Mount Vernon, Knox Co., OH, to 1865; Columbus, Franklin Co., OH, 1865–67; New Albany, Floyd Co., IN, 1867–76; Logansport, Cass Co., IN, 1876–88; and Seattle, WA, after 1888. Brother of Colonel John C. Carpenter (67 PA Infantry).
Buried: Gettysburg National Cemetery, Gettysburg, PA
References: Obituary, *Seattle Post-Intelligencer,* Feb. 19, 1908. Letters Received, Volunteer Service Branch, Adjutant General's Office, File C47(VS) 1864, National Archives. Pension File and Military Service File, National Archives. William Kepler. *History of the Three Months' and Three Years' Service of the 4th Regiment Ohio Volunteer Infantry in the War for the Union.* Cleveland, OH, 1886. Edmund J. Raus, Jr. *A Generation on the March: The Union Army at Gettysburg.* Gettysburg, PA, 1996. Death Notice, *Journal of the American Medical Association,* Vol. 50.

William Biddle Cassilly

1 Lieutenant, RQM, 10 OH Infantry (3 months), May 8, 1861. Honorably mustered out, Aug. 15, 1861. Lieutenant Colonel, Benton Cadets, MO In-

fantry, Sept. 2, 1861. Honorably mustered out, Jan. 8, 1862. Lieutenant Colonel, 69 OH Infantry, April 17, 1862. Colonel, 69 OH Infantry, Aug. 10, 1862. GSW left arm, Stone's River, TN, Dec. 31, 1862. Upon the recommendation of his brigade commander, Colonel Timothy R. Stanley, who described him at Stone's River as "so drunk as to be unfitted to command," he was dismissed, effective Dec. 31, 1862. Colonel Stanley commented further, "A man who will come to the field of battle, having the lives of so many in his keeping, in such a situation, no matter what his social position, is totally unfit for any command."
  Born: April 1824 Pittsburgh, PA
  Died: July 22, 1888 Cincinnati, OH
  Education: Attended Woodward High School, Cincinnati, OH
  Occupation: Merchant and insurance agent
  Miscellaneous: Resided Cincinnati, OH
  Buried: Spring Grove Cemetery, Cincinnati, OH (Section 57, Lot 2)
  References: Obituary, *Cincinnati Commercial Gazette,* July 24, 1888. John A. Gano, et al. *Old Woodward Memorial.* Cincinnati, OH, 1884. Military Service File, National Archives. *Official Records,* Series I, Vol. 20, Part 1, p. 421.

Zachariah Morris Chandler

2 Lieutenant, Co. B, 78 OH Infantry, Dec. 2, 1861. Captain, Co. B, 78 OH Infantry, Dec. 13, 1861. Major, 78 OH Infantry, Sept. 7, 1862. Lieutenant Colonel, 78 OH Infantry, Oct. 1, 1862. Colonel, 78 OH Infantry, Nov. 29, 1862. Discharged for disability, July 23, 1863, due to "chronic ulceration of the bowels and diarrhea."
  Born: Aug. 11, 1810 Putnam, Muskingum Co., OH
  Died: July 10, 1895 Zanesville, OH
  Occupation: School teacher and bookkeeper
  Miscellaneous: Resided Zanesville, Muskingum Co., OH
  Buried: Woodlawn Cemetery, Zanesville, OH (Section CC, Lot 9)
  References: Obituary, *Zanesville Daily Courier,* July 11, 1895. Pension File and Military Service File, National Archives. Letters Received, Volunteer Service Branch, Adjutant General's Office, File D209(VS)1863, National Archives. Thomas M. Stevenson. *History of the 78th Regiment Ohio Veteran Volunteer Infantry.* Zanesville, OH, 1865.

William Alden Choate

Captain, Co. B, 38 OH Infantry, Aug. 12, 1861. Lieutenant Colonel, 38 OH Infantry, Feb. 6, 1862. Colonel, 38 OH Infantry, Nov. 25, 1863. GSW Jonesboro, GA, Sept. 1, 1864, "severely wounded while in the act of raising the colors of his regiment

William Alden Choate (T. F. Saltsman, Photographer, Cor. Union & College Sts., Nashville, Tennessee; Roger D. Hunt Collection, USAMHI [RG98S-CWP82.49]).

from the ground, where they had fallen in consequence of the wounding of his color bearer."
  Born: Jan. 18, 1834 Tiffin, Seneca Co., OH
  Died: Sept. 12, 1864 DOW Atlanta, GA
  Occupation: Lawyer
  Miscellaneous: Resided Napoleon, Henry Co., OH
  Buried: Forest Hill Cemetery, Napoleon, OH
  References: Genevieve Eicher. *Henry County, OH.* Napoleon, OH, 1979. Ephraim O. Jameson. *The Choates in America, 1643–1896: John Choate and his Descendants.* Boston, MA, 1896. Obituary, *Napoleon North-West,* Sept. 29, 1864. Pension File and Military Service File, National Archives. *Official Records,* Series 1, Vol. 38, Part 1, p. 812.

Charles W. Clancy

Captain, Co. B, 52 OH Infantry, Aug. 11, 1862. Lieutenant Colonel, 52 OH Infantry, Feb. 19, 1863. GSW right leg, Kenesaw Mountain, GA, June 27, 1864. Taken prisoner Peach Tree Creek, GA, July 19, 1864. Confined Macon, GA, and Charleston, SC. Paroled Sept. 28, 1864. *Colonel,* 52 OH Infantry, May 31, 1865. Honorably mustered out, June 3, 1865.
  Born: April 3, 1832 Morgan Co., OH

Charles W. Clancy (Nixon B. Stewart. *Dan McCook's Regiment, 52nd Ohio Volunteer Infantry*. Alliance, Ohio, 1900).

Died: March 7, 1892 Smithfield, OH
Occupation: Physician
Offices/Honors: Ohio House of Representatives, 1888–92
Miscellaneous: Resided McConnellsville, Morgan Co., OH, to 1859; New Alexandria, Jefferson Co., OH, 1859–60; and Smithfield, Jefferson Co., OH, 1860–92
Buried: Northern Cemetery, Smithfield, OH
References: John A. Caldwell. *History of Belmont and Jefferson Counties, OH*. Wheeling, WV, 1880. Pension File and Military Service File, National Archives. Obituary, *Steubenville Daily Herald*, March 8, 1892. Nixon B. Stewart. *Dan McCook's Regiment, 52nd Ohio Volunteer Infantry*. Alliance, OH, 1900.

Stephen Russell Clark

2 Lieutenant, Co. G, 86 OH Infantry (3 months), May 27, 1862. Honorably mustered out, Sept. 25, 1862. 1 Lieutenant, Co. C, 5 Independent Battalion, OH Cavalry, Aug. 18, 1863. Dismissed March 21, 1864, for "improperly enlisting a minor." Captain, Co. B, 13 OH Cavalry, Feb. 26, 1864. Major, 13 OH Cavalry, Sept. 8, 1864. Lieutenant Colonel, 13 OH Cavalry, March 22, 1865. *Colonel*, 13 OH Cavalry, June 6, 1865. Honorably mustered out, Aug. 10, 1865. Bvt. Colonel, USV, March 13, 1865, for efficient and gallant conduct during the late campaign.

Stephen Russell Clark (M. Witt, Photographer, 81 South High St., Columbus, Ohio; Roger D. Hunt Collection, USAMHI [RG98S-CWP207.63]).

Born: Sept. 13, 1835 Meadville, PA
Died: Dec. 16, 1922 Pittsburgh, PA
Education: Attended Allegheny College, Meadville, PA
Occupation: Farmer and student before war. Traveling salesman and Methodist clergyman after war.
Miscellaneous: Resided Sullivan, Ashland Co., OH, to 1867; Orrville, Wayne Co., OH, 1867–72; Apple Creek, Wayne Co., OH; Newcomerstown, Tuscarawas Co., OH; Bloomfield, Muskingum Co., OH; Seville, Medina Co., OH; Roscoe, Coshocton Co., OH; Delaware, Delaware Co., OH; and Bellevue, Allegheny Co., PA
Buried: Oak Grove Cemetery, Delaware, OH (Forest Section, Lot 33)
References: Pension File and Military Service File, National Archives. Obituary Circular, Whole No. 1275, Ohio MOLLUS. Letters Received, Volunteer Service Branch, Adjutant General's Office, File P669(VS)1864, National Archives. Obituary, *Delaware Daily Journal Herald*, Dec. 18, 1922.

Melvin Clarke

Lieutenant Colonel, 36 OH Infantry, July 30, 1861. Colonel, 36 OH Infantry, Sept. 7, 1862. Struck by cannon ball which almost entirely severed his body, Antietam, MD, Sept. 17, 1862.

Melvin Clarke (L. M. Strayer Collection).

Born: Nov. 15, 1818 Ashfield, MA
Died: Sept. 17, 1862 KIA Antietam, MD
Occupation: Lawyer
Miscellaneous: Resided Marietta, Washington Co., OH
Buried: Mound Cemetery, Marietta, OH
References: *History of Washington County, OH.* Cleveland, OH, 1881. Obituary, *Marietta Republican,* Sept. 25, 1862. Military Service File, National Archives. Geraldine Muscari, "Marietta Home Handsome After 113 Years: Its Builder Died War Hero's Death," *Parkersburg (WV) News,* Feb. 25, 1968. Geraldine Muscari, "Pvt. Hechler's Tale of Antietam Retold," *Parkersburg (WV) News,* March 10, 1968. Geraldine Muscari, "Like Father Like Son, Civil War Victims," *Parkersburg (WV) News,* March 17, 1968.

Armstead Thompson Mason Cockerill

1 Lieutenant, Co. D, 24 OH Infantry, June 3, 1861. Captain, Co. D, 24 OH Infantry, Sept. 28, 1861. Lieutenant Colonel, 24 OH Infantry, Dec. 31, 1862. *Colonel,* 24 OH Infantry, Oct. 23, 1863. Honorably mustered out, June 24, 1864.
Born: 1841 OH
Died: April 24, 1870 West Union, OH
Occupation: Musician and band leader
Offices/Honors: Assessor of Internal Revenue
Miscellaneous: Son of Bvt. Brig. Gen. Joseph

Armstead Thompson Mason Cockerill (courtesy John C. Rutherford).

R. Cockerill. Resided West Union, Adams Co., OH, to 1865 and 1868–70; and Hamilton, Butler Co., OH, 1865–68.
Buried: Old West Union Cemetery, West Union, OH
References: Pension File and Military Service File, National Archives. William B. Brown. *Family History of Jeremiah Fenton (1764–1841) of Adams County, OH, and His Descendants.* Des Moines, IA, 1910. Letters Received, Volunteer Service Branch, Adjutant General's Office, File C414(VS)1863, National Archives.

Augustus Henry Coleman

Major, 11 OH Infantry (3 months), April 29, 1861. Major, 11 OH Infantry (3 years), July 6, 1861. Lieutenant Colonel, 11 OH Infantry, Jan. 9, 1862. *Colonel,* 11 OH Infantry, April 23, 1862. GSW right arm and side, Antietam, MD, Sept. 17, 1862.
Born: Oct. 29, 1829 Troy, OH
Died: Sept. 17, 1862 KIA Antietam, MD
Education: Attended U.S. Military Academy, West Point, NY (Class of 1851)
Occupation: Farmer
Miscellaneous: Resided Troy, Miami Co., OH
Buried: Rose Hill Cemetery, Troy, OH (Lots 67–68)
References: Joshua H. Horton and Solomon Teverbaugh. *A History of the 11th Regiment Ohio Vol-*

Augustus Henry Coleman (Rick Brown Collection).

William Oliver Collins (Ken Lawrence Collection).

unteer Infantry. Dayton, OH, 1866. Whitelaw Reid. *Ohio in the War: Her Statesmen Generals and Soldiers*. Cincinnati, OH, 1868. *Genealogical and Biographical Record of Miami County, OH*. Chicago, IL, 1900. *History of Miami County, OH*. Chicago, IL, 1880.

William Oliver Collins

Colonel, 7 OH Cavalry, Oct. 1, 1861. Incomplete regiment consolidated with 6 OH Cavalry, Dec. 19, 1861. Lieutenant Colonel, 6 OH Cavalry, Dec. 19, 1861. Lieutenant Colonel, 11 OH Cavalry, Sept. 20, 1862. Commanded Fort Laramie, WY, Oct. 13, 1863–July 28, 1864. Commanded Western Subdistrict, District of Nebraska, Oct. 5, 1864–Feb. 1865. Honorably mustered out, April 1, 1865.

Born: Aug. 23, 1809 Somers, CT
Died: Oct. 26, 1880 Hillsboro, OH
Education: Graduated Amherst (MA) College, 1833
Occupation: Lawyer
Offices/Honors: Ohio Senate, 1860–62. U.S. Collector of Internal Revenue, 6 District of Ohio, 1865–68.
Miscellaneous: Resided Hillsboro, Highland Co., OH
Buried: Hillsboro Cemetery, Hillsboro, OH (Section E, Lot 138)
References: Agnes Wright Spring. *Caspar Collins, the Life and Exploits of an Indian Fighter of the Sixties*. New York City, NY, 1927. Elsie Johnson Ayres. *The Hills of Highland*. Hillsboro, OH, 1971. Obituary, *Hillsboro Gazette*, Oct. 28, 1880. Robert H. Jones. *Guarding the Overland Trails: The 11th Ohio Cavalry in the Civil War*. Spokane, WA, 2005. Pension File and Military Service File, National Archives. Letters Received, Volunteer Service Branch, Adjutant General's Office, Files C63(VS) 1861 and M4103(VS)1864, National Archives. W. Cooper. *Sketches of the Senators and Representatives in the Fifty-fourth General Assembly of the State of Ohio*. Columbus, OH, 1861.

John MacNeill Connell

Colonel, 17 OH Infantry (3 months), May 13, 1861. Honorably mustered out, Aug. 15, 1861. Colonel, 17 OH Infantry (3 years), Aug. 16, 1861. Commanded 1 Brigade, 1 Division, Centre Wing, Army of the Cumberland, Nov.–Dec. 1862. Commanded 1 Brigade, 3 Division, 14 Army Corps, Army of the Cumberland, July 25–Oct. 9, 1863. Having been elected to the Ohio Senate and his regiment being "much below half of maximum strength," he resigned Nov. 12, 1863, as "the condition of my health almost makes it a necessity that I should not be in the field during the coming winter."

Born: Nov. 7, 1829 Lancaster, OH
Died: April 17, 1882 Lancaster, OH

John MacNeill Connell (courtesy The Excelsior Brigade, Alexandria, Virginia).

Occupation: Lawyer
Offices/Honors: Chief Clerk, U.S. Comptroller's Office, Washington, DC, 1857–60. Ohio Senate, 1862–64. Assessor of Internal Revenue, 1865–68.
Miscellaneous: Resided Lancaster, Fairfield Co., OH; Fort Wayne, Allen Co., IN, 1850–55; Wooster, Wayne Co., OH, 1855–57; and Cleveland, OH
Buried: Elmwood Cemetery, Lancaster, OH
References: *American Biography, A New Cyclopedia.* Vol. 49. New York City, NY, 1931. Obituary, *Lancaster Gazette,* April 20, 1882. Pension File and Military Service File, National Archives. Albert A. Graham. *History of Fairfield and Perry Counties, OH.* Chicago, IL, 1883. Ben Douglas. *History of the Lawyers of Wayne County.* Wooster, OH, 1900. Charles T. Develling. *History of the 17th Regiment Ohio Veteran Volunteer Infantry.* Zanesville, OH, 1889.

Robert Allen Constable

Lieutenant Colonel, 75 OH Infantry, Dec. 18, 1861. Taken prisoner, McDowell, VA, May 9, 1862. Confined Salisbury (NC) Prison. Paroled Aug. 17, 1862. Colonel, 75 OH Infantry, Dec. 3, 1862. Resigned Jan. 12, 1863, since "I can not conscientiously endorse and carry out the Emancipation Proclamation of our Commander-in-Chief, the President of the United States."

Born: March 20, 1830 Athens, OH
Died: July 7, 1888 Athens, OH
Education: Attended Ohio University, Athens, OH
Occupation: Lawyer
Miscellaneous: Resided Athens, Athens Co., OH
Buried: West Union Street Cemetery, Athens, OH (Section 2, Lot 95)
References: Mary L. Bowman. *Civil War Veterans of Athens County, OH: Biographical Sketches.* Athens, OH, 1989. *History of Hocking Valley, OH.* Chicago, IL, 1883. Obituary, *Athens Messenger,* July 12, 1888. Pension File and Military Service File, National Archives. Letters Received, Volunteer Service Branch, Adjutant General's Office, Files C31(VS)1863, R116(VS)1863, and S38(VS)1863, National Archives.

William Craig Cooper

1 Lieutenant, Co. B, 4 OH Infantry (3 months), May 4, 1861. Honorably mustered out, Aug. 21, 1861. Colonel, 142 OH Infantry, May 13, 1864. Honorably mustered out, Sept. 2, 1864.
Born: Dec. 18, 1832 Clinton Twp., Knox Co., OH
Died: Aug. 29, 1902 Mount Vernon, OH
Occupation: Lawyer
Offices/Honors: Ohio House of Representatives, 1872–74. U.S. House of Representatives, 1885–91.

William Craig Cooper (post-war) (*Biographical Cyclopedia and Portrait Gallery with an Historical Sketch of the State of Ohio.* Vol. 1. Cincinnati, Ohio, 1883).

Miscellaneous: Resided Mount Vernon, Knox Co., OH

Buried: Mound View Cemetery, Mount Vernon, OH (Section 1, Lot 32)

References: *The Biographical Record of Knox County, OH.* Chicago, IL, 1902. Pension File, National Archives. Obituary, *Mount Vernon Democratic Banner,* Sept. 2, 1902. *Biographical Cyclopedia and Portrait Gallery with an Historical Sketch of the State of Ohio.* Vol. 1. Cincinnati, OH, 1883. *Biographical Encyclopedia of Ohio of the Nineteenth Century.* Cincinnati and Philadelphia, 1876.

Charles S. Cotter

Captain, Cotter's Independent Battery, OH Light Artillery, April 25, 1861. Honorably mustered out, Sept. 3, 1861. Captain, Battery A, 1 OH Light Artillery, Sept. 2, 1861. Dismissed March 7, 1862, on charges of "disobedience of orders, conduct to the prejudice of good order and military discipline,

Charles S. Cotter (photograph by Hoag & Quick's Art Palace, No. 100 4th St. opp. Post Office, Cincinnati, Ohio; Cincinnati Museum Center-Cincinnati Historical Society Library).

and breach of arrest." Dismissal revoked April 19, 1862, by order of President Lincoln. Major, 1 OH Light Artillery, June 10, 1862. Chief of Artillery, Staff of Major Gen. Alexander McD. McCook, commanding 1 Corps, Army of the Ohio, Oct. 1862. Taken prisoner, Perryville, KY, Oct. 8, 1862. Paroled Oct. 10, 1862. Chief of Artillery, Staff of Major Gen. Alexander McD. McCook, commanding 20 Army Corps, Army of the Cumberland, Feb. 20–May 1863. Commanded Garrison Artillery, Post of Nashville, TN, Aug.8–Nov. 14, 1863. Commanded 1 Brigade, 1 Division, Reserve Artillery, Army of the Cumberland, Nov. 14–Dec. 1, 1863. Commanded Reserve Artillery, Post of Chattanooga, TN, Dec. 1, 1863–Nov. 1864. Lieutenant Colonel, 1 OH Light Artillery, Oct. 20, 1864. Colonel, 1 OH Light Artillery, Nov. 27, 1864. Chief of Artillery, Staff of Major Gen. James B. Steedman, commanding District of the Etowah, Department of the Cumberland, Dec. 1864–July 1865. Honorably mustered out, Aug. 9, 1865.

Charles S. Cotter (photograph by Hoag & Quick's Art Palace, No. 100 4th St. opp. Post Office, Cincinnati, Ohio; Library of Congress [LC-USZ62-129688]).

Born: Sept. 20, 1827 OH
Died: Jan. 16, 1886 Columbus, OH
Occupation: Silver plater
Offices/Honors: Superintendent of the Ohio State House, 1884–86
Miscellaneous: Resided Ravenna, Portage Co., OH; and Columbus, OH
Buried: Maple Grove Cemetery, Ravenna, OH (Section 8, Lot 497)
References: Richard J. Staats. *A Grassroots History of the American Civil War, Volume III: Captain Cotter's Battery.* Bowie, MD, 2002. Obituary, *Ravenna Democratic Press,* Jan. 21, 1886. John Fitch. *Annals of the Army of the Cumberland.* Philadelphia, PA, 1864. Pension File and Military Service File, National Archives. Letters Received, Volunteer Service Branch, Adjutant General's Office, File M629(VS)1862, National Archives. Henry M. Davidson. *History of Battery A, 1st Regiment Ohio Volunteer Light Artillery.* Milwaukee, WI, 1865.

John Cradlebaugh

Colonel, 114 OH Infantry, Aug. 22, 1862. GSW mouth and neck, Vicksburg, MS, May 22, 1863. Resigned Oct. 20, 1863, due to "the difficulty I have in speaking on account of the loss of a portion of my tongue and palate by a wound and the doubt I have of my physical ability to endure the exposure and fatigue of a campaign."

John Cradlebaugh (Massachusetts MOLLUS Collection, USAMHI [Vol. 72, p. 3570]).

Born: Feb. 22, 1819 Circleville, OH
Died: Feb. 19, 1872 Eureka, NV
Education: Attended Kenyon College, Gambier, OH. Attended Miami University, Oxford, OH.
Occupation: Lawyer
Offices/Honors: Ohio Senate, 1852–54. U.S. District Judge, Utah Territory, 1858–61. U.S. House of Representatives, 1861–63.
Miscellaneous: Resided Circleville, Pickaway Co., OH; Carson City, NV; and Eureka, Eureka Co., NV. As U.S. District Judge in 1859 attempted to prosecute the ringleaders of the Mountain Meadows Massacre.
Buried: Forest Cemetery, Circleville, OH (Section 8, Lot 2)
References: James L. Harrison, compiler. *Biographical Directory of the American Congress, 1774–1949.* Washington, DC, 1950. Obituary, *Circleville Democrat and Watchman,* March 8, 1872. Military Service File, National Archives. Letters Received, Volunteer Service Branch, Adjutant General's Office, File C1265(VS)1862, National Archives. Dan L. Thrapp. *Encyclopedia of Frontier Biography.* Glendale, CA, 1988. *General Catalogue of the Graduates and Former Students of Miami University During Its First Century, 1809–1909.* Oxford, OH, 1909. Will Bagley. *Blood of the Prophets: Brigham Young and the Massacre at Mountain Meadows.* Norman, OK, 2002.

John Cradlebaugh (Massachusetts MOLLUS Collection, USAMHI [Vol. 118, p. 6090]).

William Craig

1 Lieutenant, 8 U.S. Infantry, Oct. 19, 1858. Captain, AQM, USA, May 17, 1861. Authorized as Colonel, 63 OH Infantry, Sept. 27, 1861, but failed to receive permission from the Adjutant General to command a volunteer regiment. Incomplete 63 OH Infantry consolidated with 22 OH Infantry, Jan. 18, 1862. Assistant Depot Quartermaster, Fort Union, NM, Sept. 21, 1862–Feb. 1863. Submitted resignation, March 1, 1863, since "The duties are distasteful to me, and I have lost my health in the attempt to perform every duty imposed upon me, and acquit myself with credit in a branch of the service for which I have no taste." Resignation finally accepted, April 5, 1864.

Born: March 1829 Newport, IN
Died: May 27, 1886 Santa Fe, NM
Education: Attended Wabash College, Crawfordsville, IN. Graduated U.S. Military Academy, West Point, NY, 1853.
Occupation: Regular Army (Captain, AQM, resigned April 5, 1864). Engaged in ranching and mining after war.
Miscellaneous: Resided Hermosilla, Pueblo Co., CO; and Santa Fe, NM after war.
Buried: Santa Fe National Cemetery, Santa Fe, NM (Section K, Plot 321)
References: Obituary, *Santa Fe Daily New Mexican,* May 27, 1886. Obituary, *Army and Navy Journal,* June 26, 1886. Charles Leib. *Nine Months in the Quartermaster's Department; or The Chances for Making a Million.* Cincinnati, OH, 1862. George W. Cullum. *Biographical Register of the Officers and Graduates of the U.S. Military Academy.* Third Edition. Boston and New York, 1891. Pension File, National Archives. Letters Received, Appointment, Commission and Personal Branch, Adjutant General's Office, File 1115(ACP)1876, National Archives. Letter W. Craig to Adjutant General C.P. Buckingham, Sept. 30, 1861, (Series 147–10: 124), Correspondence to the Governor and Adjutant General of Ohio, 1861–66, Ohio Historical Society. Letter William E. Gilmore to Governor David Tod, Jan. 24, 1862, (Series 147–24: 189), Correspondence to the Governor and Adjutant General of Ohio, 1861–66, Ohio Historical Society.

Harvey Crampton

Private, Co. F, 75 OH Infantry, Oct. 7, 1861. 1 Lieutenant, Co. F, 75 OH Infantry, Dec. 14, 1861. Resigned May 15, 1862, due to "private business of importance, requiring my immediate attention and presence, and the state of my health (right scrotal hernia) unfitting me for active service." Colonel, 146 OH Infantry, May 12, 1864. Honorably mustered out, Sept. 7, 1864.

Born: 1829? OH
Died: July 20, 1906 Leavenworth, KS
Occupation: Carpenter before war. Contractor and builder after war.
Miscellaneous: Resided Franklin, Warren Co., OH; Kansas City, MO; and Leavenworth, KS
Buried: Leavenworth National Cemetery, Leavenworth, KS (Section 21, Row 5, Site 27)
References: Pension File and Military service File, National Archives. Funeral announcement, *Leavenworth Times,* July 22, 1906.

William R. Creighton

Captain, Co. A, 7 OH Infantry (3 months), April 22, 1861. Lieutenant Colonel, 7 OH Infantry (3 months), May 7, 1861. Lieutenant Colonel, 7 OH Infantry (3 years), June 19, 1861. Colonel, 7 OH Infantry, May 20, 1862. GSW left side and arm, Cedar Mountain, VA, Aug. 9, 1862. Commanded 1 Brigade, 2 Division, 12 Army Corps, Army of the Potomac, Feb.–March 1863. Commanded 1 Brigade, 2 Division, 12 Army Corps, Army of the Cumberland, Nov. 24–27, 1863. GSW heart, Ringgold, GA, Nov. 27, 1863.

Born: June 1837 Pittsburgh, PA
Died: Nov. 27, 1863 DOW Ringgold, GA
Occupation: Printer
Miscellaneous: Resided Cleveland, OH
Buried: Woodland Cemetery, Cleveland, OH (Section 14)

William Craig (Charles Leib. *Nine Months in the Quartermaster's Department; or The Chances for Making a Million.* Cincinnati, Ohio, 1862).

William R. Creighton.

William R. Creighton (Roger D. Hunt Collection, USAMHI [RG98S-CWP207.66]).

References: David D. Van Tassel and John J. Grabowski, editors. *The Encyclopedia of Cleveland History.* Bloomington, IN, 1987. Maurice Joblin, publisher. *Cleveland, Past and Present; Its Representative Men.* Cleveland, OH, 1869. Lawrence Wilson, editor. *Itinerary of the 7th Ohio Volunteer Infantry, 1861–64.* New York and Washington, 1907. George L. Wood. *The Seventh Regiment: A Record.* New York City, NY, 1865. Pension File and Military Service File, National Archives. Obituary, *Cleveland Leader,* Dec. 1, 1863. Funeral account, *Cleveland Leader,* Dec. 9, 1863.

Le Roy Crockett

1 Lieutenant, Co. K, 65 NY Infantry, Aug. 3, 1861. Honorably discharged Dec. 9, 1861, to accept promotion. Major, 72 OH Infantry, Dec. 10, 1861. Taken prisoner, Shiloh, TN, April 4, 1862. Lieutenant Colonel, 72 OH Infantry, April 6, 1862. Confined Montgomery, AL. Paroled Oct. 12, 1862. *Colonel,* 72 OH Infantry, Nov. 29, 1862. Having erroneously been put on a list of "officers absent from duty more than 60 days on account of wounds and sickness contracted in the line of duty," he was discharged for disability, Dec. 1, 1862. Reinstated Dec. 22, 1862. GSW leg, Vicksburg, MS, May 19, 1863.

Born: Oct. 21, 1832 OH
Died: Dec. 10, 1863 Green Springs, OH (chronic diarrhea)
Occupation: Farmer
Miscellaneous: Resided Lowell, Seneca Co., OH
Buried: Lowell School Cemetery, Lowell, OH
References: Charles S. Candage. *Crockett Genealogy, 1610–1988.* Camden, ME, 1989. Richard L. Manion and Nan Card. *Sandusky County, Ohio, Civil War Soldiers.* Fremont, OH, 1992. Obituary, *Fremont Weekly Journal,* Dec. 18, 1863. Military Service File, National Archives. Letters Received, Volunteer Service Branch, Adjutant General's Office, File O387(VS)1862, National Archives.

John Fitz Roy DeCourcy

Colonel, 16 OH Infantry, Sept. 22, 1861. Commanded 26 Brigade, 7 Division, Army of the Ohio, April 14–Oct. 10, 1862. Commanded 4 Brigade, Cumberland Division, District of Western Virginia, Army of the Ohio, Oct.–Nov. 1862. Commanded 3 Brigade, 9 Division, Left Wing, 13 Army Corps, Army of the Tennessee, Nov.–Dec. 1862. Commanded 3 Brigade, 3 Division, Yazoo Expedition, Army of the Tennessee, Dec. 1862–Jan. 1863. Commanded 3 Brigade, 9 Division, 13 Army Corps, Army of the Tennessee, Jan.–Feb. 1863. Commanded 2 Brigade, 9 Division, 13 Army Corps, Army of the Tennessee, Feb. 1863. Member

John Fitz Roy DeCourcy (The Western Reserve Historical Society, Cleveland, Ohio).

of the Military Commission for the trial of Clement L. Vallandigham, May 1863. Commanded 3 Brigade, 2 Division, 9 Army Corps, Army of the Ohio, Aug.–Sept. 1863. Commanded Independent Brigade, 9 Army Corps, Army of the Ohio, Sept. 1863. Arrested and relieved from command by Major General Burnside, Sept. 9, 1863, for writing a letter described as "a tissue of vanity, consisting of puerile personal details, and closing with a sentence highly insubordinate in its nature," to his commanding officer, Brig. Gen. James M. Shackelford, in response to a request for cooperation against the Confederate forces at Cumberland Gap, TN. "In consequence of the extremely severe censure of my conduct," and the lack of a Court of Inquiry "to save my character as an officer and a gentleman," he submitted his resignation, Oct. 16, 1863. Resignation accepted, Feb. 19, 1864, and "under the peculiar circumstances of the case," he was discharged to date Oct. 16, 1863. On March 3, 1864, however, his previous discharge was revoked, and he was honorably discharged to date March 3, 1864.

Born: March 30, 1821 Island of Corfu, Greece
Died: Nov. 20, 1890 Florence, Italy
Other Wars: Crimean War (Major in the Turkish Contingent; Knight of the Order of the Medjidie, 4th Class)
Occupation: Served in the British 47th Regiment Foot. Held the premier baronetage of Ireland, succeeding his cousin as the 31st Baron Kingsale in 1874.
Miscellaneous: Commenting on "the unnecessarily harsh and irksome discipline" enforced by DeCourcy, a soldier in his brigade described him as "a brave but not always judicious soldier of fortune," who "had no personal attachments with any of his subordinates"
Buried: Cimitero agli Allori, Florence, Italy
References: Obituary, *London Times,* Nov. 25, 1890. Military Service File, National Archives. Letters Received, Volunteer Service Branch, Adjutant General's Office, File D963(VS)1863, National Archives. Joseph N. Ashburn. *History of the 86th Regiment Ohio Volunteer Infantry.* Cleveland, OH, 1909. Enos Pierson, compiler. *Proceedings of Eleven Reunions, Held by the 16th Regiment, O.V.I.* Millersburg, OH, 1887. Frank H. Mason. *The Forty-second Ohio Infantry, a History of the Organization of That Regiment in the War of the Rebellion.* Cleveland, OH, 1876.

Hermin G. DePuy

Captain, Co. E, 8 OH Infantry (3 months), April 24, 1861. Colonel, 8 OH Infantry (3 months), May 4, 1861. Colonel, 8 OH Infantry (3 years), July 9, 1861. Resigned Nov. 9, 1861, owing to a severe injury to his spine and right side caused by his horse running away.

Born: Dec. 8, 1818 Northumberland Co., PA
Died: July 15, 1890 Wabash, IN
Other Wars: Mexican War (2 Lieutenant, Co. A, 2 KY Infantry; GSW leg Chapultepec, Mexico)
Occupation: Lawyer, insurance agent and farmer
Miscellaneous: Resided Sandusky, Erie Co., OH, to 1863; and Wabash, Wabash Co., IN, after 1863. Brother-in-law of Brig. Gen. John Beatty.
Buried: Matlock Cemetery, near Wabash, IN
References: Obituary, *Wabash Plain Dealer,* July 18 and July 25, 1890. *History of Wabash County, IN.* Chicago, IL, 1884. Pension File and Military Service File, National Archives. Letters Received, Volunteer Service Branch, Adjutant General's Office, File D651(VS)1862, National Archives. Franklin Sawyer. *A Military History of the 8th Regiment Ohio Volunteer Infantry.* Cleveland, OH, 1881.

Charles A. DeVilliers

Major, Brigade Inspector, 2 Brigade, Ohio Militia, May 28, 1861. Lieutenant Colonel, 8 OH Infantry, June 26, 1861. Colonel, 11 OH Infantry, July 7, 1861. Taken prisoner, Scary Creek, WV, July 17, 1861. Confined Richmond, VA. Escaped and re-

William F. Scott. *Philander P. Lane, Colonel of Volunteers in the Civil War, Eleventh Ohio Infantry.* New York City, NY, 1920. Charles Lanman, editor. *Journal of Alfred Ely.* New York City, NY, 1862. *Roster 11th Ohio Infantry Association, Proceedings 29th Reunion 1901, Proceedings 30th Reunion 1902.* Dayton, OH, 1902. Terry Lowry. *The Battle of Scary Creek: Military Operations in the Kanawha Valley, April–July 1861.* Charleston, WV, 1982. Court-martial Case Files, 1809–1894, File II-856, National Archives.

Moses Riley Dickey

Lieutenant Colonel, 15 OH Infantry (3 months), April 27, 1861. Colonel, 15 OH Infantry (3 years), Aug. 7, 1861. Resigned Oct. 24, 1862, due to "general debility" from "a constantly recurring masked form of intermittent fever with chronic diarrhea."
   Born: Nov. 4, 1827 Richland Co., OH
   Died: July 15, 1913 Mansfield, OH
   Other Wars: Mexican War (Private, Co. A, 3 OH Infantry)
   Occupation: Lawyer and judge
   Offices/Honors: Judge of the Court of Common Pleas, 1876–81
   Miscellaneous: Resided Mansfield, Richland Co., OH; Cleveland, OH; and Roanoke, Roanoke Co., VA

Charles A. DeVilliers (photograph by E. & H. T. Anthony, 501 Broadway, New York; L. M. Strayer Collection).

turned to regiment, Oct. 28, 1861. Commanded Post of Point Pleasant, WV, Dec. 1861–Jan. 1862. Dismissed April 23, 1862, for habitually abusing officers under his command, fraudulently obtaining money from the regimental sutler, and seizing cattle and other goods from private citizens for his own benefit.
   Born: 1820 or 1826 France
   Died: Date and place of death unknown. Known to use multiple aliases, he was arrested and jailed (as August Wever) in Baltimore, MD, in 1866 for passing a worthless check. Whereabouts after this date unknown; may have returned to France.
   Occupation: French army officer and adventurer
   Buried: Place of burial unknown
   References: *Appletons' Cyclopedia of American Biography.* Thomas P. Lowry. *Tarnished Eagles: The Courts-Martial of Fifty Union Colonels and Lieutenant Colonels.* Mechanicsburg, PA, 1997. Joshua H. Horton and Solomon Teverbaugh. *A History of the 11th Regiment Ohio Volunteer Infantry.* Dayton, OH, 1866. Military Service File, National Archives.

Moses Riley Dickey.

Buried: Mansfield Cemetery, Mansfield, OH (Section OS12, Lot 996)

References: Obituary, *The Mansfield News,* July 15, 1913. *Biographical Cyclopedia and Portrait Gallery with an Historical Sketch of the State of Ohio.* Vol. 6. Cincinnati, OH, 1895. Military Service File, National Archives. Alexis Cope. *The 15th Ohio Volunteers and Its Campaigns, War of 1861–65.* Columbus, OH, 1916.

Charles William Doubleday

Colonel, 2 OH Cavalry, Sept. 5, 1861. Appointed Acting Brigadier General, Department of Kansas, by Major General David Hunter, Feb. 15, 1862. Commanded Doubleday's Brigade, Department of Kansas, Feb. 15–June 16, 1862. Commanded Post of Fort Scott, KS, March–May 1862. Resigned June 16, 1862, "on account of continued ill health caused by the changeable climate incident to this locality."

Born: Jan. 28, 1829 Leicestershire, England

Died: Nov. 4, 1912 Arlington, VA

Occupation: Adventurer before war. Author of *Reminiscences of the Filibuster War in Nicaragua,* documenting his participation in filibustering expeditions to Nicaragua in 1854–55. Proprietor of railroad sleeping car company after war.

Miscellaneous: Resided Cleveland, OH; Arlington, Arlington Co., VA; and Williamstown, Berkshire Co., MA

Buried: Westlawn Cemetery, Williamstown, MA

References: *Appletons' Cyclopedia of American Biography.* Margaret B. Curfman. *Doubleday Families of America.* Wichita, KS, 1972. Military Service File, National Archives. Obituary Circular, Whole No. 718, District of Columbia MOLLUS. Gertrude V. R. Wickham. *The Pioneer Families of Cleveland, 1796–1840.* Cleveland, OH, 1914. Eleanor Lee Templeman. *Arlington Heritage: Vignettes of a Virginia County.* New York City, NY, 1959. Luman H. Tenney. *War Diary of Luman Harris Tenney, 1861–1865.* Cleveland, OH, 1914. Charles W. Doubleday. *Reminiscences of the Filibuster War in Nicaragua.* New York and London, 1886. Death notice, *Washington Evening Star,* Nov. 4, 1912.

Thomas Drummond

2 Lieutenant, 2 U.S. Cavalry, April 26, 1861. 1 Lieutenant, 2 U.S. Cavalry, May 30, 1861. 1 Lieutenant, 5 U.S. Cavalry, Aug. 3, 1861. Lieutenant

Charles William Doubleday (post-war) (District of Columbia MOLLUS Collection, USAMHI [RG127S-DCC.151]).

Thomas Drummond (courtesy Olaf).

Colonel, 4 IA Cavalry, Dec. 31, 1861. Resigned volunteer commission, June 3, 1862, since "my health is impaired and I need rest." Captain, 5 U.S. Cavalry, July 17, 1862. Provost Marshal, Cavalry Corps, Army of the Potomac, June 13–August 3, 1863. *Colonel,* 8 OH Cavalry, Jan. 20, 1865. Did not join regiment since its reduced strength did not permit muster of a colonel. GSW Five Forks, VA, April 1, 1865.
> **Born:** May 9, 1832 Brooke Co., WV
> **Died:** April 2, 1865 DOW Five Forks, VA
> **Occupation:** Newspaper editor
> **Offices/Honors:** Iowa House of Representatives, 1858–60. Iowa Senate, 1860–62.
> **Miscellaneous:** Resided Vinton, Benton Co., IA
> **Buried:** Methodist Cemetery, St. Clairsville, OH
> **References:** Emory H. English, "Thomas Drummond," *Annals of Iowa,* Third Series, Vol. 30, No. 5 (July 1950). George F. Price. *Across the Continent with the Fifth Cavalry.* New York City, NY, 1883. William F. Scott. *The Story of a Cavalry Regiment, the Career of the 4th Iowa Veteran Volunteers, from Kansas to Georgia.* New York City, NY, 1893. Pension File and Military Service File, National Archives. Letters Received, Volunteer Service Branch, Adjutant General's Office, File O58(VS) 1865, National Archives. Steve Meyer. *Iowans Called to Valor.* Garrison, IA, 1993.

Samuel H. Dunning

Colonel, 5 OH Infantry (3 months), April 25, 1861. Colonel, 5 OH Infantry (3 years), June 11, 1861. Resigned Aug. 13, 1862, due to "continued ill health, ... believing that I shall be unable longer to undergo the privations and exposure incident to active service in the field." Provost Marshal, Board of Enrollment, 2nd District of Ohio, Feb. 21–July 10, 1865.
> **Born:** Aug. 12, 1822 Washington, DC
> **Died:** Jan. 9, 1893 Cincinnati, OH
> **Occupation:** Marble dealer and monument builder
> **Miscellaneous:** Resided Cincinnati, OH
> **Buried:** Spring Grove Cemetery, Cincinnati, OH (Section 47, Lot 25)
> **References:** Pension File and Military Service File, National Archives. Obituary, *Cincinnati Commercial Gazette,* Jan. 10, 1893. "Question and Answer OCWGJ 2007-20: 5th OVI, Col. Dunning and Owl Symbol," *Ohio Civil War Genealogy Journal,* Vol. 12, No. 1 (2008).

Ephraim Ralph Eckley

Lieutenant Colonel, 26 OH Infantry, June 10, 1861. Colonel, 80 OH Infantry, Dec. 29, 1861.

Ephraim Ralph Eckley (Review of Reviews Collection, USAMHI).

Commanded 2 Brigade, 3 Division, Army of the Mississippi, June 1862. Commanded 2 Brigade, 7 Division, Left Wing, 13 Army Corps, Army of the Tennessee, Nov. 1, 1862–Dec. 18, 1862. Commanded 2 Brigade, 7 Division, 16 Army Corps, Army of the Tennessee, Dec. 22, 1862–Jan. 20, 1863. Commanded 2 Brigade, 7 Division, 17 Army Corps, Army of the Tennessee, Jan. 20, 1863–Feb. 12, 1863. Resigned Feb. 24, 1863, having "been elected a member of the 38th Federal Congress, whose term commences on the 4th of March next."
> **Born:** Dec. 9, 1811 near Mount Pleasant, Jefferson Co., OH
> **Died:** March 27, 1908 Carrollton, OH
> **Education:** Attended Vermillion Institute, Hayesville, OH
> **Occupation:** Lawyer
> **Offices/Honors:** Ohio Senate, 1843–47, 1849–51. Ohio House of Representatives, 1854–56. U.S. House of Representatives, 1863–69.
> **Miscellaneous:** Resided Carrollton, Carroll Co., OH
> **Buried:** Grand View Cemetery, Carrollton, OH (Section B, Row 8)
> **References:** *Commemorative Biographical Record of the Counties of Harrison and Carroll, OH.* Chicago, IL, 1891. James L. Harrison, compiler. *Biographical Directory of the American Congress, 1774–1949.* Washington, DC, 1950. Pension File and Military Service File, National Archives. Obit-

uary, *Carroll Chronicle,* April 3, 1908. Lizzie H. Johns, compiler. *Records of the Eckley Family in America.* Alhambra, CA, 1962. David F. Fryer. *History of the 80th Ohio Veteran Volunteer Infantry.* Newcomerstown, OH, 1904.

Bernhard Eith

Captain, Co. H, 28 OH Infantry, June 13, 1861. Resigned March 1, 1862, due to inguinal hernia of the left side received by a fall from a horse at Gauley Bridge, WV, Jan. 6, 1862. Colonel, 8 OH Volunteer Militia, Sept. 3, 1862. Honorably mustered out, Oct. 3, 1862.
Born: Aug. 11, 1823 Germany
Died: Dec. 19, 1875 Cincinnati, OH (committed suicide by shooting)
Occupation: Hotelkeeper and restaurant keeper
Miscellaneous: Resided Cincinnati, OH
Buried: Walnut Hills Cemetery, Cincinnati, OH (Section 13, Lot 1321, unmarked)
References: Pension File and Military Service File, National Archives. Obituary, *Cincinnati Daily Gazette,* Dec. 21, 1875. Obituary, *Cincinnati Freie Presse,* Dec. 21, 1875. Obituary, *Cincinnati Volksfreund,* Dec. 21, 1875. Letters Received, Volunteer Service Branch, Adjutant General's Office, File B1688(VS)1862, National Archives.

Lyman S. Elliott

Lieutenant Colonel, 47 OH Infantry, Aug. 23, 1861. Colonel, 47 OH Infantry, July 18, 1862. Commanded 1 Brigade, District of the Kanawha, Department of the Ohio, Dec. 1862. Facing charges of "conduct subversive of good order and military discipline, disobedience of orders, conduct unbecoming an officer and a gentleman, and inefficiency and incapacity to fill the position of colonel of a regiment in the U.S. army," he resigned Jan. 13, 1863, since "I have three lawsuits pending, two in St. Louis, MO, and one in Belleville, IL, involving above twelve thousand dollars," and ... "it now demands my immediate attention."
Born: Aug. 23, 1816 Erie Co., NY
Died: June 5, 1865 Chicago, IL
Occupation: Hotelkeeper, steamboat steward, omnibus operator, and railroad travelling agent
Miscellaneous: Resided Adrian, Lenawee Co., MI; Buffalo, NY; Cincinnati, OH; Louisville, KY; Indianapolis, IN; St. Louis, MO; and Chicago, IL
Buried: Oakwood Cemetery, Adrian, MI (Block 17, Lot 40)
References: John I. Knapp and Richard I. Bonner. *Illustrated History and Biographical Record of Lenawee County, MI.* Adrian, MI, 1903. Pension File and Military Service File, National Archives. Joseph A. Saunier, editor. *A History of the 47th Regiment Ohio Veteran Volunteer Infantry.* Hillsboro, OH, 1903. Albert Castel. *Tom Taylor's Civil War.* Lawrence, KS, 2000.

John Ferguson

Captain, Co. F, 26 OH Infantry, June 29, 1861. Major, 30 OH Infantry, July 31, 1861. Colonel, 64 OH Infantry, Jan. 21, 1862. Commanded 1 Convalescent Brigade, Bowling Green, KY, Dec.10, 1862–Jan. 22, 1863. Dismissed March 11, 1863, for "absence without the proper authority and beyond the time granted, drunkenness, disorderly and scandalous conduct, contempt of arrest and gross neglect of duty." Colonel, 172 OH Infantry, May 1, 1864. Honorably mustered out, Sept. 3, 1864.
Born: July 4, 1816 Cambridge, OH
Died: Oct. 5, 1886 Cambridge, OH
Education: Attended Madison College, Antrim, OH
Occupation: Lawyer
Offices/Honors: Ohio Senate, 1852–54
Miscellaneous: Resided Cambridge, Guernsey Co., OH
Buried: Old City Cemetery, Cambridge, OH
References: Obituary, *Cambridge Jeffersonian,* Oct. 14, 1886. Cyrus P. B. Sarchet. *History of Guernsey County, OH.* Indianapolis, IN, 1911. Pension File and Military Service File, National Archives. Letters Received, Volunteer Service Branch, Adjutant General's Office, File O749 (VS)1863, National Archives. Wilbur F. Hinman. *The Story of the Sherman Brigade.* Alliance, OH, 1897. Jim Leeke, editor. *A Hundred Days to Richmond.* Bloomington, IN, 1999.

Lyman S. Elliott (John I. Knapp and R. I. Bonner. *Illustrated History and Biographical Record of Lenawee County, MI.* Adrian, Michigan, 1903).

John Ferguson (Wilbur F. Hinman. *The Story of the Sherman Brigade.* Alliance, Ohio, 1897).

Robert Pressly Findley (photograph by John L. Gihon's Photographic Art Galleries, 1024 Chestnut Street, Philadelphia, Pennsylvania; L. M. Strayer Collection).

Robert Pressly Findley

2 Lieutenant, Co. K, 74 OH Infantry, Dec. 20, 1861. Captain, Co. K, 74 OH Infantry, Feb. 27, 1862. Cashiered Feb. 12, 1863, upon charges of "Disobedience of Orders and Violation of the 77th Article of War" for refusing to turn his company out for a nighttime roll call, he was restored to command, March 26, 1863, "upon consideration of mitigating circumstances" and the recommendation of members of the court-martial and the petition of sixteen officers of his regiment. Major, 74 OH Infantry, Dec. 19, 1864. Lieutenant Colonel, 74 OH Infantry, May 18, 1865. Honorably mustered out, July 10, 1865. *Colonel,* 74 OH Infantry, July 12, 1865.

Born: Aug. 21, 1836 Antrim, Guernsey Co., OH
Died: Sept. 15, 1898 Cincinnati, OH
Occupation: School teacher before war. Newspaper editor and book agent after war.
Miscellaneous: Resided Xenia, Greene Co., OH; and Cincinnati, OH
Buried: Lebanon Cemetery, Lebanon, OH (Lot 277)
References: Obituary, *Cincinnati Enquirer,* Sept. 16, 1898. Obituary, *Lebanon Western Star,* Sept. 22, 1898. Letters Received, Volunteer Service Branch, Adjutant General's Office, File F812(VS) 1863, National Archives. Pension File and Military Service File, National Archives. Court-martial Case Files, 1809–1894, File KK-760, National Archives. Obituary Circular, Whole No. 409, Ohio MOLLUS. Theodore W. Blackburn. *Letters from the Front: A Union "Preacher" Regiment (74th Ohio) in the Civil War.* Dayton, OH, 1981.

Samuel Sparks Fisher

Colonel, 138 OH Infantry, May 14, 1864. Honorably mustered out, Sept. 1, 1864.

Born: April 11, 1832 near Centreville, St. Joseph Co., MI
Died: Aug. 14, 1874 near Middletown, PA (drowned Conewago Falls, Susquehanna River, while on a recreational canoe trip)
Education: Graduated Philadelphia (PA) Central High School, 1851
Occupation: Patent attorney
Offices/Honors: U.S. Commissioner of Patents, 1869–71
Miscellaneous: Resided Cincinnati, OH
Buried: Spring Grove Cemetery, Cincinnati, OH (Section 77, Lot 106)
References: *In Memoriam Samuel S. Fisher.* Cincinnati, OH, 1874. *Biographical Encyclopedia of Ohio of the Nineteenth Century.* Cincinnati and Philadelphia, 1876. Obituary, *Cincinnati Daily Gazette,* Aug. 17, 1874. Philip A. Fisher. *The Fisher Genealogy.* Everett, MA, 1898. Military Service File,

Samuel Sparks Fisher.

National Archives. Jim Leeke, editor. *A Hundred Days to Richmond*. Bloomington, IN, 1999.

William T. Fitch

Captain, Co. A, 29 OH Infantry, Aug. 14, 1861. Major, 29 OH Infantry, Dec. 13, 1862. Colonel, 29 OH Infantry, June 18, 1863. GSW right leg,

William T. Fitch (John P. Gurnish Collection).

Rocky Face Ridge, GA, May 8, 1864. Discharged for disability, Oct. 13, 1864, on account of wounds.
Born: 1823? England
Died: Dec. 25, 1894 Washington, DC
Occupation: Farmer and pension claim agent
Offices/Honors: Assistant Doorkeeper, U.S. House of Representatives, 1873–94
Miscellaneous: Resided Brooklyn, NY; Jefferson, Ashtabula Co., OH; Madison, Lake Co., OH; and Washington, DC
Buried: Middle Ridge Cemetery, Madison, OH
References: Pension File and Military Service File, National Archives. Obituary, *Brooklyn Daily Eagle*, Dec. 31, 1894. Obituary, *Painesville Telegraph*, Jan. 2, 1895. Letters Received, Volunteer Service Branch, Adjutant General's Office, File F170(VS) 1862, National Archives. John H. SeCheverell. *Journal History of the 29th Ohio Veteran Volunteers, 1861–65. Its Victories and Its Reverses*. Cleveland, OH, 1883.

William Pitt Nelson Fitzgerald

Colonel, 51 OH Infantry, Oct. 14, 1861. Resigned Oct. 23, 1861.
Born: July 1, 1805 Highgate, Franklin Co., VT
Died: Aug. 22, 1867 Washington, DC
Education: Attended U.S. Military Academy, West Point, NY (Class of 1828). Attended Yale Law School, New Haven, CT.
Occupation: U.S. Patent Office examiner and lawyer
Miscellaneous: Resided Ogdensburg, St. Lawrence Co., NY; Washington, DC; and New York City, NY
Buried: Glenwood Cemetery, Washington, DC (Section A, Lot 45)
References: Grace Goodyear Kirkman. *Genealogy of the Goodyear Family*. San Francisco, CA, 1899. U.S. Military Academy Cadet Application Papers, National Archives. Death notice, *New York Times*, Aug. 24, 1867. Fred McDavitt. "The 51st Ohio Volunteer Infantry: A Regimental History," *Civil War: The Magazine of the Civil War Society*, Vol. 12 (March 1988).

William Floto

Colonel, 11 OH Volunteer Militia, Sept. 3, 1862. Honorably mustered out, Oct. 2, 1862.
Born: July 24, 1811 Kassel, Germany
Died: Dec. 14, 1885 Chicago, IL
Occupation: Watchmaker and merchant
Miscellaneous: Resided Cincinnati, OH; and Chicago, IL
Buried: Graceland Cemetery, Chicago, IL (Section R, Lot 746)
References: Obituary, *Cincinnati Volksfreund*, Dec. 17, 1885. Obituary, *Chicago Daily Tribune*,

Dec. 15, 1885. Letters Received, Volunteer Service Branch, Adjutant General's Office, File B1688(VS) 1862, National Archives.

Thomas H. Ford

Colonel, 32 OH Infantry, July 26, 1861. Taken prisoner, Harper's Ferry, WV, Sept. 15, 1862, and paroled same day. Dismissed Nov. 8, 1862, based on the decision of the Military Commission appointed to investigate the circumstances of the abandonment of Maryland Heights and the surrender of Harper's Ferry that he "conducted the defense of Maryland Heights without ability, abandoned his position without sufficient cause, and has shown throughout such a lack of military capacity as to disqualify him ... for a command in the service." Dismissal rescinded, Jan. 26, 1863, and he was "discharged on tender of his resignation, to take effect Nov. 8, 1862."

Born: Aug. 23, 1814 Rockingham Co., VA
Died: Feb. 29, 1868 Washington, DC
Other Wars: Mexican War (Captain, 3 OH Infantry)
Occupation: Lawyer
Offices/Honors: Lieutenant Governor of Ohio, 1855–57
Miscellaneous: Resided Mansfield, Richland Co., OH
Buried: Mansfield Cemetery, Mansfield, OH (Section OS1, Lot 130)
References: Albert A. Graham, compiler. *History of Richland County, OH: Its Past and Present.* Mansfield, OH, 1880. Abraham J. Baughman. *History of Richland County, OH, From 1808 to 1908.* Chicago, IL, 1908. Paul R. Teetor. *A Matter of Hours: Treason at Harper's Ferry.* Rutherford, NJ, 1982. Military Service File, National Archives. Letters Received, Volunteer Service Branch, Adjutant General's Office, File F426(VS)1862, National Archives. Ebenezer Z. Hays, editor. *History of the 32nd Ohio Veteran Volunteer Infantry.* Columbus, OH, 1896.

Thomas H. Ford (Ebenezer Z. Hays, editor. *History of the 32nd Ohio Veteran Volunteer Infantry.* Columbus, Ohio, 1896).

Freeman E. Franklin

Captain, Co. A, 8 OH Infantry (3 months), April 22, 1861. Lieutenant Colonel, 8 OH Infantry (3 months), May 4, 1861. Honorably mustered out, Aug. 24, 1861. Major, 34 OH Infantry, Sept. 2, 1861. Lieutenant Colonel, 34 OH Infantry, May 14, 1862. Colonel, 34 OH Infantry, July 18, 1863. Commanded 3 Brigade, 3 Division, Department of West Virginia, July 18–Sept. 23, 1863. Commanded 3 Brigade (Cavalry), 3 Division, Department of West Virginia, Dec. 25, 1863–Jan. 8, 1864. Dismissed Aug. 1, 1864, on a charge of "Conduct Unbecoming an Officer and a Gentleman" for lying to several officers in his regiment as to his role in having these officers brought before a Board of Examiners and

Freeman E. Franklin (photograph by Hover & Stahl's, Charleston, West Virginia; L. M. Strayer Collection).

on a charge of "Speaking Disrespectfully of his Superior Officer" for saying that "General Duffie misrepresents things sometimes," to refute General Duffie's statement that Colonel Franklin requested the examination of the officers. Disability resulting from dismissal removed, Jan. 30, 1865.

Born: Dec. 5, 1822 Genesee Co., NY
Died: Sept. 27, 1870 Calhoun Station, Madison Co., MS
Education: Graduated Eclectic Medical Institute, Cincinnati, OH, 1853
Occupation: Physician and lawyer
Offices/Honors: Mississippi House of Representatives (Speaker), 1870
Miscellaneous: Resided Tiffin, Seneca Co., OH; and Yazoo City, Yazoo Co., MS
Buried: Greenwood Cemetery, Jackson, MS
References: Pension File and Military Service File, National Archives. Charles F. Ritter and Jon L. Wakelyn. *American Legislative Leaders, 1850–1910.* Westport, CT, 1989. Letters Received, Volunteer Service Branch, Adjutant General's Office, File A812(VS)1864, National Archives. Harvey W. Felter. *History of the Eclectic Medical Institute, Cincinnati, Ohio.* Cincinnati, OH, 1902.

Daniel French

2 Lieutenant, Co. F, 65 OH Infantry, Oct. 4, 1861. Captain, Co. F, 65 OH Infantry, Nov. 6, 1861. Lieutenant Colonel, 65 OH Infantry, Nov. 30, 1861. Resigned Aug. 8, 1862, being "incapable of performing the duties of his office, because of physical disability resulting from chronic nephritis." Colonel, 120 OH Infantry, Sept. 10, 1862. Resigned Feb. 18, 1863, due to physical disability from "chronic diarrhea and hemorrhoids contracted in the Mexican War," which "entirely unfit him for duty."

Born: Aug. 18, 1822 OH
Died: Feb. 24, 1874 Millersburg, OH
Other Wars: Mexican War (1 Lieutenant, Co. I, 15 U.S. Infantry)
Occupation: Blacksmith and railway mail agent
Miscellaneous: Resided Millersburg, Holmes Co., OH
Buried: Oak Grove Cemetery, Millersburg, OH
References: Pension File and Military Service File, National Archives. Obituary, *Holmes County Republican,* Feb. 26, 1874. Wilbur F. Hinman. *The Story of the Sherman Brigade.* Alliance, OH, 1897. Frank L. Byrne and Jean Powers Soman, editors. *Your True Marcus: The Civil War Letters of a Jewish Colonel.* Kent, OH, 1985.

John Christian Fry

1 Lieutenant, Co. H, 20 OH Infantry (3 months), May 13, 1861. Captain, Co. H, 20 OH

Daniel French (Wilbur F. Hinman. *The Story of the Sherman Brigade.* Alliance, Ohio, 1897).

John Christian Fry (Dennis M. Keesee Collection, USAMHI [RG98S-CWP74.95]).

Lt. Col. John Christian Fry (left) and RQM Peter M. Hitchcock, 20 Ohio Infantry (USAMHI [RG98S-CWP20.57]).

Infantry (3 months), May 27, 1861. Captain, Co. B, 20 OH Infantry (3 years), Aug. 18, 1861. Major, 20 OH Infantry, May 23, 1862. Provost Marshal, Staff of Major Gen. John A. Logan (3 Division, 17 Army Corps, Army of the Tennessee), May 4–Nov. 7, 1863. Lieutenant Colonel, 20 OH Infantry, Jan. 8, 1864. *Colonel,* 20 OH Infantry, Jan. 8, 1864. Shell wound shoulder, Atlanta, GA, July 22, 1864. Honorably discharged, to date Sept. 18, 1864, "on account of physical disability, and by reason of expiration of his term of service."
Born: Aug. 4, 1839 Sidney, OH
Died: Dec. 21, 1872 Sidney, OH
Occupation: Dry goods merchant
Miscellaneous: Resided Sidney, Shelby Co., OH; and Denver, CO. Brother-in-law of Colonel Harrison Wilson (20 OH Infantry).
Buried: Graceland Cemetery, Sidney, OH (Section 2, Lot 21)
References: Pension File and Military Service File, National Archives. Obituary, *Sidney Journal,* Dec. 27, 1872. Letters Received, Volunteer Service Branch, Adjutant General's Office, File F318(VS)1863, National Archives.

James Perry Fyffe

Colonel, 59 OH Infantry, Sept. 26, 1861. Commanded 2 Brigade, 3 Division, Left Wing, 14 Army Corps, Army of the Cumberland, Nov. 5, 1862–Jan. 9, 1863. Commanded 2 Brigade, 3 Division, 21 Army Corps, Army of the Cumberland, Jan. 9–March 2, 1863. Resigned Oct. 6, 1863, due to failing health from "scrofulous inflammation of the cervical glands attended with suppuration."
Born: March 23, 1820 KY
Died: Jan. 5, 1864 Georgetown, OH
Other Wars: Mexican War (1 Lieutenant, Co. G, 1 OH Infantry, June 26, 1846–June 12, 1847. 1 Lieutenant, Co. C, 2 OH Infantry, Sept. 11, 1847–July 25, 1848)
Occupation: Lawyer and probate judge
Miscellaneous: Resided Georgetown, Brown Co., OH
Buried: Old Georgetown Cemetery, Georgetown, OH
References: Pension File and Military Service File, National Archives. Letters Received, Volunteer Service Branch, Adjutant General's Office, File F570(VS)1863, National Archives. James L. McDonough, "The Last Day at Stone's River—Experiences of a Yank and a Reb," *Tennessee Historical Quarterly,* Vol. 40, No. 1 (Spring 1981).

James Perry Fyffe (The National Archives [BA-41]).

Charles B. Gambee

Captain, Co. A, 55 OH Infantry, Sept. 30, 1861. Major, 55 OH Infantry, Oct. 2, 1862. Lieutenant Colonel, 55 OH Infantry, March 5, 1863. Colonel, 55 OH Infantry, May 8, 1863. GSW left breast, Resaca, GA, May 15, 1864.

Born: April 5, 1827 Seneca Co., NY
Died: May 15, 1864 KIA Resaca, GA
Occupation: Dry goods merchant
Miscellaneous: Resided Bellevue, Sandusky Co., OH
Buried: Bellevue Cemetery, Bellevue, OH
References: Hartwell Osborn and Others. *Trials and Triumphs: The Record of the 55th Ohio Volunteer Infantry.* Chicago, IL, 1904. Pension File and Military Service File, National Archives. Obituary, *Fremont Weekly Journal,* June 10, 1864. Edmund J. Raus, Jr. *A Generation on the March—The Union Army at Gettysburg.* Gettysburg, PA, 1996.

Conrad Garis

2 Lieutenant, Co. C, 20 OH Infantry, Sept. 8, 1861. 1 Lieutenant, Co. C, 20 OH Infantry, Feb. 28, 1862. Resigned April 24, 1862, on account of "permanent and increasing ill health" due to hemorrhage of the lungs. Colonel, 168 OH Infantry, May 2, 1864. GSW left arm, left shoulder, and left side, Cynthiana, KY, June 11, 1864. Honorably mustered out, Sept. 8, 1864.

Born: June 9, 1831 PA

Conrad Garis (Richard F. Carlile Collection, copied by Richard A. Baumgartner).

Died: Nov. 17, 1889 Washington Court House, OH
Occupation: Farmer, carpenter and coal dealer
Offices/Honors: Sheriff of Fayette Co., OH, 1869–73. Treasurer of Fayette Co., OH, 1876–78.
Miscellaneous: Resided Bloomingburg, Fayette Co., OH; and Washington Court House, Fayette Co., OH
Buried: Washington Cemetery, Washington Court House, OH (Section 8, Lot 258)
References: Pension File and Military Service File, National Archives. Obituary, *Washington Court House Cyclone and Fayette Republican,* Nov. 20, 1889. Jim Leeke, editor. *A Hundred Days to Richmond.* Bloomington, IN, 1999. Charles Whittlesey. *War Memoranda. Cheat River to the Tennessee, 1861–62.* Cleveland, OH, 1884. William A. Penn. *Rattling Spurs and Broad-Brimmed Hats: The Civil War in Cynthiana and Harrison Co., KY.* Midway, KY, 1995.

Alfred West Gilbert

Lieutenant Colonel, 39 OH Infantry, July 27, 1861. Commanded 1 Demi-Brigade, 1 Brigade, 2 Division, Army of the Mississippi, June 1862. Colonel, 39 OH Infantry, July 9, 1862. Resigned Oct.

Charles B. Gambee (Hartwell Osborn. *Trials and Triumphs: The Record of the 55th Ohio Volunteer Infantry.* Chicago, Illinois, 1904).

Alfred West Gilbert (photograph by Hoag & Quick's Art Palace, No. 100 4th St., opp. Post Office, Cincinnati, Ohio).

1, 1862, in order "to return to my business and family and to a position where, in a more quiet, but perhaps not less effective way, I may still help forward the cause of my country." Before learning of the acceptance of his resignation, commanded regiment in action at Corinth, MS, Oct. 4, 1862, where he suffered a severe concussion when he was thrown violently from his horse.

Born: Feb. 9, 1816 Philadelphia, PA
Died: Oct. 24, 1900 Cincinnati, OH
Education: Graduated Cincinnati (OH) College, 1837
Occupation: Surveyor and civil engineer
Offices/Honors: Cincinnati City Engineer, 1849–55, 1859–61, and 1863–67
Miscellaneous: Resided Cincinnati, OH; and Venice (now Ross), Butler Co., OH
Buried: Richards-Gilbert Cemetery, near Ross, Butler Co., OH
References: William E. Smith and Ophia D. Smith, editors. *Colonel A. W. Gilbert, Citizen-Soldier of Cincinnati.* Cincinnati, OH, 1934. Obituary, *Cincinnati Enquirer,* Oct. 25, 1900. Pension File and Military Service File, National Archives. Charles H. Smith. *History of Fuller's Ohio Brigade.* Cleveland, OH, 1909. Obituary, *Hamilton Daily Democrat,* Oct. 25, 1900.

William Edward Gilmore

Colonel, 22 OH Infantry (3 months), May 23, 1861. Honorably mustered out, Aug. 19, 1861. Lieutenant Colonel, 63 OH Infantry, Nov. 19, 1861. Resigned July 17, 1862, because "the consolidation of the 63rd and 22nd produced feelings among the officers of the two original organizations which have not been, and I am satisfied, cannot be harmonized; and the discipline and efficiency of the regiment has been materially impaired by the results of that discord. While I solemnly assert that I have endeavored to reconcile all conflicting sentiments in the regiment, yet I believe my withdrawal from it will accomplish more towards that desirable end than any influence I can exert being present."

Born: Nov. 3, 1824 Chillicothe, OH
Died: Jan. 7, 1908 Chillicothe, OH
Education: Attended Ohio University, Athens, OH. Graduated Lane Theological Seminary, Cincinnati, OH, 1846. Graduated Cincinnati (OH) Law College, 1848.

William Edward Gilmore (post-war) (collection of the Ross County Historical Society).

Occupation: Lawyer, historian and poet
Offices/Honors: Mayor of Springfield, MO, 1870–71; Postmaster of Chillicothe, OH, 1884–88
Miscellaneous: Resided Chillicothe, Ross Co., OH; and Springfield, Greene Co., MO, 1866–73. Author of a biography of Edward Tiffin, first governor of Ohio.
Buried: Grandview Cemetery, Chillicothe, OH (Section 9, Lot 184)
References: Henry H. Bennett, editor. *The County of Ross*. Madison, WI, 1902. Obituary, *Scioto Gazette,* Jan. 7, 1908. Pension File and Military Service File, National Archives. Letter William E. Gilmore to Governor David Tod, Jan. 24, 1862, (Series 147-24: 189), Correspondence to the Governor and Adjutant General of Ohio, 1861–66, Ohio Historical Society. William Coyle, editor. *Ohio Authors and Their Books.* Cleveland and New York, 1962. William T. Coggeshall. *The Poets and Poetry of the West.* New York City, NY, 1864.

Isaac Newton Gilruth

2 Lieutenant, Co. F, 27 OH Infantry, Aug. 2, 1861. 1 Lieutenant, Co. K, 27 OH Infantry, March 28, 1862. Provost Marshal, Post of Decatur, AL, March 9–April 20, 1864. Captain, Co. F, 27 OH Infantry, April 20, 1864. Provost Marshal, District of Marietta, GA, Aug. 18–Nov. 13, 1864. Major, 27 OH Infantry, Jan. 28, 1865. Lieutenant Colonel, 27 OH Infantry, May 29, 1865. *Colonel,* 27 OH Infantry, May 31, 1865. Honorably mustered out, July 11, 1865.
Born: May 24, 1841 Scioto Co., OH
Died: Sept. 20, 1899 Yazoo City, MS
Occupation: Cotton planter and merchant
Miscellaneous: Resided Wheelersburg, Scioto Co., OH; and Yazoo City, Yazoo Co., MS
Buried: Glenwood Cemetery, Yazoo City, MS (Section 13, Lot 177)
References: *Biographical and Historical Memoirs of Mississippi.* Chicago, IL, 1891. Obituary, *Yazoo Sentinel,* Sept. 21, 1899. Obituary, *Yazoo City Herald,* Sept. 22, 1899. Pension File and Military Service File, National Archives. Obituary circular, Whole No. 452, Ohio MOLLUS. Charles H. Smith. *History of Fuller's Ohio Brigade.* Cleveland, OH, 1909.

Joseph Good

Captain, Co. B, 108 OH Infantry, Aug. 25, 1862. Provost Marshal, Post of Gallatin, TN, Dec. 12, 1862–March 31, 1863. Provost Marshal, Post of Frankfort, KY, April 1863. Major, 108 OH Infantry, July 31, 1863. Lieutenant Colonel, 108 OH Infantry, March 30, 1864. *Colonel,* 108 OH Infantry, May 18, 1865. Honorably mustered out, June 9, 1865.

Joseph Good (post-war) (Album of Portraits of Companions of the Commandery of the State of Ohio MOLLUS. Cincinnati, OH, 1893).

Isaac Newton Gilruth (USAMHI [RG98S-CWP 28.80]).

Born: Nov. 11, 1841 Cincinnati, OH
Died: Sept. 17, 1893 Cincinnati, OH
Occupation: Commission merchant
Miscellaneous: Resided Cincinnati, OH
Buried: Spring Grove Cemetery, Cincinnati, OH (Section 86, Lot 140)
References: Obituary Circular, Whole No. 270, Ohio MOLLUS. Obituary, *Cincinnati Enquirer,* Sept. 18, 1893. Military Service File, National Archives.

John Brown Groesbeck

Colonel, 39 OH Infantry, Aug. 16, 1861. Commanded 1 Brigade, 1 Division, Army of the Mississippi, Feb. 23–April 24, 1862. Commanded 1 Brigade, 2 Division, Army of the Mississippi, April 24–July 8, 1862. Resigned July 8, 1862, feeling "justified in asking to be permitted to return to my former pursuits and habits of life, more congenial to my taste," having "entered the army from a sense of duty" and having served one year without being "absent from my regiment a single day."
Born: March 3, 1820 Cincinnati, OH
Died: April 12, 1879 New York City, NY (committed suicide by drowning)
Education: Attended Woodward High School, Cincinnati, OH
Occupation: Lawyer, banker and stock speculator
Miscellaneous: Resided Cincinnati, OH; and New York City, NY. Brother-in-law of Major General Joseph Hooker.
Buried: Spring Grove Cemetery, Cincinnati, OH (Section 22, Lot 55)
References: "Col. Groesbeck Disappears," *New York Times,* April 27, 1879. "Col. Groesbeck's Body Found," *New York Times,* May 21, 1879. Charles H. Smith. *History of Fuller's Ohio Brigade.* Cleveland, OH, 1909. Barrington S. Havens. *Some Descendants of Nicolas Groesbeck.* N.p., 1979. William E. Smith and Ophia D. Smith, editors. *Colonel A. W. Gilbert, Citizen-Soldier of Cincinnati.* Cincinnati, OH, 1934. John A. Gano, et al. *Old Woodward Memorial.* Cincinnati, OH, 1884. Military Service File, National Archives.

John C. Groom

Major, 84 OH Infantry, June 11, 1862. Colonel, 100 OH Infantry, Aug. 28, 1862. Under arrest for disobedience of orders, he resigned May 13, 1863, since "the members of the Court have commands that are now in the front and need their presence. Therefore, I cannot ask to deprive the Country of their services to establish my innocence or guilt at so critical a moment."
Born: Jan. 14, 1818 Fairview Twp., York Co., PA

John Brown Groesbeck (Massachusetts MOLLUS Collection, USAMHI [Vol. 80, p. 4045]).

Died: June 26, 1895 Columbus, OH
Other Wars: Mexican War (1 Lieutenant, Co. E, 4 OH Infantry)
Occupation: Lawyer and hardware merchant
Offices/Honors: Ohio House of Representatives, 1876–78, 1880–82
Miscellaneous: Resided Circleville, Pickaway Co., OH; Kansas City, MO, 1858–61; and Columbus, Franklin Co., OH
Buried: Forest Cemetery, Circleville, OH (Section 11)
References: Obituary, *Circleville Democrat and Watchman,* July 5, 1895. Pension File and Military Service File, National Archives. Letters Received, Volunteer Service Branch, Adjutant General's Office, File O213(VS)1862, National Archives.

Theodore Haffner

2 Lieutenant, Co. K, 9 OH Infantry, April 23, 1861. 1 Lieutenant, Co. K, 9 OH Infantry, May 27, 1861. Resigned July 5, 1862, due to "family affairs of an important and urgent nature." In forwarding the resignation, brigade commander Robert L. McCook added the comment, "The man is of no account whatever, and only fills the place that should be held by a good man." Colonel, 6

OH Volunteer Militia, Sept. 2, 1862. Resigned Sept. 14, 1862.
Born: 1824? Bavaria
Died: Date and place of death unknown
Miscellaneous: Resided Cincinnati, OH; and St. Joseph, Buchanan Co., MO
Buried: Place of burial unknown
References: Military Service File, National Archives. Letters Received, Volunteer Service Branch, Adjutant General's Office, File B1688(VS)1862, National Archives.

Joel Haines

Captain, Co. C, 17 OH Infantry, Sept. 2, 1861. Resigned June 6, 1862, on account of inability to discharge the duties of a soldier because of pulmonary disease. Colonel, 132 OH Infantry, May 15, 1864. Honorably mustered out, Sept. 10, 1864.
Born: June 9, 1814 West Middleburg, OH
Died: Oct. 21, 1886 West Middleburg, OH
Occupation: Farmer and cabinet maker before war. Dry goods merchant, grocer and tin manufacturer after war.
Miscellaneous: Resided West Middleburg, Logan Co., OH. Held thirteen patents as an inventor, including one for an improved fruit jar.
Buried: Middleburg Cemetery, Middleburg, OH
References: *History of Logan County, OH.* Chicago, IL, 1880. Obituary, *Bellefontaine Republican*, Oct. 22, 1886. Pension File and Military Service File, National Archives. Rendall Rhoades, "The Celebrated Haines' Patent Fruit Jar," *Hayes Historical Journal*, Vol. 7, No. 4 (Summer 1988). Letters Received, Volunteer Service Branch, Adjutant General's Office, File H222(VS)1862, National Archives. Charles T. Develling. *History of the 17th Regiment Ohio Veteran Volunteer Infantry.* Zanesville, OH, 1889.

Albert S. Hall

Captain, Co. F, 24 OH Infantry, June 3, 1861. Major, 24 OH Infantry, Dec. 20, 1861. GSW head, Shiloh, TN, April 7, 1862. Lieutenant Colonel, 24 OH Infantry, May 14, 1862. Colonel, 105 OH Infantry, Aug. 11, 1862. Commanded 10 Division, 1 Army Corps, Army of the Ohio, Oct. 8–Oct. 18, 1862. Commanded 33 Brigade, 10 Division, 1 Army Corps, Army of the Ohio, Oct. 18–Nov. 5, 1862. Commanded 1 Brigade, 5 Division, Centre, 14 Army Corps, Army of the Cumberland, Nov. 5, 1862–Jan. 9, 1863. Commanded 2 Brigade, 5 Division, 14 Army Corps, Army of the Cumberland, Jan. 9–June 8, 1863. Commanded 2 Brigade, 4 Division, 14 Army Corps, Army of the Cumberland, June 8–July 8, 1863.
Born: Oct. 20, 1830 Charlestown, OH
Died: July 10, 1863 Murfreesboro, TN (typhoid fever)
Education: Attended Geauga Seminary, Chester, OH
Occupation: Lawyer
Miscellaneous: Resided Jefferson, Ashtabula Co., OH; and Warren, Trumbull Co., OH

Joel Haines (post-war).

Albert S. Hall (photograph by F. L. Le Roy, Warren, Ohio; Roger D. Hunt Collection, USAMHI [RG98S-CWP26.18]).

Albert S. Hall gravestone (photograph by Stein's Photographic Gallery, Ravenna, Ohio).

Buried: Charlestown Cemetery, Charlestown, OH

References: Obituary, *Portage County Democrat,* July 15, 1863. Pension File and Military Service File, National Archives. Albion W. Tourgee. *The Story of a Thousand: Being a History of the Service of the 105th Ohio Volunteer Infantry.* Buffalo, NY, 1896.

Benton Halstead

Private, Co. D, 69 OH Infantry, Oct. 11, 1861. Sergeant Major, 69 OH Infantry, Nov. 13, 1861. 1 Lieutenant, Co. F, 79 OH Infantry, Aug. 29, 1862. Captain, Co. F, 79 OH Infantry, April 27, 1863. GSW Resaca, GA, May 14, 1864. Colonel, 197 OH Infantry, May 29, 1865. Honorably mustered out, July 31, 1865.

Born: March 11, 1834 Butler Co., OH
Died: Feb. 26, 1919 Washington, DC
Education: Attended Farmers' (later Belmont) College, College Hill, OH
Occupation: Lawyer
Miscellaneous: Resided Cincinnati, OH; and Washington, DC. Inventor of a typewriter which he patented. Brother of prominent journalist Murat Halstead.

Benton Halstead (L. M. Strayer Collection).

Buried: Arlington National Cemetery, Arlington, VA (Section 15A, Lot 65)

References: *National Cyclopedia of American Biography.* William L. Halstead. *The Story of the Halsteads of the U. S.* Ann Arbor, MI, 1934. Military Service File, National Archives. Letters Received, Volunteer Service Branch, Adjutant General's Office, File O527(VS)1865, National Archives. Obituary, *Washington Post,* Feb. 27, 1919.

Leonard Armstrong Harris

Captain, Co. I, 2 OH Infantry, April 17, 1861. Colonel, 2 OH Infantry, Aug. 8, 1861. Commanded 9 Brigade, 3 Division, District of the Ohio, Aug. 10–Sept. 29, 1862. Commanded 9 Brigade, 3 Division, 1 Army Corps, Army of the Ohio, Sept. 29–Nov. 5, 1862. Resigned Dec. 24, 1862, due to "an injury in the back" that ... "has increased to such an extent that I am now satisfied from the advice of my physicians and my feelings that I will never be fit for duty." Colonel, 137 OH Infantry, May 10, 1864. Honorably mustered out, Aug. 19, 1864.

Born: Oct. 11, 1824 Cincinnati, OH
Died: July 5, 1890 Cincinnati, OH
Occupation: Locksmith and magistrate before war
Offices/Honors: Mayor of Cincinnati, OH, 1863–66. U.S. Collector of Internal Revenue, 1866–70. Member of the Board of Managers of the National Homes for Disabled Volunteer Soldiers, 1878–90.

Leonard A. Harris (post-war) (Maurice Joblin & Co. *Cincinnati Past and Present; or, Its Industrial History as Exhibited in the Life-Labors of Its Leading Men.* Cincinnati, Ohio, 1872).

Miscellaneous: Resided Cincinnati, OH
Buried: Spring Grove Cemetery, Cincinnati, OH (Section 103, Lot 160)
References: *Biographical Cyclopedia and Portrait Gallery with an Historical Sketch of the State of Ohio.* Vol. 5. Cincinnati, OH, 1891. Maurice Joblin & Co. *Cincinnati Past and Present; or, Its Industrial History as Exhibited in the Life-Labors of Its Leading Men.* Cincinnati, OH, 1872. Obituary Circular, Whole No. 168, Ohio MOLLUS. Pension File and Military Service File, National Archives. *Biographical Encyclopedia of Ohio of the Nineteenth Century.* Cincinnati and Philadelphia, 1876. *Society of the Army of the Cumberland. Twenty-first Reunion, Toledo, OH, 1890.* Cincinnati, OH, 1891. Obituary, *Cincinnati Enquirer,* July 6, 1890.

James Findlay Harrison

Colonel, 11 OH Infantry (3 months), April 25, 1861. Having resigned May 29, 1861 in anticipation of being re-elected colonel of the three-years' organization, he learned that the Governor would not confirm his appointment, if re-elected, due to an episode of drunkenness triggered by the death of his young son. Commanded a brigade of "Squirrel Hunters," called out in Sept. 1862 for the defense of Cincinnati. Colonel, Volunteer ADC, Staff of Brig. Gen. William H. Lytle, commended for gallantry at Chickamauga, GA, Sept. 20, 1863. Private, Unassigned, 1 Ohio Cavalry, Sept. 21, 1864. Conditional 2 Lieutenant, 185 Ohio Infantry, Jan. 5, 1865. Captain, Co. E, 187 OH Infantry, March 2, 1865. Facing charges of being "so grossly drunk as to be entirely unfitted for duty" and then breaking his arrest, he resigned, with his "immediate and unconditional" resignation being accepted April 20, 1865, "for the good of the service."
Born: March 9, 1825 Cincinnati, OH
Died: Feb. 14, 1907 Mound City, KS
Education: Attended U.S. Military Academy, West Point, NY (Class of 1845)
Other Wars: Mexican War (1 Lieutenant, Co. K, 1 OH Infantry). 1 Lieutenant, 10 U.S. Infantry, March 3, 1855. Resigned Aug. 8, 1855.
Occupation: Lawyer before war. Farmer and surveyor after war.
Miscellaneous: Resided Terre Haute, Vigo Co., IN; Dayton, OH; and La Cygne and Mound City, Linn Co., KS, after 1866. Grandson of President William Henry Harrison and first cousin of President Benjamin Harrison. Nephew of Colonel William H. H. Taylor (5 OH Cavalry).
Buried: Woodland Cemetery, Mound City, KS (National Cemetery Plot, Section 1, Site 69)
References: *Portrait and Biographical Record of Southeastern Kansas.* Chicago, IL, 1894. Obituary, *Linn County Republic,* Feb. 22, 1907. Letter J. Findlay Harrison to Governor David Tod, Jan. 28, 1862, (Series 147–26: 160), Correspondence to the Governor and Adjutant General of Ohio, 1861–66, Ohio Historical Society. Pension File (Mexican War) and Military Service File, National Archives. Letters Received, Volunteer Service Branch, Adjutant General's Office, File O238(VS)1865, National Archives. Reginald B. Henry. *Genealogies of the Families of the Presidents.* Rutland, VT, 1935. Joshua H. Horton and Solomon Teverbaugh. *A History of the 11th Regiment Ohio Volunteer Infantry.* Dayton, OH, 1866.

Joseph D. Hatfield

Major, 89 OH Infantry, Aug. 26, 1862. Colonel, 89 OH Infantry, Oct. 2, 1862. Tried by court-martial on charges of "Conduct prejudicial to good order and military discipline, Conduct calculated to produce mutiny, Speaking disrespectfully of his superior officer, Protecting the utterance of treasonable sentiments, and Incompetence," he was acquitted of all charges except the charge of incompetence, for which he was dismissed, June 6, 1863.
Born: Sept. 15, 1815 OH
Died: April 14, 1872 Withamsville, OH
Occupation: Farmer and Baptist preacher
Offices/Honors: Superintendent of Clermont County Infirmary, Batavia, OH, 1868–72

James Findlay Harrison (Schwing & Rudd, Photographers, Army of the Cumberland; William A. Gladstone Collection).

Miscellaneous: Resided Amelia, Clermont Co., OH; Withamsville, Clermont Co., OH; and Batavia, Clermont Co., OH
Buried: Odd Fellows Cemetery, Amelia, OH
References: Pension File and Military Service File, National Archives. Bryan P. Weaver with H. Lee Fenner. *Sacrifice at Chickamauga: A History of the 89th Ohio Volunteer Infantry Regiment*. Palos Verdes Peninsula, CA, 2003. *History of Clermont County, OH*. Philadelphia, PA, 1880.

Joseph G. Hawkins

Major, 13 OH Infantry (3 months), April 30, 1861. Major, 13 OH Infantry (3 years), June 26, 1861. Lieutenant Colonel, 13 OH Infantry, Oct. 25, 1861. Colonel, 13 OH Infantry, May 13, 1862. GSW breast and neck, Stone's River, TN, Dec. 31, 1862.
Born: Jan. 11, 1828 Goshen, CT
Died: Dec. 31, 1862 KIA Stone's River, TN
Other Wars: Mexican War (Private, Co. E, 4 OH Infantry)
Occupation: Grocer and farmer
Miscellaneous: Resided Hudson, Summit Co., OH; and Marysville, Union Co., OH
Buried: Oakdale Cemetery, Marysville, OH

Joseph G. Hawkins (U.S. Military Academy Library).

References: *History of Union County, OH*. Chicago, IL, 1883. Pension File and Military Service File, National Archives.

Chauncey Gillett Hawley

Lieutenant Colonel, 117 OH Infantry, Aug. 21, 1862. Colonel, 1 OH Heavy Artillery, Aug. 1, 1863. Commanded Post of Covington and Newport (KY), District of Ohio, Department of the Ohio, Aug. 1863 and Jan. 6–March 1864. Commanded 1 Brigade, 4 Division, District of East Tennessee, Army of the Cumberland, March 17–June 1865. Honorably mustered out, July 25, 1865.
Born: May 11, 1828 Austinburg, Ashtabula Co., OH
Died: May 25, 1903 Girard, KS
Occupation: Lawyer and probate judge
Offices/Honors: Ohio Senate, 1856–58. Postmaster, Girard, KS, 1874–83.
Miscellaneous: Resided Ironton, Lawrence Co., OH; Fort Scott, Bourbon Co., KS; and Girard, Crawford Co., KS, after 1869
Buried: Girard Cemetery, Girard, KS (Section 4, Lot 38)

Chauncey Gillett Hawley (post-war) (Alvin M. Woolson. *First Ohio Volunteer Heavy Artillery, Company M.* Toledo, Ohio, 1914).

References: Pension File and Military Service File, National Archives. William C. Cuthbertson. *The Genesis of Girard.* N.p., 1980. Alvin M. Woolson. *First Ohio Volunteer Heavy Artillery, Company M.* Toledo, OH, 1914. Letters Received, Volunteer Service Branch, Adjutant General's Office, File B224(VS)1864, National Archives.

Nathaniel Haynes

Captain, Co. K, 100 OH Infantry, Aug. 7, 1862. Resigned Jan. 18, 1863, upon the death of his business partner to "immediately take charge and personally attend to the property and business of the firm." Colonel, 169 OH Infantry, May 15, 1864. Honorably mustered out, Sept. 4, 1864.

Born: 1832? NY
Died: Nov. 27, 1869 London, Ontario, Canada
Occupation: Engaged in the lumber trade and the manufacture of sash and blinds
Miscellaneous: Resided Fremont, Sandusky Co., OH
Buried: Oakwood Cemetery, Fremont, OH (Section 26, Lot 2)
References: Obituary, *Fremont Journal,* Dec. 3, 1869. Military Service File, National Archives. Jim Leeke, editor. *A Hundred Days to Richmond.* Bloomington, IN, 1999. Richard L. Manion and Nan Card. *Sandusky County, Ohio, Civil War Soldiers.* Fremont, OH, 1992.

Nathaniel Haynes (Sandusky County Kin Hunters Collection, USAMHI [RG98S-CWP144.35]).

William Henry Hayward

Lieutenant Colonel, 1 OH Light Artillery, Nov. 25, 1861. Chief of Ordnance, Mountain Department, March–April 17, 1862. Commanded Artillery Brigade, 1 Division, Department of the Rappahan-

William Henry Hayward (post-war) (George W. Tibbitts. *A Brief Sketch of the Cleveland Grays.* Cleveland, Ohio, 1903).

nock, May 1862. Chief of Artillery, 3 Division, 3 Army Corps, Army of the Potomac, Nov. 1862–March 1863. Resigned April 1, 1863, due to physical disability from "phthisis pulmonalis (hereditary) developed by an attack of pneumonia two months ago." Colonel, 150 OH Infantry, May 5, 1864. Commanded 1 Brigade, Haskin's Division, Defenses North of the Potomac, 22 Army Corps, Department of Washington, May 12–July 6, 1864. Commanded 2 Brigade, Hardin's Division, Defenses North of the Potomac, 22 Army Corps, Department of Washington, July–Aug. 1864. Honorably mustered out, Aug. 23, 1864.
Born: Dec. 6, 1822 Lebanon, CT
Died: March 1, 1904 Cleveland, OH
Occupation: Member of a printing and bookbinding firm
Miscellaneous: Resided Cleveland, OH
Buried: Woodland Cemetery, Cleveland, OH (Section 9, Lot 1)
References: Maurice Joblin, publisher. *Cleveland, Past and Present; Its Representative Men.* Cleveland, OH, 1869. Obituary Circular, Whole No. 613, Ohio MOLLUS. Obituary, *Cleveland Press,* March 1, 1904. David D. Van Tassel and John J. Grabowski, editors. *Dictionary of Cleveland Biography.* Bloomington, IN, 1996. Military Service File, National Archives. Letters Received, Volunteer Service Branch, Adjutant General's Office, File O815(VS)1863, National Archives. William J. Gleason. *Historical Sketch of the 150th Regiment Ohio Volunteer Infantry.* Cleveland, OH, 1899.

Jefferson Jackson Hibbets
1 Sergeant, Co. A, 32 OH Infantry, Aug. 27, 1861. 1 Lieutenant, Co. A, 32 OH Infantry, Nov. 6, 1861. Captain, Co. A, 32 OH Infantry, April 10, 1862. Captain, Co. K, 32 OH Infantry, July 1, 1862. GSW head, Maryland Heights, MD, Sept. 12, 1862. Taken prisoner and paroled, Harper's Ferry, WV, Sept. 15, 1862. Captain, Co. A, 32 OH Infantry, Jan. 13, 1863. Lieutenant Colonel, 32 OH Infantry, July 27, 1863. Acting AIG, Staff of Major Gen. Frank P. Blair, Jr., commanding 17 Army Corps, Army of the Tennessee, May 24–Aug. 18, 1864. Colonel, 32 OH Infantry, May 18, 1865. Commanded 1 Brigade, 4 Division, 17 Army Corps, June 26–July 9, 1865. Honorably mustered out, July 20, 1865.
Born: April 1840 Minerva, OH
Died: July 19, 1887 Kansas City, MO
Occupation: Merchant and real estate agent
Offices/Honors: Postmaster of Chetopa, KS, 1872–75
Miscellaneous: Resided Minerva, Stark Co., OH, to 1868; Chetopa, Labette Co., KS; and Kansas City, MO

Jefferson Jackson Hibbets (Ebenezer Z. Hays, editor. *History of the 32nd Ohio Veteran Volunteer Infantry.* Columbus, Ohio, 1896).

Buried: Oak Hill Cemetery, Chetopa, KS (Block 18, Lot 4)
References: Pension File and Military Service File, National Archives. Obituary, *Washington National Tribune,* Aug. 11, 1887. Ebenezer Z. Hays, editor. *History of the 32nd Ohio Veteran Volunteer Infantry.* Columbus, OH, 1896.

David Jordan Higgins
Captain, Co. C, 24 OH Infantry, June 1, 1861. Colonel, 24 OH Infantry, Jan. 1, 1863. Dismissed Oct. 3, 1863, for "cowardice in the face of the enemy" at Chickamauga, GA, Sept. 19–20, 1863. Pleading physical disability due to rheumatic disease in the back and hips, he obtained suspension of the dismissal order while a court of inquiry investigated his case. Since the court of inquiry found that he was "unfitted for the command of a regiment by reason of his physical condition," his dismissal was revoked, and his resignation was accepted to date Oct. 23, 1863.
Born: Sept. 18, 1817 Otisfield, ME
Died: Feb. 2, 1917 Pasadena, CA
Occupation: Methodist clergyman
Miscellaneous: Resided Columbiana Co., OH, to 1863; Hastings, Dakota Co., MN, 1863–76; Paynesville, Stearns Co., MN, 1876–77; Atwater, Kandiyohi Co., MN, 1877–79; Montevideo, Chippewa Co., MN, 1879–82; Reads Landing, Wabasha Co., MN, 1882–83; Minneapolis, MN, 1883–89, 1895–1900; Brooklyn Center, Hennepin Co., MN, 1889–93; and Pasadena, CA

David Jordan Higgins (an author at the age of 99) (David J. Higgins. *Human Nature: A Psychological Study*. New York and Cincinnati, 1916).

Buried: Mountain View Cemetery, Altadena, CA (Lot 573)

References: Pension File and Military Service File, National Archives. Obituary, *Los Angeles Times*, Feb. 3, 1917. Katharine C. Higgins. *Richard Higgins and His Descendants*. Worcester, MA, 1918.

Jesse Hildebrand

Colonel, 77 OH Infantry, Oct. 5, 1861. Commanded 3 Brigade, 5 Division, Army of the Tennessee, March 1–May 12, 1862. Commanded Alton Military Prison and Post of Alton, IL, Sept. 1862–April 1863.

Born: May 29, 1800 Cold Springs, PA

Died: April 18, 1863 Alton, IL (pneumonia)

Occupation: Stage line operator and railway mail agent

Offices/Honors: Sheriff of Washington Co., OH, 1850–52. Major General, Ohio State Militia.

Miscellaneous: Resided Marietta, Washington Co., OH

Buried: Mound Cemetery, Marietta, OH

References: *History of Washington County, OH*. Cleveland, OH, 1881. Obituary, *Marietta Republican*, April 23, 1863. Letters Received, Volunteer Service Branch, Adjutant General's Office, File

Jesse Hildebrand (photograph by Cadwallader & Tappen, Photographers, Marietta, Ohio; USAMHI).

M2458(VS)1862, National Archives. Military Service File, National Archives.

Joseph Hinson

Private, Co. G, 1 OH Infantry (3 months), April 29, 1861. Honorably mustered out, Aug. 1, 1861. 1 Lieutenant, Co. D, 33 OH Infantry, Aug. 27, 1861. Detailed as Acting Signal Officer, Jan. 23, 1862. Returned to regiment, May 1862. Captain, Co. D, 33 OH Infantry, March 24, 1862. GSW left arm (amputated), Chickamauga, GA, Sept. 19, 1863. Major, 33 OH Infantry, Jan. 28, 1865. Lieutenant Colonel, 33 OH Infantry, May 18, 1865. *Colonel*, 33 OH Infantry, June 26, 1865. Honorably mustered out, July 12, 1865. Bvt. Colonel, USV, March 13, 1865, for meritorious services.

Born: March 5, 1842 Waverly, OH

Died: Dec. 2, 1904 Tacoma, WA

Occupation: Bookkeeper and commercial traveler. Engaged in fruit growing after moving to Tacoma, WA.

Miscellaneous: Resided Waverly, Pike Co., OH; Menasha, Winnebago Co., WI; San Francisco, CA; and Tacoma, Pierce Co., WA, 1888–1904

Buried: Tacoma Cemetery, Tacoma, WA (Section 4, Block A, Lot 26)

Joseph Hinson (J. Willard Brown. *The Signal Corps, U.S.A, in the War of the Rebellion.* Boston, Massachusetts, 1896).

References: Pension File and Military Service File, National Archives. Lois J. Lambert. *Heroes of the Western Theater: 33rd Ohio Veteran Volunteer Infantry.* Milford, OH, 2008. Letters Received, Volunteer Service Branch, Adjutant General's Office, File H168(VS)1864, National Archives. Obituary Circular, Whole No. 113, Washington MOLLUS. Obituary, *Tacoma Daily Ledger,* Dec. 3, 1904. Benjamin W. Dwight. *History of the Descendants of Elder John Strong.* Albany, NY, 1871. J. Willard Brown. *The Signal Corps, U.S.A, in the War of the Rebellion.* Boston, MA, 1896.

John E. Hudson

1 Lieutenant, Co. C, 10 OH Infantry (3 months), April 19, 1861. Captain, Co. C, 10 OH Infantry (3 years), June 3, 1861. Major, 10 OH Infantry, Jan. 20, 1863. Honorably mustered out, June 17, 1864. Captain, Co. C, 181 OH Infantry, Oct. 4, 1864. Lieutenant Colonel, 181 OH Infantry, Oct. 15, 1864. Colonel, 181 OH Infantry, June 16, 1865. Honorably mustered out, July 14, 1865.
Born: 1838? Ireland
Died: June 21, 1889 Ogden, UT
Occupation: Wool merchant and commercial traveler
Miscellaneous: Resided Cincinnati, OH; Nashville, Davidson Co., TN; and Ogden, Weber Co., UT
Buried: Aultorest Memorial Park, Ogden, UT (Block 15, Lot 8)

John E. Hudson (L. M. Strayer Collection).

References: Military Service File, National Archives. Obituary, *Ogden Standard,* June 22, 1889. Obituary and funeral account, *Salt Lake Tribune,* June 22, 23, and 25, 1889.

John H. Humphrey

Captain, Co. G, 45 OH Infantry, Aug. 14, 1862. Lieutenant Colonel, 45 OH Infantry, Oct. 12, 1864. Honorably mustered out, June 12, 1865. *Colonel,* 45 OH Infantry, June 16, 1865.
Born: July 20, 1832 Bucks Co., PA
Died: June 23, 1904 Delaware, OH
Education: Attended Ohio Wesleyan University, Delaware, OH
Occupation: Farmer before war. Hardware merchant and traveling salesman after war.
Miscellaneous: Resided Radnor Twp., Delaware Co., OH; and Delaware, Delaware Co., OH
Buried: Oak Grove Cemetery, Delaware, OH (Mount Hope Section, Lot 8)
References: Robert B. Powers. *A Record of My Paternal Ancestors.* Delaware, OH, 1967. Pension File and Military Service File, National Archives. Obituary, *Delaware Semi-Weekly Gazette,* June 28, 1904.

Samuel Henry Hunt

Colonel, 144 OH Infantry, May 2, 1864. Honorably mustered out, Aug. 31, 1864.

John H. Humphrey.

Born: Dec. 29, 1829 near Worthington, OH
Died: March 31, 1905 Upper Sandusky, OH
Occupation: Dry goods merchant until 1868 after which time he engaged in the grain and wool business
Miscellaneous: Resided Upper Sandusky, Wyandot Co., OH
Buried: Oak Hill Cemetery, Upper Sandusky, OH
References: Obituary, *Wyandot Chief*, April 3, 1905. Obituary, *Wyandot County Republican*, April 7, 1905. *History of Wyandot County, OH*. Chicago, IL, 1884. Pension File, National Archives. Daniel A. Masters. *No Greater Glory: The 144th Ohio Volunteer Infantry in the Civil War*. CD-ROM. Maumee, OH, 2002. Letters Received, Volunteer Service Branch, Adjutant General's Office, File H2409(VS)1865, National Archives.

Gustavus Swan Innis

Colonel, 133 OH Infantry, May 6, 1864. Commanded Post of Fort Powhatan, VA, June 18–Aug. 10, 1864. Honorably mustered out, Aug. 20, 1864.
Born: Feb. 4, 1819 Franklinton, Franklin Co., OH
Died: Jan. 2, 1899 Columbus, OH
Occupation: Farmer, civil engineer, and surveyor
Offices/Honors: Warden of the Ohio Penitentiary, 1874–75
Miscellaneous: Resided Clinton Twp., Franklin Co., OH; Marion Twp., Franklin Co., OH; and Columbus, Franklin Co., OH
Buried: Greenlawn Cemetery, Columbus, OH (Section F, Lot 3)
References: Pension File, National Archives. Obituary, *Ohio State Journal*, Jan. 3, 1899. *Centennial Biographical History of the City of Columbus and Franklin County, OH*. Chicago, IL, 1901. *Biographical Encyclopedia of Ohio of the Nineteenth Century*. Cincinnati and Philadelphia, 1876. Sylvester M. Sherman. *History of the 133rd Ohio Volunteer Infantry and Incidents Connected With Its Service During the War of the Rebellion*. Columbus, OH, 1896. Jim Leeke, editor. *A Hundred Days to Richmond*. Bloomington, IN, 1999.

Gustavus Swan Innis (post-war).

James Irvine

Captain, Co. A, 16 OH Infantry (3 months), April 24, 1861. Colonel, 16 OH Infantry, May 3, 1861. Honorably mustered out, Aug. 18, 1861. Captain, Co. M, 9 OH Cavalry, Dec. 2, 1863. Major, 9 OH Cavalry, May 31, 1865. Honorably mustered out, July 20, 1865.
Born: Dec. 24, 1822 Wooster, OH
Died: June 23, 1882 Coshocton, OH
Other Wars: Mexican War (Captain, Co. G, 4 OH Infantry)
Occupation: Lawyer
Miscellaneous: Resided Coshocton, Coshocton Co., OH
Buried: Oak Ridge Cemetery, Coshocton, OH
References: Norman N. Hill, Jr., compiler. *History of Coshocton County, OH: Its Past and Present*. Newark, OH, 1881. Obituary, *Coshocton Age*, July 1, 1882. L. Boyd, compiler. *The Irvines and Their Kin*. Chicago, IL, 1908. Pension File and Military Service File, National Archives. William D. Hamil-

William Smith Irwin.

James Irvine (David A. Neuhardt Collection; copied by Richard A. Baumgartner).

ton. *Recollections of a Cavalryman of the Civil War After Fifty Years.* Columbus, OH, 1915.

William Smith Irwin

Lieutenant Colonel, 121 OH Infantry, Aug. 18, 1862. Resigned and discharged for disability, March 17, 1863, due to phthisis pulmonalis. Colonel, 136 OH Infantry, May 2, 1864. Commanded 2 Brigade, Defenses South of the Potomac, 22 Army Corps, May 16–July 10, 1864. Commanded 3 Brigade, Defenses South of the Potomac, 22 Army Corps, July 10–Aug. 22, 1864. Honorably mustered out, Aug. 31, 1864.

Born: Aug. 16, 1827 near Hayesville, Ashland Co., OH
Died: Jan. 15, 1889 Mount Gilead, OH
Occupation: Lawyer, farmer, and real estate agent
Offices/Honors: Auditor of Morrow Co., OH, 1858–62
Miscellaneous: Resided Mansfield, Richland Co., OH; and Mount Gilead, Morrow Co., OH
Buried: Rivercliff Cemetery, Mount Gilead, OH
References: *History of Morrow County and Ohio.* Chicago, IL, 1880. Pension File and Military Service File, National Archives. Obituary, *Mount Gilead Union Register,* Jan. 23, 1889.

William Smith Irwin (photograph by Ball & Thomas' Photographic Art Gallery, 120 West Fourth Street, near Race, Cincinnati, Ohio; courtesy Henry Deeks).

Lyman J. Jackson

Captain, Co. E, 17 OH Infantry (3 months), April 27, 1861. Honorably mustered out, Aug. 16, 1861. Captain, Co. G, 31 OH Infantry, Sept. 23, 1861. Major, 11 OH Infantry, Jan. 9, 1862. Resigned Oct. 31, 1862, citing his inability to "perform my duty here with proper efficiency," due to the dissatisfaction caused by his irregular appointment. Colonel, 159 OH Infantry, May 10, 1864. Honorably mustered out, Aug. 24, 1864.

Born: Jan. 12, 1834 West Rushville, Fairfield Co., OH
Died: Jan. 25, 1887 New Lexington, OH
Education: Graduated St. Joseph's College, Somerset, OH, 1857
Occupation: Lawyer
Offices/Honors: Ohio Senate, 1878–82
Miscellaneous: Resided New Lexington, Perry Co., OH
Buried: Maplewood Cemetery, New Lexington, OH
References: Albert A. Graham. *History of Fairfield and Perry Counties, OH.* Chicago, IL, 1883. Pension File and Military Service File, National Archives. Obituary, *New Lexington Tribune,* Jan. 27, 1887. Letters Received, Volunteer Service Branch, Adjutant General's Office, File O119(VS)1862, National Archives. Joshua H. Horton and Solomon Teverbaugh. *A History of the 11th Regiment Ohio Volunteer Infantry.* Dayton, OH, 1866.

Anderson D. Jaynes

Colonel, 141 OH Infantry, May 12, 1864. Honorably mustered out, Sept. 3, 1864.

Born: Nov. 26, 1829 Lawrence Co., OH
Died: Oct. 12, 1886 Winchendon, MA
Occupation: Merchant and iron furnace operator before war. Banker, railroad promoter, and business executive after war.
Miscellaneous: Resided Albany, Athens Co., OH, before war; and Sedalia, Pettis Co., MO, after war
Buried: Crown Hill Cemetery, Sedalia, MO (Block 12, Lot 1)
References: *The United States Biographical Dictionary and Portrait Gallery of Eminent and Self-Made Men.* Missouri volume. New York, Chicago, St. Louis, and Kansas City, 1878. Howard L. Conard, editor. *Encyclopedia of the History of Missouri.* New York, Louisville, and St. Louis, 1901. Chancy R. Barns, editor. *The Commonwealth of Missouri: A Centennial Record.* St. Louis, MO, 1877. Obituary, *St. Louis Globe-Democrat,* Oct. 14, 1886. *History of Pettis County, MO.* N.p., 1882. Military Service File, National Archives.

Howard Daniel John

1 Sergeant, Co. F, 2 OH Infantry (3 months), April 17, 1861. 1 Lieutenant, Co. F, 2 OH Infantry, June 29, 1861. Honorably mustered out, July 31, 1861. Captain, Co. B, 86 OH Infantry (3 months), June 7, 1862. Honorably mustered out, Sept. 25, 1862. Captain, Co. C, 129 OH Infantry, July 18, 1863. Colonel, 129 OH Infantry, Aug. 10, 1863. Honorably mustered out, March 10, 1864.

Born: Feb. 8, 1826 York Springs, PA
Died: Aug. 24, 1882 Springfield, OH
Occupation: Carpenter
Miscellaneous: Resided Springfield, Clark Co., OH
Buried: Ferncliff Cemetery, Springfield, OH (Section H, Lot 174)
References: Pension File and Military Service File, National Archives. *Vital Statistics, Early Clark County, Ohio, Families.* Vol. 1. Springfield, OH, 1985.

Frederick Charles Jones

Captain, ADC, Staff of Brig. Gen. Joshua H. Bates, April–Aug. 1861. Lieutenant Colonel, 31 OH Infantry, Oct. 1861. Lieutenant Colonel, 24 OH Infantry, Feb. 18, 1862. Colonel, 24 OH Infantry, May 14, 1862. GSW right side, Stone's River, TN, Dec. 31, 1862.

Born: Dec. 16, 1834 near Greensboro, Greene Co., PA
Died: Dec. 31, 1862 KIA Stone's River, TN
Education: Graduated Woodward High School, Cincinnati, OH, 1853
Occupation: Lawyer
Miscellaneous: Resided Cincinnati, OH
Buried: Spring Grove Cemetery, Cincinnati, OH (Section 21, Soldiers' Circle B, Center, unmarked)
References: Whitelaw Reid. *Ohio in the War: Her Statesmen Generals and Soldiers.* Cincinnati, OH, 1868. Adolphus E. Jones, editor. *In Memoriam, Cincinnati 1881, Containing Proceedings of the Memorial Association.* Cincinnati, OH, 1881. Elias R. Monfort, Henry B. Furness, and Frederick H. Alms, editors. *GAR War Papers, Papers Read Before Fred C. Jones Post, No. 401, Department of Ohio, GAR.* Cincinnati, OH, 1891. Letter Fred C. Jones to Adjutant General C.P. Buckingham, March 1, 1862, (Series 147–28: 1), Correspondence to the Governor and Adjutant General of Ohio, 1861–66, Ohio Historical Society. Military Service File, National Archives. William B. Hazen. *A Narrative of Military Service.* Boston, MA, 1885.

Henry Ewing Jones

Sergeant, Co. G, 1 OH Infantry (3 months), April 29, 1861. Honorably mustered out, Aug. 1,

Anderson D. Jaynes (post-war) (Chancy R. Barns, editor. *The Commonwealth of Missouri: A Centennial Record*. St. Louis, Missouri, 1877).

Frederick C. Jones (Tom Molocea Collection).

Frederick C. Jones (photograph by Van Loo & French, Cincinnati, Ohio; L. M. Strayer Collection, copied by Richard A. Baumgartner).

Henry Ewing Jones (Thomas J. Williams. *An Historical Sketch of the 56th Ohio Volunteer Infantry During the Great Civil War*. Columbus, Ohio, 1899).

1861. 1 Lieutenant, Adjutant, 56 OH Infantry, Oct. 17, 1861. Acting AAG, 2 Brigade, 12 Division, 13 Army Corps, Dec. 1862–Feb. 1863. Captain, Co. H, 56 OH Infantry, Feb. 6, 1863. Acting AIG, 2 Brigade, 12 Division, 13 Army Corps, Department of the Tennessee, May 6–July 28, 1863. Acting AIG, 2 Brigade, 3 Division, 13 Army Corps, Department of the Gulf, Staff of Colonel James R. Slack, July 28, 1863–April 28, 1864. Captain, Co. D, 56 OH Infantry, Aug. 8, 1863. Captain, Co. A, 56 OH Infantry, Nov. 5, 1864. Lieutenant Colonel, 56 OH Infantry, Jan. 18, 1865. Commanded Post of Algiers, LA, Department of the Gulf, Dec. 1864–June 1865. Commanded Post of Algiers, LA, Eastern District of Louisiana, Department of Louisiana, July–Sept. 1865. *Colonel,* 56 OH Infantry, April 20, 1866. Honorably mustered out, April 25, 1866.

Born: Sept. 28, 1836 Nashville, TN
Died: Sept. 13, 1876 Portsmouth, OH
Education: Graduated Denison University, Granville, OH, 1859
Occupation: Lawyer
Miscellaneous: Resided Portsmouth, Scioto Co., OH
Buried: Greenlawn Cemetery, Portsmouth, OH (Section 5, Lot 40)
References: Nelson W. Evans. *A History of Scioto County with Pioneer Record of Southern Ohio.* Portsmouth, OH, 1903. Obituary, *Portsmouth Times,* Sept. 16, 1876. *Report of the Proceedings of the Society of the Army of the Tennessee at the Eleventh Annual Meeting.* Cincinnati, OH, 1885. Thomas J. Williams. *An Historical Sketch of the 56th Ohio Volunteer Infantry During the Great Civil War.* Columbus, OH, 1899. Military Service File, National Archives.

James Andres Jones

Lieutenant Colonel, 25 OH Infantry, June 10, 1861. Colonel, 25 OH Infantry, June 26, 1861. Commanded Post of Beverly, WV, Jan. 1862 and April 1862. Resigned May 16, 1862, since "I cannot stand the exposure and fatigue of a campaign," being "afflicted with a bronchial difficulty, and at present unfit for duty."

Born: Dec. 20, 1812 Otsego Co., NY
Died: May 20, 1893 Norwalk, OH
Other Wars: Mexican War (Captain, 15 U.S. Infantry; Bvt. Major, Aug. 20, 1847, for gallant and meritorious conduct at the battles of Contreras and Churubusco, Mexico)
Occupation: Livery stable keeper and tailor
Miscellaneous: Resided Norwalk, Huron Co., OH. His second wife was widow of Colonel George P. Webster (98 OH Infantry).
Buried: Woodlawn Cemetery, Norwalk, OH (Section 3, Lot 214)

James Andres Jones (Firelands Historical Society, Inc., Norwalk, Ohio, copied by Matt Burr).

References: Obituary, *Norwalk Daily Reflector,* May 22, 1893. Pension File and Military Service File, National Archives. Edward C. Culp. *The 25th Ohio Veteran Volunteer Infantry in the War for the Union.* Topeka, KS, 1885. Letters Received, Adjutant General's Office, File J51(AGO)1847, National Archives.

Toland Jones

Captain, Co. A, 113 OH Infantry, Aug. 11, 1862. Lieutenant Colonel, 113 OH Infantry, Feb. 23, 1865. *Colonel,* 113 OH Infantry, June 8, 1865. Honorably mustered out, July 6, 1865.

Born: Jan. 10, 1820 near London, OH
Died: Feb. 18, 1894 London, OH
Education: Attended Denison University, Granville, OH, and The Ohio Medical College, Cincinnati, OH
Occupation: Physician
Offices/Honors: Ohio Senate, 1866–68
Miscellaneous: Resided London, Madison Co., OH
Buried: Kirkwood Cemetery, London, OH
References: *In Memory of Toland Jones, the Beloved Physician and the Honored Soldier.* London, OH, 1894. Obituary Circular, Whole No. 262, Ohio MOLLUS. Pension File and Military Service

Toland Jones (photograph by Nason's Excelsior Gallery, Over Kinney & Stutson's Store, Main St., London, Ohio; Roger D. Hunt Collection, USAMHI [RG98S-CWP207.71]).

William Graham Jones (Massachusetts MOLLUS Collection, USAMHI [Vol. 56, p. 2788]).

File, National Archives. Howard A. Kelly. *Cyclopedia of American Medical Biography.* N.p., 1912. *Portrait and Biographical Record of Fayette, Pickaway, and Madison Counties, OH.* Chicago, IL, 1892. Obituary, *Madison County Democrat*, Feb. 21, 1894. Francis M. McAdams. *Every-Day Soldier Life, or A History of the 113th Ohio Volunteer Infantry.* Columbus, OH, 1884. Letters Received, Volunteer Service Branch, Adjutant General's Office, File J99(VS)1864, National Archives.

William Graham Jones

2 Lieutenant, 10 U.S. Infantry, Dec. 29, 1860. Taken prisoner, San Antonio, TX, May 8, 1861. Exchanged Feb. 20, 1862. 1 Lieutenant, 10 U.S. Infantry, May 14, 1861. Acting ADC, Staff of Brig. Gen. Andrew Porter, March–June 1862. Lieutenant Colonel, 71 PA Infantry, June 18, 1862. Resigned Sept. 4, 1862, "in consideration of the fact that I am not now in command of the regiment, Col. Wistar having joined." Acting ADC, Staff of Major General Edwin V. Sumner, Sept. 1862–March 1863. Colonel, 36 OH Infantry, April 18, 1863. Captain, 10 U.S. Infantry, June 1, 1863. GSW pelvis, Chickamauga, GA, Sept. 19, 1863.
 Born: Feb. 23, 1837 Cincinnati, OH
 Died: Sept. 19, 1863 KIA Chickamauga, GA
 Education: Graduated U.S. Military Academy, West Point, NY, 1860
 Occupation: U.S. Army (Captain, 10 U.S. Infantry)

William Graham Jones (with Captain Wesley Merritt, seated) (photograph by Brady's National Photographic Portrait Gallery, Broadway & Tenth Street, New York; courtesy Steve Meadow).

Miscellaneous: Resided Cincinnati, OH
Buried: Spring Grove Cemetery, Cincinnati, OH (Section 47, Lot 83)
References: Whitelaw Reid. *Ohio in the War: Her Statesmen Generals and Soldiers.* Cincinnati, OH, 1868. Obituary, *Cincinnati Daily Commercial,* Sept. 25, 1863. George W. Cullum. *Biographical Register of the Officers and Graduates of the U.S. Military Academy.* Third Edition. Boston and New York, 1891. Pension File and Military Service File, National Archives. Letters Received, Commission Branch, Adjutant General's Office, File J32(CB) 1863, National Archives. *Biographical Encyclopedia of Ohio of the Nineteenth Century.* Cincinnati and Philadelphia, 1876.

Gustav Kaemmerling

Captain, Co. F, 9 OH Infantry (3 months), April 23, 1861. Captain, Co. F, 9 OH Infantry (3 years), May 27, 1861. Major, 9 OH Infantry, Nov. 1, 1861. Lieutenant Colonel, 9 OH Infantry, March 8, 1862. Colonel, 9 OH Infantry, May 6, 1862. Commanded 2 Brigade, 3 Division, 14 Army Corps, Army of the Cumberland, Jan. 14–Feb. 16, 1864. Although confirmed as Brig. Gen., USV, April 7, 1864, to rank from Jan. 25, 1864, he declined due to ill-health from chronic diarrhea and rheumatism. Honorably mustered out, June 7, 1864. By order dated Aug. 10, 1864, he was dishonorably dismissed, to date June 7, 1864, for "taking to the State of Ohio veterans and recruits of his regiment for discharge, (they not being entitled to the same,) in violation of the orders of the War Department." However, the belated dismissal order was revoked, Jan. 31, 1865, since Kaemmerling "ceased to belong to the military service" from the date of his muster out.
Born: Dec. 9, 1819 Muelheim an der Ruhr, Prussia
Died: April 7, 1902 Tell City, IN
Occupation: Pork and beef packer before war. Miller after war.
Miscellaneous: Resided Cincinnati, OH, to 1865; Tell City, Perry Co., IN, 1865–75 and 1880–1902; and Louisville, KY, 1875–80
Buried: Greenwood Cemetery, Tell City, IN (Division 1, Block 44, Lot 1)
References: Pension File and Military Service File, National Archives. *History of Warrick, Spencer and Perry Counties, IN.* Chicago, IL, 1885. Obituary Circular, Whole No. 154, Indiana MOLLUS. Obituary, *Cincinnati Enquirer,* April 8, 1902. Constantin Grebner. *"We Were the Ninth," A History of the Ninth Regiment, Ohio Volunteer Infantry.* Translated and edited by Frederic Trautmann. Kent, OH, 1987. Letters Received, Volunteer Service Branch, Adjutant General's Office, File P1643(VS)1864, National Archives. *The Union Army.* Vol. 8. Madison, WI, 1908. Wilhelm Kaufmann. *The Germans in the American Civil War.* Translated by Steven Rowan and edited by Don Heinrich Tolzmann with Werner D. Mueller and Robert E. Ward. Carlisle, PA, 1999.

John Kell

Captain, Co. F, 1 OH Infantry (3 months), April 17, 1861. Honorably mustered out, Aug. 16, 1861. Lieutenant Colonel, 2 OH Infantry, Aug. 27, 1861. Colonel, 2 OH Infantry, Dec. 24, 1862. GSW Stone's River, TN, Dec. 31, 1862.
Born: April 1817 Germany
Died: Dec. 31, 1862 KIA Stone's River, TN
Other Wars: Mexican War (Captain, Co. I, 3 OH Infantry)
Occupation: Tailor and postmaster
Miscellaneous: Resided Steubenville, Jefferson Co., OH; and Franklin, Warren Co., OH
Buried: Woodhill Cemetery, Franklin, OH (Section 4, Lot 17)
References: J. Morrow. *History of Warren County, OH.* Chicago, IL, 1882. Dallas R. Bogan. *Warren County's Involvement in the Civil War.* Springboro, OH, 1991. Pension File and Military Service File, National Archives.

Gustav Kaemmerling (Frederick Hill Meserve. Historical Portraits, A Part of the Collection of Americana of Frederick Hill Meserve. New York City, NY, 1913–1915; courtesy New York State Library).

John Kell (Mary Frances Hassett. *Historical Souvenir of Franklin, the Loveliest Village in Ohio, 1796–1913.* Dayton, Ohio, 1913).

John Kennett

Colonel, 4 OH Cavalry, Aug. 30, 1861. Commanded Cavalry Division, Army of the Ohio, Sept. 5–Nov. 5, 1862. Commanded Cavalry Division, Left Wing, 14 Army Corps, Army of the Cumberland, Nov. 5, 1862–Jan. 9, 1863. Resigned Jan. 23, 1863, due to "continued physical debility" caused by "stricture of the urethra of long standing, that has given rise to chronic cystitis and organic disease of the kidneys."
  Born: March 9, 1809 St. Petersburg, Russia
  Died: Dec. 12, 1898 Avondale, OH
  Education: Attended Phillips Academy, Andover, MA
  Occupation: Tobacco merchant before war. Insurance agent after war.
  Miscellaneous: Resided Cincinnati, OH; and Avondale, Hamilton Co., OH. Father of Bvt. Brig. Gen. Henry G. Kennett.
  Buried: Spring Grove Cemetery, Cincinnati, OH (Section 47, Lot 77, unmarked)
  References: Obituary, *Cincinnati Enquirer,* Dec. 13, 1898. Pension File and Military Service File, National Archives. *Biographical Catalogue of Phillips Academy, Andover, MA, 1778–1830.* Andover, MA, 1903. Lucien Wulsin. *The Story of the 4th Regiment*

John Kennett (photograph by Hoag & Quick's Art Palace, No. 100 4th St., opp. Post Office, Cincinnati, Ohio; Ken Turner Collection).

Ohio Veteran Volunteer Cavalry. Cincinnati, OH, 1912. Nancy Pape-Findley. *The Invincibles: The Story of the 4th Ohio Veteran Volunteer Cavalry.* Tecumseh, MI, 2002. John Kennett, "History of the First Cavalry Division from November 1, 1862, to January 1, 1863," *GAR War Papers, Papers Read Before Fred C. Jones Post, No. 401, Department of Ohio, GAR.* Cincinnati, OH, 1891. Obituary Circular, Whole No. 412, Ohio MOLLUS.

Peter Kinney

Colonel, 56 OH Infantry, Sept. 11, 1861. Taken prisoner near Lafayette Station, TN, June 25, 1862. Exchanged Sept. 21, 1862. Commanded 1 Brigade, 2 Division, Army of the Southwest, Department of the Missouri, Oct. 1862. As the aftermath to a riot within the regiment, Dec. 17, 1862, he shot and killed ringleader Sergeant Frank Wallace of Co. D, for which act no charges were brought against him. Commanded 2 Brigade, 2 Division, District of Eastern Arkansas, Department of the Missouri,

Peter Kinney (photograph by L. Janney, East Side of Market Street, Bet. Front and Second, Over City Bank, Portsmouth, Ohio; Howard Lanham Collection, USAMHI [RG98S-CWP209.88]).

Dec. 1862–Jan. 1863. Commanded 2 Brigade, 12 Division, 13 Army Corps, Army of the Tennessee, Jan. 22–April 2, 1863. Resigned April 2, 1863, due to physical disability from chronic rheumatism and cancer of the face. Commanded Post of Portsmouth, OH, during Morgan's Raid, July 1863.
Born: Dec. 16, 1805 Scioto Co., OH
Died: Aug. 13, 1877 Portsmouth, OH
Occupation: Banker
Miscellaneous: Resided Portsmouth, Scioto Co., OH; and Clay Twp., Scioto Co., OH
Buried: Greenlawn Cemetery, Portsmouth, OH (Section 6, Lot 19)
References: *Biographical Encyclopedia of Ohio of the Nineteenth Century.* Cincinnati and Philadelphia, 1876. Nelson W. Evans. *A History of Scioto County with Pioneer Record of Southern Ohio.* Portsmouth, OH, 1903. W. J. Comley and W. D'Eggville. *Ohio: The Future Great State. Her Manufacturers.* Cincinnati and Cleveland, 1875. Pension File and Military Service File, National Archives. Obituary, *Portsmouth Times,* Aug. 18, 1877. Eugene B. Willard, Supervising Editor. *A Standard History of the Hanging Rock Iron Region of Ohio.* Chicago, IL, 1916. Thomas J. Williams. *An Historical Sketch of the 56th Ohio Volunteer Infantry During the Great Civil War.* Columbus, OH, 1899.

Robert Kirkup

2 Lieutenant, Co. D, 5 OH Infantry (3 months), April 20, 1861. 2 Lieutenant, Co. D, 5 OH Infantry (3 years), June 10, 1861. 1 Lieutenant, Co. D, 5 OH Infantry, Jan. 9, 1862. Captain, Co. D, 5 OH Infantry, Aug. 2, 1862. GSW left arm, Cedar Mountain, VA, Aug. 9, 1862. Lieutenant Colonel, 5 OH Infantry, Sept. 26, 1864. *Colonel,* 5 OH Infantry, July 20, 1865. Honorably mustered out, July 26, 1865.
Born: Aug. 18, 1831 Scotland
Died: April 11, 1924 Cincinnati, OH
Occupation: Brass finisher and later brass foundry operator
Miscellaneous: Resided Cincinnati, OH
Buried: Spring Grove Cemetery, Cincinnati, OH (Section 73, Lot 182, unmarked)
References: Pension File and Military Service File, National Archives. Obituary, *Cincinnati Enquirer,* April 12, 1924.

Philander Parmele Lane

Captain, Co. K, 11 OH Infantry, July 7, 1861. Preferred charges which eventually led to the dismissal of Colonel Charles A. DeVilliers. Acquitted of charges preferred in retaliation by DeVilliers in March 1862. Colonel, 11 OH Infantry, Sept. 17, 1862. Resigned Oct. 26, 1863, since "an absence of nearly two and a half years from my business has placed my pecuniary affairs in such a position that my immediate presence is necessary to prevent further complication and avoid future disaster."
Born: Oct. 5, 1821 Nassau, Rensselaer Co., NY
Died: Dec. 6, 1899 Norwood, Hamilton Co., OH
Occupation: Iron worker and machinist before war. Manufacturer of engines and milling machinery after war.
Miscellaneous: Resided Cincinnati, OH
Buried: Spring Grove Cemetery, Cincinnati, OH (Section 22, Lot 67)
References: William F. Scott. *Philander P. Lane, Colonel of Volunteers in the Civil War, Eleventh Ohio Infantry.* New York City, NY, 1920. *Biographical Cyclopedia and Portrait Gallery with an Historical Sketch of the State of Ohio.* Vol. 3. Cincinnati, OH, 1884. Obituary, *Cincinnati Enquirer,* Dec. 7, 1899. Pension File and Military Service File, National Archives. Joshua H. Horton and Solomon Teverbaugh. *A History of the 11th Regiment Ohio Volunteer Infantry.* Dayton, OH, 1866. Obituary Circular, Whole No. 447, Ohio MOLLUS.

Albert Langworthy

Captain, Co. A, 49 OH Infantry, Aug. 22, 1861. GSW forehead, Serratt's Hill, MS, May 30, 1862. Resigned June 22, 1862, since "the health of my

Robert Kirkup (at the regimental boulder on Gettysburg battlefield, Sept. 17, 1887) (L. M. Strayer Collection).

family is such that my return is necessary," and "my own health has become much impaired by attacks of flux." Colonel, 99 OH Infantry, Aug. 11, 1862. Dismissed Sept. 4, 1862, by direction of the President, for "bad conduct before the enemy," at the request of Governor David Tod, who, according to Langworthy's account, "thought things were going wrong in Kentucky, and that I was to blame." His dismissal was revoked, Feb. 10, 1865, and he was mustered out and honorably discharged, as of the date of his dismissal.

Born: April 14, 1828 Troy, NY
Died: Jan. 7, 1893 Dunkirk, NY
Occupation: Druggist before war. Physician after war.
Miscellaneous: Resided Findlay, Hancock Co., OH; and Greenwich, Washington Co., NY
Buried: Greenwich Cemetery, Greenwich, NY

Philander P. Lane (courtesy Philip W. Stichter, copied by Richard A. Baumgartner).

References: William F. Langworthy, compiler. *The Langworthy Family.* Rutland, VT, 1940. Obituary, *The (Greenwich) People's Journal,* Jan. 12, 1893. Pension File and Military Service File, National Archives. Letters Received, Volunteer Service Branch, Adjutant General's Office, File O212(VS) 1862, National Archives. Kevin B. McCray. *A Shouting of Orders: A History of the 99th Ohio Volunteer Infantry Regiment.* N.p., 2003.

Walter E. Lawrence

Major, 1 OH Light Artillery, Sept. 13, 1861. Commanded Artillery Reserve, Army of the Ohio, July–Oct. 1862. Chief of Artillery, Staff of Major Gen. George H. Thomas, 14 Army Corps, Army of the Cumberland, Feb. 5–Dec. 1863. Commanded Post of Bridgeport, AL, Dec. 1863–March 1864. Lieutenant Colonel, 1 OH Light Artillery, March 18, 1864. Commanded Fortress Rosecrans, Murfreesboro, TN, April–Nov. 1864. *Colonel,* 1 OH Light Artillery, Oct. 20, 1864.

Born: 1819? England
Died: Nov. 26, 1864 Murfreesboro, TN (abscess of the liver)
Occupation: U.S. Custom House clerk and salesman
Miscellaneous: Resided Cleveland, OH
Buried: Woodland Cemetery, Cleveland, OH (Section 7, Lot 26)
References: Pension File and Military Service File, National Archives. Funeral account, *Cleveland*

Leader, Dec. 5, 1864. U.S. Census records, 1850 and 1860. *Reminiscences of the Cleveland Light Artillery.* Cleveland, OH, 1906.

William Lawrence

Colonel, 84 OH Infantry, June 7, 1862. Honorably mustered out, Sept. 20, 1862.
Born: June 26, 1819 Mount Pleasant, OH
Died: May 8, 1899 Kenton, OH
Education: Graduated Franklin College, New Athens, OH, 1838. Graduated Cincinnati (OH) Law School, 1840.
Occupation: Lawyer, judge and author
Offices/Honors: Ohio House of Representatives, 1846–48. Ohio Senate, 1849–51 and 1854. U.S. House of Representatives, 1865–71 and 1873–77. First Comptroller of the U.S. Treasury, 1880–85.
Miscellaneous: Resided Bellefontaine, Logan Co., OH
Buried: Bellefontaine Cemetery, Bellefontaine, OH
References: *Dictionary of American Biography.* William Horatio Barnes. *The American Government: Biographies of Members of the House of Representatives of the Forty-third Congress.* New York City, NY, 1874. J. Fletcher Brennan, editor. *Biographical Cyclopedia and Portrait Gallery with an Historical Sketch of the State of Ohio.* Cincinnati, OH, 1879. James L. Harrison, compiler. *Biographical Directory of the American Congress, 1774–1949.* Washington, DC, 1950. Obituary, *Bellefontaine Republican,* May 9, 1899. *Franklin College Register: Biographical and Historical.* Wheeling, WV, 1908. Military Service File, National Archives.

Orris A. Lawson

1 Lieutenant, Co. A, 3 OH Infantry (3 months), April 24, 1861. Captain, Co. A, 3 OH Infantry (3 months), May 3, 1861. Captain, Co. A, 3 OH Infantry (3 years), June 13, 1861. Major, 3 OH Infantry, Feb. 12, 1862. Lieutenant Colonel, 3 OH Infantry, Sept. 16, 1862. Colonel, 3 OH Infantry, Nov. 29, 1862. Taken prisoner near Rome, GA, May 3, 1863. Confined Libby Prison, Richmond, VA. Paroled March 21, 1864. Honorably mustered out, June 21, 1864.
Born: Dec. 28, 1827 Franklin Co., OH
Died: March 7, 1907 Galena, OH
Occupation: Carpenter before war. Carpenter and grocer after war.
Miscellaneous: Resided Parkersburg, Wood Co., WV, 1856–60; Columbus, Franklin Co., OH, 1860–72; and Galena, Delaware Co., OH, 1872–1907
Buried: Galena Cemetery, Galena, OH
References: Pension File and Military Service File, National Archives. Obituary, *Delaware Journal-Herald,* March 7, 1907. John Beatty. *The Citizen-Soldier; or Memoirs of a Volunteer.* Cincin-

William Lawrence (U.S. House of Representatives, 1867) (The National Archives [B-2344]).

Orris A. Lawson (Ohio Historical Society).

nati, OH, 1879. Civil War Papers of Orris A. Lawson, Ohio Historical Society, Columbus, OH. Allan Peskin, "The Civil War: Crucible of Change," *Timeline: A Publication of the Ohio Historical Society,* Vol. 3, No. 3 (June-July 1986).

Andrew Legg

Captain, Co. E, 12 OH Infantry, June 26, 1861. Resigned June 20, 1862, since "I am suffering from an internal injury received a number of years ago." Colonel, 135 OH Infantry, May 11, 1864. Honorably mustered out, Sept. 1, 1864.

Born: Aug. 16, 1821 near Hebron, Licking Co., OH

Died: Jan. 22, 1875 Marshalltown, IA

Occupation: Master carpenter and builder

Miscellaneous: Resided Newark, Licking Co., OH; and Marshalltown, Marshall Co., IA

Buried: Riverside Cemetery, Marshalltown, IA (Section N, Lot 26)

References: Pension File and Military Service File, National Archives.

Wilson Cooper Lemert

1 Lieutenant, Co. G, 7 IN Infantry, Sept. 1, 1861. Captain, Co. G, 7 IN Infantry, Dec. 20, 1861. Resigned June 3, 1862, due to "diseased condition of the lungs," which "incapacitates me for the service." Captain, Co. K, 86 OH Infantry (3 months), May 27, 1862. Major, 86 OH Infantry, June 10, 1862. Honorably mustered out, Sept. 25, 1862. Colonel, 86 OH Infantry (6 months), July 13, 1863. Commanded Post of Cumberland Gap, TN, Sept. 10, 1863–Jan. 25, 1864. Commanded Independent Brigade, 9 Army Corps, Army of the Ohio, Sept. 10–Oct. 12, 1863. Commanded 3 Brigade, 2 Division, 9 Army Corps, Army of the Ohio, Oct. 12–Dec. 1863. Honorably mustered out, Feb. 10, 1864.

Born: March 4, 1837 Texas Twp., Crawford Co., OH

Died: April 24, 1915 Orlando, FL

Education: Attended Heidelberg College, Tiffin, OH. Graduated Ohio Wesleyan University, Delaware, OH, 1858. Attended Cincinnati (OH) Law School.

Occupation: Lawyer before war. Industrialist and financier after war.

Miscellaneous: Resided Greensburg, Decatur Co., IN; and Bucyrus, Crawford Co., OH

Buried: Oakwood Cemetery, Bucyrus, OH (Section B, Lot 97)

References: Amy L. Hake, compiler. *The Lemert Family in America: The Story of Lewis Lemert and His Descendants.* Schenectady, NY, 1968. William

Wilson Cooper Lemert (Joseph N. Ashburn. *History of the 86th Regiment Ohio Volunteer Infantry.* Cleveland, OH, 1909).

Andrew Legg (Z. P. McMillen, Photographer, Over Wilder's Book Store, Newark, Ohio).

H. Perrin. *History of Crawford County and Ohio*. Chicago, IL, 1881. Pension File and Military Service File, National Archives. *A Centennial Biographical History of Crawford County, OH*. Chicago, IL, 1902. Obituary, *Bucyrus Evening Telegraph*, April 24, 1915. Joseph N. Ashburn. *History of the 86th Regiment Ohio Volunteer Infantry*. Cleveland, OH, 1909. Obituary Circular, Whole No. 1063, Ohio MOLLUS.

Lewis Law Lewton

Captain, Co. K, 170 OH Infantry, May 13, 1864. Colonel, 170 OH Infantry, Aug. 15, 1864. Honorably mustered out, Sept. 10, 1864.
Born: Dec. 25, 1816 Fayette Co., PA
Died: Jan. 16, 1888 Glen Ellen, Sonoma Co., CA
Occupation: Lawyer and banker
Offices/Honors: Prosecuting Attorney, Harrison Co., OH, 1854–56. Ohio House of Representatives, 1868–70.
Miscellaneous: Resided Cadiz, Harrison Co., OH; and Napa City, Napa Co., CA, after 1878
Buried: Sonoma Mountain Cemetery, Sonoma, Sonoma Co., CA
References: Allen Gardiner. *The Lewton Family*. Topeka, KS, 1974. Lyman L. Palmer. *History of Napa and Lake Counties, CA*. San Francisco, CA, 1881. Military Service File, National Archives.

George T. Limberg

Captain, Co. I, 15 KY Infantry, Dec. 14, 1861. Resigned March 29, 1862, since "my health is declining." Appointed Colonel, 108 OH Infantry, July 23, 1862. Commissioned Lieutenant Colonel, 108 OH Infantry, Aug. 22, 1862, since the regiment failed to complete organization. Commanded 39 Brigade, 12 Division, Army of the Ohio, Sept. 26–Oct. 15, 1862. Dismissed Oct. 17, 1862, for taking "eight horses belonging to A.R. Scott, residing near Shelbyville, Shelby Co., KY, with the intent to defraud said A.R. Scott of his property." The disability resulting from the dismissal was removed, Oct. 30, 1863, when the testimony upon which he was found guilty was determined to be false. Colonel, 108 OH Infantry, Nov. 24, 1863. Dismissed May 16, 1864, for "fraudulent conduct, enlisting, under false promises, Augustus Grending, a recruit who had been previously discharged for physical disability, and who was manifestly unfit for service." Dismissal revoked Sept. 6, 1864, upon evidence that he did not recruit Private Grending, and he was honorably discharged the service, as of the date of dismissal, "with pay and allowances due him for actual service rendered, deducting therefrom the expense incurred by the Government, by reason of the enlistment of Private Grending."
Born: 1838? Prussia
Died: April 5, 1866 Grenada, Nicaragua
Occupation: Lawyer
Miscellaneous: Resided Covington, Kenton Co., KY
Buried: God-to-Lovo Churchyard, Grenada, Nicaragua
References: Pension File and Military Service File, National Archives. Letters Received, Volunteer Service Branch, Adjutant General's Office, File C930(VS)1864, National Archives. Kirk C. Jenkins. *The Battle Rages Higher: The Union's 15th Kentucky Infantry*. Lexington, KY, 2003.

William R. Lloyd

Lieutenant Colonel, 6 OH Cavalry, Oct. 23, 1861. Colonel, 6 OH Cavalry, Dec. 19, 1861. Commanded 2 Brigade, 2 Division, 1 Army Corps, Army of Virginia, July 1862. Provost Marshal, 11 Army Corps, Army of the Potomac, Jan. 1863. In reaction to being passed over, despite being senior colonel, for command of the brigade and resenting being called before an unexpected Board of Examination, he resigned April 2, 1863, protesting "an apparent unwillingness, if not an absolute refusal,

William R. Lloyd (Roger D. Hunt Collection, USAMHI [RG98S-CWP21.63]).

on the part the commanding generals of the Division and Corps to assign me to the duty which my rank and commission, in my opinion, entitle me." He also protested, to no avail, the wording of the order discharging him, which, in addition to mentioning his resignation, continued "and the Board of Examination having reported him as incompetent to fill the position he holds."
    Born: Dec. 3, 1818 Chillicothe, OH
    Died: Nov. 9, 1877 Steubenville, OH
    Occupation: Lawyer and probate judge
    Miscellaneous: Resided Centre Twp., Carroll Co., OH; and Steubenville, Jefferson Co., OH
    Buried: Union Cemetery, Steubenville, OH (Section St. Paul, Lot 26)
    References: Obituary, *Steubenville Daily Gazette*, Nov. 9, 1877. John A. Caldwell. *History of Belmont and Jefferson Counties, OH.* Wheeling, WV, 1880. Military Service File, National Archives. Letters Received, Volunteer Service Branch, Adjutant General's Office, File L251(VS)1863, National Archives. Richard J. Staats. *The History of the 6th Ohio Volunteer Cavalry, 1861–65: A Journal of Patriotism, Duty and Bravery.* Westminster, MD, 2006.

Richard Long, Jr.

    1 Sergeant, Co. B, 26 OH Infantry, June 17, 1861. 2 Lieutenant, Co. K, 73 OH Infantry, Oct. 14, 1861. 1 Lieutenant, Adjutant, 73 OH Infantry, Nov. 26, 1861. Major, 73 OH Infantry, Dec. 20, 1861. Lieutenant Colonel, 73 OH Infantry, June 21, 1862. Provost Marshal, Staff of Brig. Gen. Robert C. Schenck, 1 Division, 1 Army Corps, Army of Virginia, June 26–July 13, 1862. Provost Marshal, Staff of Major Gen. Oliver O. Howard, 11 Army Corps, Army of the Potomac, July 26–Sept.25, 1863. Provost Marshal, Staff of Major General Oliver O. Howard, 11 Army Corps, Army of the Cumberland, Sept. 25–Dec. 20, 1863. *Colonel,* 73 OH Infantry, Feb. 17, 1864. Resigned June 27, 1864, being unfit for duty due to "attacks of congestion of the brain which threatens apoplexy, they being accompanied by intense pain of head, with convulsive twitchings of left side of face."
    Born: 1837 OH
    Died: April 4, 1889 Pittsburgh, PA (run over and fatally injured by railroad engine)
    Occupation: Railroad agent. Inventor and manufacturer of Long's Truss Rail Joint.
    Miscellaneous: Resided Chillicothe, Ross Co., OH; Groveport, Franklin Co., OH; Columbus, OH; and Chicago, IL
    Buried: Grandview Cemetery, Chillicothe, OH (Section 4, Lots 63–65)
    References: Edmund J. Raus, Jr. *A Generation on the March—The Union Army at Gettysburg.* Gettysburg, PA, 1996. Obituary, *Pittsburgh Dispatch,*

Richard Long, Jr. (photograph by F. A. Simonds, Chillicothe, Ohio; collection of the Ross County Historical Society).

April 5, 1889. Obituary, *Chillicothe Advertiser,* April 12, 1889. Samuel H. Hurst. *Journal-History of the 73rd Ohio Volunteer Infantry.* Chillicothe, OH, 1866. Military Service File, National Archives.

DeWitt Clinton Loudon

    Lieutenant Colonel, 70 OH Infantry, Oct. 3, 1861. Commanded Post of LaGrange, TN, April 3–June 8, 1863. *Colonel,* 70 OH Infantry, April 26, 1864. Discharged for disability, Aug. 9, 1864, due to intermittent fever, peritonitis and diarrhea.
    Born: May 29, 1827 Georgetown, OH
    Died: Sept. 19, 1897 Georgetown, OH
    Education: Graduated Ohio University, Athens, OH, 1850
    Other Wars: Mexican War (QM Sergeant, 1 OH Infantry)
    Occupation: Lawyer and surveyor before war. Lawyer and common pleas judge after war.
    Miscellaneous: Resided Georgetown, Brown Co., OH
    Buried: Confidence Cemetery, Georgetown, OH

Richard Long, Jr. (dedicatory sheet music).

References: *Biographical Encyclopedia of Ohio of the Nineteenth Century.* Cincinnati and Philadelphia, 1876. Obituary Circular, Whole No. 371, Ohio MOLLUS. Pension File and Military Service File, National Archives. Letters Received, Volunteer Service Branch, Adjutant General's Office, File L670(VS)1864, National Archives. *Report of the Proceedings of the Society of the Army of the Tennessee at the Twenty-Ninth Meeting.* Cincinnati, OH, 1898. Thomas W. Connelly. *History of the 70th Ohio Regiment.* Cincinnati, OH, 1902.

Frank Clarence Loveland

Private, Co. D, 6 OH Cavalry, Oct. 26, 1861. Sergeant, Co. D, 6 OH Cavalry, Dec. 14, 1861. Commissary Sergeant, 6 OH Cavalry, March 1, 1862. Sergeant Major, 6 OH Cavalry, June 1, 1862. 2 Lieutenant, Co. E, 6 OH Cavalry, Jan. 30, 1863. 1 Lieutenant, Co. E, 6 OH Cavalry, Feb. 6, 1863. Shell wound left leg, Cold Harbor, VA, May 31, 1864. Captain, Co. B, 6 OH Cavalry, July 25, 1864. Lieutenant Colonel, 6 OH Cavalry, April 20, 1865. *Colonel,* 6 OH Cavalry, July 30, 1865. Honorably mustered out, Aug. 7, 1865.
  Born: Aug. 26, 1839 Wellington, OH
  Died: June 21, 1916 Suffern, NY
  Education: Attended Oberlin (OH) College
  Occupation: Dry goods merchant and U.S. Pension agent

DeWitt Clinton Loudon (post-war) (Album of Portraits of Companions of the Commandery of the State of Ohio MOLLUS. Cincinnati, Ohio, 1893).

Frank Clarence Loveland (Ken Lawrence Collection).

Miscellaneous: Resided Oberlin, Lorain Co., OH; and New York City, NY
Buried: Greenwood Cemetery, Wellington, OH (Section 12, Lot 390)
References: *National Cyclopedia of American Biography*. John B. Loveland and George Loveland. *Genealogy of the Loveland Family in the United States of America from 1635 to 1895*. Fremont, OH, 1895. William H. Powell, editor. *Officers of the Army and Navy (Volunteer) Who Served in the Civil War*. Philadelphia, PA, 1893. Pension File and Military Service File, National Archives. Letters Received, Volunteer Service Branch, Adjutant General's Office, File O1304(VS)1864, National Archives. Obituary, *Wellington Enterprise,* June 28, 1916. Obituary, *New York Times,* June 25, 1916. Richard J. Staats. *The History of the 6th Ohio Volunteer Cavalry, 1861–65: A Journal of Patriotism, Duty and Bravery*. Westminster, MD, 2006.

John Gilbert Lowe

Colonel, 131 OH Infantry, May 14, 1864. Honorably mustered out, Aug. 25, 1864.
Born: Sept. 25, 1817 Lebanon, Warren Co., OH
Died: July 30, 1892 Dayton, OH
Education: Graduated Miami University, Oxford, OH, 1838
Occupation: Lawyer
Miscellaneous: Resided Dayton, Montgomery Co., OH. Step-father of Bvt. Brig. Gen. Gates P. Thruston.
Buried: Woodland Cemetery, Dayton, OH (Section 55, Lot 5)
References: Obituary, *Dayton Daily Journal,* Aug. 1, 1892. *The Alumni and Former Student Catalogue of Miami University, 1809–1892*. Oxford, OH, 1892. John F. Edgar. *Pioneer Life in Dayton and Vicinity, 1796–1840*. Dayton, OH, 1896.

John Williamson Lowe

Colonel, 12 OH Infantry (3 months), May 2, 1861. Colonel, 12 OH Infantry (3 years), June 28, 1861. GSW forehead, Carnifex Ferry, WV, Sept. 10, 1861.
Born: Nov. 15, 1809 New Brunswick, NJ
Died: Sept. 10, 1861 KIA Carnifex Ferry, WV
Other Wars: Mexican War (Captain, Co. C, 2 OH Infantry)
Occupation: Lawyer
Miscellaneous: Resided Batavia, Clermont Co., OH; and Xenia, Greene Co., OH
Buried: Woodland Cemetery, Xenia, OH
References: Carl M. Becker, "John William Lowe: Failure in Inner-Direction," *Ohio History,* Volume 73, No. 2 (Spring 1964). John Gilmary Shea, editor. *The Fallen Brave: A Biographical Memorial of the American Officers Who Have Given

John Williamson Lowe (U.S. Military Academy Library).

Their Lives for the Preservation of the Union*. New York City, NY, 1861. Whitelaw Reid. *Ohio in the War: Her Statesmen Generals and Soldiers*. Cincinnati, OH, 1868. Terry Lowry. *The Battle of Scary Creek: Military Operations in the Kanawha Valley, April–July 1861*. Charleston, WV, 1982.

Jackson A. Lucy

Captain, Co. A, 32 OH Infantry, Aug. 27, 1861. Resigned March 12, 1862, since "my business is in a deranged condition and requires personal attention." Colonel, 115 OH Infantry, Sept. 12, 1862. Commanded Post of Covington, KY, Dec. 7, 1862–Aug. 25, 1863. Discharged July 6, 1864 upon "an adverse report of a Board of Examination," which specifically noted that "he has failed to secure proper respect from his command and neglected entirely to obtain a sufficient military knowledge to instruct his officers and men."
Born: 1825 Columbiana, OH
Died: Dec. 3, 1899 Stamping Ground, KY
Occupation: Homeopathic physician
Miscellaneous: Resided Carrollton, Carroll Co., OH (1860); Monmouth, Warren Co., IL (1870); Midway, Woodford Co., KY (1880); Lexington, Fayette Co., KY; and Stamping Ground, Scott Co., KY
Buried: Lexington Cemetery, Lexington, KY (Section J, Lot 128)
References: Obituary, *Lexington Daily Leader,* Dec. 4, 1899. Obituary, *Lexington Herald,* Dec. 5,

Jackson A. Lucy (Leon Van Loo, Successor to Charles Waldack, 24 Fourth Street, Over Smith and Ditson's Hall, Cincinnati, Ohio; courtesy Richard A. Baumgartner).

1899. Military Service File, National Archives. Letters Received, Volunteer Service Branch, Adjutant General's Office, Files H2123(VS)1864 and M1786(VS)1864, National Archives. Ebenezer Z. Hays, editor. *History of the 32nd Regiment Ohio Veteran Volunteer Infantry.* Columbus, OH, 1896.

John Miner Carey Marble

Colonel, 151 OH Infantry, May 13, 1864. Commanded 2 Brigade, Haskin's Division, 22 Army Corps, Department of Washington, June 8–July 8, 1864. Commanded 1 Brigade, Hardin's Division, 22 Army Corps, Department of Washington, July 25–Aug. 16, 1864. Honorably mustered out, Aug. 27, 1864.
Born: July 27, 1833 Mehoopany, PA
Died: April 29, 1912 New York City, NY
Occupation: Merchant before war. Banker and financier after war.
Miscellaneous: Resided Delphos, Allen Co., OH, to 1874; Van Wert, Van Wert Co., OH, 1874–88; and Los Angeles, CA, 1888–1912
Buried: Inglewood Park Cemetery, Inglewood, CA (Magnolia Plot, Lot 52)
References: James M. Guinn. *A History of California and an Extended History of Los Angeles and Environs.* Los Angeles, CA, 1915. Pension File, National Archives. Obituary Circular, Whole No. 1066, California MOLLUS. Obituary, *Los Angeles Times,* April 30, 1912.

Caleb Marker

Private, Co. E, 5 OH Cavalry, Sept. 2, 1861. 1 Lieutenant, Co. E, 5 OH Cavalry, Oct. 30, 1861. Captain, Co. E, 5 OH Cavalry, March 5, 1863. Discharged for disability, Nov. 28, 1863, due to the effects of typhoid pneumonia. Colonel, 156 OH Infantry, May 17, 1864. Honorably mustered out, Sept. 1, 1864.
Born: Dec. 10, 1827 Butler Co., OH
Died: June 27, 1869 New Paris, OH
Occupation: Farmer, saw mill operator and trader
Miscellaneous: Resided New Paris, Preble Co., OH
Buried: Old New Paris Cemetery, New Paris, OH
References: Pension File and Military Service File, National Archives. Letters Received, Volunteer Service Branch, Adjutant General's Office, File M2364(VS)1863, National Archives. Obituary, *The (Richmond, IN) Humming Bird,* July 3, 1869.

Isaac Harrison Marrow

Captain, Co. A, 3 OH Infantry (3 months), April 19, 1861. Colonel, 3 OH Infantry (3 months), April 27, 1861. Colonel, 3 OH Infantry (3 years), June 12, 1861. Commanded 17 Brigade, 3 Division, Army of the Ohio, Dec. 1861. Threatened with

Caleb Marker (L. M. Strayer Collection).

charges to be preferred by Lt. Col. John Beatty, he resigned Feb. 4, 1862, since "my health will not justify me to undergo the exposure incidental to camp life." Captain, Additional ADC, March 18, 1862. Assigned to staff of Major Gen. David Hunter. Resigned May 9, 1863, due to "continued ill health."
Born: March 6, 1825 Baltimore, MD
Died: May 13, 1912 Chicago, IL
Other Wars: Mexican War (1 Lieutenant, Co. G, MD and DC Infantry)
Occupation: Railroad conductor before war. U.S. Customs inspector after war.
Miscellaneous: Resided Columbus, OH, 1854–72; Cleveland, OH, 1872–77; Cincinnati, OH, 1877–83; Washington, DC, 1883–93; Toledo, OH, 1893–1910; Chicago, IL, 1910–12
Buried: Greenlawn Cemetery, Columbus, OH (Section K, Lot 5, unmarked)
References: Pension File and Military Service File, National Archives. Letters Received, Commission Branch, Adjutant General's Office, File M229(CB)1863, National Archives. Obituary, *Ohio State Journal*, May 14, 1912. John Beatty. *The Citizen-Soldier; or Memoirs of a Volunteer.* Cincinnati, OH, 1879.

Lucius P. Marsh

Commissioned *Colonel*, 62 OH Infantry, Sept. 28, 1861. Commission revoked upon a report, dated Oct. 21, 1861, from the Military Committee of Muskingum Co., OH, that he had been for several days "grossly intoxicated" and "utterly incapable" of attending to his duties. Captain, Co. A, 159 OH Infantry, May 9, 1864. Dismissed Aug. 4, 1864, for "habitual drunkenness and neglect of duty."
Born: June 29, 1823 Carroll, Chautauqua Co., NY
Died: July 5, 1893 Denver, CO
Education: Attended Denison University, Granville, OH
Occupation: Lawyer and judge
Offices/Honors: Judge of the Court of Common Pleas for 11 years
Miscellaneous: Resided Zanesville, Muskingum Co., OH; and Denver, CO, after 1879
Buried: Fairmount Cemetery, Denver, CO (Block 5, Lot 129)
References: *History of the City of Denver, Arapahoe County, and Colorado.* Chicago, IL, 1880. Obituary, *Rocky Mountain News*, July 6, 1893. Letter Military Committee to Governor William Dennison, Oct. 21, 1861, (Series 147-14: 26), Correspondence to the Governor and Adjutant General of Ohio, 1861–66, Ohio Historical Society. Military Service File, National Archives.

John Grant Marshall

Colonel, 89 OH Infantry, Aug. 26, 1862. Dismissed Oct. 2, 1862, for "conduct unbecoming an officer," on the recommendation of Governor David Tod, who described him as "a habitual drunkard and entirely unfit for his position." Dismissal revoked Jan. 25, 1869, upon the recommendation of Gen. Ulysses S. Grant, and he was honorably discharged upon tender of resignation as of the date of dismissal.
Born: May 3, 1823 Trumbull Co., OH
Died: April 14, 1878 Columbus, OH
Other Wars: Mexican War (2 Lieutenant, Co. G, 4 OH Infantry)
Occupation: Lawyer
Offices/Honors: Ohio House of Representatives, 1870–71. Democratic candidate for Lieutenant Governor of Ohio, 1862.
Miscellaneous: Resided Georgetown, Brown Co., OH. First cousin of Gen. Ulysses S. Grant.
Buried: Old Georgetown Cemetery, Georgetown, OH (unmarked)
References: *Biographical Encyclopedia of Ohio of the Nineteenth Century.* Cincinnati and Philadelphia, 1876. Pension File and Military Service File, National Archives. Obituary, *Ohio State Journal*, April 15, 1878. Obituary, *Brown County News*, May 1, 1878. Letters Received, Volunteer Service Branch, Adjutant General's Office, File O249(VS)1862, National Archives. Arthur H. Grant. *The Grant Family.* Poughkeepsie, NY, 1898.

Rodney Mason

Lieutenant Colonel, 2 OH Infantry, April 23, 1861. Honorably mustered out, July 31, 1861. Assistant Adjutant General, Staff of Governor William Dennison, Aug. 1861–Jan. 1862. Colonel, 71 OH Infantry, Oct. 15, 1861. Accused of misconduct in the disorderly retreat of his regiment at Shiloh, TN, April 6, 1862, he was cashiered Aug. 22, 1862, for "repeated acts of cowardice in the face of the enemy," as an immediate reaction to his alleged misconduct, Aug. 18, 1862, in surrendering the Post of Clarksville, TN, to an inferior enemy force. Order cashiering him was revoked, March 22, 1866, and he was mustered out to date Aug. 22, 1862.
Born: Oct. 20, 1824 Springfield, OH
Died: Jan. 22, 1893 Jackson, MI
Education: Attended Miami University, Oxford, OH. Graduated Jefferson College, Canonsburg, PA, 1844.
Occupation: Patent attorney
Miscellaneous: Resided Springfield, Clark Co., OH, to 1865; Washington, DC, 1865–83; and Detroit, MI, 1883–93. Brother of Bvt. Brig. Gen. Edwin C. Mason.

Buried: Sackets Harbor Cemetery, Sackets Harbor, NY

References: *Biographical and Historical Catalogue of Washington and Jefferson College*. Cincinnati, OH, 1889. Obituary, *Detroit Evening News,* Jan. 23, 1893. Noah A. Trudeau, "Fields Without Honor: Two Affairs in Tennessee," *Civil War Times Illustrated,* Vol. 31, No. 3 (July-August 1992). Letters Received, Volunteer Service Branch, Adjutant General's Office, File M2313(VS)1862, National Archives. Military Service File, National Archives.

William Bion Mason

2 Lieutenant, Co. B, 77 OH Infantry, Oct. 11, 1861. Captain, Co. B, 77 OH Infantry, Dec. 2, 1861. GSW Corinth Road, TN, April 8, 1862. Major, 77 OH Infantry, Aug. 26, 1862. Colonel, 77 OH Infantry, April 18, 1863. Commanded Post of Alton, IL, April-June, 1863. Commanded Post of Little Rock, AR, Aug.-Sept. 30, 1864. Honorably mustered out, Dec. 31, 1864.

Born: Aug. 16, 1823 Adams Twp., Washington Co., OH

Died: Nov. 11, 1885 Marietta, OH

Education: Attended Allegheny College, Meadville, PA

Occupation: School teacher and clerk before war. Farmer and merchant after war.

Offices/Honors: Recorder, Washington Co., OH, 1855-61. Treasurer, Washington Co., OH, 1867-69. Postmaster, Marietta, OH, 1870-78.

Miscellaneous: Resided Lowell, Washington Co., OH; and Marietta, Washington Co., OH

Buried: Oak Grove Cemetery, Marietta, OH (Section 19, Lot 109)

References: Mary E. Mason. *The Family of Hugh Mason, William Mason and Allied Families*. Parkersburg, WV, 1930. Edna W. Mason. *Descendants of Capt. Hugh Mason in America*. New Haven, CT, 1937. Obituary, *Marietta Semi-Weekly Register,* Nov. 13, 1885. Pension File and Military Service File, National Archives.

Stanley Matthews

Lieutenant Colonel, 23 OH Infantry, June 7, 1861. Colonel, 51 OH Infantry, Oct. 23, 1861. Provost Marshal, Nashville, TN, Feb.-June 1862. Nominated as Brig. Gen., U.S. Volunteers, April 11, 1862. Nomination tabled by U.S. Senate, July 16, 1862. Commanded 23 Independent Brigade, Army of the Ohio, July 17-Aug. 1862. Commanded 23 Brigade, 5 Division, Army of the Ohio, Aug.-Sept. 1862. Commanded 23 Brigade, 5 Division, 2 Army Corps, Army of the Ohio, Sept.-Nov. 1862. Commanded 3 Brigade, 3 Division, Left Wing, 14 Army Corps, Army of the Cumberland, Nov. 5-Dec.31, 1862. Commanded 3 Brigade, 3 Division, 21 Army Corps, Jan. 9-April 11, 1863. Resigned April 11, 1863, in order to accept the office of Superior Court Judge in Cincinnati.

Born: July 21, 1824 Cincinnati, OH

Died: March 22, 1889 Washington, DC

Education: Attended Woodward High School, Cincinnati, OH. Graduated Kenyon College, Gambier, OH, 1840.

Occupation: Lawyer and judge

Offices/Honors: Ohio Senate, 1856-58. U.S. Senate, 1877-79. Associate Justice, U.S. Supreme Court, 1881-89.

Miscellaneous: Resided Cincinnati, OH; and Washington, DC

Buried: Spring Grove Cemetery, Cincinnati, OH (Section 36, Lot 106)

References: *Dictionary of American Biography.* J. Fletcher Brennan, editor. *Biographical Cyclopedia and Portrait Gallery with an Historical Sketch of the State of Ohio*. Cincinnati, OH, 1879. James Landy. *Cincinnati Past and Present*. Cincinnati, OH, 1872. *Society of the Army of the Cumberland. Twentieth Reunion, Chattanooga, TN, 1889*. Cincinnati, OH, 1890. *Biographical Encyclopedia of Ohio of the Nineteenth Century*. Cincinnati and Philadelphia, 1876. *History of Cincinnati and Hamilton County, OH*. Cincinnati, OH, 1894. Military Service File, National Archives.

Frederick John Mayer

Colonel, 6 OH Volunteer Militia, Sept. 14, 1862. Honorably mustered out, Oct. 2, 1862.

Born: Feb. 10, 1822 Stuttgart, Germany

William Bion Mason (USAMHI [RG98S-CWP 92.38]).

Stanley Matthews (Rutherford B. Hayes Presidential Center).

Died: June 22, 1882 Cincinnati, OH
Occupation: Saddler
Offices/Honors: Hamilton County (OH) Commissioner, 1862–64. Postmaster, Cincinnati, OH, 1864–66. Hamilton County (OH) Treasurer, 1871–72.
Miscellaneous: Resided Cincinnati, OH
Buried: Spring Grove Cemetery, Cincinnati, OH (Section 22, Lot 42, unmarked)
References: Charles F. Goss. *Cincinnati: The Queen City, 1788–1912*. Chicago and Cincinnati, 1912. Obituary, *Cincinnati Freie Presse*, June 23, 1882. Obituary, *Cincinnati Volksfreund*, June 24, 1882. Letters Received, Volunteer Service Branch, Adjutant General's Office, File B1688(VS)1862, National Archives.

Richard William McClain

Captain, Co. D, 16 OH Infantry (3 months), April 24, 1861. Honorably mustered out, Aug. 18, 1861. Major, 51 OH Infantry, Aug. 28, 1861. Lieutenant Colonel, 51 OH Infantry, Oct. 15, 1861. GSW abdomen, Stone's River, TN, Jan. 2, 1863. Colonel, 51 OH Infantry, April 14, 1863. Provost Marshal, McMinnville, TN, July 1863. Taken prisoner Chickamauga, GA, Sept. 20, 1863. Confined Libby Prison, Richmond, VA. Paroled March 21, 1864. Resigned Sept. 30, 1864, because "I have suffered and still continue to suffer great pecuniary loss," and also because "my family is large and helpless, their home comforts and education have been almost entirely neglected during my absence."

Richard William McClain (J. C. Price, Photographer, New Philadelphia, Ohio; courtesy Brad and Donna Pruden).

Born: Nov. 26, 1823 Linton Twp., Coshocton Co., OH
Died: March 31, 1880 near West Lafayette, OH
Other Wars: Mexican War (Sergeant, Co. B, 3 OH Infantry)
Occupation: Farmer
Offices/Honors: Treasurer of Coshocton Co., OH, 1871–75
Miscellaneous: Resided West Lafayette, Coshocton Co., OH
Buried: Fairfield Cemetery, West Lafayette, OH
References: Pension File and Military Service File, National Archives. Norman N. Hill, Jr., compiler. *History of Coshocton County, OH: Its Past and Present*. Newark, OH, 1881. Obituary, *Coshocton Age*, April 3, 1880. Obituary, *Coshocton Democrat*, April 6, 1880. Fred McDavitt. "The 51st Ohio Volunteer Infantry: A Regimental History," *Civil War: The Magazine of the Civil War Society*, Vol. 12 (March 1988).

George Wythe McCook

Colonel, 157 OH Infantry, May 15, 1864. Honorably mustered out, Sept. 2, 1864.
Born: July 21, 1822 Canonsburg, PA
Died: Dec. 28, 1877 New York City, NY
Education: Graduated Franklin College, New Athens, OH, 1840
Other Wars: Mexican War (Lieutenant Colonel, 3 OH Infantry)

George Wythe McCook (post-war) (*Franklin College Register: Biographical and Historical.* Wheeling, West Virginia, 1908).

Occupation: Lawyer
Offices/Honors: Attorney General of Ohio, 1854–56. Unsuccessful candidate for governor of Ohio, 1871.
Miscellaneous: Resided Steubenville, Jefferson Co., OH. Brother of Major Gen. Alexander M. McCook, Brig. Gen. Robert L. McCook, Brig. Gen. Daniel McCook, and Bvt. Brig. Gen. Edwin S. McCook.
Buried: Union Cemetery, Steubenville, OH (Section A, Lot 24)
References: John A. Caldwell. *History of Belmont and Jefferson Counties, OH.* Wheeling, WV, 1880. Obituary, *New York Times,* Dec. 29, 1877. *Franklin College Register: Biographical and Historical.* Wheeling, WV, 1908. *Appletons' Cyclopedia of American Biography.*

Alexander McIlvain

1 Lieutenant, Co. I, 1 OH Infantry (3 months), April 17, 1861. Honorably mustered out, Aug. 2, 1861. 2 Lieutenant, Co. A, 64 OH Infantry, Oct. 1, 1861. Captain, Co. A, 64 OH Infantry, Oct. 15, 1861. Major, 64 OH Infantry, July 1, 1862. Lieutenant Colonel, 64 OH Infantry, Aug. 11, 1862. Colonel, 64 OH Infantry, March 12, 1863. GSW Rocky Face Ridge, GA, May 9, 1864.
Born: 1818 PA
Died: May 9, 1864 KIA Rocky Face Ridge, GA
Occupation: Building contractor and plasterer

Alexander McIlvain (U.S. Military Academy Library).

Miscellaneous: Resided Mansfield, Richland Co., OH
Buried: Mansfield Cemetery, Mansfield, OH (Section 5, Lot 710)
References: Pension File and Military Service File, National Archives. Wilbur F. Hinman. *The Story of the Sherman Brigade.* Alliance, OH, 1897.

Arnold McMahan

1 Lieutenant, Co. C, 21 OH Infantry (3 months), April 25, 1861. Honorably mustered out, Aug. 12, 1861. Captain, Co. C, 21 OH Infantry (3 years), Sept. 19, 1861. Major, 21 OH Infantry, June 15, 1863. Taken prisoner Chickamauga, GA, Sept. 20, 1863. Confined at Libby Prison, Richmond, VA. Paroled March 14, 1864. Lieutenant Colonel, 21 OH Infantry, March 1, 1864. GSW left breast, Bentonville, NC, March 19, 1865. Commanded 3 Brigade, 1 Division, 14 Army Corps, Army of the Cumberland, March 19–28, 1865. *Colonel,* 21 OH Infantry, July 12, 1865. Honorably mustered out, July 25, 1865. Bvt. Colonel, USV, March 13, 1865, for meritorious services.
Born: March 10, 1835 Monaghan, Ireland
Died: Aug. 5, 1891 East Toledo, OH
Other Wars: Private, Co. A, 2 U.S. Infantry, May 3, 1858–Oct. 12, 1859

Pren Metham (courtesy Robert J. Van Dorn).

Arnold McMahan (Archibald Gracie. *The Truth About Chickamauga.* Boston and New York, 1911).

Occupation: School teacher and merchant before war. Real estate broker, insurance broker and lawyer after war.
Miscellaneous: Resided Perrysburg, Wood Co., OH, before war; and East Toledo, Lucas Co., OH, after war.
Buried: Fort Meigs Union Cemetery, Perrysburg, OH (Block 4, Lot 65)
References: Pension File and Military Service File, National Archives. Obituary, *Perrysburg Journal,* Aug. 8, 1891. Silas S. Canfield. *History of the 21st Regiment Ohio Volunteer Infantry in the War of the Rebellion.* Toledo, OH, 1893. Letters Received, Volunteer Service Branch, Adjutant General's Office, File M980(VS)1864, National Archives. Archibald Gracie. *The Truth About Chickamauga.* Boston and New York, 1911. Arnold McMahan Papers, Center for Archival Collections, Bowling Green (OH) State University.

Pren Metham

2 Lieutenant, Co. F, 80 OH Infantry, Nov. 2, 1861. Captain, Co. F, 80 OH Infantry, Dec. 31, 1861. Major, 80 OH Infantry, Jan. 15, 1863. Lieutenant Colonel, 80 OH Infantry, July 24, 1863. *Colonel,* 80 OH Infantry, Jan. 4, 1864. Honorably mustered out, April 7, 1865.
Born: April 5, 1830 near Nellie, Coshocton Co., OH

Died: Feb. 14, 1917 Madison, FL
Occupation: Farmer
Miscellaneous: Resided Nellie, Coshocton Co., OH
Buried: Valley View Cemetery, Warsaw, OH
References: William J. Bahmer. *Centennial History of Coshocton County, OH.* Chicago, IL, 1909. Pension File and Military Service File, National Archives. Obituary, *Coshocton Morning Tribune,* Feb. 16, 1917. Norman N. Hill, Jr., compiler. *History of Coshocton County, OH: Its Past and Present.* Newark, OH, 1881. David F. Fryer. *History of the 80th Ohio Veteran Volunteer Infantry.* Newcomerstown, OH, 1904.

Seraphim Meyer

Colonel, 107 OH Infantry, Sept. 6, 1862. Bayonet wound right wrist, Chancellorsville, VA, May 2, 1863. Taken prisoner Chancellorsville, VA, May 2, 1863. Confined Libby Prison, Richmond, VA. Paroled May 23, 1863. Having been found by a Board of Examination to be lacking in "sufficient knowledge of tactics and of military administrative duties," he resigned Feb. 17, 1864, citing "the greatly impaired state of my health, which is rapidly declining." In forwarding his resignation, Brig. Gen. Adelbert Ames commented, "The good of the service and the welfare of his regiment demand the immediate acceptance of this resignation."
Born: Nov. 27, 1815 Bourbach le Bas, Alsace, France
Died: April 12, 1894 Santa Cruz, CA

Seraphim Meyer (post-war) (Jacob Smith. *Camps and Campaigns of the 107th Regiment Ohio Volunteer Infantry*. N.p., 1910).

Occupation: Lawyer and judge
Offices/Honors: Judge of the Court of Common Pleas, 9th District of Ohio, 1877–92
Miscellaneous: Resided Canton, Stark Co., OH; San Jose, Santa Clara Co., CA; and Santa Cruz, Santa Cruz Co., CA. Father of Bvt. Brig. Gen. Edward S. Meyer.
Buried: Holy Cross Cemetery, Santa Cruz, CA
References: William H. Perrin, editor. *History of Stark County, OH*. Chicago, IL, 1881. William B. Neff. *The Bench and Bar of Northern Ohio*. Cleveland, OH, 1921. Pension File and Military Service File, National Archives. Death notice, *Santa Cruz Surf,* April 14, 1894. Obituary, *Canton Repository*, April 17, 1894. Richard A. Baumgartner. *Buckeye Blood: Ohio at Gettysburg*. Huntington, WV, 2003. Letters Received, Volunteer Service Branch, Adjutant General's Office, File N218 (VS)1862, National Archives. Jacob Smith. *Camps and Campaigns of the 107th Regiment Ohio Volunteer Infantry*. N.p., 1910.

Hiram Miller

1 Lieutenant, Co. H, 15 OH Infantry (3months), April 23, 1861. Captain, Co. H, 15 OH Infantry, May 6, 1861. Honorably mustered out, Aug. 29, 1861. Captain, Co. C, 15 OH Infantry (3 years), Sept. 11, 1861. Resigned July 27, 1862, due to "bad health, producing mental depression to the extent of unfitting me for properly discharging the duties of my position." Colonel, 163 OH Infantry, May 13, 1864. Commanded 2 Brigade, Haskin's Division, 22 Army Corps, Department of Washington, May 16–June 8, 1864. Honorably mustered out, Sept. 10, 1864.
Born: March 1829 Richland Co., OH
Died: Nov. 23, 1878 Columbus, OH
Other Wars: Mexican War (Private, Co. F, 1 OH Infantry, and Sergeant, Co. G, 2 OH Infantry)
Occupation: Traveling agent for wholesale grocery house
Miscellaneous: Resided Mansfield, Richland Co., OH
Buried: Mansfield Cemetery, Mansfield, OH (Section OS7, Lot 408)
References: Pension File and Military Service File, National Archives. Obituary, *Richland Shield and Banner,* Nov. 30, 1878. Alexis Cope. *The 15th Ohio Volunteers and Its Campaigns, War of 1861–65*. Columbus, OH, 1916.

Minor Millikin

1 Lieutenant, Captain Burdsall's Independent Co., OH Cavalry, June 5, 1861. Honorably mustered out, Aug. 23, 1861. Major, 1 OH Cavalry, Aug. 24, 1861. Colonel, 1 OH Cavalry, Jan. 11, 1862. Discharged March 15, 1862, upon adverse report of a Board of Examination. Reinstated June 6, 1862, upon re-examination, after President Lincoln declared the proceedings of the original board void. GSW neck, Stone's River, TN, Dec. 31, 1862.
Born: July 9, 1834 Hamilton, OH
Died: Dec. 31, 1862 KIA Stone's River, TN
Education: Attended Hanover (IN) College. Graduated Miami University, Oxford, OH, 1854. Attended Harvard University Law School, Cambridge, MA.
Occupation: Lawyer and newspaper editor
Miscellaneous: Resided Hamilton, Butler Co., OH
Buried: Greenwood Cemetery, Hamilton, OH (Millikin Section, Aisle between Lots 185 and 205, Grave 21)
References: *Memorial Record of Butler County, OH*. Chicago, IL, 1894. Gideon T. Ridlon. *Saco Valley Settlements and Families*. Portland, ME, 1895. *Biographical Encyclopedia of Ohio of the Nineteenth Century*. Cincinnati and Philadelphia, 1876. William L. Curry, compiler. *Four Years in the Saddle: History of the 1st Regiment Ohio Volunteer Cavalry*. Columbus, OH, 1898. Whitelaw Reid. *Ohio in the War: Her Statesmen Generals and Soldiers*. Cincinnati, OH, 1868. Alexander C. Mc-Clurg, "An American Soldier, Minor Millikin,"

Hiram Miller (A. Whissemore, Photographer, Mansfield, Ohio).

Military Essays and Recollections: Papers Read Before the Commandery of the State of Illinois, MOLLUS. Vol. 2. Chicago, IL, 1894. Letters Received, Volunteer Service Branch, Adjutant General's Office, Files M309(VS)1862 and M590(VS)1862, National Archives. Military Service File, National Archives.

John Thomas Mitchell

Private, Co. A, 66 OH Infantry, Oct. 19, 1861. 1 Sergeant, Co. A, 66 OH Infantry, Nov. 7, 1861. 2 Lieutenant, Co. A, 66 OH Infantry, May 24, 1862. GSW left shoulder, Cedar Mountain, VA, Aug. 9, 1862. 1 Lieutenant, Co. A, 66 OH Infantry, April 9, 1863. Captain, Co. A, 66 OH Infantry, May 8, 1864. Captain, Co. I, 66 OH Infantry, Sept. 15, 1864. Major, 66 OH Infantry, April 8, 1865. Lieutenant Colonel, 66 OH Infantry, April 12, 1865. *Colonel,* 66 OH Infantry, July 13, 1865. Honorably mustered out, July 15, 1865.

Born: June 30, 1843 Mount Morris, IL
Died: Jan. 20, 1896 Urbana, OH
Occupation: Dry goods merchant
Miscellaneous: Resided Urbana, Champaign Co., OH; and New York City, NY
Buried: Oakdale Cemetery, Urbana, OH
References: Obituary Circular, Whole No. 316, Ohio MOLLUS. Pension File and Military Service File, National Archives. Obituary, *Urbana Citizen and Gazette,* Jan. 21, 1896. David T. Thackery. *A*

Hiram Miller (A. Whissemore, Photographer, Mansfield, Ohio).

Light and Uncertain Hold: A History of the 66th Ohio Volunteer Infantry. Kent, OH, and London, 1999.

Alpheus S. Moore

Private, Co. F, 2 OH Infantry (3 months), April 17, 1861. Honorably mustered out, July 31, 1861. Captain, Co. A, 44 OH Infantry, Aug. 31, 1861. Major, 44 OH Infantry, April 19, 1863. Major, 8 OH Cavalry, Jan. 8, 1864. Lieutenant Colonel, 8 OH Cavalry, April 11, 1864. Colonel, 8 OH Cavalry, May 9, 1864. Shell wound breast, Lynchburg, VA, June 16, 1864. Commanded 1 Brigade, 2 Cavalry Division, Army of West Virginia, July and Oct.–Nov. 1864. Facing charges that he illegally sold captured property and improperly restricted access to regimental papers and baggage, he was allowed to resign, Jan. 4, 1865, upon the recommendation of Major Gen. George Crook, who commented, "I am led to believe that the charges cannot be substantiated, and the best interests of the service will be promoted by permitting him to resign."

Born: March 22, 1839 Dayton, OH
Died: Feb. 14, 1921 Altadena, CA
Education: Graduated Denison University, Granville, OH, 1859

Minor Millikin (photograph by Webster & Bro., Louisville, Kentucky; Richard F. Carlile Collection, copied by Richard A. Baumgartner).

Occupation: School teacher and Baptist clergyman

Miscellaneous: Resided Springfield, Clark Co., OH; Bloomington, McLean Co., IL; Sidney, Shelby Co., OH; Defiance, Defiance Co., OH; Salem, Columbiana Co., OH; Humboldt, Allen Co., KS; and Pasadena, Los Angeles Co., CA

Buried: Forest Lawn Memorial Park, Glendale, CA (Slumberland Section, Lot 44)

References: Horace L. Moore. *Andrew Moore and His Descendants.* Lawrence, KS, 1903. Pension File and Military Service File, National Archives. Letters Received, Volunteer Service Branch, Adjutant General's Office, File W25(VS)1865, National Archives. *Memorial Volume of Denison University, 1831–1906.* Granville, OH, 1907.

Oscar Fitzallen Moore

Lieutenant Colonel, 33 OH Infantry, July 31, 1861. Colonel, 33 OH Infantry, July 16, 1862. GSW left leg, Perryville, KY, Oct. 8, 1862. Taken prisoner and paroled, Perryville, KY, Oct. 8, 1862. Resigned July 20, 1864, due to a "shattered constitution" and also to give "my prompt personal attention" to legal matters "which on account of my absence still remain undisposed of."

Born: Jan. 27, 1817 Lagrange, Jefferson Co., OH
Died: June 24, 1885 Waverly, OH
Education: Graduated Washington (PA) College, 1836. Attended Cincinnati (OH) Law School.
Occupation: Lawyer
Offices/Honors: Ohio House of Representatives, 1850–51. Ohio Senate, 1852–54. U.S. House of Representatives, 1855–57.
Miscellaneous: Resided Portsmouth, Scioto Co., OH
Buried: Greenlawn Cemetery, Portsmouth, OH (Section 13, Lot 22)
References: *Biographical Cyclopedia and Portrait Gallery with an Historical Sketch of the State of Ohio.* Vol. 3. Cincinnati, OH, 1884. Lois J. Lambert. *Heroes of the Western Theater: 33rd Ohio Veteran Volunteer Infantry.* Milford, OH, 2008. *History of the Lower Scioto Valley, OH.* Chicago, IL, 1884. *Biographical Record of the Scioto Valley.* N.p., 1894. James L. Harrison, compiler. *Biographical Directory of the American Congress, 1774–1949.* Washington,

Oscar Fitzallen Moore (post-war) (L. M. Strayer Collection).

DC, 1950. *Biographical and Historical Catalogue of Washington and Jefferson College, 1802–89.* Cincinnati, OH, 1889. Pension File and Military Service File, National Archives. Letters Received, Volunteer Service Branch, Adjutant General's Office, File M2656(VS)1863, National Archives.

Thomas Moore

Colonel, 167 OH Infantry, May 16, 1864. Honorably mustered out, Sept. 8, 1864.

Born: July 27, 1822 Quebec, Canada
Died: July 29, 1892 Hamilton, OH
Education: Attended Miami University, Oxford, OH
Occupation: Lawyer
Offices/Honors: Ohio Senate, 1860–62
Miscellaneous: Resided Hamilton, Butler Co., OH
Buried: Greenwood Cemetery, Hamilton, OH (Hill Section, Lot 400)
References: Pension File, National Archives. Stephen D. Cone. *Biographical and Historical Sketches, A Narrative of Hamilton and Its Residents.* Hamilton, OH, 1896. Obituary, *Hamilton Daily Democrat,* July 29, 1892. W. Cooper. *Sketches of the Senators and Representatives in the Fifty-fourth General Assembly of the State of Ohio.* Columbus, OH, 1861.

Thomas Watson Moore

Captain, Co. F, 36 OH Infantry, Aug. 24, 1861. Resigned March 5, 1862, since "my business requires my immediate attention." Colonel, 148 OH Infantry, May 18, 1864. Honorably mustered out, Sept. 14, 1864.

Born: March 22, 1825 Allegheny Co., PA
Died: Feb. 20, 1909 Moore's Junction, Washington Co., OH
Occupation: Steamboat engineer and railroad contractor before war. Merchant, farmer and banker after war.
Offices/Honors: Ohio House of Representatives, 1880–84
Miscellaneous: Resided Tunnel, Washington Co., OH; and Marietta, Washington Co., OH
Buried: Tunnel Cemetery, Tunnel, OH
References: *History of Washington County, OH.* Cleveland, OH, 1881. Obituary, *Marietta Daily Times,* Feb. 20, 1909. Obituary Circular, Whole No. 789, Ohio MOLLUS. Pension File and Military Service File, National Archives.

Thomas Clarkson Morris

Sergeant, Co. B, Benton Cadets, MO Infantry, Oct. 4, 1861. Honorably mustered out, Jan. 8, 1862. Captain, Co. K, 80 OH Infantry, March 22, 1862.

Thomas Moore (post-war) (Stephen D. Cone. *Biographical and Historical Sketches, A Narrative of Hamilton and Its Residents.* Hamilton, Ohio, 1896).

Thomas Watson Moore (L. M. Strayer Collection).

Thomas Clarkson Morris (photograph by Crew's Gallery, Alliance, Ohio; L. M. Strayer Collection).

Major, 80 OH Infantry, Jan. 28, 1865. Lieutenant Colonel, 80 OH Infantry, May 20, 1865. *Colonel, 80 OH Infantry, June 16, 1865.* Honorably mustered out, Aug. 13, 1865.
Born: March 28, 1827 near Brownsville, PA
Died: July 9, 1893 Alliance, OH
Occupation: Farmer
Offices/Honors: Sheriff of Columbiana Co., OH, 1870–73
Miscellaneous: Resided Knox Twp., Columbiana Co., OH; Lisbon, Columbiana Co., OH; and Alliance, Stark Co., OH
Buried: Quaker Hill Cemetery, Sebring, OH
References: Obituary, *Alliance Daily Review,* July 11, 1893. Nevin O. Winter. *A History of Northwest Ohio.* Chicago and New York, 1917. Pension File and Military Service File, National Archives. Letters Received, Volunteer Service Branch, Adjutant General's Office, File M1881(VS)1863, National Archives. *History of Columbiana County, OH.* Philadelphia, PA, 1879. David F. Fryer. *History of the 80th Ohio Veteran Volunteer Infantry.* Newcomerstown, OH, 1904.

Thomas Morton

Captain, Co. C, 20 OH Infantry (3 months), April 22, 1861. Colonel, 20 OH Infantry, May 23, 1861. Honorably mustered out, Aug. 18, 1861. Colonel, 81 OH Infantry, Sept. 24, 1861. Commanded Post of Danville, MO, Feb. 1862. Commanded 2 Brigade, 2 Division, Army of the Tennessee, April 6–15, 1862. Commanded Post of Corinth, MS, June–Aug. 1862. Commanded Post of Hamburg,

Thomas Morton (Michael W. Waskul Collection).

TN, Aug.–Sept. 1862. Commanded 2 Brigade, Dodge's Division, District of Corinth, Army of the Tennessee, Oct. 1862. Commanded 2 Brigade, 2 Division, 16 Army Corps, Army of the Tennessee, April 1863. Commanded Post of Pulaski, TN, April–May 1864. Resigned July 30, 1864, "for reasons of physical disability," due to "fistula in ano (incomplete external), complicated with hemorrhoids, which have produced considerable debility and emaciation."
Born: Aug. 15, 1826 Preble Co., OH
Died: Sept. 14, 1905 Middletown, IN
Other Wars: Mexican War (Private, Co. F, U.S. Mounted Rifles)
Occupation: Carpenter and stock dealer
Miscellaneous: Resided Eaton, Preble Co., OH; and Middletown, Henry Co., IN
Buried: Mound Hill Union Cemetery, Eaton, OH (Section 11, Lot 420)
References: J. A. Young. *Fall Creek Township, Henry County, Indiana, in the War of the Rebellion and the War with Mexico.* New Castle, IN, 1887. Military Service File, National Archives. Obituary, *Eaton Register,* Sept. 21, 1905. Letters Received, Volunteer Service Branch, Adjutant General's Office, File I210(VS)1863, National Archives. William H. Chamberlin. *History of the 81st Regiment Ohio Infantry Volunteers during the War of the Rebellion.* Cincinnati, OH, 1865.

Samuel R. Mott

Captain, Co. E, 20 OH Infantry (3 months), April 27, 1861. Honorably mustered out, Aug. 18, 1861. Captain, Co. C, 31 OH Infantry, Sept. 3, 1861. Colonel, 118 OH Infantry, Sept. 17, 1862. Commanded 2 Brigade, 4 Division, 23 Army Corps, Army of the Ohio, June 24–July 8, 1863. Commanded 2 Brigade, 1 Division, 23 Army Corps, Army of the Ohio, July 20–Aug. 6, 1863. Commanded 1 Brigade, 2 Division, 23 Army Corps, Army of the Ohio, Oct. 20, 1863–Feb. 2, 1864. Facing charges of "conduct prejudicial to good order and military discipline, incompetence, and conduct unbecoming an officer and gentleman," highlighted by episodes of playing poker with fellow officers for large sums of money, he resigned Feb. 10, 1864, "for the purpose of avoiding the disgrace of undergoing a trial by court-martial on the charges." In approving his resignation, Brig. Gen. Henry M. Judah expressed his belief, "...that most of the irregularities with which Col. Mott stands charged are the results of ignorance and loose ideas of discipline."

Born: Jan. 26, 1818 Knox Co., OH
Died: Jan. 15, 1896 St. Marys, OH
Other Wars: Texas War for Independence, 1836
Occupation: Lawyer and dry goods merchant
Offices/Honors: Ohio House of Representatives, 1848–49
Miscellaneous: Resided St. Marys, Auglaize Co., OH. Uncle of Bvt. Brig. Gen. Samuel R. Mott (57 Ohio Infantry).
Buried: Elm Grove Cemetery, St. Marys, OH
References: Pension File and Military Service File, National Archives. Charles W. Williamson. *History of Western Ohio and Auglaize County.* Columbus, OH, 1905. Letters Received, Commission Branch, Adjutant General's Office, File M1565(CB)1864, National Archives. Obituary, *Lima Times-Democrat,* Jan. 16, 1896.

William Mungen

Lieutenant Colonel, 57 OH Infantry, Sept. 27, 1861. Colonel, 57 OH Infantry, Dec. 16, 1861. Shell wound head, Arkansas Post, AR, Jan. 10, 1863. Resigned April 16, 1863, due to "chronic dysentery of more than four months standing."

Born: May 12, 1821 Baltimore, MD
Died: Sept. 9, 1887 Findlay, OH
Occupation: Lawyer and newspaper editor
Offices/Honors: Auditor of Hancock Co., OH, 1847–51. Ohio Senate, 1852–54. U.S. House of Representatives, 1867–71.

Samuel R. Mott (far left, with officers of the 118th Ohio Infantry, including Lt. Col. Thomas L. Young, second from left, and Major Lester Bliss, seated behind child) (Ronn Palm Collection).

William Mungen (U.S. House of Representatives, 1867) (Brady-Handy Collection, Library of Congress [LC-DIG-cwpbh-00277]).

Miscellaneous: Resided Findlay, Hancock Co., OH
Buried: Maple Grove Cemetery, Findlay, OH (Block A, Lot 25)
References: *Biographical Encyclopedia of Ohio of the Nineteenth Century.* Cincinnati and Philadelphia, 1876. J. A. Kimmell. *Twentieth Century History of Findlay and Hancock County, OH.* Chicago, IL, 1910. *History of Hancock County, OH.* Chicago, IL, 1886. Pension File and Military Service File, National Archives. Obituary, *Findlay Weekly Jeffersonian,* Sept. 15, 1887. William H. Barnes. *The Fortieth Congress of the United States: Historical and Biographical.* New York City, NY, 1869. James L. Harrison, compiler. *Biographical Directory of the American Congress, 1774–1949.* Washington, DC, 1950.

James Madison Nash

1 Sergeant, Co. B, 19 OH Infantry (3 months), April 27, 1861. Sergeant Major, 19 OH Infantry, June 8, 1861. 1 Lieutenant, Adjutant, 19 OH Infantry, July 4, 1861. Honorably mustered out, Aug. 31, 1861. Captain, Co. B, 19 OH Infantry (3 years), Sept. 13, 1861. Major, 19 OH Infantry, June 20, 1863. GSW left hand, Pickett's Mills, GA, May 27, 1864. Lieutenant Colonel, 19 OH Infantry, Feb. 20, 1865. *Colonel,* 19 OH Infantry, May 31, 1865. Honorably mustered out, Oct. 24, 1865.
Born: Jan. 4, 1833 Ferrisburgh, VT
Died: Sept. 30, 1896 Canfield, OH
Occupation: Newspaper editor and clerk
Offices/Honors: Clerk of Courts, Mahoning Co., OH, 1866–72
Miscellaneous: Resided Canfield, Mahoning Co., OH
Buried: Canfield Village Cemetery, Canfield, OH
References: Obituary Circular, Whole No. 342, Ohio MOLLUS. Pension File and Military Service File, National Archives. Obituary, *Mahoning Dispatch,* Oct. 2, 1896. *History of Trumbull and Mahoning Counties, OH.* Cleveland, OH, 1882. Letters Received, Volunteer Service Branch, Adjutant General's Office, File N7(VS)1865, National Archives.

James McCleery Neibling

Lieutenant Colonel, 21 OH Infantry (3 months), April 27, 1861. Honorably mustered out, Aug. 12, 1861. Lieutenant Colonel, 21 OH Infantry (3 years), Sept. 5, 1861. Colonel, 21 OH Infantry, Dec. 20, 1862. Commanded 3 Brigade, 1 Division, 14 Army Corps, Army of the Cumberland, March 12–May 3, 1864. Shell wound right forearm (amputated), New Hope Church, GA, May 28, 1864. Resigned Dec. 6, 1864, due to the severe neuralgic pain from his amputated arm.
Born: April 11, 1827 Lancaster, OH
Died: Feb. 21, 1869 Findlay, OH
Other Wars: Mexican War (Corporal, Co. G, 2 OH Infantry)
Occupation: Merchant
Offices/Honors: Sheriff, Hancock Co., OH, 1856–61. Postmaster, Findlay, OH, 1867–69.
Miscellaneous: Resided Findlay, OH
Buried: Maple Grove Cemetery, Findlay, OH (Block B, Lot 33)
References: Robert C. Neibling. *The Neibling Family History.* Montgomery, AL, 1972. *Centennial Biographical History of Hancock County, OH.* New York and Chicago, 1903. Pension File and Military Service File, National Archives. Obituary, *Hancock Courier,* Feb. 25, 1869. Letters Received, Volunteer Service Branch, Adjutant General's Office, File M4072(VS)1864, National Archives. Silas S. Canfield. *History of the 21st Regiment Ohio Volunteer Infantry in the War of the Rebellion.* Toledo, OH, 1893. *The Union Army.* Vol. 8 (Ohio Edition). Madison, WI, 1908. *History of Hancock County, OH.* Chicago, IL, 1886.

Michael P. Nolan

Captain, Co. G, 11 OH Infantry (3 months), April 22, 1861. Honorably mustered out, Aug. 26, 1861. *Lieutenant Colonel,* 50 OH Infantry, Dec. 21, 1861. Regiment did not complete organization. Discharged April 23, 1862, upon consolidation of regiment with 61 OH Infantry. *Colonel,* 109 OH In-

James Madison Nash (Massachusetts MOLLUS Collection, USAMHI [Vol. 109, p. 5648]).

James McCleery Neibling (Silas S. Canfield. *History of the 21st Regiment Ohio Volunteer Infantry in the War of the Rebellion.* Toledo, Ohio, 1893).

James Madison Nash (courtesy Marcus S. McLemore).

fantry, Sept. 6, 1862. Mustered as 2 Lieutenant, 109 OH Infantry, effective Sept. 6, 1862. Regiment did not complete organization. Honorably mustered out, Feb. 5, 1863, upon consolidation of regiment with 113 OH Infantry.

Born: June 28, 1823 Dublin, Ireland
Died: Nov. 30, 1891 Dayton, OH

James McCleery Neibling (courtesy Robert J. Van Dorn).

Michael P. Nolan (post-war) (*Biographical Cyclopedia and Portrait Gallery with an Historical Sketch of the State of Ohio*. Vol. 1. Cincinnati, Ohio, 1883).

Occupation: Lawyer
Offices/Honors: U.S. Commissioner for several years after the war
Miscellaneous: Resided Dayton, Montgomery Co., OH
Buried: Woodland Cemetery, Dayton, OH (Section 105, Lot 2684)
References: Frank Conover. *Centennial Portrait and Biographical Record of the City of Dayton and of Montgomery County, OH*. N.p., 1897. *Biographical Cyclopedia and Portrait Gallery with an Historical Sketch of the State of Ohio*. Vol. 1. Cincinnati, OH, 1883. *History of Montgomery County, OH*. Chicago, IL, 1882. Pension File and Military Service File, National Archives. Obituary, *Dayton Evening Herald*, Dec. 1, 1891. Letters Received, Volunteer Service Branch, Adjutant General's Office, Files W365(VS)1862 and N248(VS)1863, National Archives.

Jesse Smith Norton

Colonel, 21 OH Infantry (3 months), April 27, 1861. GSW both hips, Scary Creek, WV, July 17, 1861. Taken prisoner and paroled (with anticipated exchange for CSA Colonel George S. Patton), Scary Creek, WV, July 17, 1861. Honorably mustered out, Aug. 12, 1861. Colonel, 21 OH Infantry (3 years), Sept. 19, 1861. Reprimanded for being absent from his command at a clambake with known Alabama secessionists while stationed at Huntsville, AL, in April 1862, he was then relieved from duty, July 4, 1862, for parole violation upon notification that the Norton/Patton exchange had never occurred.

Jesse Smith Norton (Silas S. Canfield. *History of the 21st Regiment Ohio Volunteer Infantry in the War of the Rebellion*. Toledo, Ohio, 1893).

Finally exchanged Aug. 27, 1862 and returned to duty, he resigned Dec. 20, 1862, since "I am in embarrassed circumstances with debts to a large amount hanging over me and property of various kinds pledged as security, which will be sacrificed during the month of January unless I can be permitted to give it prompt attention."

Born: Aug. 1, 1825 NY
Died: Nov. 4, 1886 Toledo, OH
Occupation: Banker before war. Railroad contractor and hardware and produce merchant after war.
Offices/Honors: Lucas County (OH) Commissioner, 1867–75
Miscellaneous: Resided Perrysburg, Wood Co., OH, before war; and Toledo, Lucas Co., OH, after war
Buried: Woodlawn Cemetery, Toledo, OH (Section 4, Lot 21)
References: Obituary, *Toledo Blade*, Nov. 4–5, 1886. Pension File and Military Service File, National Archives. Silas S. Canfield. *History of the 21st Regiment Ohio Volunteer Infantry in the War of the Rebellion*. Toledo, OH, 1893. Terry Lowry. *The Battle of Scary Creek: Military Operations in the Kanawha Valley, April–July 1861*. Charleston, WV, 1982.

Wesley Owens

1 Lieutenant, 2 U.S. Cavalry, March 21, 1861. 1 Lieutenant, 5 U.S. Cavalry, Aug. 3, 1861. Acting AAG, Maryland State Troops, Dec. 24, 1861–March 8, 1862. Captain, 5 U.S. Cavalry, Jan. 15, 1862. Assigned to duty as Lieutenant Colonel, AIG, 3 Army Corps, Army of the Potomac, Jan. 1–March 23, 1863. Taken prisoner, Flemming's Crossroads, VA, May 4, 1863. Confined Libby Prison, Richmond, VA, but soon paroled through the intercession of USMA classmate Fitzhugh Lee. Acting Assistant Provost Marshal General, Providence, RI, March 15–Sept. 19, 1864. Colonel, 8 OH Cavalry, May 12, 1865. Honorably mustered out of volunteer service, July 30, 1865. Bvt. Major, USA, May 27, 1862, for gallant and meritorious services at the battle of Hanover Courthouse, VA. Bvt. Lieutenant Colonel, USA, March 13, 1865, for gallant and meritorious services during the rebellion.

Born: Oct. 1, 1832 Newark, OH
Died: Aug. 11, 1867 Suisun, CA
Education: Attended Kenyon College, Gambier, OH. Graduated U.S. Military Academy, West Point, NY, 1856.
Occupation: U.S. Army (Captain, 5 U.S. Cavalry)
Miscellaneous: Resided Suisun, Solano Co., CA. Brother-in-law of Brig. Gen. George D. Bayard.
Buried: Suisun-Fairfield District Cemetery, Fairfield, CA
References: Cullum File, U.S. Military Academy Library. Pension File and Military Service File, National Archives. George W. Cullum. *Biographical Register of the Officers and Graduates of the U.S. Military Academy.* Third Edition. Boston and New York, 1891. George F. Price. *Across the Continent with the Fifth Cavalry.* New York City, NY, 1883. Letters Received, Commission Branch, Adjutant General's Office, Files O19(CB)1863 and H949 (CB)1867, National Archives. Letters Received, Volunteer Service Branch, Adjutant General's Office, File O459(VS)1865, National Archives.

James Wallace Paramore

Major, 3 OH Cavalry, Sept. 27, 1861. Charged with "misbehavior before the enemy" for his conduct in a skirmish near Corinth, MS, May 9, 1862, he was released from arrest without trial and returned to duty, June 20, 1862. Colonel, 3 OH Cavalry, Jan. 6, 1863. Commanded 2 Cavalry Brigade, Army of the Cumberland, Feb. 14–April 1863. Commanded 2 Brigade, 2 Cavalry Division, Army of the Cumberland, April–June 8, 1863. Dismissed July 1, 1863, for mutinous conduct "in ordering an armed resistance to the execution of the orders of his brigade commander," Col. Eli Long, technically

Wesley Owens (photograph by Charles D. Fredricks & Co., "Specialite," 587 Broadway, New York).

James Wallace Paramore (post-war) (Logan U. Reavis. *St. Louis: The Future Great City of the World.* Centennial Edition. St. Louis, Missouri, 1876).

his junior in rank, whose orders concerning captured horses he resented because they were not issued through him. "In view of the acknowledged valuable services rendered by this officer previous to dismissal," his dismissal was revoked, April 1, 1867, and he was honorably discharged as of the date of dismissal.

Born: Dec. 27, 1830 near Mansfield, OH
Died: May 17, 1887 St. Louis, MO
Education: Attended Denison University, Granville, OH. Attended Albany (NY) Law School.
Occupation: Lawyer and newspaper editor before war. Business executive engaged in cotton warehousing and railroad construction enterprises after war.
Miscellaneous: Resided Mansfield, Richland Co., OH, and Washington, Franklin Co., MO, before war; Nashville, TN, and St. Louis, MO, after war
Buried: Bellefontaine Cemetery, St. Louis, MO (Block 293, Lot 3142)
References: Obituary, *St. Louis Globe-Democrat*, May 18, 1887. J. Thomas Scharf. *History of St. Louis City and County*. Philadelphia, PA, 1883. Logan U. Reavis. *St. Louis: The Future Great City of the World*. Centennial Edition. St. Louis, MO, 1876. Obituary Circular, Whole No. 25, Missouri MOLLUS. Letters Received, Volunteer Service Branch, Adjutant General's Office, File O424(VS)1863, National Archives. Military Service File, National Archives. Thomas Crofts. *History of the Service of the 3rd Ohio Veteran Volunteer Cavalry in the War for the Preservation of the Union from 1861-65*. Toledo, OH, 1910. Nancy Pape-Findley. *The Invincibles: The Story of the 4th Ohio Veteran Volunteer Cavalry*. Tecumseh, MI, 2002.

Horace Park

2 Lieutenant, Co. F, 43 OH Infantry, Oct. 1, 1861. 1 Lieutenant, Co. F, 43 OH Infantry, Dec. 31, 1861. Captain, Co. F, 43 OH Infantry, Feb. 8, 1862. Provost Marshal, Memphis, TN, Jan.–Feb. 1863. Major, 43 OH Infantry, March 28, 1863. Detached as Superintendent of Repairs, Nashville and Decatur Railroad, Nov. 1863–April 1864. Lieutenant Colonel, 43 OH Infantry, Feb. 14, 1865. Colonel, 43 OH Infantry, April 26, 1865. Honorably mustered out, July 13, 1865.

Born: Aug. 6, 1833 Milan Twp., Franklin Co., OH
Died: March 22, 1907 Kenton, OH
Occupation: Prospector and miner in California before war. Gunsmith and dealer in sportsmen's supplies after war.
Offices/Honors: A well-known sportsman, he authored *The Sportsman's Hand Book* in 1885 and served as Superintendent of the Ohio State Fish Hatchery, Sandusky, OH, in his later years

Miscellaneous: Resided Columbus, Franklin Co., OH; and Kenton, Hardin Co., OH
Buried: Grove Cemetery, Kenton, OH (Section 1C, Lot 8)
References: Obituary Circular, Whole No. 727, Ohio MOLLUS. Obituary, *Ohio State Journal*, March 23, 1907. Pension File and Military Service File, National Archives. Obituary, *Kenton News-Republican*, March 22, 1907. Charles H. Smith. *History of Fuller's Ohio Brigade*. Cleveland, OH, 1909.

Job Reeder Parker

Captain, Co. A, 48 OH Infantry, Sept. 18, 1861. Lieutenant Colonel, 48 OH Infantry, Jan. 23, 1862. GSW left arm, Arkansas Post, AR, Jan. 11, 1863. Shell wound face, Vicksburg, MS, May 22, 1863. By special order dated Dec. 28, 1863, he was mustered out, to date June 20, 1863, "he having performed no duty with his regiment since that date, and having failed to file the necessary certificates of physical disability." By special order dated March 9, 1864, the discharge (described now as honorable) was amended to date Aug. 19, 1863. As an apparent remedy for the bureaucratic mishaps of the previous year during which he was first assumed to have resigned and then charged with being absent without leave, he was commissioned Colonel, 48 OH Infantry, March 18, 1864, and mustered in April 12, 1864. Commanded 2 Brigade, 4 Division, 13 Army Corps, Army of the Gulf, April 19–May 11, 1864. Honorably mustered out, Jan. 17, 1865, having been rendered supernumerary by consolidation of regiment with 83 OH Infantry.

Born: 1832? Hopetown, Ross Co., OH
Died: Dec. 5, 1865 Highland, OH
Education: Attended Ohio Wesleyan University, Delaware, OH
Occupation: School teacher
Miscellaneous: Resided Princeton, Bureau Co., IL; and Highland, Highland Co., OH
Buried: Sugar Grove Cemetery, Wilmington, OH (Section 3, Lot 57)
References: Pension File and Military Service File, National Archives. Letters Received, Volunteer Service Branch, Adjutant General's Office, File P1103(VS)1863, National Archives. John A. Bering. *History of the 48th Ohio Veteran Volunteer Infantry*. Hillsboro, OH, 1880. S.E. Williams, "Col. Job Reeder Parker," *http://www.48ovvi.org/oh48parker.html*.

Edwin Augustus Parrott

Lieutenant Colonel, 1 OH Infantry (3 months), April 17, 1861. Honorably mustered out, Aug. 16, 1861. Lieutenant Colonel, 1 OH Infantry (3 years), Aug. 17, 1861. Acting AIG, Staff of Major Gen.

Horace Park (photograph by Baldwin Gallery, Columbus, Ohio; L. M. Strayer Collection).

Job Reeder Parker.

Provost Marshal General, Columbus, OH, April 29, 1863–Feb. 15, 1864, and also Superintendent of the Volunteer Recruiting Service, Columbus, OH, Oct. 6, 1863–Feb. 15, 1864. Resigned Feb. 15, 1864, due to the death of his father.
Born: Nov. 30, 1830 Dayton, OH
Died: Sept. 20, 1931 Princeton, NJ
Education: Graduated Ohio Wesleyan University, Delaware, OH, 1849. Attended Harvard University Law School, Cambridge, MA.
Occupation: Lawyer and iron manufacturer
Offices/Honors: Ohio House of Representatives, 1860–62 and 1866–68. Speaker, Ohio House of Representatives, 1866–68.
Miscellaneous: Resided Dayton, OH; and Princeton, NJ
Buried: Princeton Cemetery, Princeton, NJ (Map 1, Section Q, Lot 9)
References: Augustus W. Drury. *History of the City of Dayton and Montgomery County, OH.* Chicago, IL, 1909. *Biographical Encyclopedia of Ohio of the Nineteenth Century.* Cincinnati and Philadelphia, 1876. Charles F. Ritter and Jon L. Wakelyn. *American Legislative Leaders, 1850–1910.* Westport, CT, 1989. Obituary, *New York Times,* Sept. 21, 1931. Pension File and Military Service File, National Archives. Letters Received, Volunteer Service Branch, Adjutant General's Office, Files M1014(VS)1863 and W964(VS)1863, National Archives. *The Union Army.* Vol. 8 (Ohio Edition). Madison, WI, 1908. W. Cooper. *Sketches of the*

Horace Park (courtesy Steve Meadow).

Alexander M. McCook, 2 Division, Army of the Ohio, Feb. 10–May 31, 1862. Colonel, 1 OH Infantry, June 1, 1862. Commanded 3 Brigade, 2 Division, 20 Army Corps, Army of the Cumberland, Jan. 27, 1863–April 16, 1863. Acting Assistant

Edwin Augustus Parrott.

Edwin Augustus Parrott (The National Archives [B-6219]).

Senators and Representatives in the Fifty-fourth General Assembly of the State of Ohio. Columbus, OH, 1861.

John Halliday Patrick

Lieutenant Colonel, 5 OH Infantry (3 months), April 25, 1861. Lieutenant Colonel, 5 OH Infantry (3 years), June 11, 1861. Colonel, 5 OH Infantry, Aug. 2, 1862. Commanded 1 Brigade, 2 Division,

John Halliday Patrick (photograph by Winder's Gem Gallery, 160 Fifth Street, bet. Race & Elm, Cincinnati, Ohio; Roger D. Hunt Collection, USAMHI [RG98S-CWP207.65]).

12 Army Corps, Army of the Cumberland, Nov. 30, 1863–Jan. 18, 1864. Shell wound abdomen, New Hope Church, GA, May 25, 1864.
    Born: March 11, 1820 Edinburgh, Scotland
    Died: May 25, 1864 KIA New Hope Church, GA
    Occupation: Tailor
    Miscellaneous: Resided Cincinnati, OH
    Buried: Wesleyan Cemetery, Cincinnati, OH (Section B, Lot 72)
    References: Whitelaw Reid. *Ohio in the War: Her Statesmen Generals and Soldiers.* Cincinnati, OH, 1868. Pension File and Military Service File, National Archives. Funeral account, *Cincinnati Daily Commercial,* June 20, 1864.

George Tod Perkins

2 Lieutenant, Co. B, 19 OH Infantry, April 24, 1861. Honorably mustered out, Aug. 29, 1861. Major, 105 OH Infantry, Aug. 15, 1862. GSW left thigh, Chickamauga, GA, Sept. 20, 1863. Lieutenant Colonel, 105 OH Infantry, Jan. 30, 1864. *Colonel,* 105 OH Infantry, Feb. 18, 1864. Honorably mustered out, June 3, 1865. Bvt. Colonel, USV, March 13, 1865, for gallantry and good conduct as commander of his regiment during the campaigns of the past year.

George Tod Perkins (G. W. Manly, Photographer, Akron, Ohio; John P. Gurnish Collection).

Born: May 5, 1836 near Akron, OH
Died: Sept. 8, 1910 Akron, OH
Education: Attended Marietta (OH) College
Occupation: Iron manufacturer and banker. President of B. F. Goodrich Rubber Co., 1888–1907.
Miscellaneous: Resided Youngstown, Mahoning Co., OH; and Akron, Summit Co., OH. Nephew of Ohio Governor David Tod.
Buried: Glendale Cemetery, Akron, OH (Section 24, Lot 9)
References: Harriet Taylor Upton and Harry Gardner Cutler. *History of the Western Reserve.* Chicago and New York, 1910. Samuel A. Lane. *Fifty Years and Over of Akron and Summit County.* Akron, OH, 1892. Obituary, *Akron Beacon Journal,* Sept. 8, 1910. Albion W. Tourgee. *The Story of a Thousand: Being a History of the Service of the 105th Ohio Volunteer Infantry.* Buffalo, NY, 1896. *Society of the Army of the Cumberland, Thirty-ninth Reunion, Chattanooga, TN, October 18,19, 1911.* Chattanooga, TN, 1912. *The Union Army.* Vol. 8 (Ohio Edition). Madison, WI, 1908. Obituary Circular, Whole No. 855, Ohio MOLLUS. Letters Received, Volunteer Service Branch, Adjutant General's Office, File W2126(VS)1863, National Archives. Military Service File, National Archives.

Edward Herrick Phelps

Paymaster General, Staff of Governor William Dennison, April 16–Aug. 23, 1861. Lieutenant Col-

Edward Herrick Phelps (L. M. Strayer Collection).

onel, 38 OH Infantry, Sept. 10, 1861. Colonel, 38 OH Infantry, Feb. 9, 1862. Commanded 3 Brigade, 3 Division, 14 Army Corps, Army of the Cumberland, Oct. 10–Nov. 25, 1863. GSW breast, Missionary Ridge, TN, Nov. 25, 1863.
Born: Dec. 17, 1827 Richville, St. Lawrence Co., NY
Died: Nov. 25, 1863 KIA Missionary Ridge, TN
Occupation: Lawyer
Miscellaneous: Resided Defiance, Defiance Co., OH. Brother-in-law of Bvt. Brig. Gen. George E. Welles.
Buried: Forest Cemetery, Toledo, OH
References: *History of Defiance County, OH.* Chicago, IL, 1883. Obituary, *Toledo Blade,* Dec. 7, 1863. Pension File and Military Service File, National Archives.

Charles B. Phillips

Colonel, 130 OH Infantry, May 3, 1864. Commanded Fort Powhatan, VA, Aug. 11–Sept. 7, 1864. Honorably mustered out, Sept. 22, 1864.
Born: May 9, 1820 Onondaga Co., NY
Died: March 4, 1900 Blissfield, MI
Occupation: Wholesale hardware merchant, Toledo Car Works operator, and real estate oper-

Edward Herrick Phelps (courtesy Henry Deeks).

Charles B. Phillips (post-war) (Denison B. Smith. "*Memorial of Gen. Charles B. Phillips," Addresses, Memorials, and Sketches.* The Maumee Valley Pioneer Association: Toledo, Ohio, 1900).

ator. For many years actively identified with the militia system of Ohio, serving in every grade from corporal to brigadier general.

Miscellaneous: Resided Toledo, Lucas Co., OH; and Blissfield, Lenawee Co., MI

Buried: Woodlawn Cemetery, Toledo, OH (Section 13, Lot 44, unmarked)

References: Denison B. Smith, "Memorial of Gen. Charles B. Phillips," *Addresses, Memorials, and Sketches.* Published by The Maumee Valley Pioneer Association. Toledo, OH, 1900. Pension File and Military Service File, National Archives. Clark Waggoner, editor. *History of the City of Toledo and Lucas County.* New York City, NY, 1888. Obituary, *Toledo Blade,* March 5, 1900.

James Elliott Philpott

2 Lieutenant, Co. A, 80 OH Infantry, Nov. 5, 1861. 2 Lieutenant, Adjutant, 80 OH Infantry, Feb. 1, 1862. 1 Lieutenant, Adjutant, 80 OH Infantry, March 21, 1862. GSW left arm, Iuka, MS, Sept. 19, 1862. Taken prisoner and paroled, Jan. 1863. Resigned July 12, 1863, due to "a sense of justice to my constituents at home, as a civil officer, a sense of honor to the surety on my official bond, justice in behalf of my clients whose causes in court have been long continued, as well as justice and duty in consideration of my obligations to the surety on

James Elliott Philpott (post-war) (from unidentified and undated newspaper clipping).

my bond as guardian, and the promptings of the ties of consanguinity refreshened by the memories which remind me of the sacred honor which binds me to a full discharge of my duties to the orphan (his nephew) whose property and personal care is now intrusted to my charge." Having adjusted all his business satisfactorily, he somehow secured from Governor David Tod a commission as *Colonel,* 80 OH Infantry, Aug. 15, 1863, upon the death of Colonel Bartilson, and returned with it to the regiment. His unexpected promotion, however, met strong opposition from more senior officers in the regiment, and being unable to obtain an order removing the disability caused by his resignation, he returned to civil life. Conditional 2 Lieutenant, 184 OH Infantry, Jan. 5, 1865. Captain, Co. A, 186 OH Infantry, Feb. 26, 1865. Dismissed March 8, 1865, for "fraud in local bounties, in requiring $1050.00 to be given him as a consideration for procuring commissions for two men as lieutenants in his company." Order of dismissal revoked, Oct. 13, 1865, and he was honorably discharged to date, Aug. 28, 1865.

Born: July 5, 1836 New Providence, Clark Co., IN

Died: Sept. 4, 1927 St. Cloud, FL

Occupation: Lawyer

Offices/Honors: County Recorder, Carroll Co., OH

Miscellaneous: Resided Carrollton, Carroll Co., OH; Lincoln, Lancaster Co., NE; and St. Cloud, Osceola Co., FL

Buried: Mount Peace Cemetery, St. Cloud, FL

References: *Portrait and Biographical Album of Lancaster County, NE.* Chicago, IL, 1888. Pension File and Military Service File, National Archives. Letters Received, Volunteer Service Branch, Adjutant General's Office, File E350(VS)1863, National Archives. David F. Fryer. *History of the 80th Ohio Veteran Volunteer Infantry.* Newcomerstown, OH, 1904. Noland (Hubbard) Bowling. *Meet Your Ancestors: Some Descendants of Edward Philpott (1597?–1678), William Barton (1605?–1674), Francis Posey (1600–1654), William Smoote (ca 1597–1673), Moses Hobart (1709–1780), and Moses Hubbard (1774–1856).* Utica, KY, 1985. Alfred T. Andreas. *History of Nebraska.* Chicago, IL, 1882. Obituary, *Lincoln Evening State Journal,* Sept. 5, 1927.

James Pickands

Corporal, Co. E, 1 OH Infantry (3 months), April 29, 1861. Sergeant, 1 OH Infantry, June 1, 1861. 1 Sergeant, Co. E, 1 OH Infantry, July 2, 1861. Honorably mustered out, Aug. 1, 1861. Captain, Co. E, 84 OH Infantry, June 2, 1862. Honorably mustered out, Sept. 20, 1862. Major, 124 OH Infantry, Oct. 30, 1862. Lieutenant Colonel, 124 OH

James Pickands.

Infantry, Jan. 1, 1863. GSW left leg, Pickett's Mills, GA, May 27, 1864. *Colonel,* 124 OH Infantry, June 20, 1865. Honorably mustered out, July 9, 1865.

Born: Dec. 15, 1839 Akron, OH

Died: July 14, 1896 Cleveland, OH

Occupation: Capitalist extensively involved in the iron and coal industry. Had charge of the largest fleet of iron ore vessels on the Great Lakes.

Offices/Honors: Mayor of Marquette, MI, 1875–76

Miscellaneous: Resided Cleveland, OH; and Marquette, Marquette Co., MI, 1867–82

Buried: Lake View Cemetery, Cleveland, OH (Section 10, Lot 81B)

References: Obituary Circular, Whole No. 337, Ohio MOLLUS. Obituary, *Cleveland Press,* July 15, 1896. *Society of the Army of the Cumberland. Twenty-seventh Reunion, Columbus, Ohio, 1897.* Cincinnati, OH, 1898. David D. Van Tassel and John J. Grabowski, editors. *The Encyclopedia of Cleveland History.* Bloomington, IN, 1987. Wilfred H. Alburn and Miriam R. Alburn. *This Cleveland of Ours.* Chicago, Cleveland, and Indianapolis, 1933. George W. Lewis. *The Campaigns of the 124th Regiment Ohio Volunteer Infantry.* Akron, OH, 1894. Military Service File, National Archives.

Francis Bates Pond

Captain, Co. H, 17 OH Infantry (3 months), April 27, 1861. Lieutenant Colonel, 17 OH Infantry,

Francis Bates Pond (post-war) (J. Landy, Photographer, 208 Fourth St., Cor. Plum, Cincinnati, Ohio; Roger D. Hunt Collection, USAMHI [RG98S-CWP207.70]).

May 14, 1861. Honorably mustered out, Aug. 16, 1861. Lieutenant Colonel, 62 OH Infantry, Sept. 28, 1861. Colonel, 62 OH Infantry, Oct. 31, 1861. Commanded 1 Brigade, 1 Division, 10 Army Corps, Army of the James, April 28–May 2, June 11–14, July 28–Aug. 16, Sept. 1–13, Sept. 24–29, and Oct. 4–26, 1864. GSW right temple, Deep Bottom, VA, Aug. 16, 1864. Commanded 3 Division, 10 Army Corps, Army of the James, Sept. 13–24, 1864. Resigned Nov. 5, 1864, since "the exposure incident to a soldier's life has so seriously impaired my constitution that I am satisfied that my longer continuance in the service would be of greater detriment to me and my family than benefit to the service."
Born: Aug. 9, 1825 Ellisburg, NY
Died: Nov. 2, 1883 Malta, OH
Education: Graduated Oberlin (OH) College, 1846
Occupation: Lawyer
Offices/Honors: Ohio House of Representatives, 1868–70. Attorney General of Ohio, 1870–74. Ohio Senate, 1880–83.
Miscellaneous: Resided Malta, Morgan Co., OH
Buried: Malta Union Cemetery, Malta, OH
References: Daniel S. Pond. *A Genealogical Record of Samuel Pond and His Descendants.* New London, OH, 1875. *Biographical Cyclopedia and Portrait Gallery with an Historical Sketch of the State of Ohio.* Vol. 6. Cincinnati, OH, 1895. W. Darwin Crabb. *Biographical Sketches of the State Officers and of the Members of the Sixtieth General Assembly of the State of Ohio.* Columbus, OH, 1872. Pension File and Military Service File, National Archives.

Christian L. Poorman

2 Lieutenant, Co. D, 43 OH Infantry, Nov. 21, 1861. Captain, Co. D, 43 OH Infantry, Dec. 21, 1861. Lieutenant Colonel, 98 OH Infantry, Aug. 12, 1862. Colonel, 98 OH Infantry, Oct. 8, 1862. Resigned June 12, 1863, due to the reduced strength (250 men for duty) of his regiment and also his wife's poor health. "As the publisher of a paper in a county carried last fall by the anti-war party, I believe I can do more good for the government during the next political contest in Ohio, if at home, than I can in command of 250 men in the field."
Born: Oct. 28, 1825 Mechanicsburg, PA
Died: March 6, 1912 Shadyside, Belmont Co., OH
Education: Attended Cincinnati (OH) Law School
Occupation: Lawyer and newspaper editor before war. Newspaper editor and publisher after war.
Offices/Honors: Auditor, Belmont Co., OH, 1858–62. Ohio House of Representatives, 1886–90. Secretary of State of Ohio, 1892.
Miscellaneous: Resided St. Clairsville, Belmont Co., OH; and Bellaire, Belmont Co., OH
Buried: Greenwood Cemetery, Bellaire, OH
References: *National Cyclopedia of American Biography. History of the Upper Ohio Valley.* Madison, WI, 1891. *Biographical Encyclopedia of Ohio of the Nineteenth Century.* Cincinnati and Philadelphia, 1876. Obituary, *St. Clairsville Gazette,* March 14, 1912. Pension File and Military Service File, National Archives. Letters Received, Volunteer Service Branch, Adjutant General's Office, File P165(VS) 1863, National Archives.

Frederick Anton Poschner

Colonel, 47 OH Infantry, Aug. 15, 1861. Resigned July 17, 1862, due to "continued ill health, resulting from an utter prostration of the nervous system."
Born: 1818? (or 1813?) Vienna, Austria
Died: Aug. 11, 1873 Dayton, OH
Occupation: Civil engineer
Miscellaneous: Resided Louisville, KY; and Cincinnati, OH

Christian L. Poorman (post-war) (Gibson L. Cranmer. *History of the Upper Ohio Valley*. Madison, Wisconsin, 1891).

Buried: Dayton National Cemetery, Dayton, OH (Section A, Row 14, Grave 56)
References: Pension File and Military Service File, National Archives. Joseph A. Saunier, editor. *A History of the 47th Regiment Ohio Veteran Volunteer Infantry*. Hillsboro, OH, 1903. Albert Castel. *Tom Taylor's Civil War*. Lawrence, KS, 2000. Letters Received, Volunteer Service Branch, Adjutant General's Office, File C504(VS)1862, National Archives. Adolf E. Zucker, editor. *The Forty-Eighters: Political Refugees of the German Revolution of 1848*. New York City, NY, 1950.

Edwin H. Powers

Private, Co. E, 55 OH Infantry, Sept. 15, 1861. Captain, Co. E, 55 OH Infantry, Dec. 30, 1861. Acting AIG, Staff of Brig. Gen. Nathaniel C. McLean, 2 Brigade, 1 Division, 11 Army Corps, Army of the Potomac, March 20–May 2, 1863. GSW right hand, Chancellorsville, VA, May 2, 1863. Acting AIG, Staff of Brig. Gen. Adolph Von Steinwehr, 2 Division, 11 Army Corps, Army of the Potomac (and Army of the Cumberland after Sept. 25, 1863), Aug. 1, 1863–Jan. 9, 1864. Captain, Co. K, 55 OH Infantry, March 9, 1864. Lieutenant Colonel, 55 OH Infantry, July 4, 1864. Colonel, 55 OH Infantry, June 6, 1865. Honorably mustered out, July 11, 1865.
Born: Nov. 13, 1831 Brandon, VT
Died: May 21, 1897 Silver Cliff, CO
Occupation: Lawyer and mine operator
Offices/Honors: Prosecuting Attorney, Saginaw Co., MI, 1867–69
Miscellaneous: Resided Berlin Heights, Erie Co., OH; and Augusta, Richmond Co., GA, before war. Resided Saginaw, Saginaw Co., MI; Denver, CO; Chicago, IL; and Silver Cliff, Custer Co., CO, after war.

Edwin H. Powers (photograph by Webster & Bro., Louisville, Kentucky).

Buried: New Hampton Cemetery, New Hampton, IA
References: Pension File and Military Service File, National Archives. Obituary, *New Hampton Tribune*, May 25, 1897. Obituary, *Silver Cliff Rustler*, May 26, 1897. Obituary, *Rocky Mountain News*, May 22, 1897. Hartwell Osborn and Others. *Trials and Triumphs: The Record of the 55th Ohio Volunteer Infantry*. Chicago, IL, 1904. Letters Received, Volunteer Service Branch, Adjutant General's Office, File 5403(VS)1889, National Archives.

George Augustus Purington

1 Sergeant, Co. G, 19 OH Infantry (3 months), April 27, 1861. Honorably mustered out, Aug. 31, 1861. Captain, Co. A, 2 OH Cavalry, Aug. 27, 1861. Major, 2 OH Cavalry, Sept. 10, 1861. Lieutenant Colonel, 2 OH Cavalry, July 10, 1863. *Colonel,* 2 OH Cavalry, May 9, 1864. Commanded 1 Brigade, 3 Cavalry Division, Middle Military Division, Sept. 19–Oct. 6, 1864. Honorably mustered out, Nov. 1, 1864. Bvt. Major, USA, March 2, 1867, for gallant and meritorious services in the battle of the Wilderness, VA. Bvt. Lieutenant Colonel, USA, March 2, 1867, for gallant and meritorious services in the battle of Winchester, VA. Bvt. Colonel, USA, March 2, 1867, for gallant and meritorious services in the battle of Cedar Creek, VA.

Edwin H. Powers.

Born: July 21, 1838 Athens, OH
Died: May 31, 1896 Metropolis, IL
Education: Attended Western Reserve College, Hudson, OH
Occupation: Regular Army (Lieutenant Colonel, 3 U.S. Cavalry, retired July 17, 1895)
Miscellaneous: Resided Hudson, Summit Co., OH; and Metropolis, Massac Co., IL
Buried: Jefferson Barracks National Cemetery, St. Louis, MO (Section OPS2, Grave 2124C)
References: Obituary Circular, Whole No. 149, Missouri MOLLUS. William H. Powell and Edward Shippen, editors. *Officers of the Army and Navy (Regular) Who Served in the Civil War.* Philadelphia, PA, 1892. Obituary, *St. Louis Post-Dispatch,* June 1, 1896. Constance Wynn Altshuler. *Cavalry Yellow & Infantry Blue: Army Officers in Arizona Between 1851 and 1886.* Tucson, AZ, 1991. Pension File and Military Service File, National Archives. Letters Received, Appointment, Commission and Personal Branch, Adjutant General's Office, File 2330(ACP)1877, National Archives. Letters Received, Volunteer Service Branch, Adjutant General's Office, File M1737(VS)1864, National Archives. Luman H. Tenney. *War Diary of Luman Harris Tenney, 1861–1865.* Cleveland, OH, 1914.

David Putman

2 Lieutenant, Co. E, 69 OH Infantry, Oct. 10, 1861. Captain, Co. E, 69 OH Infantry, Dec. 16,

George Augustus Purington (post-war) (Pennsylvania MOLLUS Collection, USAMHI [RG641S-MOL-PA4.106]).

David Putman (post-war) (*History of Darke County, OH.* Chicago, Illinois, 1880).

1861. Suffering from "disease of the stomach and bowels" and feeling that his claims for promotion had been unjustly disregarded, he resigned, June 20, 1863. Colonel, 152 OH Infantry, May 11, 1864. Honorably mustered out, Sept. 2, 1864.
Born: Aug. 4, 1821 New Madison, Darke Co., OH
Died: June 9, 1912 Palestine, OH
Occupation: Merchant, farmer and insurance agent before war. Lawyer and insurance agent after war.
Miscellaneous: Resided German and Palestine, Darke Co., OH. Brother-in-law of Major Gen. James G. Blunt.
Buried: Palestine Cemetery, Palestine, OH
References: *A Biographical History of Darke County, OH.* Chicago, IL, 1900. *History of Darke County, OH.* Chicago, IL, 1880. Pension File and Military Service File, National Archives. Jim Leeke, editor. *A Hundred Days to Richmond.* Bloomington, IN, 1999.

Owen Perkins Ransom

Colonel, 1 OH Cavalry, Aug. 17, 1861. Due to "habits and intemperate excesses," described by Major Minor Millikin, "of such a character as entirely to negative my faith in, and respect for your other good qualities," he resigned Dec. 16, 1861, stating "that he did so at (Governor) Dennison's request and upon the advice of a friend at whose solicitation the appointment had been made."
Born: Dec. 2, 1817 CT
Died: Jan. 10, 1880 Newport, KY
Education: Attended Wesleyan University, Middletown, CT. Graduated U.S. Military Academy, West Point, NY, 1838.
Other Wars: Florida War, 1838–42 (1 Lieutenant, 2 U.S. Dragoons)
Occupation: Civil engineer, employed in the survey, location, and construction of various railroads
Miscellaneous: Resided Cincinnati, OH; and Newport, Campbell Co., KY
Buried: Highland Cemetery, Fort Mitchell, KY (Section 1, Large Circle, Grave 115)
References: George W. Cullum. *Biographical Register of the Officers and Graduates of the U.S. Military Academy.* Third Edition. Boston and New York, 1891. *Annual Reunion,* Association of the Graduates of the USMA, 1880. Obituary, *Cincinnati Enquirer,* Jan. 11, 1880. U.S. Military Academy Cadet Application Papers, National Archives. Letter O. P. Ransom to Governor William Dennison, Dec. 8, 1861, (Series 147–19: 120), Correspondence to the Governor and Adjutant General of Ohio, 1861–66, Ohio Historical Society. Whitelaw Reid. *Ohio in the War: Her Statesmen Generals and Soldiers.* Cincinnati, OH, 1868. William L. Curry, compiler. *Four Years in the Saddle: History of the 1st Regiment Ohio Volunteer Cavalry.* Columbus, OH, 1898. Cullum File, U.S. Military Academy Library. Military Service File, National Archives. *Alumni Record of Wesleyan University.* 3rd Edition. Hartford, CT, 1883.

Cyrus Reasoner

1 Lieutenant, Co. A, 15 OH Infantry, Sept. 9, 1861. Captain, Co. H, 15 OH Infantry, May 4, 1862. Placed in arrest for permitting straggling, he resigned July 1, 1862, "in justice to the service and to myself." In forwarding his resignation, Brig. Gen. Richard W. Johnson commented, "Capt. R. is inefficient as an officer and his resignation should by all means be accepted." Colonel, 160 OH Infantry, May 17, 1864. Honorably mustered out, Sept. 7, 1864.
Born: March 8, 1824 New Concord, OH
Died: Feb. 11, 1908 Columbus, OH
Occupation: Carpenter and builder
Miscellaneous: Resided New Concord, Muskingum Co., OH, before war. Resided Columbus, OH; and Marshfield, Webster Co., MO, after war
Buried: Greenlawn Cemetery, Columbus, OH (Section 43, Lot 100)
References: Marie C. and Donald O. Anderson. *The Reasoner Story, 1665–1990.* Midvale, UT, 1990. Pension File and Military Service File, National Archives. Obituary, *Ohio State Journal,* Feb. 12, 1908. Alexis Cope. *The 15th Ohio Volunteers and Its Campaigns, War of 1861–65.* Columbus, OH, 1916. Jim Leeke, editor. *A Hundred Days to Richmond.* Bloomington, IN, 1999. Letters Received, Volunteer Service Branch, Adjutant General's Office, File R411(VS)1862, National Archives.

William Pitt Reid

Colonel, 121 OH Infantry, Sept. 11, 1862. Commanded 34 Brigade, 10 Division, 1 Army Corps, Army of the Ohio, Oct. 8–18, 1862. Commanded 34 Brigade, District of Western Kentucky, Department of the Ohio, Dec. 1862–Jan. 1863. Commanded Reid's Brigade, Baird's Division, Army of Kentucky, Feb.–June 1863. Commanded 2 Brigade, 1 Division, Reserve Corps, Army of the Cumberland, June 8–Sept. 9, 1863. Suffering from chronic bronchitis, he resigned Nov. 4, 1863, "on account of continued ill health, which entirely unfits me for duty in the field."
Born: Jan. 8, 1825 Oxford Twp., Delaware Co., OH
Died: Jan. 18, 1879 Delaware, OH
Occupation: Lawyer
Offices/Honors: Ohio Senate, 1874–76
Miscellaneous: Resided Delaware, Delaware Co., OH

Buried: Oak Grove Cemetery, Delaware, OH (Evergreen Ridge Section, Lot 17)
References: James R. Lytle, editor. *Twentieth Century History of Delaware County, OH.* Chicago, IL, 1908. *History of Delaware County, OH.* Chicago, IL, 1880. Obituary, *Delaware Gazette,* Jan. 23, 1879. Pension File and Military Service File, National Archives. Letters Received, Volunteer Service Branch, Adjutant General's Office, File O221(VS) 1863, National Archives.

Robert Reily

Major, 75 OH Infantry, Sept. 18, 1861. Lieutenant Colonel, 75 OH Infantry, Dec. 3, 1862. Colonel, 75 OH Infantry, March 1, 1863. GSW right leg (amputated), Chancellorsville, VA, May 2, 1863.
Born: June 1, 1820 Butler Co., OH
Died: May 3, 1863 DOW Chancellorsville, VA
Occupation: Dry goods merchant
Miscellaneous: Resided Cincinnati, OH; and Wyoming, Hamilton Co., OH. Brother-in-law of Colonel Lewis D. Campbell (69 OH Infantry). Brother of CSA Colonel James Reily (4 TX Cavalry).
Buried: Spring Grove Cemetery, Cincinnati, OH (Section 46, Lot 39)
References: James McBride. *Pioneer Biography: Sketches of the Lives of Some of the Early Settlers of Butler County, Ohio.* Cincinnati, OH, 1869. Pension File and Military Service File, National Archives. Obituary, *Cincinnati Commercial,* May 11, 1863. James Barnett, William R. Northlich, and Adelia Brownell, "Wyoming Honors Its Founder, Robert Reily," *Cincinnati Historical Society Bulletin,* Vol. 23, No. 3 (July 1965). "Ohioans Honor Col. Robert Reily, 75th Ohio Infantry," *Civil War News,* Vol. 21, No. 11 (Dec. 1995). James E. Campbell. *Military Record of Samuel Campbell and His Descendants.* N.p., 1919. Letters Received, Volunteer Service Branch, Adjutant General's Office, File R116(VS)1863, National Archives.

Charles Hendee Rippey

2 Lieutenant, Co. D, 17 OH Infantry (3 months), April 25, 1861. Honorably mustered out, Aug. 15, 1861. Captain, Co. D, 17 OH Infantry, Sept. 16, 1861. Lieutenant Colonel, 90 OH Infantry, Aug. 9, 1862. Colonel, 90 OH Infantry, April 14, 1863. The strength of his regiment being reduced to 360 men present for duty (below the level requiring a colonel), he resigned Oct. 20, 1863. In recommending acceptance of his resignation, Major Gen.

Robert Reily (James E. Campbell. *Military Record of Samuel Campbell and His Descendants.* N.p., 1919).

Charles Hendee Rippey (L. M. Strayer Collection).

John M. Palmer explained, "He now says with a great show of reason that he is wasting, with reference to the future, a most important period of his life, a period which he ought to devote to that profession which he had selected before he left college."
  Born: Feb. 19, 1839 Logan, OH
  Died: Sept. 23, 1919 San Diego, CA
  Education: Attended Ohio University, Athens, OH
  Occupation: Lawyer
  Miscellaneous: Resided Logan, Hocking Co., OH, to 1879; Columbus, OH, 1879–83; Asbury Park, Monmouth Co., NJ, 1883–84; Boston, MA, 1884–85; Quincy, Norfolk Co., MA, 1885–88; San Diego, CA, 1888–1919
  Buried: Santa Barbara Cemetery, Santa Barbara, CA (Summit Plaza Section, Lot 692)
  References: Pension File and Military Service File, National Archives. Obituary Circular, Whole No. 1324, California MOLLUS. Obituary, *San Diego Union*, Sept. 25, 1919. Obituary, *San Diego Sun*, Sept. 24, 1919. Henry O. Harden. *History of the 90th Ohio Volunteer Infantry in the War of the Great Rebellion*. Stoutsville, OH, 1902. Letter H. C. Whitman to Governor David Tod, Feb. 2, 1862, (Series 147–35: 107), Correspondence to the Governor and Adjutant General of Ohio, 1861–66, Ohio Historical Society.

Oliver P. Robie

Private, Captain Burdsall's Independent Co., OH Cavalry, June 5, 1861. 1 Sergeant, Captain Burdsall's Independent Co., OH Cavalry, Aug. 6, 1861. Honorably mustered out, Aug. 23, 1861. Captain, Co. A, 4 OH Cavalry, Sept. 10, 1861. Taken prisoner and paroled, Lexington, KY, Oct. 18, 1862. Major, 4 OH Cavalry, Nov. 22, 1862. Lieutenant Colonel, 4 OH Cavalry, Feb. 26, 1863. Exchanged and returned to regiment, March 10, 1863. Commanded 2 Brigade, 2 Cavalry Division, Army of the Cumberland, April 10–11, 1863. *Colonel*, 4 OH Cavalry, Nov. 3, 1864. Honorably mustered out, Nov. 30, 1864.
  Born: 1833? Portland, ME
  Died: March 16, 1874 San Francisco, CA (committed suicide by gunshot to head)
  Occupation: After the war took a position in the San Francisco Custom House, which he held until 1871, after which he was engaged in the manufacture of neckties
  Miscellaneous: Resided Cincinnati, OH; and San Francisco, CA
  Buried: San Francisco National Cemetery, San Francisco, CA (Section OSA, Plot 72, Grave 6)
  References: Military Service File, National Archives. Obituary, *San Francisco Examiner*, March

Oliver P. Robie (photograph by Hoag & Quick's Art Palace, No. 100 4th St. opp. Post Office, Cincinnati, Ohio; Richard F. Carlile Collection).

16, 1874. Obituary, *San Francisco Chronicle*, March 17, 1874. Lucien Wulsin. *The Story of the 4th Regiment Ohio Veteran Volunteer Cavalry*. Cincinnati, OH, 1912. Nancy Pape-Findley. *The Invincibles: The Story of the 4th Ohio Veteran Volunteer Cavalry*. Tecumseh, MI, 2002.

Aaron Black Robinson

Captain, Co. I, 121 OH Infantry, Aug. 22, 1862. GSW left arm, Chickamauga, GA, Sept. 20, 1863. GSW knee, Kenesaw Mountain, GA, June 27, 1864. Major, 121 OH Infantry, Aug. 29, 1864. Lieutenant Colonel, 121 OH Infantry, Jan. 28, 1865. *Colonel*, 121 OH Infantry, May 18, 1865. Honorably mustered out, June 8, 1865.
  Born: Nov. 10, 1833 Darby Twp., Union Co., OH
  Died: March 31, 1917 Marysville, OH
  Education: Graduated Jefferson College, Canonsburg, PA, 1857. Attended Cincinnati (OH) Law School.
  Occupation: Lawyer, manufacturer of woolen goods, and dry goods merchant
  Offices/Honors: Ohio House of Representatives, 1880–84
  Miscellaneous: Resided Marysville, Union Co., OH

Oliver P. Robie (Richard F. Carlile Collection).

Aaron Black Robinson (William L. Curry. *History of Jerome Township, Union County, OH*. Columbus, Ohio, 1913).

Buried: Oakdale Cemetery, Marysville, OH (Section C)

References: *Memorial Record of the Counties of Delaware, Union, and Morrow, OH*. Chicago, IL, 1895. *History of Union County, OH*. Chicago, IL, 1883. Obituary, *Marysville Evening Tribune*, March 31, 1917. *Biographical and Historical Catalogue of Washington and Jefferson College*. Cincinnati, OH, 1889. Military Service File, National Archives. William L. Curry. *History of Jerome Township, Union County, Ohio*. Columbus, OH, 1913.

Isaac Newton Ross

Colonel, 90 OH Infantry, July 16, 1862. Shell wound of right side, Stone's River, TN, Jan. 2, 1863. Resigned April 14, 1863, due to "long and continued sickness" being "unfit for any military duty on account of chronic diarrhea and lumbago."

Born: Aug. 22, 1824 Hanover, NH

Died: March 26, 1881 Holden, MA

Occupation: Merchant before war. Railroad superintendent and farmer after war.

Offices/Honors: Ohio House of Representatives, 1862–64. Massachusetts House of Representatives, 1871–72.

Isaac Newton Ross (post-war) (David F. Estes. *The History of Holden, MA*. Worcester, Masschusetts, 1894).

Miscellaneous: Resided Darbyville, Pickaway Co., OH; Greenfield, Franklin Co., MA; Worcester, Worcester Co., MA; and Holden, Worcester Co., MA
Buried: Cremated at LeMoyne Crematory, Washington, PA. Disposition of cremains unknown.
References: David F. Estes. *The History of Holden, MA.* Worcester, MA, 1894. *Col. Isaac N. Ross: In Memoriam.* Worcester, MA, 1881. Obituary, *Worcester Daily Spy,* March 28 and 30, 1881. *The Ohio Legislature: Biographical Notices of the Members of the Fifty-fifth General Assembly of the State of Ohio.* Columbus, OH, 1862. Pension File and Military Service File, National Archives. Henry O. Harden. *History of the 90th Ohio Volunteer Infantry in the War of the Great Rebellion.* Stoutsville, OH, 1902.

Benjamin F. Rosson
Colonel, 147 OH Infantry, May 16, 1864. Honorably mustered out, Aug. 30, 1864.
Born: 1825? KY
Died: March 4, 1873 Troy, OH
Other Wars: Mexican War (Corporal, Co. C, 3 KY Infantry)
Occupation: Dentist

Benjamin F. Rosson (post-war) (*Roster of the 147th Regiment Ohio Volunteer Infantry.* West Milton, Ohio, 1913).

Miscellaneous: Resided Troy, Miami Co., OH
Buried: Oxford Cemetery, Oxford, OH
References: Pension File and Military Service File, National Archives. Obituary, *Miami Union,* March 8, 1873. *Roster of the 147th Regiment Ohio Volunteer Infantry.* West Milton, OH, 1913.

Michael Clarkson Ryan
Colonel, 50 OH Infantry, Sept. 30, 1861. Regiment did not complete organization.
Born: April 1820 Lancaster, PA
Died: Oct. 23, 1861 Hamilton, OH
Education: Graduated Miami University, Oxford, OH, 1839. Graduated Cincinnati (OH) Law School, 1842.
Occupation: Lawyer and newspaper editor
Offices/Honors: Prosecuting Attorney, Butler Co., OH, 1848–52
Miscellaneous: Resided Hamilton, Butler Co., OH. One of the founders of the Beta Theta Pi fraternity.
Buried: Greenwood Cemetery, Hamilton, OH (Hill Section, Lot 446)
References: Stephen D. Cone. *Biographical and Historical Sketches, A Narrative of Hamilton and Its Residents.* Hamilton, OH, 1896. Jim Blount, compiler. *Greenwood Biographies.* N.p., 1990. William Raimond Baird. *Betas of Achievement.* New York City, NY, 1914. *The Alumni and Former Student Catalogue of Miami University, 1809–1892.* Oxford, OH, 1892. Letter M. C. Ryan to Adjutant General C. P. Buckingham, Sept. 30, 1861, (Series 147-12: 109), Correspondence to the Governor and Adjutant General of Ohio, 1861–66, Ohio Historical Society.

Harley H. Sage
2 Lieutenant, Co. B, 13 OH Infantry (3 years), May 29, 1861. Resigned Sept. 6, 1861, "my reasons being very important ones of a private and domestic nature." Private, Co. E, 43 OH Infantry, Oct. 7, 1861. Captain, Co. E, 43 OH Infantry, Dec. 31, 1861. Major, 43 OH Infantry, Oct. 12, 1862. Resigned March 27, 1863, due to "sickness and death in my family." In urging acceptance of his resignation, Colonel (later Brig. Gen.) Wager Swayne commented, "This officer ... by the use of politicians obtained his commission after all other officers of the regiment had sent in their urgent testimony to his unfitness." Colonel, 155 OH Infantry, May 8, 1864. Honorably mustered out, Aug. 27, 1864. Colonel, 179 OH Infantry, Sept. 28, 1864. Honorably mustered out, June 17, 1865.
Born: Feb. 23, 1835 Pickaway Co., OH
Died: Dec. 4, 1905 Dayton, OH
Education: Attended Kenyon College, Gambier, OH

Occupation: Watch maker before war. Commercial traveler, Supervisor of Dayton Asylum for the Insane, deputy court clerk, and lawyer after war.
Miscellaneous: Resided London, Madison Co., OH, and Circleville, Pickaway Co., OH, before war; Circleville, OH, 1865–78; and Dayton, Montgomery Co., OH, after 1878
Buried: Dayton National Cemetery, Dayton, OH (Section O, Row 1, Grave 21)
References: Frank Conover. *Centennial Portrait and Biographical Record of the City of Dayton and of Montgomery County, OH.* N.p., 1897. Pension File and Military Service File, National Archives. Letters Received, Volunteer Service Branch, Adjutant General's Office, File S1530(VS)1864, National Archives.

Charles Henry Sargent

Appointed Colonel, 52 OH Infantry, Oct. 10, 1861. Regiment did not complete organization and was consolidated into 61 OH Infantry, April 23, 1862. By War Department Special Order No. 550, June 7, 1862, he was mustered into U.S. Service to date, Feb. 1, 1862, and honorably mustered out to date, May 28, 1862. Appointed Provost Marshal, 1 District of Ohio, April 30, 1863, but appointment canceled, May 12, 1863.
Born: April 25, 1819 Cleveland, OH
Died: Dec. 12, 1891 Cincinnati, OH
Education: Attended Norwich (VT) University
Occupation: Merchant before war. Traveling agent for the Cincinnati Enquirer newspaper after war.
Offices/Honors: Brig. Gen., Ohio Volunteer Militia, 1857–58. Assistant Adjutant General, Staff of Ohio Governor William Allen, 1874–75.
Miscellaneous: Resided Cincinnati, OH
Buried: Spring Grove Cemetery, Cincinnati, OH (Section 45, Lot 32)
References: Obituary, *Cincinnati Enquirer,* Dec. 13, 1891. Edwin F. Sargent. *Sargent Record.* St. Johnsbury, VT, 1899. William A. Ellis, editor. *History of Norwich University, 1819–1911, Her History, Her Graduates, Her Roll of Honor.* Montpelier, VT, 1911. Letters Received, Volunteer Service Branch, Adjutant General's office, File S616(VS)1862, National Archives. Henry A. Ford and Mrs. Kate B. Ford, compilers. *History of Cincinnati, OH.* Cleveland, OH, 1881.

Miles J. Saunders

2 Lieutenant, Co. I, 13 OH Infantry (3 months), April 27, 1861. Honorably mustered out, Aug. 18, 1861. Colonel, 170 OH Infantry, May 14, 1864. Resigned July 1, 1864, "on account of bad health aggravated by the changes and exposures necessary in this service, which has terminated in bealing (sic) in the head and discharges from my ears which if long continued will totally destroy my hearing."
Born: Dec. 15, 1831 Greensburg, PA
Died: Dec. 11, 1906 Alliance, OH
Occupation: Dry goods merchant
Miscellaneous: Resided Hopedale, Harrison Co., OH, to 1898; and Alliance, Stark Co., OH, after 1898
Buried: Hopedale Cemetery, Hopedale, OH
References: Obituary, *Cadiz Republican,* Dec. 20, 1906. Military Service File, National Archives.

Newton Schleich

Brig. Gen., Ohio State Militia, April 23, 1861. Commanded 1 Brigade, Army of Occupation, Department of the Ohio, June–July 24, 1861. Honorably mustered out, July 30, 1861. Colonel, 61 OH Infantry, April 1, 1862. Facing charges of cowardice at the battle of Freeman's Ford, VA, Aug. 22, 1862, he resigned Sept. 23, 1862, because "the relations between myself and some few of the officers of the regiment are such that the public service must be prejudiced by our all remaining in the same regiment."
Born: March 6, 1827 Fairfield Co., OH

Newton Schleich (Massachusetts MOLLUS Collection, USAMHI [Vol. 91, p. 4676]).

Died: Sept. 22, 1879 Lancaster, OH
Occupation: Lawyer
Offices/Honors: Ohio Senate, 1858–62
Miscellaneous: Resided Lancaster, Fairfield Co., OH. Described by Colonel John Beatty (3 OH Infantry) as "a rampant demagogue... He is what might be called a tremendous little man, swears terribly, and imagines that he thereby shows his snap."
Buried: Forest Rose Cemetery, Lancaster, OH
References: Pension File and Military Service File, National Archives. *The Biographical Encyclopedia of Ohio of the Nineteenth Century.* Cincinnati and Philadelphia, 1876. Obituary, *Lancaster Gazette,* Sept. 25, 1879. W. Cooper. *Sketches of the Senators and Representatives in the Fifty-fourth General Assembly of the State of Ohio.* Columbus, OH, 1861. Robert G. Carroon, editor. *From Freeman's Ford to Bentonville: The 61st Ohio Volunteer Infantry.* Shippensburg, PA, 1998. John Beatty. *The Citizen-Soldier; or Memoirs of a Volunteer.* Cincinnati, OH, 1879.

Jonas Schoonover

2 Lieutenant, Co. H, 29 OH Infantry, Oct. 15, 1861. Captain, Co. H, 29 OH Infantry, Nov. 8, 1861. GSW shoulder Cedar Mountain, VA, Aug. 9, 1862. Major, 29 OH Infantry, Jan. 18, 1865. Lieutenant Colonel, 29 OH Infantry, Jan. 28, 1865. *Colonel,* 29 OH Infantry, July 12, 1865. Honorably mustered out, July 13, 1865.
Born: April 28, 1825 Chili, Monroe Co., NY
Died: Aug. 5, 1887 Akron, OH
Occupation: Farmer
Miscellaneous: Resided Northampton, Summit Co., OH; and Akron, Summit Co., OH
Buried: Glendale Cemetery, Akron, OH (Section O, Lot 41)
References: Pension File and Military Service File, National Archives. Obituary, *Akron City Times,* Aug. 10, 1887. *Schoonover Mastertree, Part 1,* compiled by Roger Schoonover and revised by Mary Schoonover, http://www.geocities.com/mfs53211/mastertree1.html. John H. SeCheverell. *Journal History of the 29th Ohio Veteran Volunteers, 1861–65. Its Victories and its Reverses.* Cleveland, OH, 1883.

Charles B. Seidel

Private, Co. I, 1 OH Infantry (3 months), April 17, 1861. Honorably mustered out, Aug. 2, 1861. Captain, Co. E, 3 OH Cavalry, Sept. 24, 1861. Major, 3 OH Cavalry, Jan. 16, 1862. Taken prisoner and paroled, Lexington, KY, Oct. 18, 1862. Lieutenant Colonel, 3 OH Cavalry, June 7, 1863. GSW right hip, Alpine, GA, Sept. 12, 1863. Colonel, 3 OH Cavalry, Sept. 24, 1863. Commanded Post of Columbia, TN, April 16–May 21, 1864. Honorably mustered out, Jan. 18, 1865.
Born: April 10, 1835 Berlin, Germany
Died: March 14, 1916 Lyndon, KY
Occupation: Miller before war. Miller, carriage painter, and U.S. Internal Revenue official after war.
Miscellaneous: Resided Mansfield, Richland Co., OH, to 1868; Louisville, KY; and Lyndon, Jefferson Co., KY

Charles B. Seidel (post-war) (Thomas Crofts. *History of the Service of the 3rd Ohio Veteran Volunteer Cavalry in the War for the Preservation of the Union from 1861–65.* Toledo, Ohio, 1910).

Jonas Schoonover (post-war) (John P. Gurnish Collection).

Buried: Cave Hill Cemetery, Louisville, KY (Section 14, Lot 284)

References: Pension File and Military Service File, National Archives. Obituary, *Louisville Courier-Journal,* March 16, 1916. Thomas Crofts. *History of the Service of the 3rd Ohio Veteran Volunteer Cavalry in the War for the Preservation of the Union from 1861–65.* Toledo, OH, 1910.

Dudley Seward

Sergeant, Co. G, 19 OH Infantry (3 months), April 22, 1861. Honorably mustered out, Aug. 31, 1861. 1 Lieutenant, Co. A, 2 OH Cavalry, Aug. 16, 1861. Captain, Co. A, 2 OH Cavalry, Sept. 10, 1861. Major, 2 OH Cavalry, Sept. 18, 1862. Lieutenant Colonel, 2 OH Cavalry, April 22, 1865. Colonel, 2 OH Cavalry, June 20, 1865. Commanded 4 Sub-District of Missouri, Department of the Missouri, July 1865. Honorably mustered out, Sept. 11, 1865.

Born: Jan. 14, 1819 Utica, NY

Died: May 24, 1882 Akron, OH

Occupation: Captain, 8 U.S. Cavalry, July 28, 1866. Honorably mustered out, Dec. 28, 1870. Claims collector, manufacturer, and justice of the peace in later years.

Offices/Honors: Sheriff, Summit Co., OH, 1853–57

Miscellaneous: Resided Akron, Summit Co., OH

Buried: Glendale Cemetery, Akron, OH (Section C, Lot 550)

References: Pension File and Military Service File, National Archives. Samuel A. Lane. *Fifty Years and Over of Akron and Summit County.* Akron, OH, 1892. Obituary, *Akron Daily Beacon,* May 24, 1882. Letters Received, Appointment, Commission and Personal Branch, Adjutant General's Office, File 3668(ACP)1871, National Archives. Guy V. Henry. *Military Record of Civilian Appointments in the United States Army.* New York City, NY, 1869. Constance Wynn Altshuler. *Cavalry Yellow & Infantry Blue: Army Officers in Arizona Between 1851 and 1886.* Tucson, AZ, 1991.

John Sherman

Colonel, 64 OH Infantry, Sept. 20, 1861. Resigned Dec. 2, 1861, at the urgent request of President Lincoln, to continue as a United States Senator.

Born: May 10, 1823 Lancaster, OH

Died: Oct. 22, 1900 Washington, DC

Occupation: Statesman

Offices/Honors: U.S. House of Representatives, 1855–61. U.S. Senate, 1861–77 and 1881–97. U.S. Secretary of the Treasury, 1877–81. U.S. Secretary of State, 1897–98.

Dudley Seward (photograph by G. W. Manly, Wood's Block, Akron, Ohio; John P. Gurnish Collection).

John Sherman (Brady-Handy Collection, Library of Congress [LC-DIG-cwpbh-03047]).

Miscellaneous: Resided Mansfield, Richland Co., OH; and Washington, DC. Brother of Major Gen. William T. Sherman.

Buried: Mansfield Cemetery, Mansfield, OH (Section OS5, Lot 1104)

References: *Dictionary of American Biography*. Winfield S. Kerr. *John Sherman, His Life and Public Services*. Boston, MA, 1908. John Sherman. *John Sherman's Recollections of Forty Years in the House, Senate and Cabinet: An Autobiography*. Chicago and New York, 1895. Abraham J. Baughman. *History of Richland County, OH, From 1808 to 1908*. Chicago, IL, 1908. Wilbur F. Hinman. *The Story of the Sherman Brigade*. Alliance, OH, 1897.

Edward Siber

Colonel, 37 OH Infantry, Sept. 12, 1861. Commanded 1 Provisional Brigade, District of the Kanawha, Department of the Ohio, Sept.–Dec. 1862. Commanded 3 Brigade, 2 Division, 15 Army Corps, Army of the Tennessee, July 21–Oct. 19, 1863. Commanded Post of Iuka, MS, Oct.–Nov. 1863. Resigned March 23, 1864, due to "failing health" caused by "chronic rheumatism and great nervous debility."

Born: 1820? Prussia

Died: Date and place of death unknown

Other Wars: A captain in the Prussian army, he resigned to fight for freedom in the Schleswig-Holstein army

Occupation: An accomplished German officer, who had seen active service in Prussia and Brazil

Miscellaneous: Resided Cleveland, OH; and Cincinnati, OH (1870)

Buried: Place of burial unknown

References: Military Service File, National Archives. Adolf E. Zucker, editor. *The Forty-Eighters: Political Refugees of the German Revolution of 1848*. New York City, NY, 1950. Wilhelm Kaufmann. *The Germans in the American Civil War*. Translated by Steven Rowan and edited by Don Heinrich Tolzmann with Werner D. Mueller and Robert E. Ward. Carlisle, PA, 1999. Letters Received, Volunteer Service Branch, Adjutant General's Office, File S143(VS)1861, National Archives.

Charles C. Smith

Captain, Co. G, 2 OH Cavalry, Oct. 14, 1861. Colonel, 10 OH Cavalry, Feb. 23, 1863. Commanded 2 Brigade, 3 Cavalry Division, Army of the Cumberland, April 13–July 1, 1864. Commanded Camp Cleveland, OH, Aug. 13, 1864–Jan. 1865. Discharged for disability, Jan. 13, 1865, due to typhoid fever and spinal irritation.

Born: 1829? Niagara Co., NY

Died: April 17, 1889 Norwalk, OH

Occupation: Civil engineer engaged in railroad construction

Miscellaneous: Resided Painesville, Lake Co., OH; and St. Paul, MN

Buried: Woodlawn Cemetery, Norwalk, OH (Section 2, Lot 111, unmarked)

References: Pension File and Military Service File, National Archives. Obituary, *Norwalk Daily Reflector*, April 18, 1889 and April 27, 1889. Obituary, *St. Paul Pioneer Press*, April 18, 1889. Letters Received, Volunteer Service Branch, Adjutant General's Office, File S1932(VS)1863, National Archives. Letters Received, Commission Branch, Adjutant General's Office, File S1987(CB)1864, National Archives. Abram W. Foote. *Foote Family, Comprising the Genealogy and History of Nathaniel Foote of Wethersfield, CT, and His Descendants*. Rutland, VT, 1907.

Joseph Lee Kirby Smith

1 Lieutenant, U.S. Topographical Engineers, Aug. 3, 1861. ADC, Staff of Major Gen. Nathaniel P. Banks, July 25–Aug. 25, 1861. Colonel, 43 OH Infantry, Sept. 28, 1861. Commanded 2 Brigade, 1 Division, Army of the Mississippi, March 4–April 24, 1862. Commanded 1 Brigade, 2 Division, Army of the Mississippi, July 8–Sept. 10, 1862. GSW face and neck, Corinth, MS, Oct. 4, 1862. Bvt. Colonel, USA, Oct. 4, 1862, for gallant and meritorious services at the battle of Corinth, MS.

Born: July 25, 1836 Syracuse, NY

Died: Oct. 12, 1862 DOW Corinth, MS

Education: Graduated U.S. Military Academy, West Point, NY, 1857

Joseph Lee Kirby Smith (written on the back of the photograph, "This is Kirby, our darling, as he appears in his great role, of Laugh-and-grow-fat").

Joseph Lee Kirby Smith (photograph by Henry Payne, (successor to N. E. Lewis), Mount Vernon, Ohio; L. M. Strayer Collection).

Occupation: Regular Army (2 Lieutenant, U.S. Topographical Engineers)
Miscellaneous: Resided Syracuse, NY. Nephew of CSA Gen. Edmund Kirby Smith. Grand nephew of Colonel Francis S. Belton (4 U.S. Artillery).
Buried: Oakwood Cemetery, Syracuse, NY (Section 44, Lots 40–41)
References: John W. Fuller, "Our Kirby Smith," *Sketches of War History*, Vol. 2, Ohio MOLLUS. Cincinnati, OH, 1888. Melatiah Everett Dwight. *The Kirbys of New England*. New York City, NY, 1898. Charles H. Smith. *History of Fuller's Ohio Brigade*. Cleveland, OH, 1909. Whitelaw Reid. *Ohio in the War: Her Statesmen Generals and Soldiers*. Cincinnati, OH, 1868. George W. Cullum. *Biographical Register of the Officers and Graduates of the U.S. Military Academy*. Third Edition. Boston and New York, 1891. Mrs. Sarah Sumner Teall, "Onondaga's Part in the Civil War," *Annual Volume of the Onondaga Historical Association*. Syracuse, NY, 1915. Military Service File, National Archives.

Marcus M. Spiegel

2 Lieutenant, Co. C, 67 OH Infantry, Nov. 13, 1861. Captain, Co. C, 67 OH Infantry, Dec. 23, 1861. Lieutenant Colonel, 120 OH Infantry, Oct. 2, 1862. Colonel, 120 OH Infantry, Feb. 18, 1863. GSW left knee, Vicksburg, MS, May 19, 1863. Shell wound left thigh, Jackson, MS, July 12, 1863. GSW abdomen, May 3, 1864, during capture of the U.S. transport "City Belle," en route from Baton Rouge, LA, to Alexandria, LA.
Born: Dec. 8, 1829 Abenheim, Germany
Died: May 4, 1864 DOW near Cheneyville, LA
Occupation: Dry goods merchant and commission merchant
Miscellaneous: Resided Chicago, IL; East Liberty, Summit Co., OH; and Millersburg, Holmes Co., OH
Buried: Temporarily buried on the bank of the Red River, his body was not recovered, the burial site being lost by the shifting of the river
References: Frank L. Byrne and Jean Powers Soman, editors. *Your True Marcus: The Civil War Letters of a Jewish Colonel*. Kent, OH, 1985. Pension File and Military Service File, National Archives. Harry Simonhoff. *Jewish Participants in the Civil War*. New York City, NY, 1963. Letters Received, Volunteer Service Branch, Adjutant General's Office, File O259(VS)1862, National Archives.

Samuel Harris Steedman

Lieutenant Colonel, 68 OH Infantry, Oct. 1, 1861. Colonel, 68 OH Infantry, Nov. 29, 1861.

Marcus M. Spiegel (Roger D. Hunt Collection, USAMHI [RG98S-CWP155.47]).

Mustered out, July 5, 1862, by direction of the Secretary of War, in response to the following telegram from Governor David Tod, "All the company officers, save two, of the Sixty-eighth regiment O.V.I., have requested their colonel to resign; three of the captains have preferred charges of fraud and neglect of duty against him. I advise that he may be suspended from command forthwith."

Born: Oct. 17, 1803 Northumberland Co., PA
Died: April 8, 1887 Perrysburg, OH
Occupation: Dry goods merchant, contractor on the Wabash and Erie Canal, hotelkeeper, and stone quarryman
Offices/Honors: Ohio House of Representatives, 1850–51. Ohio Senate, 1854–56.
Miscellaneous: Resided Providence, Lucas Co., OH; Grand Rapids, Wood Co., OH; Napoleon, Henry Co., OH; Monclova, Lucas Co., OH; and Perrysburg, Wood Co., OH. Uncle of Major Gen. James B. Steedman.
Buried: Fort Meigs Union Cemetery, Perrysburg, OH (Block F, Lot 5)
References: Obituary, *Perrysburg Journal,* April 15, 1887. Letters Received, Volunteer Service Branch, Adjutant General's Office, File O361(VS) 1862, National Archives. Copy of letter signed by 26 commissioned officers of the 68th Regiment, Ohio Volunteer Infantry, to Colonel Samuel H. Steedman, April 3, 1862, (Series 147-37: 80), Correspondence to the Governor and Adjutant General of Ohio, 1861–66, Ohio Historical Society. Pension File and Military Service File, National Archives. Myron B. Loop. *The Long Road Home: Ten Thousand Miles Through the Confederacy with the 68th Ohio.* Edited by Richard A. Baumgartner. Huntington, WV, 2006. Harvey Scribner, editor. *Memoirs of Lucas County and the City of Toledo.* Madison, WI, 1910.

Leander Stem

Colonel, 101 OH Infantry, Aug. 30, 1862. GSW spine and taken prisoner, Stone's River, TN, Dec. 31, 1862.
Born: Sept. 19, 1825 Carroll Co., MD
Died: Jan. 5, 1863 DOW Murfreesboro, TN
Education: Attended Mount St. Mary's College, Emmitsburg, MD
Occupation: Lawyer
Miscellaneous: Resided Tiffin, Seneca Co., OH; and Green Springs, Sandusky Co., OH
Buried: Green Springs Cemetery, Green Springs, OH
References: John T. Hubbell, editor, "Stand By the Colors: The Civil War Letters of Leander Stem," *Register of the Kentucky Historical Society.* Vol. 73, No. 2-4 (April, July, October 1975). Lewis W. Day. *Story of the One Hundred and First Ohio*

Leander Stem (Sandusky County Kin Hunters Collection, USAMHI [RG98S-CWP144.41]).

Infantry, A Memorial Volume. Cleveland, OH, 1894. John Fitch. *Annals of the Army of the Cumberland.* Philadelphia, PA, 1864. David D. Bigger. *Ohio's Silver-Tongued Orator: Life and Speeches of General William H. Gibson.* Dayton, OH, 1901. Whitelaw Reid. *Ohio in the War: Her Statesmen Generals and Soldiers.* Cincinnati, OH, 1868. Richard L. Manion and Nan Card. *Sandusky County, Ohio, Civil War Soldiers.* Fremont, OH, 1992. Military Service File, National Archives.

Oscar William Sterl

2 Lieutenant, Co. K, 7 OH Infantry (3 months), April 22, 1861. 2 Lieutenant, Co. K, 7 OH Infantry (3 years), June 20, 1861. 1 Lieutenant, Co. F, 7 OH Infantry, Feb. 5, 1862. Resigned April 18, 1862. Captain, Co. A, 104 OH Infantry, Aug. 14, 1862. Major, 104 OH Infantry, Dec. 10, 1862. Lieutenant Colonel, 104 OH Infantry, Jan. 2, 1863. Commanded Post of Knoxville, TN, Jan. 30–March 8, 1864. Colonel, 104 OH Infantry, Aug. 24, 1864. Commanded 1 Brigade, 3 Division, 23 Army Corps, Army of the Ohio, Jan. 15–Feb. 2, 1865. Commanded 1 Brigade, 3 Division, 23 Army Corps, Department of North Carolina, Feb. 9–June 17, 1865. Commanded Post of Wilmington, NC, Feb. 26–March 5, 1865. Honorably mustered out, June 17, 1865.
Born: July 2, 1837 Massillon, OH
Died: Feb. 23, 1895 Rutland, VT

Oscar William Sterl (A. S. Morse, Photographer, Dept. of the Cumberland, Branch of Hqtrs., 25 Cedar St., Nashville, Tennessee; Timothy R. Brookes Collection).

Occupation: Farmer and wholesale hat and cap merchant
Miscellaneous: Resided Cleveland, OH; New York City, NY; and Rutland, Rutland Co., VT
Buried: Evergreen Cemetery, Rutland, VT (Section 20, Lot 2)
References: Pension File and Military Service File, National Archives. Obituary, *Rutland Herald*, Feb. 25, 1895. Letters Received, Volunteer Service Branch, Adjutant General's Office, File O128(VS)1862, National Archives. Nelson A. Pinney. *History of the 104th Regiment Ohio Volunteer Infantry, 1862 to 1865.* Akron, OH, 1886. Lawrence Wilson, editor. *Itinerary of the 7th Ohio Volunteer Infantry, 1861-64.* New York and Washington, 1907.

William Edward Stevens

2 Lieutenant, 78 OH Infantry, Oct. 10, 1861. Captain, Co. A, 77 OH Infantry, Nov. 23, 1861. GSW right foot, Shiloh, TN, April 6, 1862. Major, 77 OH Infantry, April 28, 1863. Lieutenant Colonel, 77 OH Infantry, April 19, 1864. *Colonel*, 77 OH Infantry, March 7, 1866. Honorably mustered out, March 8, 1866.
Born: Nov. 9, 1835 London, England
Died: Sept. 23, 1910 Minneapolis, MN
Occupation: Methodist clergyman and in later years insurance and real estate agent
Miscellaneous: Resided Columbus, Franklin Co., OH; Alton, Madison Co., IL; Moline, Rock Island Co., IL; Port Byron, Rock Island Co., IL; and Minneapolis, MN
Buried: Riverside Cemetery, Moline, IL
References: Obituary, *Minneapolis Morning Tribune*, Sept. 25, 1910. Pension File and Military Service File, National Archives. Letters Received, Volunteer Service Branch, Adjutant General's Office, File S2432(VS)1864, National Archives.

Robert Stevenson

2 Lieutenant, Co. C, 74 OH Infantry, Oct. 10, 1861. 1 Lieutenant, Co. C, 74 OH Infantry, Dec. 23, 1862. Resigned Feb. 10, 1863, due to a severe bronchial affection. Colonel, 154 OH Infantry, May 9, 1864. Honorably mustered out, Sept. 1, 1864.
Born: Feb. 3, 1823 near Xenia, OH
Died: Aug. 25, 1889 near Xenia, OH
Occupation: Farmer
Offices/Honors: Sheriff of Greene Co., OH, 1866-70. Treasurer of Greene Co., OH, 1872-76.
Miscellaneous: Resided Xenia, Greene Co., OH
Buried: Woodland Cemetery, Xenia, OH
References: Obituary, *Xenia Democrat-News*, Aug. 31, 1889. Pension File and Military Service File, National Archives. Theodore W. Blackburn. *Letters from the Front: A Union "Preacher" Regiment (74th Ohio) in the Civil War.* Dayton, OH, 1981. Joseph A. Stipp. *The History and Service of the 154th Ohio Volunteer Infantry.* Toledo, OH, 1896. Michael A. Broadstone, editor. *History of Greene County, Ohio: Its People, Industries and Institutions.* Indianapolis, IN, 1918.

Israel Stough

1 Lieutenant, Co. F, 44 OH Infantry, Sept. 14, 1861. Captain, Co. F, 44 OH Infantry, Sept. 25, 1861. Discharged for disability, Sept. 23, 1863, "suffering from sickness of a typho-malarial character, very severely." Colonel, 153 OH Infantry, May 10, 1864. Taken prisoner and paroled, Old Town, MD, Aug. 2, 1864. Honorably mustered out, Sept. 9, 1864.
Born: Jan. 28, 1829 Warrington Twp., York Co., PA
Died: Sept. 18, 1900 Chicago, IL
Education: Attended Wittenberg College, Springfield, OH
Occupation: Traveling salesman and farmer before war. Farmer, millwright and miller after war.
Miscellaneous: Resided Springfield, Clark Co., OH, before war; Patoka, Gibson Co., IN, 1864-71; Bloomfield, Greene Co., IN, 1872-79; Lyons, Greene Co., IN, 1879-88; and Chicago, IL
Buried: Oakwoods Cemetery, Chicago, IL (Section P, Division 2, Lot 279)

William Edward Stevens (courtesy Robert J. Van Dorn).

Robert Stevenson (post-war) (Joseph A. Stipp. *The History and Service of the 154th Ohio Volunteer Infantry.* Toledo, Ohio, 1896).

References: *History of Greene and Sullivan Counties, IN.* Chicago, IL, 1884. Pension File and Military Service File, National Archives. Letters Received, Volunteer Service Branch, Adjutant General's Office, File S1363(VS)1863, National Archives. Jim Leeke, editor. *A Hundred Days to Richmond.* Bloomington, IN, 1999.

Ogden Street

Captain, Co. C, 11 OH Infantry, July 7, 1861. Lieutenant Colonel, 11 OH Infantry, Sept. 18, 1862. Acting AIG, Staff of Brig. Gen. George Crook, Crook's Brigade, Baird's Division, Army of Kentucky, Department of the Cumberland, April–June, 1863. Acting AIG, 3 Brigade, 4 Division, 14 Army Corps, Army of the Cumberland, June–Aug. 14, 1863. *Colonel,* 11 OH Infantry, Oct. 26, 1863. GSW lower back, Rocky Face Ridge, GA, Feb. 25, 1864. Honorably mustered out, June 21, 1864.

Born: Oct. 18, 1838 Salem, OH
Died: Oct. 17, 1898 Dayton, OH
Education: Attended Haverford (PA) College
Occupation: Clerk and bookkeeper before war. Mechanical engineer, draftsman, and blast furnace superintendent after war.
Miscellaneous: Resided Salem, Columbiana Co., OH; Sheffield, Colbert Co., AL; Seattle, WA; and Orting, Pierce Co., WA
Buried: Dayton National Cemetery, Dayton, OH (Section L, Row 10, Grave 7)
References: Pension File and Military Service File, National Archives. *Roster 11th Ohio Infantry*

Ogden Street (*Roster 11th Ohio Infantry Association, Proceedings 23rd Reunion 1895, Proceedings 24th Reunion 1896.* Dayton, OH, 1896).

Association, Proceedings 25th Reunion 1897, Proceedings 26th Reunion 1898. Dayton, OH, 1898. Henry A. and Mary A. Street. *The Street Genealogy.* Exeter, NH, 1895. Joshua H. Horton and Solomon Teverbaugh. *A History of the 11th Regiment Ohio Volunteer Infantry.* Dayton, OH, 1866. *Biographical Catalog of the Matriculates of Haverford College, 1833–1922.* Philadelphia, PA, 1922.

Hiram Strong

Lieutenant Colonel, 93 OH Infantry, Aug. 5, 1862. Colonel, 93 OH Infantry, Feb. 22, 1863. GSW right shoulder, Chickamauga, GA, Sept. 19, 1863.

Born: Oct. 28, 1825 Centerville, OH
Died: Oct. 7, 1863 DOW Nashville, TN
Education: Graduated Miami University, Oxford, OH, 1846
Occupation: Lawyer
Miscellaneous: Resided Dayton, OH
Buried: Woodland Cemetery, Dayton, OH (Section 87, Lot 272)
References: *History of Montgomery County, OH.* Chicago, IL, 1882. The Hiram Strong Collection, Dayton (OH) Metro Library. John F. Edgar. *Pioneer Life in Dayton and Vicinity, 1796–1840.* Dayton, OH, 1896. *History of Dayton, OH.* Dayton, OH, 1889. William Sumner Dodge. *History of the Old Second Division, Army of the Cumberland.* Chicago, IL, 1864. Charlotte Reeve Conover. *The Story of Dayton.* Dayton, OH, 1917. *The Alumni and Former Student Catalogue of Miami University, 1809–1892.* Oxford, OH, 1892. Military Service File, National Archives.

Peter Tyrer Swaine

Captain, 15 U.S. Infantry, May 14, 1861. Colonel, 99 OH Infantry, Sept. 4, 1862. Commanded 2 Brigade, 1 Division, Army of Kentucky, Department of the Ohio, Oct. 1862. Commanded 2 Brigade, 3 Division, Army of Kentucky, Department of the Ohio, Oct.–Nov. 1862. GSW right arm, Stone's River, TN, Jan. 2, 1863. Commanded Post of Cincinnati, OH, Feb. 3–April 21, 1864. Commanded 4 Brigade, 2 Division, 23 Army Corps, Army of the Ohio, June 23–Aug. 11, 1864. Commanded Post of Covington and Newport, KY, Sept. 12, 1864–Feb. 1865. Honorably mustered out of volunteer service, Dec. 31, 1864, "having been rendered supernumerary by reason of the consolidation of the 50th Ohio Infantry Volunteers with the 99th Ohio Infantry Volunteers." Bvt. Colonel, USA, March 13, 1865, for faithful and meritorious services during the rebellion.

Born: Jan. 21, 1831 New York City, NY
Died: May 9, 1904 Los Nietos, CA
Education: Graduated U.S. Military Academy, West Point, NY, 1852
Occupation: Regular Army (Colonel, 22 U.S. Infantry, retired Jan. 21, 1895)
Miscellaneous: Resided Los Nietos, Los Angeles Co., CA
Buried: Rosedale Cemetery, Los Angeles, CA (Section I, Lot 97)
References: William H. Powell and Edward Shippen, editors. *Officers of the Army and Navy (Regular) Who Served in the Civil War.* Philadelphia, PA, 1892. Kevin B. McCray. *A Shouting of Orders: A History of the 99th Ohio Volunteer Infantry Regiment.* N.p., 2003. George W. Cullum. *Biographical Register of the Officers and Graduates of the U.S. Military Academy.* Third Edition. Boston and New York, 1891. *Society of the Army of the Cumberland. Thirty-second Reunion, Indianapolis, IN, Sept. 20, 21, 1904.* Cincinnati, OH, 1905. Obituary circular, Whole No. 760, California MOLLUS. Obituary, *Los Angeles Times,* May 10, 1904. Pension File and Military Service File, National Archives. Letters Received, Commission Branch, Adjutant General's Office, File S2102(CB)1865, National Archives.

Jonah R. Taylor

Colonel, 50 OH Infantry, Aug. 23, 1862. Facing charges of cowardice at Perryville, KY, Oct. 8, 1862, he resigned Oct. 16, 1862, "for the reason, my inability to command the regiment." In accepting his resignation, Major Gen. Alexander McD. McCook commented, "Col. Taylor should leave camp as soon as possible, and if I had confidence that a

Hiram Strong (Charlotte Reeve Conover. *The Story of Dayton.* Dayton, Ohio, 1917.

Peter Tyrer Swaine (1881) (G. W. Pach, Photographer, No. 841 Broadway, New York; Archibald Gracie. *The Truth About Chickamauga*. Boston and New York, 1911).

Oliver Perry Taylor (post-war) (Edwin S. Rhodes. *The First Centennial Atlas of Tuscarawas County, OH*. New Philadelphia, Ohio, 1908).

volunteer court would do him justice and sentence him to death for conduct on the 8th instant, I would have him tried, ... not having such confidence, I hope that he may be sent out of the camp at once."

Born: April 10, 1819 Cincinnati, OH
Died: Nov. 7, 1897 Chicago, IL
Occupation: Brick layer and contractor before war. Real estate operator, silver miner, and contractor after war.
Miscellaneous: Resided Cincinnati, OH, before war; Saginaw, Saginaw Co., MI, 1863–69; Omaha, Douglas Co., NE, 1869–75; Chicago, IL, 1875–87 and 1891–97; Wichita, Sedgwick Co., KS, 1887–91
Buried: Mount Olivet Cemetery, Chicago, IL (Block 34, Lot 232, unmarked)
References: Pension File and Military Service File, National Archives. Letters Received, Volunteer Service Branch, Adjutant General's Office, File T193(VS)1864, National Archives. *Portrait and Biographical Album of Sedgwick County, KS*. Chicago, IL, 1888. Death notice, *Chicago Times-Herald*, Nov. 10, 1897.

Oliver Perry Taylor

Colonel, 161 OH Infantry, May 9, 1864. Honorably mustered out, Sept. 2, 1864.

Born: April 6, 1831 New Philadelphia, OH
Died: May 14, 1914 New Philadelphia, OH
Education: Attended Franklin College, New Athens, OH. Graduated Washington College, Washington, PA, 1850.
Occupation: Lawyer and hardware merchant
Offices/Honors: Judge of Probate Court, Tuscarawas Co., OH, 1861–67
Miscellaneous: Resided New Philadelphia, Tuscarawas Co., OH
Buried: Fair Avenue Cemetery, New Philadelphia, OH (Section A, Lot 26)
References: Edwin S. Rhodes. *The First Centennial Atlas of Tuscarawas County, OH*. New Philadelphia, OH, 1908. Obituary, *Ohio Democrat and Times*, May 21, 1914. Pension File, National Archives.

William Henry Harrison Taylor

Colonel, 5 OH Cavalry, Aug. 26, 1861. Chief of Cavalry, Staff of Brig. Gen. Jeremiah C. Sullivan, District of Jackson, 16 Army Corps, Department of the Tennessee, Dec. 1862. Chief of Cavalry, Staff of Major Gen. Stephen A. Hurlbut, 16 Army Corps, Army of the Tennessee, June 11–July 24, 1863. Resigned Aug. 11, 1863, since "I am unfit for active military service" due to "chronic rheumatism of the spinal column in connection with acute disorder of the kidneys."

William Henry Harrison Taylor.

Born: Nov. 28, 1813 Richmond, VA
Died: Jan. 30, 1894 St. Paul, MN
Occupation: Private Secretary to President William Henry Harrison and, after his death, manager of the Harrison estate
Offices/Honors: Postmaster, Cincinnati, OH, 1841–45 and 1866–67. Minnesota State Librarian, 1877–94.
Miscellaneous: Resided North Bend, Hamilton Co., OH, to 1867; St. Paul, MN, 1867–94. Grand nephew of President William Henry Harrison, whose youngest daughter (Anna Tuthill Harrison) he married. Uncle of CSA Gen. Thomas T. Munford and Colonel James Findlay Harrison (11 OH Infantry).
Buried: Lakewood Cemetery, Minneapolis, MN (Section 3, Lot 81)
References: *The United States Biographical Dictionary and Portrait Gallery of Eminent and Self-Made Men.* Minnesota volume. New York and Chicago, 1879. Obituary, *St. Paul Pioneer Press,* Jan. 30, 1894. Pension File and Military Service File, National Archives. Reginald B. Henry. *Genealogies of the Families of the Presidents.* Rutland, VT, 1935. John A. Vinton. *The Symmes Memorial.* Boston, MA, 1873. Warren Upham and Mrs. Rose Barteau Dunlap, compilers. *Minnesota Biographies, 1655–1912. Minnesota Historical Society Collections, Vol. 14.* St. Paul, MN, 1912.

John T. Toland

Lieutenant Colonel, 34 OH Infantry, Sept. 2, 1861. Colonel, 34 OH Infantry, May 14, 1862. Commanded 1 Brigade, District of the Kanawha, Department of the Ohio, Sept. 25–Nov. 5, 1862. Commanded 2 Brigade, District of the Kanawha, Department of the Ohio, Jan.–March, 1863. Commanded 3 Brigade, 3 Division, 8 Army Corps, Department of West Virginia, July 8–18, 1863. GSW left breast, Wytheville, VA, July 18, 1863.
Born: Sept. 25, 1825 Ireland
Died: July 18, 1863 KIA Wytheville, VA
Occupation: Merchant dealing in dental supplies
Miscellaneous: Resided Lancaster, Fairfield Co., OH; and Cincinnati, OH
Buried: North Sixth Street Catholic Cemetery, Burlington, IA (Lot 263)
References: Whitelaw Reid. *Ohio in the War: Her Statesmen Generals and Soldiers.* Cincinnati, OH, 1868. Obituary, *Cincinnati Daily Commercial,* July 25, 1863. Pension File and Military Service

John T. Toland (L. M. Strayer Collection).

File, National Archives. *Roster Chace Mac-acheek Piatt Zouaves, 34th Regiment Ohio Veteran Volunteer Infantry.* N.p., 1906.

William Ransom Tolles

Captain, Co. B, 41 OH Infantry, Aug. 20, 1861. Lieutenant Colonel, 105 OH Infantry, Aug. 11, 1862. *Colonel,* 105 OH Infantry, July 10, 1863. Resigned Jan. 29, 1864, due to chronic diarrhea, "which disease has so deranged my system as to make it impossible for me longer to render effective service to the Government either in the camp or field."

Born: April 10, 1823 Watertown, CT
Died: Dec. 11, 1893 San Bernardino, CA
Occupation: Traveling salesman before war. Lumber merchant, rancher and fruit grower after war.
Miscellaneous: Resided Burton, Geauga Co., OH, to 1867; Breedsville, Van Buren Co., MI, 1867–74; and San Bernardino, San Bernardino Co., CA, 1874–93
Buried: Welton Cemetery, Burton, OH

Top: William Ransom Tolles (post-war) (Albion W. Tourgee. *The Story of a Thousand: Being a History of the Service of the 105th Ohio Volunteer Infantry.* Buffalo, New York, 1896). *Above:* William Ransom Tolles (Albion W. Tourgee. *The Story of a Thousand: Being a History of the Service of the 105th Ohio Volunteer Infantry.* Buffalo, New York, 1896).

References: *Illustrated History of Southern California, Embracing the Counties of San Diego, San Bernardino, Los Angeles and Orange.* Chicago, IL, 1890. Obituary, *San Bernardino Weekly Times-Index,* Dec. 15, 1893. Albion W. Tourgee. *The Story of a Thousand: Being a History of the Service of the 105th Ohio Volunteer Infantry.* Buffalo, NY, 1896. Pension File and Military Service File, National Archives. William M. Tolles and Alyce J. Morow. *Tolles in America.* Baltimore, MD, 1997. Obituary, *Geauga Republican,* Dec. 27, 1893. *http://www.illustratedredlands.com/Individuals/TollesWR.htm.*

William Henry Trimble

Lieutenant Colonel, 60 OH Infantry, Dec. 17, 1861. Colonel, 60 OH Infantry, Feb. 25, 1862. Commanded 2 Brigade, Post of Harper's Ferry, 8 Army Corps, Middle Department, Sept. 5–15, 1862. Taken prisoner and paroled, Harper's Ferry, WV, Sept. 15, 1862. Honorably mustered out, Nov. 13, 1862.

Born: Oct. 22, 1811 Hillsboro, OH
Died: Feb. 7, 1883 Hillsboro, OH
Education: Attended Miami University, Oxford, OH
Occupation: Farmer and lawyer
Offices/Honors: Ohio House of Representatives, 1845–48
Miscellaneous: Resided Hillsboro, Highland Co., OH. Son of Ohio Governor Allen Trimble.
Buried: Hillsboro Cemetery, Hillsboro, OH (Section C, Lot 150)
References: *Biographical Cyclopedia and Portrait Gallery with an Historical Sketch of the State of Ohio.* Vol. 4. Cincinnati, OH, 1887. *Biographical Encyclopedia of Ohio of the Nineteenth Century.* Cincinnati and Philadelphia, 1876. Obituary, *Hillsboro Gazette,* Feb. 15, 1883. John F. Trimble. *Trimble Families of America.* Parsons, WV, 1973. Pension File and Military Service File, National Archives. Paul R. Teetor. *A Matter of Hours: Treason at Harper's Ferry.* Rutherford, NJ, 1982.

Edward Nathan Upton

1 Lieutenant, Co. D, 46 OH Infantry, Sept. 10, 1861. Captain, Co. D, 46 OH Infantry, April 7, 1862. Acting ADC, Staff of Brig. Gen. John M. Corse, 2 Brigade, 4 Division, 15 Army Corps, Army of the Tennessee, Sept. 9, 1863–Feb. 1864. Acting AIG, 2 Brigade, 4 Division, 15 Army Corps, Army of the Tennessee, Feb.–April 29, 1864. Acting AAG, Staff of Brig. Gen. Charles C. Walcutt, 2 Brigade, 4 Division, 15 Army Corps, Army of the Tennessee, April 29–Sept. 14, 1864. Major, 46 OH Infantry, Aug. 19, 1864. Lieutenant Colonel, 46 OH Infantry, Dec. 22, 1864. *Colonel,* 46 OH In-

William Henry Trimble (R. W. Addis, Photographer, 308 Penna Avenue, Washington, DC; Nicholas Picerno Collection).

Edward Nathan Upton (Nona P. Dickson Collection, USAMHI [RG98S-CWP149.94]).

fantry, July 16, 1865. Honorably mustered out, July 22, 1865.
Born: Sept. 27, 1837 Auburn, NY
Died: April 24, 1898 Effingham, IL
Occupation: Printer and mechanic before war. Farmer and traveling salesman after war.
Miscellaneous: Resided Columbus, Franklin Co., OH, and Ewington, Effingham Co., IL, before war; Watson Twp., Effingham Co., IL, and St. Louis, MO, after war
Buried: Rinehart Cemetery, Effingham, IL
References: William H. Perrin, editor. *History of Effingham County, IL.* Chicago, IL, 1883. Newton Bateman and Paul Selby, editors. *Illinois Historical; Effingham County Biographical.* Chicago, IL, 1910. John A. Vinton. *The Upton Memorial.* Bath, ME, 1874. Pension File and Military Service File, National Archives. Letters Received, Volunteer Service Branch, Adjutant General's Office, Files U42(VS)1865 and W1875(VS)1865, National Archives.

Nelson Holmes Van Vorhes

1 Lieutenant, Co. C, 3 OH Infantry (3 months), May 4, 1861. Honorably mustered out, Aug. 21, 1861. 1 Lieutenant, RQM, 18 OH Infantry, Sept. 13, 1861. Colonel, 92 OH Infantry, Sept. 2, 1862. Commanded 1 Brigade, 2 Kanawha Division, Department of the Ohio, Dec. 30, 1862–Jan. 7, 1863. Resigned March 22, 1863, due to disability caused by typhoid pneumonia.
Born: Jan. 23, 1822 Washington Co., PA
Died: Dec. 4, 1882 Athens, OH
Occupation: Newspaper editor before war. Hardware merchant after war.
Offices/Honors: Ohio House of Representatives, 1850–54, 1856–60, 1870–74. Speaker of Ohio House of Representatives, 1856–58, 1872–74. U.S. House of Representatives, 1875–79.
Miscellaneous: Resided Athens, Athens Co., OH
Buried: West Union Street Cemetery, Athens, OH (Section 3, Lot 63)
References: Obituary, *Athens Messenger,* Dec. 7, 1882. *History of Hocking Valley, OH.* Chicago, IL, 1883. W. Darwin Crabb. *Biographical Sketches of the State Officers and of the Members of the 60th General Assembly of the State of Ohio.* Columbus, OH, 1872. Charles F. Ritter and Jon L. Wakelyn. *American Legislative Leaders, 1850–1910.* Westport, CT, 1989. James L. Harrison, compiler. *Biographical Directory of the American Congress, 1774–1949.*

Nelson Holmes Van Vorhes (post-war) (Brady-Handy Collection, Library of Congress [LC-DIG-cwpbh-04576]).

Washington, DC, 1950. Pension File and Military Service File, National Archives.

Joseph W. Vance

Colonel, 96 OH Infantry, Aug. 19, 1862. Commanded 2 Brigade, 2 Division, Army of Kentucky, Department of the Ohio, Sept. 17–Oct. 1862. Commanded 2 Brigade, 4 Division, 13 Army Corps, Department of the Gulf, March 14–April 8, 1864. GSW breast, Sabine Cross Roads, LA, April 8, 1864.

Born: July 9, 1809 Washington Co., PA
Died: April 8, 1864 KIA Sabine Cross Roads, LA
Occupation: Lawyer
Miscellaneous: Resided Mount Vernon, Knox Co., OH
Buried: Mound View Cemetery, Mount Vernon, OH (Section 16, Lot 175)
References: Norman N. Hill, Jr., compiler. *History of Knox County, OH: Its Past and Present.* Mount Vernon, OH, 1881. *The Biographical Record of Knox County, OH.* Chicago, IL, 1902. W. J. Park. *Biographical Sketch of the Park Family of Washington County, PA.* Covington, KY, 1880. Joseph T. Woods. *Services of the 96th Ohio Volunteers.* Toledo, OH, 1874. Pension File and Military Service File, National Archives.

William Henry Vodrey

Colonel, 143 OH Infantry, May 13, 1864. Honorably mustered out, Sept. 13, 1864.

Born: Aug. 1, 1832 Louisville, KY
Died: Oct. 23, 1896 East Liverpool, OH
Occupation: Pottery manufacturer
Miscellaneous: Resided East Liverpool, Columbiana Co., OH
Buried: Riverview Cemetery, East Liverpool, OH (Section 19, Lot 22)
References: William B. McCord, editor. *History of Columbiana County, OH.* Chicago, IL, 1905. *History of the Upper Ohio Valley.* Madison, WI, 1891. Harold B. Barth. *History of Columbiana County, OH.* Topeka and Indianapolis, 1926. Obituary, *East Liverpool Tribune,* Oct. 24, 1896. Pension File and Military Service File, National Archives.

William Wallace

Captain, Co. B, 15 OH Infantry (3 months), April 27, 1861. Honorably mustered out, Aug. 30, 1861. Major, 15 OH Infantry (3 years), Sept. 12, 1861. Accidental GSW left foot, Munfordville, KY, Jan. 7, 1862. Lieutenant Colonel, 15 OH Infantry, Aug. 11, 1862. Colonel, 15 OH Infantry, Oct. 25, 1862. Commanded 1 Brigade, 2 Division, Right Wing, 14 Army Corps, Army of the Cumberland, Dec. 31, 1862. Commanded 1 Brigade, 2 Division, 20 Army Corps, Army of the Cumberland, Feb. 20–March 5, 1863. Commanded Camp Chase Military Prison, Columbus, OH, May 1863–Jan. 26, 1864. Shell wound breast, Pickett's Mills, near Dallas, GA, May 27, 1864. Discharged for disability, July 19, 1864, due to "wounds received in action."

Born: April 20, 1828 York, PA
Died: Feb. 7, 1886 Philadelphia, PA
Occupation: Lawyer before war. U.S. Customs official after war, serving as gauger of the Port of Philadelphia, 1869–86.
Miscellaneous: Resided Martinsville, Belmont Co., OH, before war; and Philadelphia, PA, after war
Buried: West Laurel Hill Cemetery, Bala-Cynwyd, PA (Summit Section, Lot 165)
References: Pension File and Military Service File, National Archives. Obituary, *Philadelphia Public Ledger,* Feb. 9, 1886. Obituary, *Philadelphia Inquirer,* Feb. 9, 1886. Letters Received, Volunteer Service Branch, Adjutant General's Office, File M2392(VS)1863, National Archives. Alexis Cope. *The 15th Ohio Volunteers and Its Campaigns, War of 1861–65.* Columbus, OH, 1916.

Joseph W. Vance (Reeve & Watts, Photographers, No. 57 High Str., Over Post Office, Columbus, Ohio; courtesy The Horse Soldier, Gettysburg, Pennsylvania).

William H. Vodrey (pre-war) (courtesy the East Liverpool Historical Society and Timothy R. Brookes).

William Wallace (Alexis Cope. *The 15th Ohio Volunteers and Its Campaigns, War of 1861–65*. Columbus, Ohio, 1916).

James Washburn

Captain, Co. B, 25 OH Infantry, June 10, 1861. Resigned July 7, 1862, due to "the failing health of my wife and present sickness of other members of my family, which requires my immediate presence at home." Colonel, 116 OH Infantry, Aug. 22, 1862. Commanded 2 Brigade, Cheat Mountain Division, District of West Virginia, Department of the Ohio, Oct. 28, 1862–Jan. 1863. Commanded Post of Romney, WV, Jan.–Feb. 1863. GSW head, destroying sight in left eye, Snickers Ferry, VA, July 18, 1864. Commanded Post of Wheeling, WV, Nov. 7, 1864–July 5, 1865. Honorably mustered out, July 5, 1865.

Born: Aug. 15, 1821 Manlius, NY
Died: May 12, 1898 Richland Center, WI
Occupation: House joiner and carpenter before war. Farmer after war.
Offices/Honors: Wisconsin Assembly, 1882
Miscellaneous: Resided Woodsfield, Monroe Co., OH, to 1868; Rockbridge and Richland Center, Richland Co., WI, after 1868
Buried: Richland Center Cemetery, Richland Center, WI (Old Plat 1, Lot 47)
References: *History of Crawford and Richland Counties, WI.* Springfield, IL, 1884. Obituary, *Richland Center Republican Observer,* May 19, 1898. Pension File and Military Service File, National Archives. Thomas F. Wildes. *Record of the 116th Regiment Ohio Infantry Volunteers in the War of the Rebellion.* Sandusky, OH, 1884. Letters Received, Volunteer Service Branch, Adjutant General's Office, File W2921(VS)1864, National Archives.

Daniel Weber

1 Sergeant, Co. D, 39 OH Infantry, July 20, 1861. 2 Lieutenant, Co. D, 39 OH Infantry, July

James Washburn (Massachusetts MOLLUS Collection, USAMHI [Vol. 73, p. 3637]).

Daniel Weber (Album of Portraits of Companions of the Commandery of the State of Ohio MOLLUS. Cincinnati, Ohio, 1893).

31, 1861. 1 Lieutenant, Co. D, 39 OH Infantry, Sept. 1, 1861. 1 Lieutenant, Adjutant, 39 OH Infantry, April 12, 1862. Captain, Co. I, 39 OH Infantry, March 7, 1864. Acting AAG, Staff of Brig. Gen. John W. Fuller, 4 Division, 16 Army Corps, Army of the Tennessee, July 17–Sept. 17, 1864. Acting ADC, Staff of Brig. Gen. John W. Fuller, 1 Division, 17 Army Corps, Army of the Tennessee, Sept. 17–Oct. 1864. Major, 39 OH Infantry, Jan. 29, 1865. Lieutenant Colonel, 39 OH Infantry, Feb. 10, 1865. Colonel, 39 OH Infantry, May 18, 1865. Honorably mustered out, July 9, 1865.

Born: Dec. 13, 1833 Lancaster, PA
Died: Oct. 7, 1892 Cincinnati, OH
Occupation: Blacksmith before war. U.S. Customs official, clerk of Probate Court, and live stock commission merchant after war.
Offices/Honors: Sheriff of Hamilton Co., OH, 1869–70
Miscellaneous: Resided Cincinnati, OH
Buried: Spring Grove Cemetery, Cincinnati, OH (Section 17, Lot 25)
References: Obituary Circular, Whole No. 230, Ohio MOLLUS. Obituary, *Cincinnati Commercial Gazette*, Oct. 8, 1892. Charles H. Smith. *History of Fuller's Ohio Brigade*. Cleveland, OH, 1909. *Report of the Proceedings of the Society of the Army of the Tennessee at the Twenty-Fourth Meeting*. Cincinnati, OH, 1893. Henry A. Ford and Mrs. Kate B. Ford, compilers. *History of Cincinnati, OH*. Cleveland, OH, 1881. Pension File and Military Service File, National Archives.

George Penny Webster

Major, 25 OH Infantry, June 28, 1861. Lieutenant Colonel, 25 OH Infantry, May 16, 1862. Resigned July 30, 1862, to accept promotion. Colonel, 98 OH Infantry, Aug. 8, 1862. Commanded 34 Brigade, 10 Division, 1 Army Corps, Army of the Ohio, Sept.–Oct. 1862. GSW right hip and bowels, Perryville, KY, Oct. 8, 1862.

Born: Dec. 24, 1824 near Middletown, OH
Died: Oct. 9, 1862 DOW Perryville, KY
Other Wars: Mexican War (Sergeant Major, 1 OH Infantry)
Occupation: Lawyer
Miscellaneous: Resided Steubenville, Jefferson Co., OH. His widow Mary married Colonel James A. Jones (25 OH Infantry).
Buried: Union Cemetery, Steubenville, OH (Section K, Lot 35)
References: Whitelaw Reid. *Ohio in the War: Her Statesmen Generals and Soldiers.* Cincinnati, OH, 1868. John A. Caldwell. *History of Belmont and Jefferson Counties, OH.* Wheeling, WV, 1880.

George Penny Webster (photograph by Partridge's Gallery, Wheeling, West Virginia; courtesy Richard A. Baumgartner).

History of the Upper Ohio Valley. Madison, WI, 1891. "Death of Col. Webster," *Steubenville Daily Herald,* Oct. 8, 1897. Pension File and Military Service File, National Archives.

Charles Whittlesey

Colonel, Assistant Quartermaster General of Ohio, April 17, 1861. Chief Engineer, District of the Kanawha, Department of the Ohio, July 16–Aug. 10, 1861. Colonel, 20 OH Infantry (3 years), Aug. 21, 1861. Chief Engineer, Department of the Ohio, Sept. 23–Dec. 5, 1861. Commanded 3 Brigade, 3 Division, District of West Tennessee, Feb. 17–April 19, 1862. Resigned April 19, 1862, since "my physical constitution, which was never robust, is being permanently injured by the exposures of service," and since "my wife is about to undergo a capital surgical operation, which will probably prove fatal to her." Assistant to Major James H. Simpson, Chief Topographical Engineer, Department of the Ohio, Sept. 6–Oct. 7, 1862.

Born: Oct. 5, 1808 Southington, CT
Died: Oct. 18, 1886 Cleveland, OH
Education: Graduated U.S. Military Academy, West Point, NY, 1831
Other Wars: Black Hawk War (1832)
Occupation: Civil and mining engineer best known for his extensive geological explorations
Buried: Lake View Cemetery, Cleveland, OH (Section 14, Lot 4)
References: Maurice Joblin, publisher. *Cleveland, Past and Present; Its Representative Men.* Cleveland, OH, 1869. *Memorial of Colonel Charles Whittlesey, Late President of the Western Reserve Historical Society.* Cleveland, OH, 1887. *Biographical Encyclopedia of Ohio of the Nineteenth Century.* Cincinnati and Philadelphia, 1876. *Annual Reunion,* Association of the Graduates of the USMA, 1887. George W. Cullum. *Biographical Register of the Officers and Graduates of the U.S. Military Academy.* Third Edition. Boston and New York, 1891. Pension File and Military Service File, National Archives. Obituary, *New York Times,* Oct. 19, 1886. Charles Whittlesey. *War Memoranda. Cheat River to the Tennessee, 1861–62.* Cleveland, OH, 1884.

Charles Whittlesey (photograph by J. M. Greene, Cleveland, Ohio; L. M. Strayer Collection).

Arthur Tappan Wilcox

2 Lieutenant, Co. E, 7 OH Infantry (3 months), April 25, 1861. 1 Lieutenant, Co. E, 7 OH Infantry (3 years), June 17, 1861. Taken prisoner, Cross Lanes, WV, Aug. 26, 1861. Confined at Richmond, VA, and Charleston, SC. Paroled Aug. 17, 1862. Captain, Co. D, 7 OH Infantry, July 9, 1862. Captain, Co. E, 7 OH Infantry, March 10, 1863. Honorably mustered out, July 6, 1864. Colonel, 177 OH Infantry, Sept. 23, 1864. Commanded 2 Brigade, 3 Division, 23 Army Corps, Department

Arthur Tappan Wilcox (photograph by Union Photograph Gallery at C. V. Old's Bookstore, Sandusky, Ohio; Michael W. Waskul Collection).

of North Carolina, Feb. 25–March 6, 1865. Honorably mustered out, June 24, 1865.
Born: Dec. 28, 1834 Lorain Co., OH
Died: Oct. 24, 1902 Port Limon, Costa Rica
Education: Graduated University of Michigan, Ann Arbor, MI, 1859. Graduated University of Michigan Law School, Ann Arbor, MI, 1861.
Occupation: Lawyer and civil engineer engaged in railroad construction
Offices/Honors: Ohio House of Representatives, 1866
Miscellaneous: Resided Huron, Erie Co., OH; and Monroe, Monroe Co., MI
Buried: Limon Cemetery, Port Limon, Costa Rica
References: Lawrence Wilson, editor. *Itinerary of the 7th Ohio Volunteer Infantry, 1861–64.* New York and Washington, 1907. George L. Wood. *The Seventh Regiment: A Record.* New York City, NY, 1865. William Raimond Baird. *Betas of Achievement.* New York City, NY, 1914. Obituary, *The Michigan Alumnus,* Vol. 11, No. 1 (October 1904). Obituary, *Norwalk Daily Reflector,* Nov. 24, 1902. Obituary, *Monroe Democrat,* Oct. 31, 1902. Dispatches from U.S. Consuls in San Jose, Costa Rica, National Archives. Isaac N. Demmon, editor. *General Catalogue of Officers and Students University of Michigan, 1837–1911.* Ann Arbor, MI, 1912. Military Service File, National Archives. Letters Received, Volunteer Service Branch, Adjutant General's Office, File W834(VS)1862, National Archives. http://sanduskyhistory.blogspot.com/2009/11/colonel-arthur-t-wilcox.html.

Harrison Wilson

Corporal, Co. I, 25 OH Infantry, June 26, 1861. 2 Lieutenant, Co. I, 20 OH Infantry, Dec. 7, 1861. 1 Lieutenant, Co. I, 20 OH Infantry, Feb. 11, 1862. Captain, Co. E, 20 OH Infantry, Feb. 16, 1863. Captain, Co. F, 20 OH Infantry, May 6, 1863. Awarded 17 Army Corps, Department of the Tennessee, Medal of Honor, April 4, 1864, inscribed "Fort Donelson, Shiloh, Raymond, Champion Hills, Vicksburg." Major, 20 OH Infantry, Jan. 6, 1865. Lieutenant Colonel, 20 OH Infantry, Jan. 11, 1865. *Colonel,* 20 OH Infantry, June 21, 1865. Honorably mustered out, July 15, 1865.
Born: March 15, 1841 Cadiz, OH
Died: Nov. 28, 1929 Ojai, CA
Education: Attended Ohio University, Athens, OH
Occupation: Lawyer and judge
Offices/Honors: Circuit Court Judge, 1895–1909
Miscellaneous: Resided Harriettsville, Noble Co., OH, before war; Sidney, Shelby Co., OH, 1867–1909; Columbus, OH, 1909–12; and Ojai,

Harrison Wilson (USAMHI [RG98S-CWP20.71]).

Ventura Co., CA, 1912–29. Brother-in-law of Colonel John C. Fry (20 OH Infantry).
Buried: Graceland Cemetery, Sidney, OH (Section 2, Lot 21)
References: Harrison Wilson. *Memoirs of the Civil War.* N.p., 1923. Obituary, *Sidney Daily News,* Nov. 29, 1929. A.B.C. Hitchcock. *History of Shelby County, OH, and Representative Citizens.* Chicago, IL, 1913. *History of Noble County, OH.* Chicago, IL, 1887. Pension File and Military Service File, National Archives. John C. Hover, et al., editors. *Memoirs of the Miami Valley.* Chicago, IL, 1919. Obituary Circular, Whole No. 1320, Ohio MOLLUS. Stanley S. Phillips. *Civil War Corps Badges and Other Related Awards, Badges, Medals of the Period.* Lanham, MD, 1982.

Lewis Wilson

Colonel, 2 OH Infantry, April 17, 1861. Resigned June 20, 1861, to accept regular army commission as Captain, 19 U.S. Infantry, dated May 14, 1861. Commanded Post of Tullahoma, TN, July–Aug. 1862. Facing charges of insubordination preferred by his superior officer, Brig. Gen. John H. King, he resigned July 28, 1864, claiming "almost total loss of eyesight" caused by night blindness contracted during the Atlanta campaign.
Born: Jan. 6, 1830 Cincinnati, OH
Died: Dec. 8, 1892 Maineville, OH

Education: Attended Woodward College, Cincinnati, OH

Occupation: Carpenter, joiner, and police superintendent before war. Policeman and health officer after war.

Offices/Honors: Chief of Police, Cincinnati, OH, 1859–61

Miscellaneous: Resided Cincinnati, OH, to 1884; Xenia, Greene Co., OH; and Maineville, Warren Co., OH. An authority on the workings of secret orders, he served as Grand Reporter of the Knights of Honor of the State of Ohio, 1884–92.

Buried: Maineville Cemetery, Maineville, OH

References: Pension File, National Archives. Obituary, *Cincinnati Commercial Gazette,* Dec. 10, 1892. John A. Gano, et al. *Old Woodward Memorial.* Cincinnati, OH, 1884. George M. Roe, editor. *Our Police, A History of the Cincinnati Police Force.* Cincinnati, OH, 1890. Letters Received, Adjutant General's Office, File W519(AGO)1861, National Archives. Letters Received, Commission Branch, Adjutant General's Office, File W734(CB)1864, National Archives. Mark W. Johnson. *That Body of Brave Men: The U.S. Regular Infantry and the Civil War in the West.* Cambridge, MA, 2003.

Robert B. Wilson

Colonel, 140 OH Infantry, May 10, 1864. Honorably mustered out, Sept. 3, 1864.

Born: Oct. 23, 1832 PA

Died: March 21, 1882 New York City, NY (committed suicide by drowning)

Occupation: Manager of the Excelsior Salt Works, Pomeroy, OH, before war. Merchant and mining company executive after war.

Miscellaneous: Resided Salisbury Twp., Meigs Co., OH; and New York City, NY

Buried: Gravel Hill Pioneer Cemetery, Middleport, OH

References: Pension File and Military Service File, National Archives. Obituary, *Meigs County Telegraph,* March 29, 1882. "Not a Murder. Identification of the Drowned Man With the Mysterious Note and Five Thousand Dollars in Stock — Suicide While Drunk," *New York Herald,* March 24, 1882.

John Fox Wiltsee

Colonel, 2 OH Volunteer Militia, Sept. 4, 1862. Honorably mustered out, Oct. 4, 1862.

Born: June 15, 1823 Little Egg Harbor, NJ

Died: March 29, 1899 Cincinnati, OH

Education: Attended Woodward College, Cincinnati, OH

Occupation: Undertaker

Miscellaneous: Resided Cincinnati, OH

Buried: Spring Grove Cemetery, Cincinnati, OH (Section 46, Lot 113)

References: Charles F. Goss. *Cincinnati: The Queen City, 1788–1912.* Chicago and Cincinnati, 1912. Obituary, *Cincinnati Commercial Tribune,* March 30, 1899. Obituary, *Cincinnati Enquirer,*

Robert B. Wilson (T. T. Garlic, Photographic Artist, East Side Market Street, Over City Bank, Portsmouth, Ohio).

John Fox Wiltsee (post-war) (Cincinnati Museum Center-Cincinnati Historical Society Library).

March 30, 1899. John A. Gano, et al. *Old Woodward Memorial.* Cincinnati, OH, 1884. Letters Received, Volunteer Service Branch, Adjutant General's Office, File B1688(VS)1862, National Archives.

Samuel M. Wolff

Corporal, Co. I, 1 OH Infantry (3 months), April 29, 1861. Honorably mustered out, Aug. 2, 1861. Private, Co. A, 64 OH Infantry, Sept. 21, 1861. 2 Lieutenant, Co. A, 64 OH Infantry, Oct. 26, 1861. 1 Lieutenant, Co. H, 64 OH Infantry, July 1, 1862. Captain, Co. H, 64 OH Infantry, Jan. 3, 1863. GSW right arm, Missionary Ridge, TN, Nov. 25, 1863. Major, 64 OH Infantry, Feb. 24, 1865. Lieutenant Colonel, 64 OH Infantry, March 18, 1865. Honorably mustered out, Dec. 3, 1865. *Colonel,* 64 OH Infantry, Dec. 15, 1865.

Born: June 1, 1839 Chambersburg, PA
Died: Aug. 12, 1883 Chambersburg, PA
Occupation: Carpenter and joiner
Miscellaneous: Resided Mansfield, Richland Co., OH
Buried: Mansfield Cemetery, Mansfield, OH (Section 5, Lot 791)
References: Albert A. Graham, compiler. *History of Richland County, OH: Its Past and Present.* Mansfield, OH, 1880. Obituary, *Chambersburg Valley Spirit,* Aug. 22, 1883. Pension File and Military Service File, National Archives. Obituary, *Mansfield Herald,* Aug. 16, 1883. Wilbur F. Hinman. *The Story of the Sherman Brigade.* Alliance, OH, 1897.

Charles H. Wood

Captain, Co. B, 51 OH Infantry, Sept. 17, 1861. Acting AIG, 23 Independent Brigade, Army of the Ohio, July–Aug. 1862. Acting AIG, 23 Brigade, 5 Division, Army of the Ohio, Aug.–Sept. 1862. Acting AIG, 23 Brigade, 5 Division, 2 Army Corps, Army of the Ohio, Sept.–Nov. 1862. Acting AIG, 3 Division, Left Wing, 14 Army Corps, Army of the Cumberland, Nov. 1862–Jan. 1863. Acting AIG, 3 Division, 21 Army Corps, Army of the Cumberland, Jan.–April 1863. Major, 51 OH Infantry, March 18, 1863. Lieutenant Colonel, 51 OH Infantry, April 14, 1863. Colonel, 51 OH Infantry, Jan. 20, 1865. Commanded 1 Brigade, 1 Division, 4 Army Corps, Army of the Cumberland, June 1865. Commanded Post of Victoria, TX, Aug.–Sept. 1865. Honorably mustered out, Oct. 3, 1865.

Born: July 10, 1836 Canal Dover, OH
Died: April 8, 1867 Fremont, OH
Occupation: Merchant and general agent for the Cincinnati, Columbus and Pittsburgh Railroad

Samuel M. Wolff (A. Whissemore, Photographer, Mansfield, Ohio; from a private collection).

Charles H. Wood (J. C. Price, Photographer, Uhrichsville, Ohio; courtesy Brad & Donna Pruden).

Miscellaneous: Resided New Philadelphia, Tuscarawas Co., OH, before war; Cincinnati, OH, and Fremont, Sandusky Co., OH, after war

Buried: Oakwood Cemetery, Fremont, OH (Section 4, Lot 1)

References: Pension File and Military Service File, National Archives. Obituary, *Fremont Weekly Journal,* April 12, 1867. Letters Received, Volunteer Service Branch, Adjutant General's Office, File W654(VS)1865, National Archives. Cincinnati (OH) City Directory, 1866–67.

Thomas Worthington

Lieutenant Colonel, 46 OH Infantry, Oct. 23, 1861. Colonel, 46 OH Infantry, Jan. 28, 1862. Cashiered Oct. 1, 1862, for drunkenness on duty and insubordination. In rejecting Worthington's persistent demands for investigation of Major Gen. Sherman's performance at the battle of Shiloh, Judge Advocate General Joseph Holt, in his Feb. 15, 1865 report to President Lincoln, said, "In view of this man's well-known incompetency as an officer and the querulousness of temper which he has incessantly manifested toward his superiors, it is believed that the investigation suggested by him is not called for by his conduct and correspondence." Nevertheless, the order cashiering him was revoked, Jan. 8, 1867, and he was honorably discharged, upon tender of resignation, to date Nov. 21, 1862.

Born: March 18, 1807 near Chillicothe, OH
Died: Feb. 23, 1884 Washington, DC
Education: Graduated U.S. Military Academy, West Point, NY, 1827
Other Wars: Mexican War (1 Lieutenant, Adjutant, 2 OH Infantry)
Occupation: Flour manufacturer and farmer before war. Farmer and fruit grower after war.
Offices/Honors: Brig. Gen., Ohio Militia, 1839–46
Miscellaneous: Resided near Logan, Hocking Co., OH; Morrow, Warren Co., OH; and Washington, DC. Son of Ohio Governor Thomas Worthington.
Buried: Grandview Cemetery, Chillicothe, OH (Section 1, Lots 34–35)
References: James D. Brewer. *Tom Worthington's Civil War: Shiloh, Sherman, and the Search for Vindication.* Jefferson, NC, and London, 2001. Robert W. McCormick. "Challenge of Command: Worthington vs Sherman," *Timeline: A Publication of the Ohio Historical Society,* Vol. 8, No. 3 (June–July, 1991). *Annual Reunion,* Association of the Graduates of the USMA, 1884. *History of Warren County, OH.* Chicago, IL, 1882. George W. Cullum. *Biographical Register of the Officers and Graduates of the U.S. Military Academy.* Third Edition. Boston and New York, 1891. Pension File and Military Service File, National Archives. Letters Received, Volunteer Service Branch, Adjutant General's Office, File W1141(VS)1862, National Archives. Thomas Worthington. *Brief History of the 46th Ohio Volunteers.* Washington, DC, 1880.

Crafts James Wright

Colonel, 13 MO Infantry, Aug. 3, 1861. Commanded Post of Clarksville, TN, March 1862. Nominated as Brig. Gen., U.S. Volunteers, May 22, 1862. Nomination tabled by U.S. Senate, July 16, 1862. Designation of 13 MO Infantry changed to 22 OH Infantry, July 7, 1862. Commanded 2 Brigade, 2 Division, District of Corinth, Army of West Tennessee, June–July 1862. Responding to several reported instances of insubordination by Wright, Major Gen. Grant on Aug. 10, 1862, endorsed a recommendation for his discharge and commented, "From the day Col. Wright first reported to me for duty, to the present time, he has been the cause of more complaints from his immediate commanders than any six officers of this command. He has constantly raised the question of rank with those immediately over him ... and he is constantly raising points and occupying the time of his superior officers with a correspondence, useless to the service, and to some extent insubordinate." A Board of Examination con-

Thomas Worthington (post-war) (Thomas Worthington. *Brief History of the 46th Ohio Volunteers.* Washington, DC, 1880).

Crafts James Wright (photograph by Hoag & Quick's Art Palace, No. 100 4th St., opp. Post Office, Cincinnati, Ohio; Roger D. Hunt Collection, USAMHI [RG98S-CWP207.68]).

vened Aug. 23, 1862 recommended that he be discharged on account of physical disability. Meanwhile, suffering from "the effects of two days' constant fighting" at Shiloh and "laying on the ground at night in the rain and mud," he resigned Sept. 9, 1862, since "he is satisfied, in this debilitating climate, thus confined (to his bed), he cannot speedily recover full strength for active duty."

Born: July 13, 1808 Troy, NY
Died: July 22, 1883 Chicago, IL
Education: Graduated U.S. Military Academy, West Point, NY, 1828
Occupation: Lawyer, newspaper editor and journalist. After removing to Chicago, he was Superintendent and Steward of the U.S. Marine Hospital there.
Offices/Honors: Secretary of the Washington Peace Conference, February 1861
Miscellaneous: Resided Cincinnati, OH, before war; Glendale, Hamilton Co., OH, 1862–75; and Chicago, IL, 1875–83
Buried: Spring Grove Cemetery, Cincinnati, OH (Section 84, Lot 7)
References: *Annual Reunion,* Association of the Graduates of the USMA, 1884. George W. Cullum.

Biographical Register of the Officers and Graduates of the U.S. Military Academy. Third Edition. Boston and New York, 1891. Pension File and Military Service File, National Archives. Obituary, *Chicago Daily Tribune,* July 24, 1883. Obituary, *Cincinnati Commercial Gazette,* July 24–25, 1883. *Report of the Proceedings of the Society of the Army of the Tennessee at the Sixteenth Meeting.* Cincinnati, OH, 1885. Letters Received, Volunteer Service Branch, Adjutant General's Office, File M1287(VS)1862, National Archives. John Y. Simon, editor. *The Papers of Ulysses S. Grant.* Vol. 5: April 1–August 31, 1862. Carbondale, IL, 1973.

George Bohan Wright

Assistant Quartermaster General of Ohio, July 9, 1861. Quartermaster General of Ohio, Oct. 13, 1861. Quartermaster General and Commissary General of Ohio, April 14, 1863. Military Storekeeper of Ordnance, USA, Nov. 24, 1863. Colonel, 106 OH Infantry, Jan. 9, 1864. Having accepted the commission as colonel with the express understanding that he would be detailed to command the Columbus (OH) Arsenal, then being constructed, he resigned as colonel, effective March 5, 1864, upon learning on Feb. 11, 1864 that he was to be relieved of this command. He then resigned as military storekeeper, March 31, 1864.

George Bohan Wright (Griswold & Smith, Photographers, Johnson Building, Columbus, Ohio; Roger D. Hunt Collection, USAMHI [RG98S-CWP21.82]).

Born: Dec. 11, 1815 near Granville, OH
Died: Sept. 1, 1903 Columbus, OH
Education: Attended Western Reserve College, Hudson, OH. Attended Ohio University, Athens, OH.
Occupation: Lawyer and railroad executive
Offices/Honors: Ohio Commissioner of Railroads and Telegraphs, 1867–71
Miscellaneous: Resided Newark, Licking Co., OH, before war; Columbus, OH, 1863–73 and 1887–1903; and Indianapolis, IN, 1873–87
Buried: Cedar Hill Cemetery, Newark, OH (Section 2, Lot 268)
References: *Biographical Cyclopedia and Portrait Gallery with an Historical Sketch of the State of Ohio.* Vol. 5. Cincinnati, OH, 1891. Obituary Circular, Whole No. 584, Ohio MOLLUS. Obituary, *Ohio State Journal,* Sept. 2–3, 1903. Pension File and Military Service File, National Archives. Letters Received, Volunteer Service Branch, Adjutant General's Office, File W2531(VS)1863, National Archives. William R. Baird. *Betas of Achievement.* New York City, NY, 1914.

Samuel Nye Yeoman

Major, 90 OH Infantry, Aug. 14, 1862. Lieutenant Colonel, 90 OH Infantry, April 15, 1863. *Colonel,* 90 OH Infantry, Oct. 20, 1863. Honorably mustered out, June 13, 1865. Bvt. Colonel, USV, March 13, 1865, for gallant and meritorious services at the battle of Nashville, TN.
Born: Oct. 14, 1828 Wayne Twp., Fayette Co., OH
Died: July 18, 1890 Tate Springs, TN
Occupation: Dry goods merchant, railroad builder and coal company president
Offices/Honors: Ohio Senate, 1868–70 and 1874–76
Miscellaneous: Resided Washington Court House, Fayette Co., OH. First cousin of the father, Alva Yeoman, of Bvt. Brig. Gen. Stephen B. Yeoman.

Samuel Nye Yeoman (L. M. Strayer Collection).

Buried: Washington Cemetery, Washington Court House, OH (Section 8, Lot 199)
References: *Biographical Cyclopedia and Portrait Gallery with an Historical Sketch of the State of Ohio.* Vol. 4. Cincinnati, OH, 1887. Obituary, *Washington Court House Cyclone and Fayette Republican,* July 23, 1890. *Biographical Encyclopedia of Ohio of the Nineteenth Century.* Cincinnati and Philadelphia, 1876. Obituary Circular, Whole No. 164, Ohio MOLLUS. R. S. Dills. *History of Fayette County: Together With Historic Notes on the Northwest and the State of Ohio.* Dayton, OH, 1881. R. Glen Nye. *A Genealogy of the Nye Family: Nyes of German Origin.* N.p., 1965. Bryan Bush, "Col. Samuel N. Yeoman, 90th Ohio Volunteer Infantry," *North South Trader's Civil War,* Vol. 27, No. 4. Pension File and Military Service File, National Archives. Henry O. Harden. *History of the 90th Ohio Volunteer Infantry in the War of the Great Rebellion.* Stoutsville, OH, 1902.

MICHIGAN

Regiments

1st Cavalry

Thornton F. Brodhead	Aug. 22, 1861	DOW Sept. 2, 1862, **Bvt. Brig. Gen.**
Charles H. Town	Sept. 2, 1862	Discharged Aug. 17, 1864
Peter Stagg	Aug. 17, 1864	Mustered out March 10, 1866, **Bvt. Brig. Gen.**

2nd Cavalry

Gordon Granger	Sept. 2, 1861	Promoted **Brig. Gen., USV,** March 26, 1862
Philip H. Sheridan	May 25, 1862	Promoted **Brig. Gen., USV,** July 1, 1862
Archibald P. Campbell	Sept. 30, 1862	Discharged Sept. 29, 1864
Thomas W. Johnston	Dec. 31, 1864	Mustered out Aug. 29, 1865

3rd Cavalry

Francis W. Kellogg	Dec. 6, 1861	Resigned March 13, 1862
John K. Mizner	March 7, 1862	Mustered out Feb. 12, 1866, **Bvt. Brig. Gen.**

4th Cavalry

Robert H. G. Minty	July 31, 1862	Mustered out Aug. 15, 1865, **Bvt. Brig. Gen.**

5th Cavalry

Joseph T. Copeland	Aug. 30, 1862	Promoted **Brig. Gen., USV,** Nov. 29, 1862
Freeman Norvell	Dec. 31, 1862	Resigned Feb. 27, 1863
Russell A. Alger	June 11, 1863	Resigned Sept. 20, 1864, **Bvt. Brig. Gen.**
Ebenezer Gould	Sept. 21, 1864	Discharged Nov. 10, 1864
Smith H. Hastings	Feb. 25, 1865	Mustered out June 22, 1865

6th Cavalry

George Gray	Oct. 13, 1862	Resigned May 19, 1864
James H. Kidd	May 19, 1864	Mustered out Nov. 7, 1865, **Bvt. Brig. Gen.**

7th Cavalry

William D. Mann	Feb. 19, 1863	Resigned March 1, 1864
Allyne C. Litchfield	March 1, 1864	Resigned May 15, 1865, **Bvt. Brig. Gen.**
George G. Briggs	May 31, 1865	Mustered out Dec. 4, 1865

8th Cavalry

John Stockton	April 22, 1863	Discharged April 15, 1864
Elisha Mix	Sept. 1, 1864	Mustered out Sept. 22, 1865, **Bvt. Brig. Gen.**

9th Cavalry

James I. David	Nov. 3, 1862	Resigned Nov. 30, 1863

George S. Acker	July 2, 1864	Resigned June 27, 1865, **Bvt. Brig. Gen.**
William B. Way	June 27, 1865	Mustered out July 21, 1865

10th Cavalry

Thaddeus Foote	Nov. 11, 1863	Resigned July 25, 1864
Luther S. Trowbridge	July 25, 1864	Mustered out Sept. 1, 1865, **Bvt. Brig. Gen.**
Israel C. Smith	Sept. 2, 1865	Mustered out Nov. 11, 1865, **Bvt. Brig. Gen.**

11th Cavalry

Simeon B. Brown	Dec. 10, 1863	Resigned June 11, 1865, **Bvt. Brig. Gen.**

1st Lancers

Arthur Rankin	Sept. 4, 1861	Resigned Dec. 21, 1861

1st Light Artillery

Cyrus O. Loomis	Oct. 8, 1862	Mustered out July 29, 1865, **Bvt. Brig. Gen.**

1st Heavy Artillery
(Designation changed from 6th Infantry, July 28, 1863)

Frederick W. Curtenius	Aug. 20, 1861	Resigned June 20, 1862
Thomas S. Clark	June 21, 1862	Resigned Jan. 29, 1864
Edward Bacon	April 6, 1864	Discharged Oct. 16, 1864
Charles E. Clarke	Oct. 16, 1864	Mustered out Sept. 7, 1865

1st Engineers and Mechanics

William P. Innes	Sept. 12, 1861	Mustered out Nov. 2, 1864, **Bvt. Brig. Gen.**
John B. Yates	Nov. 3, 1864	Mustered out Sept. 22, 1865

1st Sharpshooters

Charles V. DeLand	July 7, 1863	Discharged Feb. 4, 1865, **Bvt. Brig. Gen.**

1st Infantry (3 months)

Orlando B. Willcox	May 1, 1861	Promoted **Brig. Gen., USV,** July 21, 1861

1st Infantry (3 years)

John C. Robinson	Sept. 1, 1861	Promoted **Brig. Gen., USV,** April 28, 1862
Horace S. Roberts	April 28, 1862	KIA Aug. 30, 1862
Franklin W. Whittelsey	Aug. 30, 1862	Resigned March 18, 1863
Ira C. Abbott	March 18, 1863	Resigned Dec. 22, 1864, **Bvt. Brig. Gen.**
William A. Throop	Dec. 22, 1864	Mustered out Jan. 6, 1865, **Bvt. Brig. Gen.**
George Lockley	May 30, 1865	Mustered out July 9, 1865

2nd Infantry

Israel B. Richardson	May 25, 1861	Promoted **Brig. Gen., USV,** Sept. 16, 1861
Orlando M. Poe	Sept. 16, 1861	Promoted **Brig. Gen., USV,** Feb. 16, 1863
William Humphrey	Feb. 16, 1863	Mustered out Sept. 30, 1864, **Bvt. Brig. Gen.**
Edwin J. March	Sept. 30, 1864	Resigned April 17, 1865
Frederick Schneider	April 18, 1865	Mustered out July 28, 1865

3rd Infantry

Daniel McConnell	June 10, 1861	Resigned Oct. 22, 1861
Stephen G. Champlin	Oct. 22, 1861	Promoted **Brig. Gen., USV,** Nov. 29, 1862
Byron R. Pierce	Jan. 1, 1863	Promoted **Brig. Gen., USV,** June 7, 1864

3rd Infantry (Re-organized)

Moses B. Houghton	Oct. 15, 1864	Mustered out May 25, 1866, **Bvt. Brig. Gen.**

4th Infantry

Dwight A. Woodbury	June 20, 1861	KIA July 1, 1862
Jonathan W. Childs	July 1, 1862	Resigned Nov. 25, 1862
Harrison H. Jeffords	March 12, 1863	DOW July 3, 1863
George W. Lumbard	July 3, 1863	DOW May 6, 1864

4th Infantry (Re-organized)

Jairus W. Hall	Oct. 14, 1864	Mustered out May 26, 1866, **Bvt. Brig. Gen.**

5th Infantry

Henry D. Terry	June 10, 1861	Promoted **Brig. Gen., USV,** July 17, 1862
Samuel E. Beach	Aug. 8, 1862	Discharged June 16, 1864
John Pulford	July 12, 1864	Mustered out July 5, 1865, **Bvt. Brig. Gen.**

6th Infantry
(See 1st Heavy Artillery, to which designation changed, July 28, 1863)

7th Infantry

Ira R. Grosvenor	Aug. 22, 1861	Resigned July 7, 1862
Norman J. Hall	July 14, 1862	Discharged June 4, 1864
George W. LaPointe	Nov. 18, 1864	Mustered out July 5, 1865

8th Infantry

William M. Fenton	Sept. 23, 1861	Resigned March 15, 1863
Frank Graves	May 26, 1863	Died May 6, 1864
Ralph Ely	May 7, 1864	Mustered out May 19, 1866, **Bvt. Brig. Gen.**

9th Infantry

William W. Duffield	Sept. 21, 1861	Resigned Feb. 6, 1863
John G. Parkhurst	Feb. 6, 1863	Mustered out Nov. 10, 1865, **Bvt. Brig. Gen.**

10th Infantry

Charles M. Lum	Jan. 10, 1862	Mustered out April 1, 1865
William H. Dunphy	June 7, 1865	Mustered out July 19, 1865

11th Infantry

William J. May	Sept. 24, 1861	Resigned April 1, 1862
William L. Stoughton	April 1, 1862	Mustered out Sept. 30, 1864, **Bvt. Brig. Gen.**

11th Infantry (Re-organized)

Patrick H. Keegan	March 16, 1865	Mustered out Sept. 16, 1865

12th Infantry

Francis Quinn	Jan. 8, 1862	Resigned Aug. 31, 1862
William H. Graves	Sept. 1, 1862	Resigned June 10, 1865
Dwight May	June 10, 1865	Mustered out Feb. 15, 1866, **Bvt. Brig. Gen.**

13th Infantry

Charles E. Stuart	Jan. 17, 1862	Resigned Jan. 27, 1862
Michael Shoemaker	Feb. 1, 1862	Resigned May 26, 1863
Joshua B. Culver	May 26, 1863	Mustered out Feb. 23, 1865
Willard G. Eaton	Feb. 23, 1865	KIA March 19, 1865
Joshua B. Culver	April 24, 1865	Mustered out July 25, 1865

14th Infantry

Robert P. Sinclair	Feb. 7, 1862	Resigned Nov. 10, 1862
Henry R. Mizner	Dec. 22, 1862	Mustered out July 18, 1865, **Bvt. Brig. Gen.**

15th Infantry

John M. Oliver	March 13, 1862	Promoted **Brig. Gen., USV,** Jan. 12, 1865
Frederick S. Hutchinson	May 22, 1865	Mustered out Aug. 13, 1865, **Bvt. Brig. Gen.**

16th Infantry

Thomas B. W. Stockton	Aug. 21, 1861	Resigned May 18, 1863
Norval E. Welch	June 1, 1864	KIA Sept. 30, 1864
Benjamin F. Partridge	Dec. 17, 1864	Mustered out July 8, 1865, **Bvt. Brig. Gen.**

17th Infantry

William H. Withington	Aug. 11, 1862	Resigned March 21, 1863, **Bvt. Brig. Gen.**
Constant Luce	March 21, 1863	Mustered out Dec. 1, 1864
Frederick W. Swift	Dec. 4, 1864	Mustered out June 3, 1865, **Bvt. Brig. Gen.**

18th Infantry

Charles C. Doolittle	Aug. 13, 1862	Promoted **Brig. Gen., USV,** Jan. 27, 1865
John W. Horner	March 21, 1865	Mustered out June 26, 1865

19th Infantry

Henry C. Gilbert	Sept. 5, 1862	DOW May 24, 1864
Eli A. Griffin	June 20, 1864	DOW June 16, 1864
David Anderson	June 15, 1865	Mustered out June 10, 1865

20th Infantry

Adolphus W. Williams	July 26, 1862	Discharged Nov. 21, 1863, **Bvt. Brig. Gen.**
Byron M. Cutcheon	Jan. 8, 1864	To 27th Infantry, Dec. 19, 1864, **Bvt. Brig. Gen.**
Claudius B. Grant	Dec. 20, 1864	Resigned April 12, 1865
Clement A. Lounsberry	March 11, 1865	Mustered out May 30, 1865

21st Infantry

Ambrose A. Stevens	July 25, 1862	Resigned Feb. 3, 1863, **Bvt. Brig. Gen.**
William B. McCreery	Feb. 4, 1863	Resigned Sept. 14, 1864

22nd Infantry

Moses Wisner	Aug. 22, 1862	Died Jan. 5, 1863
Heber LeFavour	Jan. 5, 1863	Mustered out June 26, 1865, **Bvt. Brig. Gen.**

23rd Infantry

Marshall W. Chapin	Sept. 1, 1862	Resigned April 15, 1864
Oliver L. Spaulding	April 16, 1864	Mustered out June 28, 1865, **Bvt. Brig. Gen.**

24th Infantry

Henry A. Morrow	Aug. 15, 1862	Mustered out July 19, 1865, **Bvt. Brig. Gen.**

25th Infantry

Orlando H. Moore	Sept. 22, 1862	Mustered out June 24, 1865

26th Infantry

Judson S. Farrar	Dec. 4, 1862	Resigned March 29, 1864
Lemuel Saviers	Sept. 12, 1864	Discharged Sept. 27, 1864
Henry H. Wells	Sept. 26, 1864	Mustered out Sept. 27, 1865, **Bvt. Brig. Gen.**

27th Infantry

Dorus M. Fox	Jan. 15, 1863	Resigned Oct. 3, 1864
William B. Wright	Nov. 18, 1864	Discharged Nov. 22, 1864
Byron M. Cutcheon	Dec. 19, 1864	Resigned March 6, 1865, **Bvt. Brig. Gen.**
Charles Waite	March 6, 1865	Mustered out July 26, 1865, **Bvt. Brig. Gen.**

28th Infantry

William W. Wheeler	Nov. 10, 1864	Mustered out July 12, 1866

29th Infantry

Thomas Saylor	Sept. 29, 1864	Mustered out Sept. 6, 1865

30th Infantry

Grover S. Wormer	Nov. 21, 1864	Mustered out June 30, 1865, **Bvt. Brig. Gen.**

Biographies

David Anderson

1 Lieutenant, Co. H, 19 MI Infantry, Aug. 9, 1862. Taken prisoner, Thompson's Station, TN, March 5, 1863. Confined Libby Prison, Richmond, VA. Paroled May 5, 1863. Captain, Co. H, 19 MI Infantry, May 1, 1863. Shell wound, New Hope Church, GA, May 25, 1864. Major, 19 MI Infantry, Nov. 13, 1864. Honorably mustered out, June 10, 1865. *Colonel,* 19 MI Infantry, June 15, 1865.

David Anderson (Roger D. Hunt Collection, USAMHI [RG98S-CWP26.79]).

Born: Nov. 26, 1824 Clarendon, Orleans Co., NY
Died: June 16, 1911 Berlamont, Van Buren Co., MI
Occupation: Lumber manufacturer and farmer
Offices/Honors: Michigan Senate, 1873–74
Miscellaneous: Resided Matteson, Branch Co., MI, before war; and Breedsville, Van Buren Co., MI, after war
Buried: Breedsville Cemetery, Breedsville, MI
References: *Michigan Biographies.* Lansing, MI, 1924. Pension File and Military Service File, National Archives. Obituary, *Bangor Advance,* June 23, 1911. William M. Anderson. *They Died to Make Men Free: A History of the 19th Michigan Infantry in the Civil War.* Berrien Springs, MI, 1980.

Edward Bacon

Major, 6 MI Infantry, Aug. 20, 1861. Lieutenant Colonel, 6 MI Infantry, June 21, 1862. Charges preferred (but not sustained) against him by Brig. Gen. Thomas Williams in July 1862 and by Major Gen. William Dwight in June 1863 are colorfully documented in his book, *Among the Cotton Thieves.* Lieutenant Colonel, 1 MI Heavy Artillery, July 28, 1863. Colonel, 1 MI Heavy Artillery, April 6, 1864. Commanded Fort Morgan, Mobile, AL, Sept.-Oct. 1864. Reported by Brig. Gen. Joseph Bailey as "thoroughly inefficient in neglecting to recommend officers for promotion, failing to enforce discipline, and omitting to secure for his regiment the advantages it had a right to claim," he was dismissed Oct. 16, 1864, for "incompetency and inefficiency, in consequence of which the regiment, which is composed of excellent material and under its former commander bore an honorable name, has fallen into discredit." Upon review of the dismissal, Judge Advocate Gen. Joseph Holt con-

cluded that "in view of the numerous testimonials from officers without motive to partiality ..., this officer may have suffered injustice from Gen. Bailey's action against him." Therefore, the dismissal was revoked, Feb. 6, 1865, and he was honorably discharged as of the date of dismissal.
Born: April 17, 1830 Rochester, NY
Died: April 25, 1901 Niles, MI
Education: Graduated University of Michigan, Ann Arbor, MI, 1850
Occupation: Lawyer
Miscellaneous: Resided Niles, Berrien Co., MI
Buried: Silverbrook Cemetery, Niles, MI (Old Ground, Section 11, Lot 300)
References: Obituary, *Niles Daily Star,* April 25, 1901. Pension File and Military Service File, National Archives. Letters Received, Volunteer Service Branch, Adjutant General's Office, Files J1015(VS)1864 and W2749(VS)1864, National Archives. Edward Bacon. *Among the Cotton Thieves.* Detroit, MI, 1867. Orville W. Coolidge, editor. *A Twentieth Century History of Berrien County, MI.* Chicago, IL, 1906. Franklin Ellis. *History of Berrien and Van Buren Counties, MI.* Philadelphia, PA, 1880. *http://www.friendsofsilverbrook.org/site3/obituaries.html.*

Samuel Elmore Beach

Lieutenant Colonel, 5 MI Infantry, Aug. 28, 1861. GSW left thigh, Williamsburg, VA, May 5, 1862. Colonel, 5 MI Infantry, Aug. 8, 1862. Honorably discharged, Aug. 7, 1863, on account of physical disability, having been absent from duty over six months. Discharge revoked, Oct. 8, 1863, and restored to his command, as of the date of discharge. Honorably discharged, June 16, 1864, having been rendered supernumerary by the consolidation of his regiment with the 3 MI Infantry.
Born: April 7, 1823 Lewiston, NY
Died: Nov. 14, 1893 Pontiac, MI
Other Wars: Mexican War (1 Lieutenant, 15 U.S. Infantry)
Occupation: Clerk, justice of the peace, and insurance agent
Offices/Honors: Oakland County (MI) Treasurer, 1851–57. Oakland County (MI) Sheriff, 1865–69.
Miscellaneous: Resided Pontiac, Oakland Co., MI
Buried: Oak Hill Cemetery, Pontiac, MI (Block 4, Lot 93)
References: Samuel W. Durant. *History of Oakland County, MI.* Philadelphia, PA, 1877. *Portrait and Biographical Album of Oakland County, MI.* Chicago, IL, 1891. Obituary, *Pontiac Republican,* Nov. 16, 1893. Pension File and Military Service File, National Archives. Letters Received, Volunteer Service Branch, Adjutant General's Office, File

Edward Bacon (Milton Chase Papers, Bentley Historical Library, University of Michigan).

Samuel Elmore Beach (courtesy Oakland County Pioneer and Historical Society. All Rights Reserved).

B896(VS)1862, National Archives. Mortimer E. Cooley. *The Cooley Genealogy: The Descendants of Ensign Benjamin Cooley.* Rutland, VT, 1941.

George Gooding Briggs

1 Lieutenant, Co. A, 7 MI Cavalry, Oct. 13, 1862. 1 Lieutenant, Adjutant, 7 MI Cavalry, July 27, 1863. Taken prisoner, Buckland Mills, VA, Oct. 19, 1863. Escaped Oct. 20, 1863. Major, 7 MI Cavalry, Nov. 29, 1864. Lieutenant Colonel, 7 MI Cavalry, Feb. 27, 1865. GSW left leg, Five Forks, VA, April 1, 1865. Colonel, 7 MI Cavalry, May 31, 1865. Commanded Cavalry Forces, South Sub-District of the Plains, Department of the Missouri, July 1865. Honorably mustered out, Dec. 4, 1865.

Born: Jan. 24, 1838 Livonia, MI
Died: Dec. 8, 1912 Grand Rapids, MI
Education: Attended Olivet (MI) College
Occupation: Dry goods merchant, barrel manufacturer, and capitalist
Offices/Honors: Michigan House of Representatives, 1869–70. Postmaster, Grand Rapids, MI, 1890–94.
Miscellaneous: Resided Battle Creek, Calhoun Co., MI, before war; and Grand Rapids, Kent Co., MI, after war
Buried: Oak Hill Cemetery, Grand Rapids, MI (Section E, Lot 77)

References: Albert Baxter. *History of the City of Grand Rapids, MI.* New York City, NY, 1891. Dwight Goss. *History of Grand Rapids and Its Industries.* Chicago, IL, 1906. *History of Kent County, MI.* Chicago, IL, 1881. *American Biographical History of Eminent and Self-Made Men.* Michigan volume. Cincinnati, OH, 1878. Pension File and Military Service File, National Archives. Obituary Circular, Whole No. 476, Michigan MOLLUS. Obituary, *Grand Rapids Herald,* Dec. 9–10, 1912. William O. Lee, compiler. *Personal and Historical Sketches and Facial History of and by Members of the 7th Regiment Michigan Volunteer Cavalry.* Detroit, MI, 1901.

Archibald P. Campbell

Captain, Co. K, 2 MI Cavalry, Sept. 20, 1861. Lieutenant Colonel, 2 MI Cavalry, July 27, 1862. Colonel, 2 MI Cavalry, Sept. 30, 1862. Commanded 1 Brigade, 1 Cavalry Division, Department of the Cumberland, April 28, 1863-Feb. 1864. Commanded 1 Cavalry Division, Department of the Cumberland, March 1864. Honorably discharged, Sept. 29, 1864, on account of physical disability due to "phthisis pulmonalis."

George Gooding Briggs (James H. Kidd. *Personal Recollections of a Cavalryman with Custer's Michigan Cavalry Brigade in the Civil War.* Ionia, Michigan, 1908).

Archibald P. Campbell (photograph by T. M. Schleier's Cartes de Visite Photograph Gallery, Corner Cherry and Union Streets, Nashville, Tennessee; Courtesy Archives of Michigan).

Born: Nov. 11, 1828 Argylshire, Scotland
Died: May 24, 1865 Clyde Twp., St. Clair Co., MI
Occupation: Farmer and lumberman
Miscellaneous: Resided Port Huron, St. Clair Co., MI
Buried: Lakeside Cemetery, Port Huron, MI
References: Pension File and Military Service File, National Archives. Obituary, *Port Huron Press,* May 31, 1865. Letters Received, Volunteer Service Branch, Adjutant General's Office, File C1912(VS) 1864, National Archives. Marshall P. Thatcher. *A Hundred Battles in the West, St. Louis to Atlanta, 1861–65, the Second Michigan Cavalry, with the Armies of the Mississippi, Ohio, Kentucky and Cumberland.* Detroit, MI, 1884.

Marshall Wright Chapin

1 Lieutenant, Co. I, 4 MI Infantry, May 16, 1861. Captain, Co. F, 4 MI Infantry, March 10, 1862. Resigned Aug. 20, 1862, to accept promotion. Colonel, 23 MI Infantry, Sept. 1, 1862. Commanded 38 Brigade, 12 Division, Army of the Ohio, Sept. 22-Nov. 1862. Commanded 1 Brigade, 3 Division, 23 Army Corps, Army of the Ohio, June 1863. Commanded Post of Carthage, TN, July 1863. Commanded 2 Brigade, 2 Division, 23 Army Corps, Army of the Ohio, Aug. 6, 1863-Feb. 8, 1864 and April 1864. Resigned April 15, 1864, on account of physical disability from "camp diarrhea."
Born: June 14, 1831 Detroit, MI
Died: April 13, 1873 Salt Lake City, UT
Occupation: Farmer
Miscellaneous: Resided Newport, Monroe Co., MI, before war; and Detroit, MI, and Monroe, Monroe Co., MI, after war.
Buried: Mount Olivet Cemetery, Salt Lake City, UT (GAR Plat, Section A, Lot 58)
References: Pension File and Military Service File, National Archives. Gilbert W. Chapin, compiler. *The Chapin Book of Genealogical Data.* Hartford, CT, 1924. Orange Chapin, compiler. *The Chapin Genealogy, Containing a Very Large Proportion of the Descendants of Deacon Samuel Chapin.* Northampton, MA, 1862.

Jonathan Webster Childs

Major, 4 MI Infantry, June 20, 1861. Lieutenant Colonel, 4 MI Infantry, Sept. 25, 1861. GSW hip, Gaines' Mill, VA, June 27, 1862. Colonel, 4 MI Infantry, July 1, 1862. Resigned Nov. 25, 1862, due to "unexpected and urgent circumstances of a private nature." In forwarding the resignation, Brig. Gen. Charles Griffin commented, "It is absolutely necessary for the interest and harmony of the regiment." Captain, Co. D, 2 USCT, Sept. 13, 1863. Commanded Post of Fort Myers, FL, April 18, 1864-Feb. 22, 1865. Commanded Post of Tallahassee, FL, Aug. 1865. Honorably mustered out, Jan. 5, 1866.

Marshall Wright Chapin (Dale R. Niesen Collection).

Jonathan Webster Childs (courtesy Archives of Michigan).

Born: March 14, 1834 Fredonia, NY
Died: May 24, 1896 Hanover, Howard Co., MD
Education: Graduated Michigan State Normal School, Ypsilanti, MI, 1855. Attended Norwich (VT) University.
Occupation: School teacher and civil engineer before war. Lawyer, surveyor of public lands, special agent for the U.S. Interior Department, and U.S. Government clerk after war.
Offices/Honors: Florida Legislature, 1868–70. Treasurer, Alachua Co., FL, 1872–74.
Miscellaneous: Resided Augusta Twp., Washtenaw Co., MI, before war; Gainesville, Alachua Co., FL, 1866–74; Washington, DC; and Hanover, Howard Co., MD
Buried: Arlington National Cemetery, Arlington, VA (Section 1, Lot 809)
References: Pension File and Military Service File, National Archives. William A. Ellis, editor. *History of Norwich University, 1819–1911, Her History, Her Graduates, Her Roll of Honor.* Montpelier, VT, 1911. Elias Child. *Genealogy of the Child, Childs and Childe Families.* Utica, NY, 1881. Martin Bertera and Ken Oberholtzer. *The 4th Michigan Volunteer Infantry at Gettysburg: The Battle for the Wheatfield.* Dayton, OH, 1997.

Thomas Scott Clark

Lieutenant Colonel, 6 MI Infantry, Aug. 20, 1861. Colonel, 6 MI Infantry, June 21, 1862. Com-

Thomas Scott Clark (Bob Coch Collection).

manded 1 Brigade, 2 Division, 19 Army Corps, Army of the Gulf, Jan. 13-Feb. 26, 1863 and May 27-July 1863. Although charged by Lieutenant Colonel Edward Bacon, May 15, 1863, with "Conduct Unbecoming an Officer and a Gentleman" for various serious offenses including drunkenness, cotton stealing, and "indecent exposure of his own person and of the person of a certain colored girl called Maria," he was never brought to trial on the charges. Colonel, 1 MI Heavy Artillery, July 28, 1863. Due to "the continued low state of my wife, who is liable to drop off at any moment," he resigned, Jan. 29, 1864, "the regiment being so scattered, there is but little for a colonel to do and I, therefore, feel as if I was a useless appendage."
Born: Aug. 27, 1827 Chillicothe, OH
Died: Jan. 23, 1907 Dayton, OH
Other Wars: Mexican War (Private, Co. E, 2 KY Infantry)
Occupation: Newspaper publisher, bookseller, and stationer before war. Merchant, postal clerk, and clerk in Michigan Auditor General's office after war.
Miscellaneous: Resided Monroe, Monroe Co., MI, to 1874; Lansing, Ingham Co., MI; and NHDVS, Dayton, OH

Thomas Scott Clark (John Fuller Collection).

Buried: Dayton National Cemetery, Dayton, OH (Section P, Row 20, Grave 32)
References: Pension File and Military Service File, National Archives. Edward Bacon. *Among the Cotton Thieves*. Detroit, MI, 1867. Talcott E. Wing, editor. *History of Monroe County, MI*. New York City, NY, 1890. Letters Received, Volunteer Service Branch, Adjutant General's Office, File H232(VS)1864, National Archives.

Charles Edward Clarke

Captain, Co. D, 6 MI Infantry, Aug. 20, 1861. Major, 6 MI Infantry, June 21, 1862. Major, 1 MI Heavy Artillery, July 28, 1863. Lieutenant Colonel, 1 MI Heavy Artillery, May 1, 1864. *Colonel,* 1 MI Heavy Artillery, Oct. 16, 1864. Commanded Post of Mobile Point, District of South Alabama, Department of the Gulf, March-April 1865. Honorably mustered out, Sept. 7, 1865.
Born: Sept. 1815 Lebanon, CT
Died: Feb. 2, 1901 New Rochelle, NY
Occupation: Steamboat captain before war. Regular Army (Captain, 17 U.S. Infantry, retired June 28, 1878)
Miscellaneous: Resided New Brighton, Beaver Co., PA; Dowagiac, Cass Co., MI; and New Rochelle, Westchester Co., NY. Brother of Sara Jane (Clarke) Lippincott, a well-known author, better known as "Grace Greenwood."
Buried: Grove Cemetery, New Brighton, PA (Section F, Lot 135)
References: Obituary, *New York Tribune*, Feb. 3, 1901. Obituary, *Boston Evening Transcript*, Feb. 4, 1901. Alfred Mathews. *History of Cass County, MI*. Chicago, IL, 1882. Letters Received, Appointment, Commission and Personal Branch, Adjutant General's Office, File 4090(ACP)1874, National Archives. Letters Received, Volunteer Service Branch, Adjutant General's Office, File C1997(VS) 1865, National Archives. Military Service File, National Archives.

Elijah Henry Crowell

Conditional 2 Lieutenant, 21 MI Infantry, July 18, 1862. Captain, Co. F, 21 MI Infantry, Aug. 14, 1862. GSW left knee, Chickamauga, GA, Sept. 20, 1863. Provost Marshal, Engineer Brigade, Department of the Cumberland, Jan. 18-Sept. 1864. *Colonel,* 21 MI Infantry, Nov. 14, 1864. Honorably mustered out, June 8, 1865.
Born: March 1829 Seneca Co., NY
Died: Jan. 14, 1901 Newark, NJ
Occupation: School teacher, carpenter and cabinet maker
Offices/Honors: Superintendent of Schools, Montcalm Co., MI, 1871–80
Miscellaneous: Resided Otisco, Ionia Co., MI; Lowell, Kent Co., MI; Greenville, Montcalm Co., MI; Owosso, Shiawassee Co., MI; and Detroit, MI
Buried: Woodmere Cemetery, Detroit, MI (Section D, Lot 226, unmarked)
References: Pension File and Military Service File, National Archives. John S. Schenck. *History of Ionia and Montcalm Counties, MI*. Philadelphia, PA, 1881. Death notice, *Newark Daily Advertiser*, Jan. 15, 1901.

Joshua B. Culver

1 Lieutenant, Adjutant, 13 MI Infantry, Jan. 17, 1862. Major, 13 MI Infantry, Oct. 16, 1862. Lieutenant Colonel, 13 MI Infantry, Feb. 26, 1863. Colonel, 13 MI Infantry, May 26, 1863. Stunned by shell explosion, Chickamauga, GA, Sept. 19, 1863. Commanded Engineer Brigade, Department of the Cumberland, July 23-Aug. 20 and Sept. 1864. Commanded Post of Dalton, GA, Nov.-Dec. 1864. Commanded 3 Brigade, Provisional Division, Army of the Tennessee (attached to District of North Carolina), Feb. 1865. Honorably mustered out, Feb. 23, 1865. Colonel, 13 MI Infantry, April 24, 1865. Commanded 2 Brigade, 1 Division, 14 Army Corps, Army of the Cumberland, June 1865. Honorably mustered out, July 25, 1865.
Born: Sept. 12, 1829 Delaware Co., NY
Died: July 17, 1883 Buffalo, NY
Other Wars: Mexican War (Corporal, Knowlton's Co., WI Infantry)
Occupation: Indian trader before war. After war engaged in insurance business and established a

Charles Edward Clarke (Milton Chase Papers, Bentley Historical Library, University of Michigan).

Joshua B. Culver (*Souvenir Roster of the Surviving Members of the 13th Michigan Infantry*. Kalamazoo, Michigan, 1909).

Frederick William Curtenius (Milton Chase Papers, Bentley Historical Library, University of Michigan).

bank. Later operated an extensive dockage and general commission business.

Offices/Honors: Register, General Land Office, Duluth, MN, 1859–61. Mayor, Duluth, MN, 1870–71 and 1883.

Miscellaneous: Resided Superior, Douglas Co., WI; Duluth, St. Louis Co., MN; and Paw Paw, Van Buren Co., MI

Buried: Forest Hill Cemetery, Duluth, MN (Section D, Block 5, Lot 6)

References: Charles E. Flandrau. *Encyclopedia of Biography of Minnesota*. N.p., 1900. Walter Van Brunt, editor. *Duluth and St. Louis County, MN*. Chicago, IL, 1921. Pension File and Military Service File, National Archives. Dwight E. Woodbridge and J. S. Pardee, editors. *History of Duluth and St. Louis County, Past and Present*. Chicago, IL, 1910. Obituary, *Duluth Tribune*, July 18, 1883. Letters Received, Volunteer Service Branch, Adjutant General's Office, File C428(VS)1865, National Archives.

Frederick William Curtenius

Colonel, 6 MI Infantry, Aug. 20, 1861. Resigned June 20, 1862, due to "my declining health" and

Frederick William Curtenius (patriotic envelope image).

"the ill health of my wife, ... coupled with impaired hearing ... and sight." Although biographies attribute his resignation to indignation over being ordered to return refugee slaves to their Southern masters, his letter of resignation to Major Gen. Benjamin F. Butler contains no mention of this reason.

Born: Sept. 30, 1806 New York City, NY

Died: July 13, 1883 Kalamazoo, MI
Education: Graduated Hamilton College, Clinton, NY, 1824
Other Wars: Mexican War (Captain, Co. A, 1 MI Infantry)
Occupation: Farmer and bank president
Offices/Honors: Michigan Senate, 1853–54 and 1867–68. Michigan Adjutant General, 1855–61. U.S. Collector of Internal Revenue, 1868–70.
Miscellaneous: Resided Kalamazoo, Kalamazoo Co., MI
Buried: Mountain Home Cemetery, Kalamazoo, MI (Section K, Lot 456)
References: Samuel W. Durant, compiler. *History of Kalamazoo County, MI*. Philadelphia, PA, 1880. *American Biographical History of Eminent and Self-Made Men*. Michigan volume. Cincinnati, OH, 1878. *Michigan Biographies*. Lansing, MI, 1924. Obituary, *New York Times,* July 14, 1883. Benjamin W. Dwight. *History of the Descendants of John Dwight of Dedham, MA*. New York City, NY, 1874. Military Service File, National Archives.

James Ira David

2 Lieutenant, Co. K, 1 MI Cavalry, July 20, 1861. 1 Lieutenant, RQM, 1 MI Cavalry, Aug. 22, 1861. Acting Quartermaster, Staff of Brig. Gen. John P. Hatch, Cavalry Brigade, Army of the Shenandoah, April-June 1862. Captain, AQM, USV, June 11, 1862. Quartermaster, Cavalry Brigade, 2 Army Corps, Army of Virginia, July-Aug. 1862. Colonel, 9 MI Cavalry, Nov. 3, 1862. "Severely afflicted with indigestion and liver complaint," he resigned Nov. 30, 1863, "my own health being very poor, unfitting me for the arduous duties of the field, and the situation and health of my family being such as imperatively to demand my presence at home."
Born: Aug. 2, 1822 Catskill, NY
Died: Oct. 13, 1892 Grosse Isle, MI
Occupation: Lumber merchant and contractor on canal and bridge projects before war. Farmer and Indian agent after war.
Offices/Honors: Michigan House of Representatives, 1859–60. Michigan Senate, 1875–76.
Miscellaneous: Resided Trenton, Wayne Co., MI; Grosse Isle, Wayne Co., MI; and Pawhuska, Osage Agency, OK
Buried: Woodmere Cemetery, Detroit, MI (Section G, Lot 122, unmarked)
References: Pension File and Military Service File, National Archives. Obituary, *Detroit Free Press,* Oct. 14, 1892. Obituary Circular, Whole No. 106, Michigan MOLLUS. *Michigan Biographies*. Lansing, MI, 1924. Letters Received, Commission Branch, Adjutant General's Office, File D452(CB) 1863, National Archives.

James Ira David (The National Archives [Photographic Prints of Quartermaster Officers]).

William Ward Duffield

Lieutenant Colonel, 4 MI Infantry, May 16, 1861. Colonel, 9 MI Infantry, Sept. 21, 1861. Commanded 23 Independent Brigade, Army of the Ohio, March 8-May 14 and July 13, 1862. Nominated as Brig. Gen., U.S. Volunteers, April 11, 1862. Nomination tabled by U.S. Senate, July 16, 1862. Commanded U.S. Forces in Kentucky, May 14-June 6, 1862. GSW left thigh and right testicle, Murfreesboro, TN, July 13, 1862. Taken prisoner and paroled, Murfreesboro, TN, July 13, 1862. Exchanged Aug. 27, 1862. Disabled by his wounds and "physically incapacitated for further usefulness and active service," he resigned Feb. 6, 1863.
Born: Nov. 19, 1823 Carlisle, PA
Died: June 22, 1907 Washington, DC
Education: Graduated Columbia University, New York City, NY, 1841
Other Wars: Mexican War (1 Lieutenant, Acting Adjutant, 2 TN Infantry)
Occupation: Civil engineer, primarily engaged in railroad construction, but also involved in coal and iron mining enterprises
Offices/Honors: Michigan Senate, 1879–80. Superintendent, U.S. Coast and Geodetic Survey, 1894–97.

William Ward Duffield (post-war) (District of Columbia MOLLUS Collection, USAMHI [RG 127S-DCC.155]).

Miscellaneous: Resided Detroit, MI; Traverse City, Leelanau Co., MI; and Washington, DC
Buried: Arlington National Cemetery, Arlington, VA (Section 3, Lot 1813)
References: *Appletons' Cyclopedia of American Biography.* Obituary, *Washington Post,* June 23, 1907. *Michigan Biographies.* Lansing, MI, 1924. Pension File and Military Service File, National Archives. Charles W. Bennett. *Historical Sketches of the 9th Michigan Infantry (General Thomas' Headquarters Guards) With an Account of the Battle of Murfreesboro, TN.* Coldwater, MI, 1913. Obituary Circular, Whole No. 498, District of Columbia MOLLUS.

William Henry Dunphy

1 Lieutenant, Co. G, 10 MI Infantry, Oct. 1, 1861. Captain, Co. G, 10 MI Infantry, March 31, 1863. Lieutenant Colonel, 10 MI Infantry, Feb. 24, 1865. *Colonel,* 10 MI Infantry, June 7, 1865. Honorably mustered out, July 19, 1865.
Born: Dec. 20, 1835 Boston, MA
Died: Sept. 13, 1871 Montague, MI
Occupation: Lumber merchant and railroad construction foreman before war. Railroad construction foreman and hotelkeeper after war.
Offices/Honors: Sheriff of St. Clair Co., MI, 1867–69
Miscellaneous: Resided Kimball, St. Clair Co., MI; Grand Rapids, Kent Co., MI; and Montague, Muskegon Co., MI

Buried: Place of burial unknown
References: Fletcher W. Hewes. *History of the 10th Regiment Michigan Volunteer Infantry.* Detroit, MI, 1864. Pension File and Military Service File, National Archives. Obituary, *Muskegon News and Reporter,* Sept. 20, 1871. Obituary, *St. Clair Republican,* Sept. 26, 1871.

Willard G. Eaton

1 Lieutenant, Co. I, 13 MI Infantry, Nov. 8, 1861. Captain, Co. I, 13 MI Infantry, Oct. 21, 1862. Major, 13 MI Infantry, June 13, 1863. *Colonel,* 13 MI Infantry, Feb. 23, 1865. GSW, Bentonville, NC, March 19, 1865.
Born: April 6, 1821 Monroe Co., NY
Died: March 19, 1865 KIA Bentonville, NC
Occupation: School teacher and clerk
Miscellaneous: Resided Otsego, Allegan Co., MI
Buried: Mountain Home Cemetery, Otsego, MI
References: Pension File and Military Service File, National Archives. Resolutions of Respect, *Detroit Advertiser and Tribune,* May 8, 1865.

Judson Smith Farrar

Captain, Co. B, 5 MI Infantry, Aug. 13, 1861. Lieutenant Colonel, 26 MI Infantry, Sept. 18, 1862. Colonel, 26 MI Infantry, Dec. 4, 1862. Suffering from chronic diarrhea and "an affection of the lungs," he resigned March 29, 1864, since "my health has become very much impaired by exposure in service during the past three years."
Born: Aug. 23, 1836 Mount Clemens, MI

Willard G. Eaton (*Souvenir Roster of the Surviving Members of the 13th Michigan Infantry.* Kalamazoo, Michigan, 1909).

Died: March 11, 1916 Mount Clemens, MI
Occupation: Druggist before war. Druggist and lumber and coal merchant after war.
Offices/Honors: Mayor, Mount Clemens, MI, 1883–85. U.S. Consul, Port Sarnia, Ontario, 1887–90. Adjutant General of Michigan, 1891–93.
Miscellaneous: Resided Mount Clemens, Macomb Co., MI
Buried: Clinton Grove Cemetery, Mount Clemens, MI (Section A, Lot 93)
References: Robert F. Eldredge. *Past and Present of Macomb County, MI.* Chicago, IL, 1905. Obituary Circular, Whole No. 537, Michigan MOLLUS. Obituary, *Mount Clemens Monitor,* March 17, 1916. Pension File and Military Service File, National Archives. Letters Received, Volunteer Service Branch, Adjutant General's Office, File F239(VS) 1864, National Archives. *http://www.online-isp.com/~maggie/macomb/farrar1.htm.*

William Matthew Fenton

Colonel, 8 MI Infantry, Sept. 23, 1861. Commanded 1 Brigade, 2 Division, Northern District, Department of the South, April-July 1862. Commanded 1 Brigade, 1 Division, 9 Army Corps, Army of the Potomac, July 25-Aug. 3, 1862, Sept. 1–8, 1862, and Dec. 15, 1862-Feb. 11, 1863. Commanded 2 Brigade, 1 Division, 9 Army Corps, Army of the Potomac, Sept. 30-Oct. 8, 1862 and Oct. 26-Dec. 15, 1862. Commanded 1 Division, 9 Army Corps, Army of the Potomac, Oct. 8- 26, 1862. Resigned March 15, 1863, due to "prostration of my health consequent upon the duties of camp life and a continued service of eighteen months in camp and the field."
Born: Dec. 19, 1808 Norwich, NY
Died: May 13, 1871 Flint, MI
Education: Graduated Hamilton College, Clinton, NY, 1826
Occupation: Lawyer
Offices/Honors: Michigan Senate, 1846–47. Lieutenant Governor of Michigan, 1848–49 and 1850–51.
Miscellaneous: Resided Fenton, Genesee Co., MI; and Flint, Genesee Co., MI. Father-in-law of Colonel William B. McCreery (21 MI Infantry).
Buried: Glenwood Cemetery, Flint, MI (Section H, Lot 80)
References: *Biographical History of Genesee County, MI.* Indianapolis, IN, 1908. *Golden Jubilee, Transactions Grand Lodge F&AM Michigan.* N.p., 1895. *American Biographical History of Eminent and Self-Made Men.* Michigan volume. Cincinnati, OH, 1878. Thomas A. Atkins. *The Fenton Family of America and Great Britain.* Yonkers, NY, 1912. *History of Genesee County, MI.* Philadelphia, PA, 1879. Military Service File, National Archives.

Judson Smith Farrar (courtesy the Rev. Linda C. Pope).

William Matthew Fenton (Massachusetts MOLLUS Collection, USAMHI [Vol. 118, p. 6086]).

William Matthew Fenton (with daughter Sarah) (courtesy Archives of Michigan).

Thaddeus Foote

Major, 6 MI Cavalry, Oct. 13, 1862. Colonel, 10 MI Cavalry, Nov. 11, 1863. Accidental GSW right foot, Greenville, TN, May 31, 1864. Facing charges involving a recruitment violation, he resigned July 25, 1864, because of his wound, since "my general health has become impaired by long service in the field," and since "I do not wish to subject the Government ... to the expense of affording me a formal trial." Commissioner, District 4, Michigan Board of Enrollment, Dec. 3, 1864. Honorably discharged, May 5, 1865.

Born: April 27, 1821 Southwick, MA
Died: Feb. 3, 1903 Grand Rapids, MI
Education: Graduated Yale University, New Haven, CT, 1844. Attended Harvard University Law School, Cambridge, MA.
Occupation: Lawyer
Offices/Honors: U.S. Pension Agent, Grand Rapids, MI, 1869–77
Miscellaneous: Resided Grand Rapids, Kent Co., MI
Buried: Fulton Street Cemetery, Grand Rapids, MI (Block 15, Lot 6)

Thaddeus Foote (Massachusetts MOLLUS Collection, USAMHI [Vol. 72, p. 3581]).

References: *Obituary Record of Graduates of Yale University Deceased During the Academical Year Ending in June 1903.* New Haven, CT, 1903. Pension File and Military Service File, National Archives. Abram W. Foote. *Foote Family: Comprising the Genealogy and History of Nathaniel Foote of Wethersfield, CT, and His Descendants.* Rutland, VT, 1907. Obituary, *Grand Rapids Herald,* Feb. 4, 1903. Ernest B. Fisher, editor. *Grand Rapids and Kent County, MI.* Chicago, IL, 1918. Letters Received, Volunteer Service Branch, Adjutant General's Office, File K502(VS)1863, National Archives. Luther S. Trowbridge. *A Brief History of the 10th Michigan Cavalry.* Detroit, MI, 1905.

Dorus Morton Fox

Major, 9 MI Infantry, Sept. 10, 1861. Commanded Post of Tullahoma, TN, Aug. 1862. Colonel, 27 MI Infantry, Jan. 15, 1863. GSW right arm, Petersburg, VA, June 17, 1864. Having endured repeated charges of recruiting (and other) irregularities (including the selling of commissions), preferred by prospective Colonel Thomas S. Sprague (deposed by Fox upon the formation of the regiment), he resigned Oct. 3, 1864, since "my health has become impaired in the service ..., the health of my family absolutely requires my presence

at home ..., and my regiment is reduced to less than half its maximum number."
Born: Nov. 29, 1817 Adams, NY
Died: Nov. 20, 1901 Des Moines, IA
Occupation: Produce dealer, steamboat line operator, and miller before war. Newspaper editor and journalist after war.
Offices/Honors: Register of U.S. Land Office, Des Moines, IA, 1889–93
Miscellaneous: Resided Lyons, Ionia Co., MI; Chicago, IL; New York City, NY; Rochester, Monroe Co., NY; Ottumwa, Wapello Co., IA; and Des Moines, Polk Co., IA. An active worker in temperance and spiritualism organizations. Author of *A History of Political Parties, National Reminiscences, and the Tippecanoe Movement* (1895).
Buried: Woodland Cemetery, Des Moines, IA (Block 21, Lot 8C, unmarked)
References: *Portrait and Biographical Album of Polk County, IA.* Chicago, IL, 1890. Obituary, *Davenport Weekly Leader,* Nov. 22, 1901. Obituary, *Iowa State Register,* Nov. 21, 1901. Letters Received, Volunteer Service Branch, Adjutant General's Office, Files P145(VS)1863 and S1008(VS)1864, National Archives. Pension File and Military Service File, National Archives. Charles W. Bennett. *Historical Sketches of the 9th Michigan Infantry (General Thomas' Headquarters Guards) With an Account of the Battle of Murfreesboro, TN.* Coldwater, MI, 1913.

Dorus Morton Fox (post-war) (Frank A. Lester. *Semi-Centennial Roster of the Ninth Michigan Infantry Veteran Volunteers.* Lansing, Michigan, 1911).

Henry Clarke Gilbert

Colonel, 19 MI Infantry, Sept. 5, 1862. Taken prisoner, Thompson's Station, TN, March 5, 1863. Confined Libby Prison, Richmond, VA. Paroled May 5, 1863. Commanded 3 Brigade, 1 Division, Reserve Corps, Army of the Cumberland, June 24-July 12, 1863. GSW breast, Resaca, GA, May 15, 1864.
Born: July 14, 1818 Syracuse, NY
Died: May 24, 1864 DOW Chattanooga, TN
Occupation: Lawyer and farmer
Offices/Honors: Indian Agent to the Chippewa Indians of Northern Michigan, 1853–57
Miscellaneous: Resided Coldwater, Branch Co., MI
Buried: Oak Grove Cemetery, Coldwater, MI (Old Plat, Lot 790)
References: *The Civil War Letters and Diaries of Henry C. Gilbert.* Transcribed and published by Alcetta Gilbert Campbell. Corvallis, OR, 1991. *American Biographical History of Eminent and Self-Made Men.* Michigan volume. Cincinnati, OH, 1878. William M. Anderson. *They Died to Make Men Free: A History of the 19th Michigan Infantry in the Civil War.* Berrien Springs, MI, 1980. Pension File and Military Service File, National Archives. Francis B. Trowbridge. *The Champion Genealogy: A History of the Descendants of Henry Champion of*

Henry Clarke Gilbert (U.S. Military Academy Library).

Saybrook and Lyme, CT. New Haven, CT, 1891. Henry C. Gilbert Papers, 1826–64. William L. Clements Library, University of Michigan, Ann Arbor, MI.

Ebenezer Gould

Major, 5 MI Cavalry, Sept. 2, 1862. Lieutenant Colonel, 5 MI Cavalry, Dec. 31, 1862. GSW right ankle, Hagerstown, MD, July 13, 1863. Commanded Dismounted Cavalry, Army of the Potomac, June-July 1864. *Colonel,* 5 MI Cavalry, Sept. 21, 1864. Discharged for disability, Nov. 10, 1864, due to chronic diarrhea.

Born: April 10, 1817 Fleming Twp., Cayuga Co., NY
Died: Sept. 7, 1877 Owosso, MI
Occupation: Lawyer and farmer
Miscellaneous: Resided Owosso, Shiawassee Co., MI
Buried: Oak Hill Cemetery, Owosso, MI (Section H)
References: Obituary, *Owosso Weekly Press,* Sept. 12, 1877. *History of Shiawassee and Clinton Counties, MI.* Philadelphia, PA, 1880. Pension File and Military Service File, National Archives. *American Biographical History of Eminent and Self-Made Men.* Michigan volume. Cincinnati, OH, 1878. Letters Received, Volunteer Service Branch, Adjutant General's Office, File L654(VS)1864, National Archives. *Pioneer Collections: Report of the Pioneer Society of the State of Michigan.* Vol. 3. Lansing, MI, 1881.

Claudius Buchanan Grant

Captain, Co. D, 20 MI Infantry, Aug. 11, 1862. Major, 20 MI Infantry, June 20, 1864. Lieutenant Colonel, 20 MI Infantry, Dec. 20, 1864. *Colonel,* 20 MI Infantry, Dec. 20, 1864. Resigned April 12, 1865, since "I consider it my duty to those at home to leave the service after having served two and a half years in the field."

Born: Oct. 25, 1835 Lebanon, York Co., ME
Died: Feb. 28, 1921 St. Petersburg, FL
Education: Graduated University of Michigan, Ann Arbor, MI, 1859
Occupation: School teacher before war. Lawyer and judge after war.
Offices/Honors: Michigan House of Representatives, 1871–74. Circuit Court Judge, 1882–89. Associate Justice, Michigan Supreme Court, 1890–1909.
Miscellaneous: Resided Ann Arbor, Washtenaw Co., MI, 1865–73; Houghton, Houghton Co., MI, 1873–86; Marquette, Marquette Co., MI, 1886–90; Detroit, MI, 1890–93 and 1910–21; and Lansing, Ingham Co., MI, 1893–1910
Buried: Forest Hill Cemetery, Ann Arbor, MI (Block 33, Lot 5)
References: *American Biographical History of Eminent and Self-Made Men.* Michigan volume.

Ebenezer Gould (Massachusetts MOLLUS Collection, USAMHI [Vol. 72, p. 3584]).

Claudius Buchanan Grant (Bob Coch Collection).

Cincinnati, OH, 1878. Obituary Circular, Whole No. 609, Michigan MOLLUS. George I. Reed, editor. *Bench and Bar of Michigan*. Chicago, IL, 1897. *Men of Progress: Embracing Biographical Sketches of Representative Michigan Men*. Detroit, MI, 1900. Pension File and Military Service File, National Archives. Letters Received, Volunteer Service Branch, Adjutant General's Office, File G522(VS) 1865, National Archives. Byron M. Cutcheon, compiler. *The Story of the 20th Michigan Infantry*. Lansing, MI, 1904. *Michigan Biographies*. Lansing, MI, 1924.

Frank Graves

Lieutenant Colonel, 8 MI Infantry, Sept. 23, 1861. Acting AIG, Staff of Brig. Gen. Horatio G. Wright, June 1862. Resigned Sept. 24, 1862, on account of "long continued ill health." Colonel, 8 MI Infantry, May 26, 1863. Taken prisoner, May 6, 1864, Wilderness, VA, and murdered by his captors, who were attracted by his fancy boots.

Born: Oct. 13, 1836 Niles, MI
Died: May 6, 1864 Wilderness, VA (murdered after being taken prisoner because he would not submit to indignity and robbery at the hands of his captors)
Education: Attended U.S. Military Academy, West Point, NY (Class of 1857)

Frank Graves (photograph by E. B. Ives, 22 Main Street, Niles, Michigan; Civil War Times Illustrated Collection, USAMHI).

Occupation: Hardware merchant
Miscellaneous: Resided Niles, Berrien Co., MI. Brother-in-law of Bvt. Major Gen. Henry A. Morrow.
Buried: Silverbrook Cemetery, Niles, MI (City Addition, Section 42, Lot 8)
References: Pension File and Military Service File, National Archives. Letters Received, Volunteer Service Branch, Adjutant General's Office, File C1844(VS)1863, National Archives. Charles Lanman. *The Red Book of Michigan; A Civil, Military and Biographical History*. Detroit, MI, 1871.

William Henry Graves

Captain, Co. K, 1 MI Infantry (3 months), May 1, 1861. GSW left leg, 1st Bull Run, VA, July 21, 1861. Captain, Co. K, 1 MI Infantry (3 years), Aug. 17, 1861. Lieutenant Colonel, 12 MI Infantry, Nov. 18, 1861. Colonel, 12 MI Infantry, Sept. 1, 1862. Commanded 1 Brigade, 3 Division, 16 Army Corps, Army of the Tennessee, July 12–Aug. 14, 1863. Commanded 1 Brigade, 2 Division, Arkansas Expedition, 16 Army Corps, Army of the Tennessee, Aug.-Sept. 1863. Commanded 3 Brigade, 2 Division, Army of Arkansas, Department of the Missouri, Sept. 13, 1863-Jan. 6, 1864. Commanded 3 Brigade, 2 Division, 7 Army Corps, Department of Arkansas, April 9–16, 1864. Commanded 1 Brigade, 2 Division, District of Little Rock, 7 Army Corps, Department of Arkansas, May 13-Sept. 10, 1864. GSW right knee, Gregory's Landing, near Augusta, AR, Sept. 4, 1864. Com-

William H. Graves (Dale R. Niesen Collection).

William H. Graves (seated left, with officers of the 12th Michigan Infantry, including Adjutant William E. Stewart, Major Phineas Graves, and Lt. Col. Dwight May, left to right) (photograph by A. J. White's Photograph Rooms, De Vall's Bluff, Arkansas; Roger D. Hunt Collection, USAMHI [RG98S-CWP58.88]).

manded 1 Brigade, 2 Division, 7 Army Corps, Department of Arkansas, Jan. 7-June 10, 1865. Resigned June 10, 1865, since "I have served my country four years and two months as a commissioned officer."

Born: Aug. 28, 1836 Adrian, MI
Died: Sept. 23, 1874 Adrian, MI
Occupation: Railroad office clerk and banker
Miscellaneous: Resided Adrian, Lenawee Co., MI; and Toledo, Lucas Co., OH, 1866–70
Buried: Oakwood Cemetery, Adrian, MI (Block 19, Lot 14)
References: Obituary, *Adrian Daily Times and Expositor*, Sept. 24, 1874. William A. Whitney and Richard I. Bonner. *History and Biographical Record of Lenawee County, MI.* Adrian, MI, 1879. *Report of the Proceedings of the Society of the Army of the Tennessee at the Eighth Annual Meeting.* Cincinnati, OH, 1877. Pension File and Military Service File, National Archives.

George Gray

Colonel, 6 MI Cavalry, Oct. 13, 1862. Commanded 2 Brigade, 3 Division, Cavalry Corps, Army of the Potomac, Sept. 1863. He resigned May 19, 1864, "being now absent from the field for more than seven months, ... in consequence of injuries received while temporarily in command of a brigade, ... with no prospect of being able to resume duty there."

Born: June 20, 1824 County Tyrone, Ireland
Died: April 19, 1892 Orange, NJ
Education: Graduated Trinity College, Dublin, Ireland
Occupation: Lawyer, being for many years General Counsel of the Northern Pacific Railroad Co.
Miscellaneous: Resided Grand Rapids, Kent Co., MI; and Orange, Essex Co., NJ
Buried: Rosedale Cemetery, Orange, NJ (Prospect Section, Lot 80)
References: Albert Baxter. *History of the City of Grand Rapids, MI.* New York and Grand Rapids, 1891. Dwight Goss. *History of Grand Rapids and Its Industries.* Chicago, IL, 1906. Obituary, *Newark Advertiser*, April 20, 1892. Obituary, *Orange Chronicle*, April 23, 1892. Military Service File,

George Gray (post-war) (James H. Kidd. *Personal Recollections of a Cavalryman with Custer's Michigan Cavalry Brigade in the Civil War.* Ionia, Michigan, 1908).

National Archives. Letters Received, Volunteer Service Branch, Adjutant General's Office, File C813(VS)1864, National Archives. Dwight Goss, "The Bench and Bar of Kent County," *Historical Collections: Collections and Researches Made by the Michigan Pioneer and Historical Society.* Vol. 35. Lansing, MI, 1907. Edward G. Longacre. *Custer and His Wolverines: The Michigan Cavalry Brigade, 1861–1865.* Conshohocken, PA, 1997.

Eli Augustus Griffin

Captain, Co. A, 6 MI Infantry, Aug. 20, 1861. GSW arm, Port Hudson, LA, May 27, 1863. Acting AIG, 1 Brigade, 2 Division, 19 Army Corps, June 1863. Resigned July 17, 1863, since "I have not been in good health for a long time and was wounded ..., from which I have not entirely recovered." Major, 19 MI Infantry, Nov. 13, 1863. *Lieutenant Colonel,* 19 MI Infantry, April 20, 1864. GSW left breast, Gilgal Church, GA, June 15, 1864. *Colonel,* 19 MI Infantry, June 20, 1864.

Born: July 1833 Poplar Ridge, Cayuga Co., NY
Died: June 16, 1864 DOW near Ackworth, GA
Occupation: Dry goods merchant
Miscellaneous: Resided Niles, Berrien Co., MI
Buried: Silverbrook Cemetery, Niles, MI (Bond Addition, Section 6, Lot 3)
References: Orville W. Coolidge. *A 20th Century History of Berrien County, MI.* Chicago and New York, 1906. William M. Anderson. *They Died to Make Men Free: A History of the 19th Michigan Infantry in the Civil War.* Berrien Springs, MI, 1980. Pension File and Military Service File, National Archives. Letters Received, Volunteer Service Branch, Adjutant General's Office, File G991(VS) 1863, National Archives. Eli Augustus Griffin Collection, Bentley Historical Library, University of Michigan, Ann Arbor, MI.

Ira Rufus Grosvenor

Colonel, 7 MI Infantry, Aug. 22, 1861. Commanded 2 Brigade, Stone's Division, Army of the Potomac, Dec. 4, 1861-Feb. 22, 1862. Resigned July 7, 1862, due to "the impoverished state of my health ..., together with the precarious state of the health of my family, and the personal care my business affairs demand."

Born: March 18, 1815 Paxton, MA
Died: April 7, 1899 Monroe, MI
Occupation: Lawyer
Offices/Honors: Michigan House of Representatives, 1871–72
Miscellaneous: Resided Monroe, Monroe Co., MI
Buried: Woodland Cemetery, Monroe, MI (Range 8 North, Lot 13)
References: Talcott E. Wing, editor. *History of Monroe County, MI.* New York City, NY, 1890. Obituary, *Monroe Democrat,* April 13, 1899. George I. Reed, editor. *Bench and Bar of Michigan.*

Eli A. Griffin (David K. Parks Collection).

Ira Rufus Grosvenor (Massachusetts MOLLUS Collection, USAMHI [Vol. 94, p. 4826]).

Ira Rufus Grosvenor (courtesy Archives of Michigan).

Chicago, IL, 1897. Pension File and Military Service File, National Archives. David G. Townshend. *The Seventh Michigan Volunteer Infantry.* Fort Lauderdale, FL, 1993. *Michigan Biographies.* Lansing, MI, 1924.

Norman Jonathan Hall

1 Lieutenant, 5 U.S. Artillery, May 14, 1861. Chief of Artillery, Hooker's Division, Army of the Potomac, Dec. 1861-March 1862. Acting AAG, Staff of Brig. Gen. John G. Barnard, May-June 1862. Colonel, 7 MI Infantry, July 14, 1862. GSW Antietam, MD, Sept. 17, 1862. Commanded 3 Brigade, 2 Division, 2 Army Corps, Army of the Potomac, Sept. 17–19, 1862, Nov.-Dec. 15, 1862 and March 20-July 18, 1863. Captain, 5 U.S. Artillery, Aug. 1, 1863. Suffering from "chronic dysentery and chills and fever," he was discharged from volunteer service, June 4, 1864, on account of physical disability. Retired from Regular Army, Feb. 22, 1865.
  Born: March 2, 1837 Geneva, NY
  Died: May 26, 1867 Brooklyn, NY
  Education: Graduated U.S. Military Academy, West Point, NY, 1859
  Occupation: Regular Army (Captain, 5 U.S. Artillery, retired Feb. 22, 1865)

Norman Jonathan Hall (photograph by J. W. Black, 173 Washington St., Boston, Masschusetts; courtesy Henry Deeks).

  Miscellaneous: Resided Raisinville, Monroe Co., MI; and Brooklyn, NY
  Buried: Post Cemetery, West Point, NY (Section 30, Row I, Grave 373)
  References: David Dorsey Finney, Jr. *Colonel Norman Jonathon Hall of the 7th Michigan Infantry, 1837–1867: A Biographical Sketch.* Howell, MI, 2001. George W. Cullum. *Biographical Register of the Officers and Graduates of the U.S. Military Academy.* Third Edition. Boston and New York, 1891. *Dedication of the New York Auxiliary State Monument on the Battlefield of Gettysburg.* Albany, NY, 1926. David G. Townshend. *The Seventh Michigan Volunteer Infantry.* Fort Lauderdale, FL, 1993. Frank B. Woodford. *Father Abraham's Children: Michigan Episodes in the Civil War.* Detroit, MI, 1961. Letters Received, Volunteer Service Branch, Adjutant General's Office, File H146(VS)1863, National Archives. Pension File and Military Service File, National Archives.

Smith Hugh Hastings

Private, Co. C, 1 MI Infantry (3 months), May 1, 1861. Honorably mustered out, Aug. 7, 1861. 1

Norman Jonathan Hall (courtesy Steve Meadow).

Lieutenant, Co. M, 5 MI Cavalry, Aug. 30, 1862. Captain, Co. M, 5 MI Cavalry, Jan. 10, 1863. GSW foot and groin, Trevilian Station, VA, June 12, 1864. Major, 5 MI Cavalry, Aug. 10, 1864. Lieutenant Colonel, 5 MI Cavalry, Nov. 11, 1864. Colonel, 5 MI Cavalry, Feb. 25, 1865. Honorably mustered out, June 22, 1865.

Born: Dec. 27, 1843 Quincy, Branch Co., MI
Died: Oct. 13, 1905 Denver, CO
Occupation: Commission merchant dealing primarily in produce, grain and gunpowder
Offices/Honors: Medal of Honor, Newbys Crossroads, VA, July 24, 1863. "While in command of a squadron in rear guard of a cavalry division, then retiring before the advance of a corps of infantry, was attacked by the enemy and, orders having been given to abandon the guns of a section of field artillery with the rear guard that were in imminent danger of capture, he disregarded the orders received and aided in repelling the attack and saving the guns."
Miscellaneous: Resided Coldwater, Branch Co., MI; and Denver, CO
Buried: Riverside Cemetery, Denver, CO (Block 5, Lot 53)

References: *History of the City of Denver, CO.* Chicago, IL, 1880. William H. Powell, editor. *Officers of the Army and Navy (Volunteer) Who Served in the Civil War.* Philadelphia, PA, 1893. Obituary, *Rocky Mountain News,* Oct. 14, 1905. George Lang, Raymond L. Collins, and Gerard F. White, compilers. *Medal of Honor Recipients, 1863–1994.* New York City, NY, 1995. Military Service File, National Archives. Letters Received, Volunteer Service Branch, Adjutant General's Office, File 6662(VS)1872, National Archives. W. F. Beyer and O. F. Keydel, editors. *Deeds of Valor.* Detroit, MI, 1906.

John Wesley Horner

1 Lieutenant, Co. K, 1 MI Infantry (3 months), May 1, 1861. Honorably mustered out, Aug. 7, 1861. Captain, Co. C, 18 MI Infantry, Aug. 8, 1862. Major, 18 MI Infantry, Aug. 13, 1862. Provost Marshal, Nashville, TN, Feb. 27, 1864-June 1864. Lieutenant Colonel, 18 MI Infantry, March 7, 1864. Provost Marshal, District of Northern Alabama, Aug. 14, 1864-March 2, 1865. Colonel, 18 MI Infantry, March 21, 1865. Commanded Post of Huntsville, AL, April-June 1865. Honorably mustered out, June 26, 1865.

Born: May 29, 1833 PA
Died: Aug. 16, 1874 Osawatomie (KS) Insane Asylum
Education: Graduated University of Michigan, Ann Arbor, MI, 1858

Smith Hugh Hastings (David D. Finney Collection).

Occupation: College professor and newspaper editor. Professor of Mental and Moral Philosophy, University of Kansas, 1867–68. Editor of *Chetopa Advance,* 1869–73.
Offices/Honors: President of Baker University, Baldwin City, KS, 1866–67
Miscellaneous: Resided Adrian, Lenawee Co., MI; Lawrence, Douglas Co., KS; and Chetopa, Labette Co., KS
Buried: Place of burial unknown
References: *University of Michigan: General Catalogue of Officers and Students, 1837–1890.* Ann Arbor, MI, 1891. Homer K. Ebright. *The History of Baker University.* Baldwin, KS, 1951. Nelson Case, editor. *History of Labette County, KS, and Its Representative Citizens.* Chicago, IL, 1901. Wilson Sterling, editor. *Quarter-Centennial History of the University of Kansas, 1866–1891.* Topeka, KS, 1891. Pension File and Military Service File, National Archives. Obituary, *Daily Kansas Tribune,* Aug. 25, 1874. Death notice, *Detroit Evening News,* Aug. 25, 1874.

Harrison H. Jeffords

1 Lieutenant, Co. K, 4 MI Infantry, June 20, 1861. Captain, Co. C, 4 MI Infantry, May 1, 1862. Colonel, 4 MI Infantry, March 12, 1863. Bayonet wound chest, Gettysburg, PA, July 2, 1863, receiving a "thrust through with a bayonet while gallantly attempting to rescue his colors from the grasp of the enemy."
Born: Aug. 21, 1837 Monroe Co., NY
Died: July 3, 1863 DOW Gettysburg, PA
Education: Graduated University of Michigan Law School, Ann Arbor, MI, 1861

Smith Hugh Hastings (David D. Finney Collection).

John Wesley Horner (Michael W. Waskul Collection).

Harrison H. Jeffords (reunion ribbon).

Occupation: Lawyer
Miscellaneous: Resided Dexter, Washtenaw Co., MI
Buried: Forest Lawn Cemetery, Dexter, MI
References: *Portrait and Biographical Album of Lenawee County, MI.* Chicago, IL, 1888. Jeffrey J. and Loree L. Kowalis. *Died At Gettysburg!* Hightstown, NJ, 1998. Obituary, *Weekly Michigan Argus*, July 17, 1863. Martin Bertera and Ken Oberholtzer. *The 4th Michigan Volunteer Infantry at Gettysburg: The Battle for the Wheatfield.* Dayton, OH, 1997. Pension File and Military Service File, National Archives. Letters Received, Volunteer Service Branch, Adjutant General's Office, File S1749(VS)1863, National Archives.

Thomas W. Johnston

2 Lieutenant, Co. M, 2 MI Cavalry, Sept. 16, 1861. Captain, Co. K, 2 MI Cavalry, Aug. 1, 1862. Captain, Co. M, 2 MI Cavalry, March 1, 1863. GSW left leg, Dandridge, TN, Dec. 24, 1863. Acting AIG, Staff of Brig. Gen. John T. Croxton, 1 Brigade, 1 Division, Cavalry Corps, Military Division of the Mississippi, Dec. 18, 1864-March 18, 1865. *Colonel,* 2 MI Cavalry, Dec. 31, 1864. Lieutenant Colonel, 2 MI Cavalry, March 7, 1865. Commanded Post of Macon, GA, July 25-Aug. 29, 1865. Honorably mustered out, Aug. 29, 1865.
Born: Nov. 10, 1838 Marshall, MI
Died: Sept. 8, 1884 Marshall, MI
Occupation: Insurance agent and grocer
Miscellaneous: Resided Marshall, Calhoun Co., MI; and Chicago, IL
Buried: Oakridge Cemetery, Marshall, MI
References: Obituary, *Marshall Statesman*, Sept. 12, 1884. Rex Miller. *Croxton's Raid.* Fort Collins, CO, 1979. Pension File and Military Service File, National Archives. Marshall P. Thatcher. *A Hundred Battles in the West, St. Louis to Atlanta, 1861–65, the Second Michigan Cavalry, with the Armies of the Mississippi, Ohio, Kentucky and Cumberland.* Detroit, MI, 1884.

Patrick H. Keegan

1 Lieutenant, Co. K, 11 MI Infantry, Aug. 24, 1861. GSW face, Stone's River, TN, Dec. 31, 1862. Captain, Co. K, 11 MI Infantry, March 14, 1863. GSW chest, Missionary Ridge, TN, Nov. 25, 1863. *Major,* 11 MI Infantry, Nov. 25, 1863. Honorably mustered out, Sept. 30, 1864. Lieutenant Colonel, 11 MI Infantry (Reorganized), March 1, 1865. Colonel, 11 MI Infantry, March 16, 1865. Commanded Post of Knoxville, TN, Sept. 1865. Honorably mustered out, Sept. 16, 1865.
Born: 1841? MI
Died: Nov. 26, 1866 Deerfield, MI

Harrison H. Jeffords (Massachusetts MOLLUS Collection, USAMHI [Vol. 118, p. 6085]).

Thomas W. Johnston (Roger D. Hunt Collection, USAMHI [RG98S-CWP160.49]).

Patrick H. Keegan (Dearborn Historical Museum).

Occupation: Farm laborer
Miscellaneous: Resided Deerfield, Lenawee Co., MI
Buried: Deerfield Township Cemetery, Deerfield, MI
References: Pension File and Military Service File, National Archives. 1860 U.S. Census, Blissfield Twp., Lenawee Co., MI. Leland W. Thornton. *When Gallantry was Commonplace: The History of the Michigan Eleventh Volunteer Infantry, 1861–64.* New York City, NY, 1991. Charles E. Belknap. *History of the Michigan Organizations at Chickamauga, Chattanooga, and Missionary Ridge, 1863.* Lansing, MI, 1899.

Francis William Kellogg

Colonel, 3 MI Cavalry, Dec. 6, 1861. Resigned March 13, 1862.
Born: May 30, 1810 Worthington, MA
Died: Jan. 13, 1879 Alliance, OH
Occupation: Lumber merchant
Offices/Honors: Michigan House of Representatives, 1857–58. U.S. House of Representatives, 1859–65, 1868–69. U.S. Collector of Internal Revenue, 1866–68.
Miscellaneous: Resided Grand Rapids, Kent Co., MI; Mobile, AL; New York City, NY; and Alliance, Stark Co., OH
Buried: Fulton Street Cemetery, Grand Rapids, MI (Block 7, Lot 9)
References: Timothy Hopkins. *The Kelloggs in the Old World and the New.* San Francisco, CA,

Francis William Kellogg (U.S. House of Representatives, 1862) (The National Archives [B-2445]).

1903. James L. Harrison, compiler. *Biographical Directory of the American Congress, 1774–1949.* Washington, DC, 1950. Edward W. Barber, "Michigan Men in Congress: The Chosen of the People," *Historical Collections: Collections and Researches Made by the Michigan Pioneer and Historical Society.* Vol. 35. Lansing, MI, 1907. William H. Barnes. *The Fortieth Congress of the United States: Historical and Biographical.* New York City, NY, 1870. *Michigan Biographies.* Lansing, MI, 1924. Military Service File, National Archives. Letters Received, Volunteer Service Branch, Adjutant General's Office, File W705(VS)1862, National Archives.

George Washington LaPointe

Corporal, Co. D, 7 MI Infantry, Aug. 22, 1861. Sergeant, Co. D, 7 MI Infantry, Nov. 25, 1861. 2 Lieutenant, Co. D, 7 MI Infantry, Sept. 18, 1862. 1 Lieutenant, Co. D, 7 MI Infantry, May 26, 1863. Captain, Co. K, 7 MI Infantry, Sept. 21, 1863. GSW right knee, Spotsylvania, VA, May 13, 1864. Captain, Co. C, 7 MI Infantry, July 6, 1864. Lieutenant Colonel, 7 MI Infantry, Oct. 13, 1864. *Colonel,* 7 MI Infantry, Nov. 18, 1864. Honorably mustered out, July 5, 1865. Bvt. Colonel, USV, April 2, 1865, for gallant and meritorious services in front of Petersburg, VA.
Born: March 14, 1842 Blissfield, MI

George Washington LaPointe (courtesy Archives of Michigan).

Died: May 18, 1927 Wilson, WI
Occupation: Sailor and factory worker before war. U.S. customs inspector and lumber merchant after war.
Miscellaneous: Resided Monroe, Monroe Co., MI, to 1866; Detroit, MI, 1866–74; Wilson, St. Croix Co., WI, after 1874
Buried: Evergreen Cemetery, Menomonie, WI
References: Pension File and Military Service File, National Archives. Augustus B. Easton, editor. *History of the St. Croix Valley.* Chicago, IL, 1909. Obituary, *Dunn County News,* May 19, 1927. David G. Townshend. *The Seventh Michigan Volunteer Infantry.* Fort Lauderdale, FL, 1993.

George Lockley

Private, Co. B, 1 MI Infantry (3 months), May 1, 1861. Honorably mustered out, Aug. 7, 1861. Sergeant, Co. G, 1 MI Infantry (3 years), Aug. 24, 1861. 1 Sergeant, Co. G, 1 MI Infantry, July 1, 1862. 2 Lieutenant, Co. G, 1 MI Infantry, Aug. 6, 1862. 1 Lieutenant, Co. G, 1 MI Infantry, Sept. 23, 1862. Captain, Co. A, 1 MI Infantry, Nov. 1, 1862. GSW right thigh, North Anna, VA, May 23, 1864. Major, 1 MI Infantry, Dec. 22, 1864. Lieutenant Colonel, 1 MI Infantry, Jan. 7, 1865. Shell wound right shoulder, Hatcher's Run, VA, Feb. 6, 1865. *Colonel,* 1 MI Infantry, May 30, 1865. Honorably mustered out, July 9, 1865.
Born: 1835? Birmingham, England
Died: Sept. 17, 1882 St. Ignace, MI
Occupation: Farmer before war. Clerk and insurance agent after war.
Offices/Honors: Postmaster, East Saginaw, MI, 1871–75
Miscellaneous: Resided Ann Arbor, Washtenaw Co., MI; East Saginaw, Saginaw Co., MI, 1866-76; and St. Ignace, Mackinac Co., MI, after 1876
Buried: Place of burial unknown
References: Pension File and Military Service File, National Archives. Obituary, *Saginaw Evening News,* Sept. 18, 1882. Obituary, *Saginaw Daily Courier,* Sept. 19, 1882. Letters Received, Volunteer Service Branch, Adjutant General's Office, File 7999(VS)1882, National Archives. James C. Mills. *History of Saginaw County, MI: Historical, Commercial, Biographical.* Saginaw, MI, 1918. George Lockley Papers, Bentley Historical Library, University of Michigan, Ann Arbor, MI. Charles W. Owen. *The First Michigan Infantry, Three Months and Three Years.* Quincy, MI, 1903.

George Lockley (George Lockley Papers, Bentley Historical Library, University of Michigan).

Clement Augustus Lounsberry

Private, Co. I, 1 MI Infantry (3 months), May 1, 1861. GSW right leg, 1st Bull Run, VA, July 21, 1861. Taken prisoner, 1st Bull Run, VA, July 21, 1861. Confined Libby Prison, Richmond, VA, and Salisbury (NC) Prison. Paroled May 28, 1862. Honorably mustered out, July 6, 1862. 1 Sergeant, Co. I, 20 MI Infantry, Aug. 19, 1862. 2 Lieutenant, Co. K, 20 MI Infantry, Feb. 1, 1863. 2 Lieutenant, Co. I, 20 MI Infantry, April 25, 1863. GSW right thigh, Horseshoe Bend, KY, May 9, 1863. Taken prisoner, Horseshoe Bend, KY, May 9, 1863. Escaped May 30, 1863. 1 Lieutenant, Co. I, 20 MI Infantry, Nov. 19, 1863. Captain, Co. H, 20 MI Infantry, May 12, 1864. GSW left leg, Spotsylvania, VA, May 12, 1864. Captain, Co. A, 20 MI Infantry, Oct. 10, 1864. Engineer Officer, 2 Brigade, 1 Division, 9 Army Corps, Army of the Potomac, Oct. 25-Dec. 31, 1864. Acting AAG, 2 Brigade, 1 Division, 9 Army Corps, Army of the Potomac, Jan. 1-May 1, 1865. *Colonel,* 20 MI Infantry, March 11, 1865. Lieutenant Colonel, 20 MI Infantry, April 29, 1865. Honorably mustered out, May 30, 1865.

Born: March 27, 1843 Wilmington, DeKalb Co., IN

Died: Oct. 3, 1926 Washington, DC

Occupation: Farm laborer before war. Newspaper editor and publisher after war, best known for publishing in the *Bismarck Tribune* the first full account of the 1876 Custer Massacre.

Offices/Honors: Auditor, Martin Co., MN, 1866-70. Postmaster, Bismarck, ND, 1876-85. Special agent, U.S. General Land Office, 1889-1905.

Miscellaneous: Resided Marengo, Calhoun Co., MI; Fairmont, Martin Co., MN; Minneapolis, MN; Bismarck, Burleigh Co., ND; Duluth, St. Louis Co., MN; Fargo, Cass Co., ND; and Washington, DC

Buried: Arlington National Cemetery, Arlington, VA (Section 2, Lot 1133)

References: Pension File and Military Service File, National Archives. Clement A. Lounsberry. *North Dakota History and People: Outlines of American History.* Chicago, IL, 1917. C. W. G. Hyde and William Stoddard, editors. *History of the Great Northwest and Its Men of Progress.* Minneapolis, MN, 1901. Letters Received, Volunteer Service Branch, Adjutant General's Office, File L572(VS) 1862, National Archives. Obituary, *The Bismarck Tribune,* Oct. 6, 1926. Obituary, *Washington Post,* Oct. 4, 1926. Byron M. Cutcheon, compiler. *The Story of the Twentieth Michigan Infantry.* Lansing, MI, 1904. http://www.arlingtoncemetery.net/calounsberry.htm.

Constant Luce

Captain, Co. A, 4 MI Infantry, May 16, 1861. Resigned Nov. 23, 1861, due to "continued ill health, which unfits me for the duties of the service." Lieutenant Colonel, 17 MI Infantry, Aug. 11, 1862. Colonel, 17 MI Infantry, March 21, 1863. Honorably mustered out, Dec. 1, 1864. Charged after his discharge with presenting a false claim against the United States, he was tried by court-martial and found guilty, Feb. 25, 1865. His sentence was eventually remitted after several months of confinement in Old Capitol Prison, Washington, DC.

Born: March 7, 1821 Pittsfield, MA

Died: Feb. 28, 1903 Monroe, MI

Occupation: Real estate agent and lawyer

Offices/Honors: Register of Deeds, Monroe Co., MI, 1852-56, 1858-60, 1868-72

Miscellaneous: Resided Monroe, Monroe Co., MI

Buried: Woodland Cemetery, Monroe, MI (Range 3 North, Lot 3)

References: Pension File and Military Service File, National Archives. Obituary, *Monroe Democrat,* March 6, 1903. Letters Received, Volunteer Service Branch, Adjutant General's Office, File B458(VS)1865, National Archives. Martha F. Mc-

Clement Augustus Lounsberry (courtesy Archives of Michigan).

Court and Thomas R. Luce. *The American Descendants of Henry Luce of Martha's Vineyard, 1640–1985.* N.p., 1985. William Christen, Gary Pritchard, David Curtis, Timothy Pack and Gregory Kolasa. *Stonewall Regiment: A History of the 17th Michigan Volunteer Infantry Regiment.* Detroit, MI, 1986. Talcott E. Wing, editor. *History of Monroe County, MI.* New York City, NY, 1890. Court-martial Case Files, 1809–1894, File NN- 3707, National Archives.

Charles Matthew Lum

Captain, Co. A, 1 MI Infantry (3 months), May 1, 1861. GSW right knee, Bull Run, VA, July 21, 1861. Honorably mustered out, Aug. 7, 1861. Colonel, 10 MI Infantry, Jan. 10, 1862. Commanded 1 Brigade, 4 Division, 14 Army Corps, Army of the Cumberland, May 5-June 8, 1863. Commanded 1 Brigade, 2 Division, 14 Army Corps, Army of the Cumberland, Aug. 22-Oct. 15, 1864. Honorably mustered out, April 1, 1865.

Born: March 1, 1830 Canandaigua, NY
Died: Sept. 18, 1899 Detroit, MI
Occupation: Artist, best known for his work as an interior decorator for the Pullman Palace Car Co.
Miscellaneous: Resided Detroit, MI
Buried: Elmwood Cemetery, Detroit, MI (Section F, Lot 89)
References: Walter F. Clowes. *The Detroit Light Guard.* Detroit, MI, 1900. Fletcher W. Hewes. *History of the 10th Regiment Michigan Volunteer Infantry.* Detroit, MI, 1864. Obituary, *Detroit Evening News,* Sept. 18, 1899. Obituary Circular, Whole No. 210, Michigan MOLLUS. Pension File, National Archives. Letters Received, Volunteer Service Branch, Adjutant General's Office, File L256(VS)1865, National Archives. *Society of the Army of the Cumberland. Twenty-eighth Reunion, Detroit, MI, Sept. 26 and 27, 1899.* Cincinnati, OH, 1900.

George Washington Lumbard

Captain, Co. E, 4 MI Infantry, June 20, 1861. Lieutenant Colonel, 4 MI Infantry, July 1, 1862. *Colonel,* 4 MI Infantry, July 3, 1863. GSW breast, Wilderness, VA, May 5, 1864.

Born: 1830? NY
Died: May 6, 1864 DOW Wilderness, VA
Occupation: Lawyer
Miscellaneous: Resided Hillsdale, Hillsdale Co., MI
Buried: Wilderness, VA (body never recovered)
References: Obituary, *Hillsdale Standard,* May 24, 1864. Pension File and Military Service File, National Archives. Martin Bertera and Ken Oberholtzer. *The 4th Michigan Volunteer Infantry at Gettysburg: The Battle for the Wheatfield.* Dayton, OH,

Charles Matthew Lum (Schuyler C. Baldwin, Photographer, Kalamazoo, Michigan; Roger D. Hunt Collection, USAMHI [RG98S-CWP80.91]).

Charles Matthew Lum (David D. Finney Collection).

George Washington Lumbard (John Fuller Collection).

1997. Edmund J. Raus, Jr. *A Generation on the March- The Union Army at Gettysburg.* Gettysburg, PA, 1996. http://www.lumbardgenealogy.com/gendata/p14.htm.

William d'Alton Mann

Captain, Co. K, 1 MI Cavalry, Aug. 29, 1861. Resigned July 5, 1862, to accept promotion. Lieutenant Colonel, 5 MI Cavalry, Aug. 21, 1862. Resigned Jan. 7, 1863, to accept promotion. Colonel, 7 MI Cavalry, Feb. 19, 1863. Having been "engaged in perfecting a new set of accoutrements for infantry and cavalry soldiers," he resigned March 1, 1864, "to give my entire personal attention" to "this enterprise which I firmly believe will prove of great value to the army."

Born: Sept. 27, 1839 Sandusky, OH
Died: May 17, 1920 Morristown, NJ
Occupation: Inventor and editor. As editor of *Town Topics: The Journal of Society,* 1891–1920, he reported the activities of New York's socially elite, but was not adverse to suppressing unsavory stories upon payment of blackmail.
Miscellaneous: Resided Blissfield, Lenawee Co., MI; Detroit, MI; Mobile, AL; and New York City, NY. Awarded patent in 1863 for an improved method of arranging the accoutrements and equipments of a soldier so as to transfer the total weight to the shoulders. Later awarded patents for a railway sleeping car and a railway refrigerator car.

Buried: Woodlawn Cemetery, New York City, NY (Section 41, Hillside Plot, Lot 8648)

References: *National Cyclopedia of American Biography.* Obituary, *New York Times,* May 18, 1920. Andy Logan. *The Man Who Robbed the Robber Barons.* London, England, 1966. John W. Leonard, editor. *Who's Who in America, 1899–1900.* Chicago, IL, 1899. Military Service File, National Archives. Letters Received, Volunteer Service Branch, Adjutant General's Office, File M2218(VS)1863, National Archives. William O. Lee, compiler. *Personal and Historical Sketches and Facial History of and by Members of the 7th Regiment Michigan Volunteer Cavalry.* Detroit, MI, 1901.

Edwin Johnson March

2 Lieutenant, Co. K, 27 MI Infantry, Dec. 8, 1863. Captain, Co. K, 27 MI Infantry, Jan. 5, 1864. Lieutenant Colonel, 2 MI Infantry, April 1, 1864. GSW head, Petersburg, VA, June 18, 1864. Colonel, 2 MI Infantry, Sept. 30, 1864. Commanded 2 Brigade, 1 Division, 9 Army Corps, Army of the Potomac, Jan. and March 1865. Resigned April 17, 1865, due to increasing disability from chronic rheumatism.

William d'Alton Mann (Massachusetts MOLLUS Collection, USAMHI [Vol. 73, p. 3601]).

Edwin Johnson March (photograph by Andrew, Hillsdale, Michigan; Roger D. Hunt Collection, USAMHI [RG98S-CWP58.83]).

Born: Sept. 15, 1836 Bridgton, ME
Died: Aug. 24, 1907 Hillsdale, MI
Occupation: Lawyer, banker, and newspaper editor
Offices/Honors: Postmaster of Hillsdale, MI, 1891–95 and 1899–1907
Miscellaneous: Resided Saco, York Co., ME, before war; and Hillsdale, Hillsdale Co., MI, after war
Buried: Oak Grove Cemetery, Hillsdale, MI (Section 16, Lot 868)
References: *In Memoriam, Founders and Makers of Michigan; a Memorial History of the State's Honored Men and Women.* Detroit and Indianapolis, 1933. Obituary, *Jonesville Independent,* Aug. 29, 1907. Pension File and Military Service File, National Archives. Letters Received, Volunteer Service Branch, Adjutant General's Office, File C2915(VS) 1864, National Archives. *Record of Service of Michigan Volunteers in the Civil War, 1861–1865.* Vol. 2 (Second Michigan Infantry). Kalamazoo, MI, 1905.

William J. May

Colonel, 11 MI Infantry, Sept. 24, 1861. Resigned April 1, 1862, due to continued ill health.
Born: 1821? PA
Died: Dec. 23, 1874 Meridian, MS
Occupation: Hotel proprietor and steamboat captain
Miscellaneous: Resided White Pigeon, St. Joseph Co., MI; Louisville, KY; and Meridian, Lauderdale Co., MS
Buried: Place of burial unknown
References: Pension File and Military Service File, National Archives. Leland W. Thornton. *When Gallantry was Commonplace: The History of the Michigan Eleventh Volunteer Infantry, 1861–64.* New York City, NY, 1991.

Daniel McConnell

Colonel, 3 MI Infantry, June 10, 1861. Resigned Oct. 22, 1861, due to ill health caused by chronic diarrhea.
Born: Aug. 11, 1828 Newbury, Berkshire, England
Died: Jan. 3, 1908 Grand Rapids, MI
Other Wars: Mexican War (1 Sergeant, Co. I, 10 U.S. Infantry)
Occupation: Dry goods merchant, jeweler, and pawn broker
Miscellaneous: Resided Grand Rapids, Kent Co., MI
Buried: Fulton Street Cemetery, Grand Rapids, MI (Block 6, Lot 21)
References: Franklin Everett. *Memorials of the Grand River Valley.* Chicago, IL, 1878. Obituary Circular, Whole No. 378, Michigan MOLLUS. Obituary, *Grand Rapids Herald,* Jan. 4, 1908. Pension File and Military Service File, National Archives. *http://thirdmichigan.blogspot.com/2009/09/daniel-mcconnell.html.*

Daniel McConnell (David W. Taylor Collection).

William Barker McCreery

Sergeant, Co. F, 2 MI Infantry, May 25, 1861. 2 Lieutenant, Co. G, 2 MI Infantry, July 10, 1861. 1 Lieutenant, RQM, 2 MI Infantry, July 22, 1861. Captain, Co. G, 2 MI Infantry, Feb. 19, 1862. GSW both legs and left wrist, Williamsburg, VA, May 5, 1862. Resigned Dec. 1, 1862, to accept promotion. Lieutenant Colonel, 21 MI Infantry, Nov. 20, 1862. Colonel, 21 MI Infantry, Feb. 4, 1863. GSW right shoulder, right arm, and left thigh, Chickamauga, GA, Sept. 20, 1863. Taken prisoner, Chickamauga, GA, Sept. 20, 1863. Confined Libby Prison, Richmond, VA. Escaped Feb. 9, 1864. Commanded Engineer Brigade, Department of the Cumberland, April–July 23 and Aug. 20–Sept. 14, 1864. Resigned Sept. 14, 1864, "on account of wounds (six in number) received at various times in action while in discharge of duty, the honorable scars of which he now wears."

Born: Aug. 27, 1836 Mount Morris, NY
Died: Dec. 9, 1896 Flint, MI
Occupation: Lawyer, lumber merchant and banker
Offices/Honors: U.S. Collector of Internal Revenue, 1871–74. Michigan State Treasurer, 1875–79. U.S. Consul, Valparaiso, Chile, 1890–92.
Miscellaneous: Resided Flint, Genesee Co., MI. Son-in-law of Colonel William M. Fenton (8 MI Infantry).
Buried: Glenwood Cemetery, Flint, MI (Section H, Lot 80)
References: Obituary Circular, Whole No. 178, Michigan MOLLUS. *American Biographical History of Eminent and Self-Made Men.* Michigan volume. Cincinnati, OH, 1878. *Cyclopedia of Michigan: Historical and Biographical.* New York and Detroit, 1890. *Society of the Army of the Cumberland. Twenty-seventh Reunion, Columbus, OH, 1897.* Cincinnati, OH, 1898. Frank B. Woodford. *Father Abraham's Children: Michigan Episodes in the Civil War.* Detroit, MI, 1961. Pension File and Military Service File, National Archives. Thomas A. Atkins. *The Fenton Family of America and Great Britain.* Yonkers, NY, 1912. Letters Received, Volunteer Service Branch, Adjutant General's Office, File M880(VS)1862, National Archives. William B. McCreery. "My Experience as a Prisoner of War, and Escape from Libby Prison," *War Papers Michigan MOLLUS,* Vol. 1. Detroit, MI, 1893.

Orlando Hurley Moore

Captain, 6 U.S. Infantry, May 26, 1861. Lieutenant Colonel, 13 MI Infantry, Jan. 17, 1862. Resigned volunteer commission, July 4, 1862, to rejoin his regular army command. Colonel, 25 MI Infantry, Sept. 22, 1862. Commanded Post of

William Barker McCreery (G. W. Clark, Photographer, Hackett's Block, Ionia, Michigan; Ken Turner Collection).

Orlando Hurley Moore (Chris Sullivan Collection, USAMHI [RG98S-CWP71.79]).

Louisville, KY, District of Louisville, Department of the Ohio, Oct. 1862. Provost Marshal, Louisville, KY, May 13-June 7, 1863. Commanded 1 Brigade, 2 Division, 23 Army Corps, Army of the Ohio, Aug. 6-Oct. 20, 1863. Discharged for disability, Feb. 23, 1864, due to "chronic bronchitis with a disposition to phthisis." His disability discharge was amended, May 2, 1864, to read "dismissed the service of the United States ... for conduct unbecoming an officer and a gentleman, and for habitual drunkenness." Then, on June 9, 1864, his dismissal was revoked and his disability discharge restored, upon evidence that the dismissal charges originated from differences with certain Kentucky officers concerning his application of Government policy on the subject of slavery while Provost Marshal of Louisville. Finally, on July 25, 1864, his disability discharge was revoked, and he was restored to his command as Colonel. Commanded 2 Brigade, 2 Division, 23 Army Corps, Army of the Ohio, Nov. 1, 1864–Feb. 2, 1865. Commanded 2 Brigade, 2 Division, 23 Army Corps, Department of North Carolina, Feb.9–27, 1865. Commanded 1 Brigade, 2 Division, 23 Army Corps, Department of North Carolina, March 6–April 4, April 20–26, and April 30–June 24, 1865. Commanded 2 Division, 23 Army Corps, Department of North Carolina, April 4–8, 1865. Honorably mustered out of volunteer service, June 24, 1865.

Born: July 13, 1827 Danville, PA
Died: Oct. 31, 1890 Dearborn, MI
Occupation: Regular Army (Lieutenant Colonel, 17 U.S. Infantry, retired April 15, 1884)
Miscellaneous: Resided Schoolcraft, Kalamazoo Co., MI; and Tulare, Tulare Co., CA
Buried: Tulare Cemetery, Tulare, CA (City Section, Block 2, Lot 1)
References: Benjamin F. Travis. *The Story of the Twenty-fifth Michigan*. Kalamazoo, MI, 1897. Obituary, *Tulare Evening Register*, Nov. 4, 1890. *Michigan Pioneer Experiences, 1710-1880, With Genealogical Data and Anecdotes*. N.p., 1933. Letters Received, Appointment, Commission and Personal Branch, Adjutant General's Office, File 4611(ACP)1874, National Archives. Military Service File, National Archives. Letters Received, Volunteer Service Branch, Adjutant General's Office, File W492(VS)1864, National Archives. Clifford L. Swanson. *The Sixth United States Infantry Regiment, 1855 to Reconstruction*. Jefferson, NC, 2001. Jessie Moore Loveridge. "I am an American," *Michigan and the Civil War: An Anthology*. Lansing, MI, 1999. Orlando H. Moore Papers, Bentley Historical Library, University of Michigan, Ann Arbor, MI.

Freeman Norvell

Captain, Co. M, 1 MI Cavalry, Nov. 20, 1861. Captain, Co. B, 1 MI Cavalry, Jan. 1, 1862.

Freeman Norvell (from a private collection).

Resigned June 14, 1862, to accept promotion. Major, 5 MI Cavalry, Aug. 27, 1862. Lieutenant Colonel, 5 MI Cavalry, Dec. 1, 1862. Colonel, 5 MI Cavalry, Dec. 31, 1862. Following a reconnaissance to Ashby's Gap, VA, Feb. 9–11, 1863, charges were preferred that he "was so drunk as to be utterly unfitted for duty, for three days in succession," resulting in his resignation, Feb. 27, 1863. Captain, AAG, USV, May 8, 1863. AAG, Staff of Brig. Gen. Joseph T. Copeland. Resigned May 10, 1864.

Born: Jan. 15, 1827 Philadelphia, PA
Died: May 13, 1881 Detroit, MI
Other Wars: Mexican War (Bvt. 1 Lieutenant, Adjutant, USMC, Sept. 13, 1847, for the storming of Chapultepec and capture of Mexico City)
Occupation: Bvt. 1 Lieutenant, USMC, dismissed June 23, 1855, for drunkenness. Employed as Secretary to his future father-in-law, Alexander H. Redfield, at Yankton Indian Agency, Dakota Territory, before war. After the war he edited *Detroit Free Press* to 1872, and then engaged in iron mining near Lake Superior.
Offices/Honors: President of the Detroit Board of Education, 1877–79
Miscellaneous: Resided Detroit, MI

Buried: Elmwood Cemetery, Detroit, MI (Section A, Lot 152)

References: John E. Norvell. *History of the Norvell and Related Families*. 3rd edition. Canandaigua, NY, 2006. Obituary, *Detroit Free Press,* May 14, 1881. Obituary, *Detroit Evening News,* May 14, 1881. Military Service File, National Archives. Letters Received, Commission Branch, Adjutant General's Office, File N188(CB)1863, National Archives. Records of General Courts-Martial and Courts of Inquiry of the Navy Department, 1799–1867, National Archives. David M. Sullivan. *The United States Marine Corps in the Civil War—The First Year.* Shippensburg, PA, 1997. Frank L. Klement, editor. "Edwin B. Bigelow, A Michigan Sergeant in the Civil War," *Michigan History,* Vol. 38, No. 3 (Sept. 1954).

Francis Quinn

Colonel, 12 MI Infantry, Jan. 8, 1862. Commanded 6 Division, Army of West Tennessee, April 6–10, 1862. Facing numerous charges including cowardice (at Shiloh, TN, April 6, 1862), neglect of duty, disobedience of orders, and incompetency, he submitted his resignation, July 25, 1862, citing ill health due to chronic diarrhea, jaundice, and other hepatic derangements, making him incapable of enduring the fatigue and exposure of camp life. Upon an improvement in his health, he attempted to withdraw his resignation, but in forwarding his petition Michigan Governor Austin Blair implored, "I do most earnestly desire that his resignation may be accepted," adding the comment, "He is the worst colonel I ever saw and has made me more trouble than all the rest together." His resignation was accepted Aug. 31, 1862.

Born: 1827 Ireland

Died: March 26, 1876 Chicago, IL

Occupation: Produce dealer and real estate agent before war. Commission merchant after war, dealing in produce and livestock.

Offices/Honors: Postmaster, Niles, MI, 1861–63

Miscellaneous: Resided Niles, Berrien Co., MI; and Hyde Park, Cook Co., IL

Buried: Silverbrook Cemetery, Niles, MI (Old Ground, Section 7, Lot 153)

References: Obituary, *Chicago Daily Tribune,* March 27, 1876. Obituary, *Niles Republican,* March 30, 1876. Pension File and Military Service File, National Archives. Robert C. Myers. "The Worst Colonel I Ever Saw," *Michigan History,* Vol. 80, No. 1 (Jan.–Feb. 1996). Thomas P. Lowry. *Tarnished Eagles: The Courts-Martial of Fifty Union Colonels and Lieutenant Colonels.* Mechanicsburg, PA, 1997. Letters Received, Volunteer Service Branch, Adjutant General's Office, File Q40(VS)1862, National Archives.

Arthur Rankin

Colonel, 1 MI Lancers, Sept. 4, 1861. Resigned Dec. 21, 1861, due to "complications existing between this country and England relative to the Trent affair, he being a member of the Canadian Parliament."

Born: 1816 Montreal, Canada

Died: March 13, 1893 Windsor, Ontario, Canada

Occupation: Surveyor, militia officer, showman, mining entrepreneur, and politician

Offices/Honors: Canadian Parliament, 1861–67

Miscellaneous: Resided Windsor, Ontario, Canada. Described in his obituary as, "Above the middle height, powerfully built and betraying none of the weaknesses of old age, his individualism was more strongly asserted in his facial contour, which indicated firmness, determination, shrewdness and an iron will. His bronzed, resolute face and gleaming eye were surrounded by an aureole of white hair and long whiskers and mustache, which gave him a resemblance to a French marshal of the *ancien regime*. Nor did his appearance belie his record. He was a gallant soldier, fire-eating duelist, belligerent politician and successful speculator and man of business."

Buried: St. Alphonsus Cemetery, Windsor, Ontario

References: *Dictionary of Canadian Biography.* Vol. 12, 1891–1900. Toronto, Buffalo, and London, 1990. Obituary, *Detroit Evening News,* March 13, 1893. Patrick T. D. Brode, "Colonel Rankin's

Arthur Rankin ("Obituary," *Detroit Free Press*, March 14, 1893).

Canadian Lancers in the American Civil War," *Detroit in Perspective: A Journal of Regional History,* Vol. 4, No. 3 (Spring 1980). Letters Received, Volunteer Service Branch, Adjutant General's Office, File L75(VS)1861, National Archives. Military Service File, National Archives. Obituary, *Detroit Free Press,* March 14, 1893. "The Canadian Regiment," *New York Tribune,* Oct. 18, 1861.

Horace Smith Roberts

Captain, Co. F, 1 MI Infantry (3 months), May 1, 1861. Lieutenant Colonel, 1 MI Infantry (3 years), Aug. 19, 1861. Colonel, 1 MI Infantry, April 28, 1862. GSW Gaines' Mill, VA, June 27, 1862. GSW abdomen, 2nd Bull Run, VA, Aug. 30, 1862.

Born: March 21, 1828 Rochester, NY
Died: Aug. 30, 1862 KIA 2nd Bull Run, VA
Other Wars: Mexican War (2 Lieutenant, Co. D, 1 MI Infantry)
Occupation: Lawyer, merchant, and U.S. Customs official
Offices/Honors: Register of Deeds, Wayne Co., MI, 1857–61
Miscellaneous: Resided Detroit, MI
Buried: Cenotaph (body never recovered), Elmwood Cemetery, Detroit, MI (Section M, Lot 134)
References: Robert B. Ross. *The Early Bench and Bar of Detroit.* Detroit, MI, 1907. *Golden Jubilee, Transactions Grand Lodge F&AM Michigan.* N.p., 1895. Pension File and Military Service File, National Archives. Edward Doubleday Harris. *A Genealogical Record of Thomas Bascom and His Descendants.* Boston, MA, 1870. George C. Hopper. "The Battle of Groveton; or, Second Bull Run," *War Papers Michigan MOLLUS,* Vol. 1. Detroit, MI, 1893. Charles Lanman. *The Red Book of Michigan.* Detroit, MI, 1871.

Lemuel Saviers

1 Sergeant, Co. C, 1 U.S. Sharpshooters, Aug. 26, 1861. 2 Lieutenant, Co. C, 1 U.S. Sharpshooters, Oct. 18, 1861. Captain, Co. F, 26 MI Infantry, Oct. 4, 1862. Major, 26 MI Infantry, June 17, 1863. Commanded Fort at Sandy Hook, New York Harbor, Department of the East, Aug. 1863. GSW left lung and shell wounds left side and lower spine, Spotsylvania, VA, May 12, 1864. *Colonel,* 26 MI Infantry, Sept. 12, 1864. Lieutenant Colonel, 26 MI Infantry, Sept. 26, 1864. Discharged for disability, Sept. 27, 1864, due to wounds received in action.

Born: Dec. 12, 1840 Antrim, OH
Died: Aug. 19, 1912 St. Louis, MI
Occupation: Carpenter and millwright before war. Capitalist, engaged in real estate and banking enterprises after war.
Offices/Honors: Quartermaster General of Michigan, 1877–81

Horace S. Roberts (photograph by Brady's National Photographic Portrait Gallery, Broadway & Tenth Street, New York; courtesy Thomas Harris).

Miscellaneous: Resided Tecumseh, Lenawee Co., MI, to 1874; and St. Louis, Gratiot Co., MI, after 1874
Buried: Oak Grove Cemetery, St. Louis, MI (Section E)
References: *Men of Progress: Embracing Biographical Sketches of Representative Michigan Men.* Detroit, MI, 1900. Obituary, *Gratiot County Herald,* Aug. 22, 1912. Pension File and Military Service File, National Archives. Letters Received, Volunteer Service Branch, Adjutant General's Office, Files M1339(VS)1862 and M2903(VS)1864, National Archives. Willard D. Tucker. *Gratiot County, Michigan. Historical, Biographical, Statistical.* Saginaw, MI, 1913.

Thomas Saylor

Captain, Co. M, 3 MI Cavalry, Oct. 14, 1861. Major, 3 MI Cavalry, July 13, 1862. Colonel, 29 MI Infantry, Sept. 29, 1864. Commanded 3 Brigade, 1 Sub-District, District of Middle Tennessee, June 17–July 21, 1865. Commanded 1 Brigade, District of Middle Tennessee and Post of Murfreesboro, Aug. 21–Sept. 6, 1865. Honorably mustered out, Sept. 6, 1865.

Lemuel Saviers (courtesy Archives of Michigan).

Thomas Saylor (Wilson, Artist, Cor. Fifth and Washington Ave., St. Louis, Missouri).

Born: July 21, 1831 Philadelphia, PA
Died: July 18, 1911 Pontiac, MI
Occupation: Saw maker before war. Lumberman and farmer after war.
Offices/Honors: Receiver, U.S. Land Office, East Saginaw, MI, 1868–71. Postmaster, East Saginaw, MI, 1875–84.
Miscellaneous: Resided East Saginaw, Saginaw Co., MI; and Bridgeport, Saginaw Co., MI
Buried: Forest Lawn Cemetery, Saginaw, MI (Section 14, Lot 203)
References: *Portrait and Biographical Record of Saginaw and Bay Counties, MI.* Chicago, IL, 1892. *History of Saginaw County, MI.* Chicago, IL, 1881. Obituary, *Saginaw Courier-Herald,* July 19, 1911. Pension File and Military Service File, National Archives.

Frederick Schneider

Sergeant, Co. A, 2 MI Infantry, May 25, 1861. 1 Sergeant, Co. A, 2 MI Infantry, Dec. 7, 1862. Sergeant Major, 2 MI Infantry, May 14, 1864. GSW right arm, Petersburg, VA, June 18, 1864. 1 Lieu-

Thomas Saylor (Roger D. Hunt Collection, USAMHI [RG98S-CWP58.92]).

Frederick Schneider (1861) (courtesy Gil Barrett).

Frederick Schneider (*Record of Service of Michigan Volunteers in the Civil War, 1861–1865*. Vol. 2 [Second Michigan Infantry]. Kalamazoo, Michigan, 1905).

tenant, Co. A, 2 MI Infantry, July 27, 1864. Taken prisoner, The Crater, Petersburg, VA, July 30, 1864, but escaped the same day. Captain, Co. A, 2 MI Infantry, Oct. 27, 1864. GSW left thigh, and taken prisoner, Hatcher's Run, VA, Oct. 27, 1864. Confined at Salisbury, NC; Danville, VA; and Libby Prison, Richmond, VA. Paroled Feb. 22, 1865. Lieutenant Colonel, 2 MI Infantry, April 18, 1865. *Colonel,* 2 MI Infantry, April 18, 1865. Honorably mustered out, July 28, 1865.

Born: Nov. 24, 1840 Saline, Washtenaw Co., MI

Died: Nov. 4, 1917 Lansing, MI

Education: Attended Bryant and Stratton's Commercial College, Detroit, MI

Occupation: Shipping clerk before war. Notary public and conveyancer after war, also engaged in real estate, insurance and foreign collection enterprises.

Offices/Honors: Chief of the Abstract Department, Michigan Auditor General's Office, 1867–90

Miscellaneous: Resided Detroit, MI; and Lansing, Ingham Co., MI

Buried: Mount Hope Cemetery, Lansing, MI (Section F, Lot 165)

References: *Portrait and Biographical Album of Ingham and Livingston Counties, MI.* Chicago, IL, 1891. *Record of Service of Michigan Volunteers in the Civil War, 1861–1865.* Vol. 2 (Second Michigan Infantry). Kalamazoo, MI, 1905. Obituary Circular, Whole No. 568, Michigan MOLLUS. Obituary, *Lansing State Journal,* Nov. 5, 1917. Frederick Schneider. *Incidental History of the Flags and Color Guard of the Second Michigan Veteran Volunteer Infantry.* Lansing, MI, 1905. Pension File and Military Service File, National Archives. Letters Received, Volunteer Service Branch, Adjutant General's Office, File S566(VS)1865, National Archives.

Michael Shoemaker

Colonel, 13 MI Infantry, Feb. 1, 1862. Commanded Post of Stevenson, AL, Aug. 21–31, 1862. Taken prisoner, Tyree Springs, TN, Sept. 7, 1862. Confined Libby Prison, Richmond, VA. Exchanged Sept. 21, 1862. Commanded 3 Brigade, 1 Division, 21 Army Corps, Army of the Cumberland, Feb. 17–March 17, 1863. Resigned May 26, 1863, since "for the last six weeks my wife has been very sick ... and I am satisfied that her life depends upon my being with her during her illness."

Born: April 6, 1818 German Flats, Herkimer Co., NY

Michael Shoemaker (J. V. Cookingham, Artist, Jackson, Michigan; courtesy Steve Meadow).

Died: Nov. 10, 1895 Jackson, MI
Occupation: Miller and farmer before war. Farmer, oil producer, and real estate agent after war.
Offices/Honors: Michigan Senate, 1848–51, 1877–78, 1883–86. U.S. Collector of Customs, Port of Detroit, MI, 1857–60.
Miscellaneous: Resided Jackson, Jackson Co., MI
Buried: Mount Evergreen Cemetery, Jackson, MI (Section S, Block 3, Range 2, Lot 5)
References: *Portrait and Biographical Album of Jackson County, MI.* Chicago, IL, 1890. *History of Jackson County, MI.* Chicago, IL, 1881. *Cyclopedia of Michigan: Historical and Biographical.* New York and Detroit, 1890. *Golden Jubilee, Transactions Grand Lodge F&AM Michigan.* N.p., 1895. *American Biographical History of Eminent and Self-Made Men.* Michigan volume. Cincinnati, OH, 1878. Obituary, *Detroit Free Press,* Nov. 11, 1895. Pension File and Military Service File, National Archives. Michael Shoemaker. "War Sketch by Col. Shoemaker. Narrative of the Capture of Colonel Michael Shoemaker of the Thirteenth Regiment of Michigan Volunteer Infantry, Near Tyree Springs, in Tennessee; His Journey to Richmond, Virginia; His Confinement and Experience in Libby Prison; His Exchange and Return by the Way of Fortress Monroe and Annapolis," *Pioneer Collections: Report of the Pioneer Society of the State of Michigan.* Vol. 3. Lansing, MI, 1881.

Robert P. Sinclair

Colonel, 14 MI Infantry, Feb. 7, 1862. "Laboring under general debility with considerable tendency to thoracic disease, and also frequent recurring attacks of diarrhea," he resigned Nov. 10, 1862, since "his continuing in the service or enduring the hardships and exposure incident to a fall and winter campaign must necessarily prove fatal to him."
Born: Oct. 17, 1814 Romulus, Seneca Co., NY
Died: March 29, 1886 Grand Rapids, MI
Education: Attended Hobart College, Geneva, NY. Attended University of Edinburgh, Scotland.
Occupation: Lawyer and real estate agent
Offices/Honors: U.S. Collector of Internal Revenue, 1866–67
Miscellaneous: Resided Grand Rapids, Kent Co., MI

Robert P. Sinclair (post-war) (Franklin Everett. *Memorials of the Grand River Valley.* Chicago, Illinois, 1878).

Buried: Oak Hill Cemetery, Grand Rapids, MI (Section K, Lot 49)

References: *History of Kent County, MI.* Chicago, IL, 1881. Franklin Everett. *Memorials of the Grand River Valley.* Chicago, IL, 1878. Pension File and Military Service File, National Archives. Obituary, *Grand Rapids Daily Democrat,* March 30, 1886.

John Stockton

Colonel, 8 MI Cavalry, April 22, 1863. Commanded Post of Hickman's Bridge, KY, June–July 1863. Dismissed April 15, 1864, for "rendering false and fraudulent accounts against the Government." Dismissal revoked, Feb. 5, 1866, and he was honorably discharged to date April 15, 1864.

Born: Dec. 24, 1790 Lancaster, PA

Died: Nov. 27, 1878 Mount Clemens, MI

Other Wars: War of 1812 (1 Lieutenant, 2 U.S. Rifles)

Occupation: Justice of the Peace

Offices/Honors: Michigan Legislative Council, 1824–31 and 1834–35. Michigan Senate, 1835–36. Michigan House of Representatives, 1840–41 and 1850.

Miscellaneous: Resided Mount Clemens, Macomb Co., MI. One of the pioneers of Macomb Co., MI, serving as its first county clerk and register of deeds.

Buried: Clinton Grove Cemetery, Mount Clemens, MI (Section A, Lot 267)

References: *American Biographical History of Eminent and Self-Made Men.* Michigan volume. Cincinnati, OH, 1878. Thomas C. Stockton. *The Stockton Family of New Jersey and Other Stocktons.* Washington, DC, 1911. *History of Macomb County, MI.* Chicago, IL, 1882. Robert F. Eldredge. *Past and Present of Macomb County, MI.* Chicago, IL, 1905. *Michigan Biographies.* Lansing, MI, 1924. Obituary, *Detroit Evening News,* Nov. 27, 1878. Pension File and Military Service File, National Archives. Letters Received, Volunteer Service Branch, Adjutant General's Office, File J222(VS) 1864, National Archives.

Thomas Baylis Whitmarsh Stockton

Colonel, 16 MI Infantry, Aug. 21, 1861. Taken prisoner Gaines' Mill, VA, June 27, 1862. Confined Libby Prison, Richmond, VA. Paroled Aug. 12, 1862. Commanded 3 Brigade, 1 Division, 5 Army Corps, Army of the Potomac, Sept. 9–Dec. 17, 1862 and Jan.–May 18, 1863. Frustrated that he had not been promoted to brigadier general, he resigned May 18, 1863, "for the purpose of accepting the po-

John Stockton (David K. Parks Collection).

Thomas Baylis Whitmarsh Stockton (R. W. Addis, Photographer, McClees' Gallery, 308 Penna. Ave., Washington, DC; Ken Turner Collection).

Thomas Baylis Whitmarsh Stockton (courtesy Olaf).

sition that Gov. Andrew Johnson of Tennessee has given me to raise three regiments to serve under him in redeeming that state from rebeldom." His hopes for promotion were, however, dashed when Johnson's authority to recruit outside of Tennessee for exclusive service in East Tennessee was revoked.

Born: June 18, 1805 Walton, NY
Died: Dec. 9, 1890 Flint, MI
Education: Graduated U.S. Military Academy, West Point, NY, 1827
Other Wars: Mexican War (Colonel, 1 MI Infantry)
Occupation: Civil engineer, mine operator, and U.S. Customs official before war. Warehouse commission merchant after war.
Miscellaneous: Resided Flint, Genesee Co., MI. Brother-in-law of Colonel John Garland (8 U.S. Infantry), whose daughter, Maria Louise, was the first wife of CSA General James Longstreet.
Buried: Glenwood Cemetery, Flint, MI (Section H, Lot 181)
References: *American Biographical History of Eminent and Self-Made Men.* Michigan volume. Cincinnati, OH, 1878. *Biographical History of Genesee County, MI.* Indianapolis, IN, 1908. Thomas C. Stockton. *The Stockton Family of New Jersey and Other Stocktons.* Washington, DC, 1911. Kim Crawford. *The 16th Michigan Infantry.* Dayton, OH, 2002. *Annual Reunion,* Association of the Graduates of the USMA, 1891. Colonel Edward Hill and Mrs. Edward Hill. *Proceedings of the Third Brigade Association, First Division, Fifth Army Corps, Army of the Potomac, 1894–1896–1897–1898.* Record No. III. New York City, NY, 1899. Pension File and Military Service File, National Archives. Letters Received, Volunteer Service Branch, Adjutant General's Office, File 2880(VS)1879, National Archives. Leroy P. Graf and Ralph W. Haskins, editors. *The Papers of Andrew Johnson.* Vol. 6, 1862–64. Knoxville, TN, 1983.

Charles Edward Stuart

Colonel, 13 MI Infantry, Jan. 17, 1862. Amid widespread rumors of his association with the Knights of the Golden Circle, he resigned Jan. 27, 1862, due to ill health.

Born: Nov. 25, 1810 Canaan Corners, Columbia Co., NY
Died: May 19, 1887 Kalamazoo, MI
Occupation: Lawyer
Offices/Honors: Michigan House of Representatives, 1842. U.S. House of Representatives, 1847–49 and 1851–53. U.S. Senate, 1853–59.
Miscellaneous: Resided Kalamazoo, Kalamazoo Co., MI
Buried: Mountain Home Cemetery, Kalamazoo, MI (Section B, Lot 48)
References: *Portrait and Biographical Record of Kalamazoo, Allegan and Van Buren Counties, MI.* Chicago, IL, 1892. Edward W. Barber, "Michigan Men in Congress: The Chosen of the People," *Historical Collections: Collections and Researches*

Charles Edward Stuart (post-war) *Portrait and Biographical Record of Kalamazoo, Allegan and Van Buren Counties, MI.* Chicago, Illinois, 1892).

Made by the Michigan Pioneer and Historical Society. Vol. 35. Lansing, MI, 1907. James L. Harrison, compiler. *Biographical Directory of the American Congress, 1774–1949.* Washington, DC, 1950. Obituary, *Kalamazoo Daily Telegraph,* May 20, 1887. Obituary, *New York Times,* May 20, 1887. *Michigan Biographies.* Lansing, MI, 1924. Henry Parsons. *Parsons Family: Descendants of Cornet Joseph Parsons, Springfield, 1636 – Northampton, 1655.* New York City, NY, 1912. Military Service File, National Archives.

Charles H. Town

Captain, Co. B, 1 MI Cavalry, Aug. 23, 1861. Major, 1 MI Cavalry, Sept. 6, 1861. Saber wounds right arm, 2nd Bull Run, VA, Aug. 30, 1862. Colonel, 1 MI Cavalry, Sept. 2, 1862. Commanded 2 Brigade, 3 Division, Cavalry Corps, Army of the Potomac, July 15–Aug. 4, 1863 and Nov. 25–Dec. 15, 1863. Discharged for disability, Aug. 17, 1864, due to wounds received in action.

Born: May 27, 1827 Elba, NY
Died: May 7, 1865 Elba, NY
Occupation: Merchant
Miscellaneous: Resided Dexter, Washtenaw Co., MI; Detroit, MI; and Elba, Genesee Co., NY
Buried: Hudson Cemetery, Hudson Mills, Washtenaw Co., MI
References: Edwin E. Towne. *The Descendants of William Towne.* Newtonville, MA, 1901. Obituary, *Batavia Republican Advocate,* May 30, 1865. Pension File and Military Service File, National Archives. Letters Received, Volunteer Service Branch, Adjutant General's Office, File P353(VS)1864, National Archives. Edward G. Longacre. *Custer and His Wolverines: The Michigan Cavalry Brigade, 1861–1865.* Conshohocken, PA, 1997. Obituary, *Weekly Michigan Argus,* June 9, 1865. Obituary, *Detroit Advertiser and Tribune,* May 13, 1865.

William B. Way

1 Lieutenant, Co. C, 1 MI Cavalry, Sept. 4, 1861. Captain, Co. C, 1 MI Cavalry, Oct. 10, 1862. Major, 9 MI Cavalry, March 12, 1863. Lieutenant Colonel, 9 MI Cavalry, July 2, 1864. Commanded 4 Brigade (dismounted), 3 Division, Cavalry Corps, Military Division of the Mississippi, Jan. 25–March 31, 1865. *Colonel,* 9 MI Cavalry, June 27, 1865. Honorably mustered out, July 21, 1865.

Born: Jan. 15, 1836 Philadelphia, PA
Died: April 7, 1882 Cincinnati, OH
Occupation: Produce dealer and farmer
Miscellaneous: Resided Detroit, MI; Drayton Plains, Oakland Co., MI; and Cincinnati, OH
Buried: Spring Grove Cemetery, Cincinnati, OH (Section 31, Lot 293)
References: Pension File and Military Service File, National Archives. Obituary, *Cincinnati Daily Gazette,* April 8, 1882. Obituary, *Detroit Evening News,* April 8 and April 14, 1882. Obituary, *Pontiac Gazette,* April 14, 1882. Letters Received, Volunteer Service Branch, Adjutant General's Office, File T38(VS)1863, National Archives.

Norval E. Welch

Major, 16 MI Infantry, Aug. 22, 1861. Lieutenant Colonel, 16 MI Infantry, July 6, 1862. Colonel, 16

Charles H. Town (G. Grelling, Artist, Detroit, Michigan; Thomas Harris Collection).

William B. Way (Richard F. Carlile Collection).

William B. Way (Massachusetts MOLLUS Collection, USAMHI [Vol. 73, p. 3638]).

Norval E. Welch (G. Grelling, Artist, Detroit, Michigan; Roger D. Hunt Collection, USAMHI [RG98S-CWP160.52]).

Norval E. Welch (courtesy Steve Meadow).

MI Infantry, June 1, 1864. Commanded 3 Brigade, 1 Division, 5 Army Corps, Army of the Potomac, July 20, 1864–Aug. 9, 1864. GSW forehead, Peebles' Farm, VA, Sept. 30, 1864.
  Born: 1835 Pittsfield, MI
  Died: Sept. 30, 1864 KIA Peebles' Farm, VA
  Education: Graduated University of Michigan Law School, Ann Arbor, MI, 1860
  Occupation: Lawyer. Early in life served as private secretary to U.S. Senator Lewis Cass.
  Offices/Honors: Recorder, City of Ann Arbor, MI, 1859
  Miscellaneous: Resided Ann Arbor, Washtenaw Co., MI
  Buried: Forest Hill Cemetery, Ann Arbor, MI (Block 34, Lot 8)
  References: Colonel Edward Hill and Mrs. Edward Hill. *Proceedings of the Third Brigade Association, First Division, Fifth Army Corps, Army of the Potomac, 1894–1896–1897–1898.* Record No. III, New York City, NY, 1900. Kim Crawford. *The 16th Michigan Infantry.* Dayton, OH, 2002. John Michael Gibney, "A Shadow Passing: The Tragic Story of Norval Welch and the Sixteenth Michigan at Gettysburg and Beyond," *The Gettysburg Magazine.* January 1992 — Issue No. 6. Obituary, *Weekly Michigan Argus,* Oct. 7, 1864. Pension File and Military Service File, National Archives. John Robertson, compiler. *Michigan in the War.* Lansing, MI, 1882. *History of Washtenaw County, MI.* Chicago, IL, 1881.

William White Wheeler

Captain, Co. B, 6 MI Infantry, Aug. 20, 1861. Acting AIG, 2 Division, 19 Army Corps, Department of the Gulf, March–April 1863. Major, 23

William White Wheeler (photograph by Brady's National Photographic Portrait Gallery, No. 352 Pennsylvania Ave., Washington, DC; Michael W. Waskul Collection).

MI Infantry, June 25, 1863. Provost Marshal General, 23 Army Corps, Army of the Ohio, May 18–Aug. 16, 1864. Lieutenant Colonel, 23 MI Infantry, Sept. 20, 1864. Colonel, 28 MI Infantry, Nov. 10, 1864. Honorably mustered out, July 12, 1866.
   Born: March 10, 1837 Vergennes, VT
   Died: Aug. 29, 1873 Chicago, IL
   Education: Attended University of Vermont, Burlington, VT. Graduated University of Michigan, Ann Arbor, MI, 1856. Graduated Albany (NY) Law School, 1858.
   Occupation: Lawyer
   Miscellaneous: Resided Niles, Berrien Co., MI; St. Joseph, Berrien Co., MI; and Chicago, IL
   Buried: Graceland Cemetery, Chicago, IL (Section A, Lot 374)
   References: Obituary, *Chicago Daily Tribune*, Aug. 30, 1873. *Catalogue of the Lambda Iota Society of the University of Vermont, 1836–1903.* N.p., N.d. William Raimond Baird. *Betas of Achievement.* New York City, NY, 1914. Franklin Ellis. *History of Berrien and Van Buren Counties, MI.* Philadelphia, PA, 1880. Military Service File, National Archives. Letters Received, Volunteer Service Branch, Adjutant General's Office, File N113(VS)1866, National Archives.

Franklin Ward Whittelsey

Captain, Co. H, 1 MI Infantry (3 months), May 1, 1861. Honorably mustered out, Aug. 7, 1861. Major, 1 MI Infantry (3 years), Aug. 17, 1861. Lieutenant Colonel, 1 MI Infantry, May 1, 1862. GSW left leg, Gaines' Mill, VA, June 27, 1862. Colonel, 1 MI Infantry, Aug. 30, 1862. Resigned March 18, 1863, since "I have not done duty with the regiment

Franklin Ward Whittelsey (photograph by Brady's National Photographic Portrait Gallery, 352 Pennsylvania Avenue, Washington, DC).

since the 3rd of August last, and my lameness (from injury to right knee) still continues and will probably cling to me through life."
   Born: May 31, 1827 Middletown, CT
   Died: Aug. 24, 1893 Middletown, CT
   Occupation: Mill operator, bookkeeper, and insurance agent
   Miscellaneous: Resided Ypsilanti, Washtenaw Co., MI, to 1868; Detroit, MI, 1868–70; Grand Rapids, Kent Co., MI, 1870–75; and Middletown, Middlesex Co., CT, 1875–93
   Buried: Washington Street Cemetery, Middletown, CT
   References: Obituary, *Middletown Tribune*, Aug. 24, 1893. Charles B. Whittelsey. *Genealogy of the Whittelsey-Whittlesey Family.* Hartford, CT, 1941. Pension File and Military Service File, National Archives. Letters Received, Volunteer Service Branch, Adjutant General's Office, File W342(VS) 1863, National Archives.

Moses Wisner

Colonel, 22 MI Infantry, Aug. 22, 1862
   Born: June 3, 1815 Springport, Cayuga Co., NY
   Died: Jan. 5, 1863 Lexington, KY (typhoid fever)

Moses Wisner (*Portrait and Biographical Album of Lenawee County, MI.* Chicago, Illinois, 1888).

Dwight Avery Woodbury (courtesy Thomas Harris).

Occupation: Lawyer
Offices/Honors: Governor of Michigan, 1859–61
Miscellaneous: Resided Pontiac, Oakland Co., MI. Brother of Colonel Reuben P. Wisner (58 NY National Guard).
Buried: Oak Hill Cemetery, Pontiac, MI (Block 4, Lot 391)
References: *American Biographical History of Eminent and Self-Made Men.* Michigan volume. Cincinnati, OH, 1878. *Cyclopedia of Michigan: Historical and Biographical.* New York and Detroit, 1890. Thaddeus D. Seeley, editor. *History of Oakland County, MI.* Chicago and New York, 1912. John H. Snook, "Governor Wisner and the Twenty-Second Michigan Volunteer Infantry," *Michigan History,* Vol. 31, No. 1 (March 1947). G. Franklin Wisner. *The Wisners in America and Their Kindred.* Baltimore, MD, 1918. Pension File and Military Service File, National Archives. *National Cyclopedia of American Biography.*

Dwight Avery Woodbury

Colonel, 4 MI Infantry, June 20, 1861. GSW forehead, Malvern Hill, VA, July 1, 1862.
Born: Dec. 18, 1828 NY
Died: July 1, 1862 KIA Malvern Hill, VA
Occupation: Railroad conductor and hotelkeeper
Miscellaneous: Resided Adrian, Lenawee Co., MI
Buried: Oakwood Cemetery, Adrian, MI (Block 9, Lot 44)

Dwight Avery Woodbury (Roger D. Hunt Collection, USAMHI [RG98S-CWP160.50]).

References: Benjamin W. Dwight. *History of the Descendants of John Dwight of Dedham, MA.* New York City, NY, 1874. Martin Bertera and Ken Oberholtzer. *The 4th Michigan Volunteer Infantry at Gettysburg: The Battle for the Wheatfield.* Dayton, OH, 1997. Pension File and Military Service File, National Archives. John Robertson. *Michigan in the War.* Lansing, MI, 1882.

William B. Wright

2 Lieutenant, Co. C, 27 MI Infantry, Aug. 13, 1862. Captain, Co. C, 27 MI Infantry, Oct. 10, 1862. Major, 27 MI Infantry, Jan. 8, 1863. Lieutenant Colonel, 27 MI Infantry, Dec. 17, 1863. GSW right shoulder and shell wound left hip, Petersburg, VA, July 30, 1864. Colonel, 27 MI Infantry, Nov. 18, 1864. Honorably discharged on account of physical disability, Nov. 22, 1864, due to wounds received in action.

Born: June 28, 1814 Middletown Point, NJ
Died: Sept. 25, 1902 Belford, NJ
Other Wars: Black Hawk War, 1832. Florida Indian War, 1838–39.
Occupation: Regular Army enlisted man, 1831–55, attaining the rank of Ordnance Sergeant. Hotelkeeper, after 1855.
Offices/Honors: Sheriff of Keweenaw Co., MI, 1881–85
Miscellaneous: Resided Eagle River, Keweenaw Co., MI, to 1899; and Keyport, Monmouth Co., NJ, 1899–1902
Buried: Cedarwood Cemetery, Hazlet, NJ (New Section, Lot 73)
References: *History of the Upper Peninsula of Michigan.* Chicago, IL, 1883. Obituary circular, Whole No. 262, Michigan MOLLUS. Pension File and Military Service File, National Archives. Letters Received, Volunteer Service Branch, Adjutant General's Office, File W2925(VS)1864, National Archives.

William B. Wright (G. Grelling, Artist, Detroit, Michigan; 27th Michigan Infantry Regiment Photograph Collection, Bentley Historical Library, University of Michigan).

John Barentse Yates

Captain, Co. A, 1 MI Engineers and Mechanics, Sept. 23, 1861. Major, 1 MI Engineers and Mechanics, May 29, 1863. Colonel, 1 MI Engineers and Mechanics, Nov. 3, 1864. Honorably mustered out, Sept. 22, 1865.

Born: Oct. 18, 1833 Schenectady, NY
Died: Oct. 20, 1899 Amherstburg, Ontario, Canada
Education: Graduated Union College, Schenectady, NY, 1852
Occupation: Civil engineer engaged in railroad construction
Miscellaneous: Resided Albion, Calhoun Co., MI; Ionia, Ionia Co., MI; Schenectady, Schenectady Co., NY; and Amherstburg, Ontario, Canada

John Barentse Yates (Charles R. Sligh. *History of the Services of the First Regiment Michigan Engineers and Mechanics During the Civil War, 1861–1865.* Grand Rapids, Michigan, 1921).

Buried: Vale Cemetery, Schenectady, NY (Section S, Lot 9, unmarked)

References: Special Collections, Schaffer Library, Union College, Schenectady, NY. Noble E. Whitford. *History of the Canal System of the State of New York.* Albany, NY, 1906. *Appletons' Cyclopedia of American Biography.* Obituary, *New York Times,* Oct. 24, 1899. Obituary, *Schenectady Evening Star,* Oct. 24, 1899. Obituary, *Washington National Tribune,* Nov. 9, 1899. Charles R. Sligh. *History of the Services of the First Regiment Michigan Engineers and Mechanics During the Civil War 1861–1865.* Grand Rapids, MI, 1921. Mark Hoffman. *"My Brave Mechanics," The First Michigan Engineers and Their Civil War.* Detroit, MI, 2007. Military Service File, National Archives.

West Virginia

Regiments

1st Cavalry

Henry Anisansel	Sept. 6, 1861	Resigned Aug. 6, 1862
Nathaniel P. Richmond	Oct. 16, 1862	Resigned March 18, 1863
Nathaniel P. Richmond	June 12, 1863	Resigned Nov. 11, 1863
Henry Capehart	Feb. 22, 1864	Mustered out July 8, 1865, **Bvt. Brig. Gen.**

2nd Cavalry

William M. Bolles	Sept. 1, 1861	Resigned June 25, 1862
John C. Paxton	June 25, 1862	Resigned May 7, 1863
William H. Powell	May 18, 1863	Promoted **Brig. Gen., USV,** Oct. 19, 1864

3rd Cavalry

David H. Strother	July 18, 1863	Resigned Sept. 10, 1864, **Bvt. Brig. Gen.**
John L. McGee	May 3, 1865	Mustered out June 30, 1865

4th Cavalry

Joseph Snider	Dec. 22, 1863	Mustered out March 11, 1864

5th Cavalry
(Designation changed from 2nd Infantry, Jan. 26, 1864)

John W. Moss	July 10, 1861	Resigned May 20, 1862
George R. Latham	May 24, 1862	To 6th Cavalry, Dec. 14, 1864, **Bvt. Brig. Gen.**

6th Cavalry
(Designation changed from 3rd Infantry, Jan. 26, 1864)

David T. Hewes	July 8, 1861	Dismissed Feb. 15, 1864
Francis W. Thompson	May 5, 1864	Mustered out Aug. 18, 1864
George R. Latham	Dec. 14, 1864	Discharged March 9, 1865, **Bvt. Brig. Gen.**

7th Cavalry
(Designation changed from 8th Infantry, Jan. 26, 1864)

John H. Oley	March 1, 1863	Mustered out Aug. 1, 1865, **Bvt. Brig. Gen.**

1st Infantry (3 months)

Benjamin F. Kelley	May 22, 1861	Promoted **Brig. Gen., USV,** May 17, 1861

1st Infantry (3 years)

Joseph Thoburn	Oct. 29, 1861	KIA Oct. 19, 1864

1st Veteran Infantry

William H. Enochs	Dec. 23, 1864	Mustered out July 21, 1865, **Bvt. Brig. Gen.**

2nd Infantry
(See 5th Cavalry, to which designation changed, Jan. 26, 1864)

2nd Veteran Infantry

Regiment not entitled to a colonel since it never attained full strength

3rd Infantry
(See 6th Cavalry, to which designation changed, Jan. 26, 1864)

4th Infantry

Joseph A. J. Lightburn	Aug. 14, 1861	Promoted **Brig. Gen., USV,** March 14, 1863
James H. Dayton	May 16, 1863	Mustered out July 4, 1864

5th Infantry

John L. Zeigler	Sept. 14, 1861	Resigned April 14, 1863
Abia A. Tomlinson	April 14, 1863	Mustered out Sept. 20, 1864

6th Infantry

Nathan Wilkinson	Oct. 6, 1861	Mustered out June 10, 1865

7th Infantry

James Evans	Nov. 3, 1861	Resigned Aug. 2, 1862
Joseph Snider	Sept. 3, 1862	Mustered out Sept. 7, 1863

8th Infantry
(See 7th Cavalry, to which designation changed, Jan. 26, 1864)

9th Infantry

Leonard Skinner	Dec. 6, 1861	Resigned Sept. 19, 1862
Isaac H. Duval	Sept. 19, 1862	Promoted **Brig. Gen., USV,** Sept. 24, 1864

10th Infantry

Thomas M. Harris	May 20, 1862	Promoted **Brig. Gen., USV,** March 29, 1865
Morgan A. Darnall	June 29, 1865	Mustered out Aug. 9, 1865

11th Infantry

John C. Rathbone	Feb. 15, 1862	Discharged Jan. 6, 1863
Daniel Frost	Feb. 9, 1863	DOW July 18, 1864
Van H. Bukey	Nov. 3, 1864	Mustered out Dec. 26, 1864, **Bvt. Brig. Gen.**

12th Infantry

John B. Klunk	Aug. 20, 1862	Resigned Sept. 1, 1863
William B. Curtis	Jan. 28, 1864	Mustered out June 16, 1865, **Bvt. Brig. Gen.**

13th Infantry

William R. Brown	Jan. 18, 1864	Mustered out June 22, 1865, **Bvt. Brig. Gen.**

14th Infantry

Andrew S. Core	Sept. 16, 1862	Discharged April 4, 1863
Daniel D. Johnson	April 5, 1863	Mustered out June 27, 1865

15th Infantry

Maxwell McCaslin	Jan. 21, 1863	Resigned Sept. 9, 1864
Milton Wells	Oct. 4, 1864	Resigned April 6, 1865, **Bvt. Brig. Gen.**

16th Infantry

James T. Close	Oct. 25, 1862	Resigned May 28, 1863

17th Infantry

Charles H. Day	March 13, 1865	Mustered out June 30, 1865

Biographies

Henry Anisansel

1 Lieutenant, Co. A, Ringgold Battalion, PA Cavalry, June 29, 1861. Resigned Aug. 27, 1861, to accept promotion. Colonel, 1 WV Cavalry, Sept. 6, 1861. Acquitted by General Court-martial of the charge of "misbehavior before the enemy" at Bloomery Gap, WV, Feb. 14, 1862, he resigned Aug. 6, 1862, on account of disability caused by a right inguinal hernia incurred in the same skirmish.

Born: 1829? Geneva, Switzerland
Died: May 21, 1905 Detroit, MI
Occupation: Trader and speculator before war. Professor of languages and music, lawyer, and bookkeeper after war.
Offices/Honors: Mayor of Canonsburg, PA, before war
Miscellaneous: Resided Canonsburg, Washington Co., PA; Jamestown, Chautauqua Co., NY; and Detroit, MI
Buried: Woodmere Cemetery, Detroit, MI (GAR Section, Lot 84)
References: Pension File and Military Service File, National Archives. Thomas P. Lowry. *Tarnished Eagles: The Courts-Martial of Fifty Union Colonels and Lieutenant Colonels.* Mechanicsburg, PA, 1997. Gary L. Ecelbarger. *Frederick W. Lander: The Great Natural American Soldier.* Baton Rouge, LA, 2000. Letters Received, Volunteer Service Branch, Adjutant General's Office, File H315(VS)1862, National Archives. Court-martial Case Files, 1809–1894, File II-693, National Archives. Death notice, *Detroit News,* May 24, 1905.

William Mather Bolles

Captain, Co. C, 18 OH Infantry (3 months), May 26, 1861. Lieutenant Colonel, 18 OH Infantry, May 29, 1861. Honorably mustered out, Aug. 28, 1861. Colonel, 2 WV Cavalry, Sept. 1, 1861. Resigned June 25, 1862, since "the severe and dangerous illness of my wife, which I have reason to fear will terminate fatally, renders my presence at home absolutely necessary for her care and the protection of my small children."

Born: Feb. 28, 1827 Brooklyn, Windham Co., CT
Died: Oct. 5, 1911 Portsmouth, OH
Education: Attended Ohio University, Athens, OH
Occupation: Engaged in iron manufacturing enterprises after early career (1848–51) as a lawyer
Miscellaneous: Resided Ironton, Lawrence Co., OH, to 1863; and Portsmouth, Scioto Co., OH, after 1863
Buried: Greenlawn Cemetery, Portsmouth, OH (Section 13, Lot 30)
References: Nelson W. Evans. *A History of Scioto County with Pioneer Record of Southern Ohio.*

William Mather Bolles (Henry A Lorberg. *Pictorial Portsmouth, Ohio. The Peerless City. Past and Present.* Cincinnati, Ohio, 1907).

Portsmouth, OH, 1903. Obituary, *Portsmouth Daily Times,* Oct. 6, 1911. Pension File and Military Service File, National Archives. George E. Williams. *A Genealogy of the Descendants of Joseph Bolles of Wells, ME.* West Hartford, CT, 1970. Joseph J. Sutton. *History of the Second Regiment West Virginia Cavalry Volunteers During the War of the Rebellion.* Portsmouth, OH, 1892. Eugene B. Willard, Supervising Editor. *A Standard History of the Hanging Rock Iron Region of Ohio.* Chicago, IL, 1916.

James Titus Close

Colonel, 16 WV Infantry, Oct. 25, 1862. Resigned May 28, 1863, to accept the position of U.S. Marshal, Eastern District of Virginia.

Born: April 14, 1829 Broadalbin Twp., Fulton Co., NY

Died: Aug. 30, 1869 Arlington, VA

Occupation: Insurance agent

Offices/Honors: Delegate to the 2nd Wheeling Convention, June 11–25 and Aug. 6–21, 1861. Senate Restored Government of Virginia, 1861–63. U.S. Marshal, Eastern District of Virginia, 1863–64.

Miscellaneous: Resided North Norwich, Chenango Co., NY; and Alexandria, VA

Buried: Place of burial unknown

References: Lewis R. Close. *Lewis Gile Close: Ancestors and Descendants.* N.p., 1955. Pension File and Military Service File, National Archives. *History of Wyandot County, OH.* Chicago, IL, 1884. Obituary, *Alexandria Gazette,* Aug. 31, 1869. Obituary, *Washington Evening Star,* Sept. 1, 1869. Letters Received, Volunteer Service Branch, Adjutant General's Office, Files C805(VS)1862 and C384(VS)1863, National Archives.

Andrew S. Core

Colonel, 14 WV Infantry, Sept. 16, 1862. Commanded Post of New Creek, WV, Defenses of the Upper Potomac, Jan.–Feb. 1863. Discharged April 4, 1863, upon adverse report of a Board of Examination, which found him "grossly incompetent."

Born: Dec. 25, 1806 near Brownsville, PA

Died: Aug. 11, 1888 Ellenboro, WV

Occupation: Dry goods merchant and farmer

Offices/Honors: Brigadier General, 23 Brigade, 3 Division, VA Militia, 1862. U.S. Collector of Internal Revenue, 2nd District of Virginia, 1863. West Virginia House of Delegates, 1869.

James Titus Close (photograph by Pein & Co. Photograph Gallery, No. 350 Pennsylvania Ave., Washington City; USAMHI [RG98S-CWP35.68]).

Andrew S. Core (Richard A. Wolfe Collection).

Miscellaneous: Resided Ellenboro, Ritchie Co., WV
Buried: Ellenboro Cemetery, Ellenboro, WV
References: Minnie K. Lowther. *History of Ritchie County.* Wheeling, WV, 1911. Minnie K. Lowther. *Ritchie County in History and Romance.* Parsons, WV, 1990. Obituary, *Ritchie Gazette,* Aug. 16, 1888. Pension File and Military Service File, National Archives. Letters Received, Volunteer Service Branch, Adjutant General's Office, File M598(VS)1863, National Archives.

Morgan Alexander Darnall

Captain, Co. A, 10 WV Infantry, Nov. 24, 1861. Honorably mustered out, March 12, 1865. Bvt. Major, USV, March 13, 1865, for uniform good conduct and ability. Lieutenant Colonel, 10 WV Infantry, April 25, 1865. Colonel, 10 WV Infantry, June 29, 1865. Commanded 1 Brigade, Independent Division, 24 Army Corps, Department of Virginia, July 1865. Honorably mustered out, Aug. 9, 1865.
Born: Nov. 28, 1826 Greenbrier Co., WV
Died: Oct. 8, 1882 French Creek, WV
Occupation: Blacksmith and farmer
Miscellaneous: Resided French Creek, Upshur Co., WV

Morgan Alexander Darnall (courtesy Upshur County [WV] Historical Society, Virginia Bly Hoover Collection).

Buried: McDowell Cemetery, near Frenchton, Upshur Co., WV
References: Marie Mollohan. *By the Banks of the Holly: Notes and Letters from the Desk of Bernard Mollohan.* Lincoln, NE, 2005. *Twelfth Annual Report of the Descendants of the French Creek Pioneers.* Buckhannon, WV, 1960. Avlyn D. Conley. *The Darnall, Darnell Family.* Baltimore, MD, 1979. W. B. Cutright. *History of Upshur County, WV.* Buckhannon, WV, 1907. Pension File and Military Service File, National Archives. Herman E. Matheny. *Major General Thomas Maley Harris ... and Roster of the 10th West Virginia Volunteer Infantry Regiment, 1861–1865.* Parsons, WV, 1963. Obituary, *Weston Republican,* Oct. 21, 1882.

Charles H. Day

Private, Co. E, 2 WV Infantry, June 19, 1861. 2 Lieutenant, Co. H, 2 WV Infantry, March 27, 1862. 1 Lieutenant, Co. E, 2 WV Infantry, Sept. 1, 1862. Acting AAG, 2 Brigade, Cheat Mountain Division, District of Western Virginia, Department of the Ohio, Oct.–Dec. 1862. 1 Lieutenant, Co. F, 2 WV Infantry, Nov. 9, 1862. 1 Lieutenant, Co. I, 2 WV Infantry, May 25, 1863. GSW left arm, Droop Mountain, WV, Sept. 6, 1863. 1 Lieutenant, Co. I, 5 WV Cavalry, Jan. 26, 1864. Discharged for disability, March 9, 1864, on account of wounds received in action. 1 Lieutenant, Adjutant, 17 WV Infantry, Aug. 15, 1864. Major, 17 WV Infantry, Sept. 10, 1864. Colonel, 17 WV Infantry, March 13, 1865. Honorably mustered out, June 30, 1865.
Born: Dec. 25, 1838 New Market, Frederick Co., MD
Died: April 1, 1921 Hampton, VA
Occupation: Printer
Miscellaneous: Resided Ritchie Court House, Ritchie Co., WV; Wheeling, Ohio Co., WV; and Occoquan, Prince William Co., VA
Buried: Hampton National Cemetery, Hampton, VA (Phoebus Addition, Section C, Grave 8630B)
References: Frank S. Reader. *History of the 5th West Virginia Cavalry.* New Brighton, PA, 1890. Pension File and Military Service File, National Archives. Letters Received, Volunteer Service Branch, Adjutant General's Office, File S464(VS)1864, National Archives.

James H. Dayton

Captain, Co. K, 4 WV Infantry, June 17, 1861. Major, 4 WV Infantry, Aug. 10, 1862. Lieutenant Colonel, 4 WV Infantry, Jan. 31, 1863. Colonel, 4 WV Infantry, May 16, 1863. Honorably mustered out, July 4, 1864.
Born: 1836 Hampshire Co., WV
Died: May 24, 1888 Kansas City, MO

James H. Dayton (L. M. Strayer Collection; copied by Richard A. Baumgartner).

James Evans (post-war) (Samuel T. Wiley. *History of Monongalia County, WV, From Its First Settlement to the Present Time.* Kingwood, WV, 1883).

Occupation: Wholesale dry goods merchant
Miscellaneous: Resided New Creek Station, Hampshire Co., WV; St. Joseph, Buchanan Co., MO; and Kansas City, MO, after 1878
Buried: Elmwood Cemetery, Kansas City, MO (Block K, Lot 40)
References: Carrie Westlake Whitney. *Kansas City, Missouri, Its History and Its People, 1808-1908.* Chicago, IL, 1908. Pension File and Military Service File, National Archives. Letters Received, Volunteer Service Branch, Adjutant General's Office, File O567(VS)1864, National Archives. Thomas H. Barton. *Autobiography of Dr. Thomas H. Barton, the Self-Made Physician of Syracuse, Ohio, Including a History of the Fourth Regt. West Va. Vol. Inf'y.* Charleston, WV, 1890.

James Evans

Colonel, 7 WV Infantry, Nov. 3, 1861. Unfit for duty for more than six months due to a partial paralysis of the left side and later a gastric disorder, he resigned Aug. 2, 1862. Provost Marshal, 2nd District of West Virginia, Sept. 9, 1863. Honorably discharged, Oct. 5, 1865.
Born: July 3, 1810 Morgantown, WV
Died: Nov. 24, 1888 Morgantown, WV
Occupation: Farmer and surveyor
Offices/Honors: Virginia House of Delegates, 1839-40. Delegate to the 1st Wheeling Convention, May 13-15, 1861. Delegate to the 2nd Wheeling Convention, June 11-25 and Aug. 6-21, 1861.

Miscellaneous: Resided Morgantown, Monongalia Co., WV
Buried: Oak Grove Cemetery, Morgantown, WV (Section A, Lot 3)
References: Samuel T. Wiley. *History of Monongalia County, WV, From Its First Settlement to the Present Time.* Kingwood, WV, 1883. Obituary, *Morgantown New Dominion*, Dec. 1, 1888. Earl L. Core. *The Monongalia Story.* Parsons, WV, 1979. Military Service File, National Archives. Letters Received, Volunteer Service Branch, Adjutant General's Office, File E144(VS)1862, National Archives.

Daniel Frost

Lieutenant Colonel, 11 WV Infantry, May 20, 1862. Commanded Post of Parkersburg, WV, Jan.-Aug. 1863. Colonel, 11 WV Infantry, Feb. 9, 1863. Commanded 3 Brigade, 1 Infantry Division, Department of West Virginia, July 1864. GSW abdomen, Snicker's Ferry, VA, July 18, 1864.
Born: Feb. 23, 1819 OH
Died: July 18, 1864 DOW Snicker's Ferry, VA
Occupation: Newspaper editor
Offices/Honors: House of Delegates Restored Government of Virginia (Speaker to May 1862), 1861-62

Miscellaneous: Resided Wheeling, Ohio Co., WV; and Ravenswood, Jackson Co., WV. Brother-in-law of Colonel John C. Rathbone (11 WV Infantry).

Buried: Mount Wood Cemetery, Wheeling, WV

References: Obituary, *Wheeling Daily Intelligencer,* July 23, 26–27, 1864. Josephine C. Frost. *The Frost Genealogy.* New York City, NY, 1912. John C. Cooley. *Rathbone Genealogy.* Syracuse, NY, 1898. Pension File and Military Service File, National Archives. Herman E. Matheny. *Wood County, WV, in Civil War Times.* Parkersburg, WV, 1987.

David T. Hewes

Colonel, 3 WV Infantry, July 8, 1861. Colonel, 6 WV Cavalry, Jan. 26, 1864. Dismissed Feb. 15, 1864, for "cowardice and improper conduct before the enemy" at McDowell, VA, May 8, 1862, and for "neglect of duty" in being absent from the regiment more than 65 days and being "extensively engaged in the purchase and sale of sheep."

Born: Dec. 8, 1809 Harrison Co., WV

Died: Sept. 1, 1876 Clarksburg, WV

Occupation: Dancing master and gentleman of leisure

Miscellaneous: Resided Clarksburg, Harrison Co., WV

Buried: Odd Fellows Cemetery, Clarksburg, WV

References: Obituary, *Clarksburg Telegram,* Sept. 9, 1876. Pension File and Military Service File, National Archives. Letters Received, Volunteer Service Branch, Adjutant General's Office, File T524(VS)1863, National Archives. Theodore F. Lang. *Loyal West Virginia from 1861 to 1865.* Baltimore, MD, 1895.

Daniel Dye Johnson

Major, 14 WV Infantry, Aug. 21, 1862. Colonel, 14 WV Infantry, April 5, 1863. Commanded 2 Brigade, 2 Division, Department of West Virginia, Feb.–March 1864. Commanded 2 Brigade, 2 Infantry Division, Department of West Virginia, July–Sept. 1864 and Dec. 1864–Jan. 1865. GSW right forearm, Winchester, VA, Sept. 19, 1864. Honorably mustered out, June 27, 1865.

Born: April 28, 1836 Long Reach, WV

Died: Dec. 18, 1893 Long Reach, WV

Education: Attended Marietta (OH) College. Graduated Columbian College (now George Washington University), Washington, DC, 1860.

Occupation: Lawyer and farmer

Offices/Honors: Delegate to the 1st Wheeling Convention, May 13–15, 1861. Delegate to the 2nd Wheeling Convention, June 11–25 and Aug. 6–21, 1861. West Virginia House of Delegates, 1866. West

Daniel Frost (photograph by Partridge's Gallery, Wheeling, West Virginia; Roger D. Hunt Collection, USAMHI [RG98S-CWP160.104]).

Daniel Dye Johnson (photograph by Cadwallader & Tappen's Gallery of Art, Front St. over the Bank, Marietta, Ohio; courtesy Henry Deeks).

Virginia Senate (President, 1872–75, 1879), 1872–79.

Miscellaneous: Resided Long Reach, Tyler Co., WV

Buried: Long Reach Cemetery, Long Reach, WV

References: George W. Atkinson and Alvaro F. Gibbens. *Prominent Men of West Virginia*. Wheeling, WV, 1890. Obituary, *Parkersburg Daily State Journal*, Dec. 19, 1893. Pension File and Military Service File, National Archives. Letters Received, Volunteer Service Branch, Adjutant General's Office, File J125(VS)1865, National Archives.

John B. Klunk

Colonel, 12 WV Infantry, Aug. 20, 1862. Resigned Sept. 1, 1863, on account of "my domestic affairs. I have a large family of children to support, with no one to govern or control them except my wife, who is very much afflicted."

Born: March 6, 1812 Baltimore, MD

Died: July 19, 1877 Chillicothe, OH

Occupation: Railroad builder and carpenter

Miscellaneous: Resided Grafton, Taylor Co., WV; and Chillicothe, Ross Co., OH

Buried: Greenlawn Cemetery, Chillicothe, OH (Section 1)

References: Charles R. Wood. *The Klunk (Clunk) Family*. Coatesville, PA, 1976. Pension File and Military Service File, National Archives. William Hewitt. *History of the Twelfth West Virginia Volunteer Infantry, The Part It Took in the War of the Rebellion, 1861–1865*. Steubenville, OH, 1892. Letters Received, Volunteer Service Branch, Adjutant General's Office, File K368(VS)1863, National Archives.

Maxwell McCaslin

Lieutenant Colonel, 15 WV Infantry, Sept. 9, 1862. Colonel, 15 WV Infantry, Jan. 21, 1863. Commanded 1 Brigade, 2 Division, Department of West Virginia, March–April 2, 1864. Resigned Sept. 9, 1864, due to physical disability from "piles ... of three years' duration ... complicated with fistula in ano and the debility attending advanced age."

Born: March 1, 1802 Martinsburg, WV

Died: Jan. 7, 1880 Paola, KS

Occupation: Bricklayer, cattle drover, politician, Indian agent, and farmer

Offices/Honors: Pennsylvania House of Representatives, 1843–45. Pennsylvania Senate (Speaker, 1854), 1849–54.

Miscellaneous: Resided Waynesburg, Greene Co., PA; Parkersburg, Wood County, WV; and Paola, Miami Co., KS

Buried: Paola Cemetery, Paola, KS (Oak Grove Addition, Row 17, Lot 58)

Maxwell McCaslin (Richard A. Wolfe Collection).

References: *The United States Biographical Dictionary*. Kansas volume. Chicago and Kansas City, 1879. William Hanna. *History of Greene County, PA*. N.p., 1882. Military Service File, National Archives. Letters Received, Volunteer Service Branch, Adjutant General's Office, File M1851(VS)1864, National Archives.

John Lowry McGee

Captain, Co. A, 1 WV Cavalry, July 18, 1861. Major, 3 WV Cavalry, March 26, 1862. Acting ADC, Staff of Major Gen. Robert H Milroy, Dec. 1862–May 1863. Acting AIG, Staff of Major Gen. Robert H. Milroy, 2 Division, 8 Army Corps, Middle Department, May–June, 1863. Honorably discharged Nov. 23, 1863, "the condition of the regiment not requiring the services of a Major." Lieutenant Colonel, 3 WV Cavalry, Oct. 4, 1864. Colonel, 3 WV Cavalry, May 3, 1865. Honorably mustered out, June 30, 1865.

Born: April 17, 1837 Weston, WV

Died: March 19, 1925 Tampa, FL (died of injuries sustained when hit by a motor truck)

Education: Graduated Baltimore College of Dental Surgery, 1859

Occupation: Dentist to 1871. Clerk, U.S. War Department, Adjutant General's Office, 1871–1920.

Miscellaneous: Resided Morgantown, Monongalia Co., WV; Burlington, Des Moines Co., IA; Washington, DC; and Riverdale, Prince Georges Co., MD
Buried: Arlington National Cemetery, Arlington, VA (Section 2, Lot 1185)
References: Pension File and Military Service File, National Archives. Obituary, *Washington Evening Star*, March 20, 1925. Letters Received, Volunteer Service Branch, Adjutant General's Office, File M1536(VS)1863, National Archives. Theodore F. Lang. *Loyal West Virginia from 1861 to 1865*. Baltimore, MD, 1895.

John William Moss

Colonel, 2 WV Infantry, July 10, 1861. Resigned May 20, 1862, "urgent domestic and pecuniary affairs requiring my presence at home." Surgeon, 14 WV Infantry, Aug. 22, 1862.
Born: Oct. 4, 1816 Fairfax Co., VA
Died: Jan. 2, 1864 Petersburg, WV (heart disease)
Education: M. D., University of Pennsylvania Medical School, Philadelphia, PA, 1838
Occupation: Physician
Offices/Honors: President of the 1st Wheeling Convention, May 13–15, 1861. Delegate to the 2nd Wheeling Convention, June 11–25 and Aug. 6–21, 1861. House of Delegates Restored Government of Virginia, 1861–62.
Miscellaneous: Resided Parkersburg, Wood Co., WV
Buried: Riverview Cemetery, Parkersburg, WV
References: George W. Atkinson and Alvaro F. Gibbens. *Prominent Men of West Virginia*. Wheeling, WV, 1890. Frank S. Reader. *History of the 5th West Virginia Cavalry*. New Brighton, PA, 1890. Military Service File, National Archives. Theodore F. Lang. *Loyal West Virginia from 1861 to 1865*. Baltimore, MD, 1895. Herman E. Matheny. *Wood County, WV, in Civil War Times*. Parkersburg, WV, 1987.

John C. Paxton

1 Lieutenant, RQM, 18 OH Infantry (3 months), June 1, 1861. Honorably mustered out, Aug. 28, 1861. Lieutenant Colonel, 2 WV Cavalry, Sept. 1, 1861. Colonel, 2 WV Cavalry, June 25, 1862. Following a failed attack upon an inferior force near Lewisburg, WV, May 2, 1863, he was dismissed, May 7, 1863, for "neglect of duty and drunkenness whilst under orders to attack the enemy," upon the recommendation of Brig. Gen. Eliakim P. Scammon. With the strong backing of West Virginia Governor Arthur I. Boreman, who stated that "a more discreet, brave, and gallant officer was not to be found in the volunteer service," his dismissal was revoked, April 14, 1869, and he was honorably discharged upon tender of resignation to date May 7, 1863.
Born: Feb. 22, 1824 Gettysburg, PA
Died: Feb. 28, 1881 Marietta, OH
Occupation: Merchant and Red River steamboat

John Lowry McGee (Theodore F. Lang. *Loyal West Virginia from 1861 to 1865*. Baltimore, Maryland, 1895).

John William Moss (Theodore F. Lang. *Loyal West Virginia from 1861 to 1865*. Baltimore, Maryland, 1895).

John C. Paxton (post-war) (Joseph J. Sutton. *History of the Second Regiment West Virginia Cavalry Volunteers During the War of the Rebellion.* Portsmouth, Ohio, 1892).

John Castelli Rathbone (courtesy John Cass Lenahan, Sr. Copy print courtesy of Linda Cunningham Fluharty).

clerk before war. Auctioneer and cigar and tobacco manufacturer after war.
   Miscellaneous: Resided Dexter City, Noble Co., OH; and Marietta, Washington Co., OH
   Buried: Mound Cemetery, Marietta, OH
   References: *History of Washington County, OH.* Cleveland, OH, 1881. *History of Noble County, OH.* Chicago, IL, 1887. Obituary, *Marietta Register,* March 3, 1881. Pension File and Military Service File, National Archives. Letters Received, Volunteer Service Branch, Adjutant General's Office, File M911(VS)1863, National Archives. Joseph J. Sutton. *History of the Second Regiment West Virginia Cavalry Volunteers During the War of the Rebellion.* Portsmouth, OH, 1892.

John Castelli Rathbone

Lieutenant Colonel, 11 WV Infantry, Oct. 17, 1861. Colonel, 11 WV Infantry, Feb. 15, 1862. Taken prisoner and paroled, Spencer Court House, WV, Sept. 2, 1862. Dismissed (with Major George C. Trimble), Jan. 6, 1863, for "cowardly conduct in surrendering their command at Spencer Court House, WV, on the 2nd September 1862," upon the recommendation of Major Gen. Jacob D. Cox, who called the Spencer affair "a burlesque upon military operations, without one redeeming feature," but in contradiction to the findings of a Court of Inquiry, which praised him as "a good, true, firm friend of the Union" and defended his actions as necessary "to prevent a useless effusion of blood and loss of life" against "an overwhelming force of the enemy." Despite President Lincoln's endorsement of April 23, 1864, "Let the order dismissing Col. Rathbone be set aside, and his resignation accepted," the order revoking his dismissal was not issued until May 18, 1866, with his honorable discharge dating back to Jan. 6, 1863.
   Born: Oct. 10, 1818 Saddle River, NJ
   Died: June 17, 1908 Tonganoxie, KS
   Occupation: Land speculator and oil producer
   Offices/Honors: Delegate to the 1st Wheeling Convention, May 13–15, 1861
   Miscellaneous: Resided Burning Springs, Wirt Co., WV; Parkersburg, Wood Co., WV; and Tonganoxie, Leavenworth Co., KS. Brother-in-law of Colonel Daniel Frost (11 WV Infantry).
   Buried: 14th Street Catholic Cemetery, Parkersburg, WV
   References: Louis Reed. "Colonel Rathbone of Burning Springs," *West Virginia History,* Vol. 23, No. 3 (April 1962). Linda Cunningham Fluharty. *Major George C. Trimble, 11th West Virginia Infantry, A Soldier's Life Revisited.* Baton Rouge, LA, 2006. *Portrait and Biographical Record of Leavenworth, Douglas and Franklin Counties, KS.* Chicago, IL, 1899. John C.

Cooley. *Rathbone Genealogy.* Syracuse, NY, 1898. Obituary, *Parkersburg Daily State Journal,* June 18, 1908. Military Service File, National Archives. Letters Received, Volunteer Service Branch, Adjutant General's Office, File C1470(VS)1862, National Archives. Herman E. Matheny. *Wood County, WV, in Civil War Times.* Parkersburg, WV, 1987.

Nathaniel Pendleton Richmond

2 Lieutenant, Co. E, 13 IN Infantry, April 25, 1861. Acting ADC, Staff of Brig. Gen. William S. Rosecrans, July–Aug. 1861. Discharged for promotion, Aug. 20, 1861. Lieutenant Colonel, 1 WV Cavalry, Sept. 7, 1861. Colonel, 1 WV Cavalry, Oct. 16, 1862. Resigned March 18, 1863, on account of physical disability due to "hemorrhoids, with which he has been afflicted for the past twelve months." Colonel, 1 WV Cavalry, June 12, 1863. Commanded 1 Brigade, 3 Division, Cavalry Corps, Army of the Potomac, July 4–9, 1863. Resigned Nov. 11, 1863, due to injuries to right hip and back caused by fall of his horse at Raccoon Ford, VA, Sept. 16, 1863. Colonel, Howard County Regiment, Indiana Legion, April 1, 1864. *Colonel,* U.S. Veteran Volunteer Infantry, March 6, 1865. Resigned May 29, 1865, since he was "not prepared to pass the examination required in infantry tactics."

Born: July 26, 1833 Indianapolis, IN
Died: June 28, 1919 Malvern, AR
Education: Attended Brown University, Providence, RI

Occupation: Lawyer and farmer
Offices/Honors: Indiana Senate, 1865–1869. Mayor of Kokomo, IN, 1873–79.
Miscellaneous: Resided Kokomo, Howard Co., IN; and Malvern, Hot Spring Co., AR, after 1882
Buried: Oakridge Cemetery, Malvern, AR (Block 5, Lot 14)
References: *Combination Atlas Map of Howard County, IN.* N.p., 1877. Obituary, *Kokomo Daily Tribune,* July 7, 1919. *Biographical History of Eminent and Self-Made Men of the State of Indiana.* Cincinnati, OH, 1880. Pension File and Military Service File, National Archives. Rebecca A. Shepherd, Charles W. Calhoun, Elizabeth Shanahan-Shoemaker, and Alan F. January, editors. *A Biographical Directory of the Indiana General Assembly.* Vol. 1, 1816–1899. Indianapolis, IN, 1980. Joshua B. Richmond. *The Richmond Family, 1594–1896.* Boston, MA, 1897.

Leonard Skinner

Colonel, 9 WV Infantry, Dec. 6, 1861. Resigned Sept. 19, 1862, since the regiment "continues to be divided and scattered ... with no prospect of getting it together, ... and I can see no propriety in taxing the Government with the additional expenses of a Colonel's pay for a regiment of this size." Colonel (later Brig. Gen.) Joseph A. J. Lightburn forwarded the resignation with the endorsement, "I approve the within resignation not because the regiment does not need a colonel, but because it does need one instructed in his duties, which qualifications are not found in the present incumbent." Appointed Major, 7 OH Cavalry, Nov. 11, 1862, but did not serve.

Born: Jan. 7, 1827 Glens Falls, NY
Died: April 10, 1898 Santa Paula, CA
Other Wars: Mexican War (Sergeant, Co. B, 1 U.S. Mounted Rifles)
Occupation: Merchant, trader, and farmer
Miscellaneous: Hartland, Huron Co., OH; Brooklyn, Poweshiek Co., IA; and Santa Paula, Ventura Co., CA, after 1876
Buried: Santa Paula Cemetery, Santa Paula, CA
References: Pension File and Military Service File, National Archives. Obituary, *Ventura Free Press,* April 15, 1898. Obituary, *Norwalk (OH) Daily Reflector,* April 19, 1898.

Joseph Snider

Colonel, 7 WV Infantry, Sept. 3, 1862. GSW forehead, Fredericksburg, VA, Dec. 13, 1862. Commanded 1 Brigade, 3 Division, 2 Army Corps, Army of the Potomac, March–April 1863 and July–Sept. 7, 1863. Honorably mustered out, Sept. 7, 1863, rendered supernumerary by consolidation of regiment. Colonel, 4 WV Cavalry, Dec. 22, 1863. Honorably mustered out, March 11, 1864.

Nathaniel Pendleton Richmond (post-war) (*Combination Atlas Map of Howard County, IN.* N.p., 1877).

Joseph Snider (Theodore F. Lang. *Loyal West Virginia from 1861 to 1865*. Baltimore, Maryland, 1895).

Born: Feb. 14, 1827 Rosedale, Monongalia Co., WV
Died: Jan. 8, 1904 Point Marion, PA
Occupation: Farmer, hotelkeeper, and politician
Offices/Honors: Delegate to the 1st Wheeling Convention, May 13–15, 1861. Delegate to the 2nd Wheeling Convention, June 11–25 and Aug. 6–21, 1861. House of Delegates Restored Government of Virginia, 1861–62. West Virginia House of Delegates, 1872–73, 1875. West Virginia Senate, 1887 and 1889.
Miscellaneous: Resided Wheeling, Ohio Co., WV; Easton, Monongalia Co., WV; and Point Marion, Fayette Co., PA
Buried: Mount Union Cemetery, near Easton, WV
References: John W. Jordan and James Hadden, editors. *Genealogical and Personal History of Fayette County, PA*. New York City, NY, 1912. Samuel T. Wiley. *History of Monongalia County, WV*. Kingwood, WV, 1883. George W. Atkinson and Alvaro F. Gibbens. *Prominent Men of West Virginia*. Wheeling, WV, 1890. Obituary, *Morgantown Evening Post*, Jan. 9, 1904. Pension File and Military Service File, National Archives. Letters Received, Volunteer Service Branch, Adjutant General's Office, File S1380(VS)1863, National Archives.

Joseph Thoburn

Surgeon, 1 WV Infantry (3 months), May 27, 1861. Honorably mustered out, Aug. 27, 1861. Colonel, 1 WV Infantry (3 years), Oct. 29, 1861. GSW arm, Kernstown, VA, March 23, 1862. Nominated as Brig. Gen., U.S. Volunteers, June 9, 1862. Nomination withdrawn, June 11, 1862. Commanded 4 Brigade, 2 Division, 3 Army Corps, Army of Virginia, Aug. 1862. GSW, 2nd Bull Run, VA, Aug. 30, 1862. Commanded 2 Brigade, 2 Division, Department of West Virginia, Nov. 1863–April 1864. Commanded 2 Brigade, 1 Infantry Division, Department of West Virginia, April–July 22, 1864. Commanded 1 Infantry Division, Department of West Virginia, July 22–Oct. 19, 1864. GSW left side of chest, Cedar Creek, VA, Oct. 19, 1864.
Born: April 29, 1825 Carrickfergus, County Antrim, Ireland
Died: Oct. 19, 1864 DOW Cedar Creek, VA
Education: Attended Starling Medical College, Columbus, OH
Occupation: Physician
Miscellaneous: Resided Belmont Co., OH; and Wheeling, Ohio Co., WV. Brother-in-law of Bvt. Brig. Gen. Benjamin R. Cowen.
Buried: Mount Wood Cemetery, Wheeling, WV
References: Thomas C. Thoburn. *My Experiences During the Civil War*. Compiled and edited by Lyle Thoburn. Cleveland, OH, 1963. *History of the Upper Ohio Valley*. Madison, WI, 1891. Obituary, *Wheeling Daily Intelligencer*, Oct. 24, 1864. Theodore F. Lang. *Loyal West Virginia from 1861 to 1895*. Baltimore, MD, 1895. Thomas F. Wildes. *Record of the 116th Regiment Ohio Infantry Volunteers in the War of the Rebellion*. Sandusky, OH, 1884. William Davis Slease. *The Fourteenth Pennsylvania Cavalry in the Civil War*. Pittsburgh, PA, 1915. Charles J. Rawling. *History of the First Regiment Virginia Infantry*. Philadelphia, PA, 1887. Pension File and Military Service File, National Archives. Charles "Bud" Fry. *The Generals of Belmont County, OH*. Apollo, PA, 1995.

Francis W. Thompson

Captain, Co. A, 3 WV Infantry, June 7, 1861. Lieutenant Colonel, 3 WV Infantry, July 20, 1861. Shell wound right shoulder, 2nd Bull Run, VA, Aug. 30, 1862. Lieutenant Colonel, 6 WV Cavalry, Jan. 26, 1864. *Colonel*, 6 WV Cavalry, May 5, 1864. Honorably mustered out, Aug. 18, 1864.
Born: Jan. 7, 1828 Morgantown, WV
Died: July 14, 1900 Morgantown, WV
Other Wars: Yakima Indian War (1 Lieutenant, Co. C, Oregon and Washington Mounted Rangers, 1855–56)

Joseph Thoburn.

Francis W. Thompson (courtesy Henry Deeks).

Occupation: Potter, miller, and justice of the peace
Miscellaneous: Resided Central, Linn Co., OR; and Morgantown, Monongalia Co., WV
Buried: Oak Grove Cemetery, Morgantown, WV (Section A, Lot 4)

References: Samuel T. Wiley. *History of Monongalia County, WV.* Kingwood, WV, 1883. Pension File and Military Service File, National Archives. Theodore F. Lang. *Loyal West Virginia from 1861 to 1865.* Baltimore, MD, 1895.

Abia Allen Tomlinson

Sergeant Major, 5 WV Infantry, Sept. 14, 1861. Major, 5 WV Infantry, Oct. 11, 1861. Lieutenant Colonel, 5 WV Infantry, March 1, 1862. Colonel, 5 WV Infantry, April 14, 1863. Commanded 1 Brigade, 3 Division, Department of West Virginia, Jan.–Feb. 1864. Honorably mustered out, Sept. 20, 1864.
Born: Nov. 13, 1832 Harrison Co., OH
Died: Feb. 2, 1913 Kansas City, MO
Occupation: Lawyer and banker
Miscellaneous: Resided Catlettsburg, Boyd Co., KY; and Kansas City, MO
Buried: Mount Washington Cemetery, Kansas City, MO (Block 2, lot 643)
References: Carrie Westlake Whitney. *Kansas City, Missouri, Its History and Its People, 1808–1908.* Chicago, IL, 1908. Pension File and Military Service File, National Archives. Theodore S. Case, editor. *History of Kansas City, MO.* Syracuse, NY, 1888.

Nathan Wilkinson

Colonel, 6 WV Infantry, Oct. 6, 1861. Commanded 2 Brigade, Railroad Division, 8 Army Corps, Middle Department, Nov. 17, 1862–March 26, 1863. Commanded 6 Brigade, 1 Division, 8

Abia Allen Tomlinson (Richard A. Wolfe Collection).

Army Corps, Middle Department, March 27–June 1863. Commanded Wilkinson's Separate Brigade, Department of West Virginia, June–Oct. 1863. Commanded 3 Brigade, 2 Division, Department of West Virginia, Oct. 30, 1863–April 13, 1864. Commanded 2 Separate Brigade, Department of West Virginia, April 23–June 8, 1864. Commanded Forces West of Piedmont, Department of West Virginia, June 9, 1864–Jan. 2, 1865. Commanded 1 Brigade, 2 Infantry Division, Department of West Virginia, Jan. 3–April 7, 1865. Commanded 1 Brigade, 1 Infantry Division, Department of West Virginia, April 30–June 3, 1865. Honorably mustered out, June 10, 1865.

Born: Feb. 23, 1811 Wilmington, DE
Died: March 18, 1889 Wheeling, WV
Occupation: Iron manufacturing company executive
Miscellaneous: Resided Wheeling, Ohio Co., WV
Buried: Greenwood Cemetery, Wheeling, WV (Section F, Lot 106)
References: Obituary, *Wheeling Register,* March 19, 1889. Genevieve Brown. *A History of the Sixth Regiment West Virginia Infantry Volunteers.* Morgantown, WV, 1936. Henry Clay McDougal. *Recollections, 1844–1909.* Kansas City, MO, 1910. Samuel Lamborn, compiler. *The Genealogy of the Lamborn Family.* Philadelphia, PA, 1894. Theodore F. Lang. *Loyal West Virginia from 1861 to 1865.* Baltimore, MD, 1895. Military Service File, National Archives. Letters Received, Volunteer Service Branch, Adjutant General's Office, File W2528(VS)1864, National Archives.

John L. Zeigler

Colonel, 5 WV Infantry, Sept. 14, 1861. Having been found incompetent by two Boards of Examination and recommended by Brig. Gen. Eliakim P. Scammon for dismissal, he resigned "unconditional and immediate," April 14, 1863. Major Gen. Robert C. Schenck accepted the resignation with the endorsement, "Col. Zeigler is not a capable officer and never can become one, but he is a true, zealous, loyal, brave man, who did good service as a partisan against the Rebels at the breaking out of the Rebellion in Western Virginia, and ought not to be dishonorably dismissed."

Nathan Wilkinson (photograph by T. H. Higgins, Wheeling, West Virginia; Roger D. Hunt Collection, USAMHI [RG98S-CWP64.79]).

Born: 1812 Franklin Co., PA
Died: June 6, 1877 Catlettsburg, KY
Occupation: Farmer, land speculator, and hotelkeeper
Miscellaneous: Resided Ceredo, Wayne Co., WV; and Catlettsburg, Boyd Co., KY
Buried: Catlettsburg Cemetery, Catlettsburg, KY
References: Jack L. Dickinson. *Wayne County, West Virginia in the Civil War.* Huntington, WV, 2003. Pension File and Military Service File, National Archives. Obituary, *The Central Methodist,* June 16, 1877. Letters Received, Volunteer Service Branch, Adjutant General's Office, File Z7(VS)1863, National Archives. William Ely. *The Big Sandy Valley: A History of the People and Country from the Earliest Settlement to the Present Time.* Catlettsburg, KY, 1887.

BIBLIOGRAPHY

Published Sources

Alburn, Wilfred H., and Miriam R. Alburn. *This Cleveland of Ours*. Chicago: S. J. Clarke Publishing, 1933.

Altshuler, Constance Wynn. *Cavalry Yellow & Infantry Blue: Army Officers in Arizona Between 1851 and 1886*. Tucson: Arizona Historical Society, 1991.

The Alumni and Former Student Catalogue of Miami University, 1809–1892. Oxford, OH: Oxford News, 1892.

Alumni Record of Wesleyan University. 3d ed. Hartford, CT: Case, Lockwood & Brainard, 1883.

American Biographical History of Eminent and Self-Made Men. Michigan volume. Cincinnati: Western Biographical Publishing, 1878.

American Biography, A New Cyclopedia. Vol. 49. New York: American Historical Society, 1931.

Anderson, Marie C., and Donald O. Anderson. *The Reasoner Story, 1665–1990*. Midvale, UT: Authors, 1990.

Anderson, William M. *They Died to Make Men Free: A History of the 19th Michigan Infantry in the Civil War*. Berrien Springs, MI: Hardscrabble, 1980.

Anderson, William P. *Anderson Family Records*. Cincinnati: W. P. Anderson, 1936.

Andreas, Alfred T. *History of the State of Nebraska*. Chicago: Western Historical, 1882.

Andrews, Alfred. *Genealogical History of John and Mary Andrews*. Chicago: A. H. Andrews, 1872.

Appler, Charles Ross. *The Appler Family History*. Berkeley Heights, NJ: C. R. Appler, 1976.

Appletons' Cyclopedia of American Biography.

Arnold, Jean Fyler. *The Fyler-Filer Family*. Franklin, NC: Genealogy Publishing Service, 1991.

Ashburn, Joseph N. *History of the 86th Regiment Ohio Volunteer Infantry*. Cleveland: A. S. Gilman Printing, 1909.

Atkins, Thomas A. *The Fenton Family of America and Great Britain*. Yonkers, NY: Gazette, 1912.

Atkinson, George W., and Alvaro F. Gibbens. *Prominent Men of West Virginia*. Wheeling, WV: W. L. Callin, 1890.

Ayres, Elsie Johnson. *The Hills of Highland*. Springfield, OH: H. K. Skinner, 1971.

Bacon, Edward. *Among the Cotton Thieves*. Detroit: Free Press Printing House, 1867.

Bagley, Will. *Blood of the Prophets: Brigham Young and the Massacre at Mountain Meadows*. Norman: University of Oklahoma Press, 2002.

Bahmer, William J. *Centennial History of Coshocton County, OH*. Chicago: S. J. Clarke Publishing, 1909.

Baird, William Raimond. *Betas of Achievement*. New York: Beta Publishing, 1914.

Barber, Edward W. "Michigan Men in Congress: The Chosen of the People," *Historical Collections: Collections and Researches Made by the Michigan Pioneer and Historical Society*. Vol. 35. Lansing, MI: Michigan Historical Commission, 1907.

Barnes, William Horatio. *The American Government: Biographies of Members of the House of Representatives of the Forty-third Congress*. New York: Nelson & Phillips, 1874.

_____. *The Fortieth Congress of the United States: Historical and Biographical*. New York: George E. Perine, 1869.

_____. *The Forty-First Congress of the United States, 1869–71*. New York: W. H. Barnes, 1872.

Barnett, James, William R. Northlich, and Adelia Brownell. "Wyoming Honors Its Founder, Robert Reily," *Cincinnati Historical Society Bulletin*. Vol. 23, No. 3 (July 1965).

Barns, Chancy R., editor. *The Commonwealth of Missouri: A Centennial Record*. St. Louis: Bryan, Brand, 1877.

Barth, Harold B. *History of Columbiana County, OH*. Topeka, KS: Historical Publishing, 1926.

Bartlett, Robert F., compiler. *Roster of the 96th Regiment, Ohio Volunteer Infantry*. Columbus, OH: Hann & Adair, 1895.

Barton, Thomas H. *Autobiography of Dr. Thomas H. Barton, the Self-Made Physician of Syracuse, Ohio, Including a History of the Fourth Regt. West Va. Vol. Inf'y*. Charleston, WV: West Virginia Printing, 1890.

Bateman, Newton, and Paul Selby, editors. *Illinois Historical; Effingham County Biographical*. Chicago: Munsell Publishing, 1910.

Baughman, Abraham J. *History of Richland County,*

OH, From 1808 to 1908. Chicago: S. J. Clarke Publishing, 1908.

_____, editor. *Centennial Biographical History of Richland and Ashland Counties, OH*. Chicago: Lewis Publishing, 1901.

Baumgartner, Richard A. *Buckeye Blood: Ohio at Gettysburg*. Huntington, WV: Blue Acorn Press, 2003.

Baxter, Albert. *History of the City of Grand Rapids, MI*. New York: Munsell, 1891.

Beatty, John. *The Citizen-Soldier; or Memoirs of a Volunteer*. Cincinnati: Wilstach, Baldwin, 1879.

Becker, Carl M. "John William Lowe: Failure in Inner-Direction," *Ohio History*. Volume 73, No. 2 (Spring 1964).

Belknap, Charles E. *History of the Michigan Organizations at Chickamauga, Chattanooga, and Missionary Ridge, 1863*. Lansing, MI: Robert Smith Printing, 1899.

Bennett, Charles W. *Historical Sketches of the 9th Michigan Infantry (General Thomas' Headquarters Guards) with an Account of the Battle of Murfreesboro, TN*. Coldwater, MI: Daily Courier Print, 1913.

Bennett, Henry H., editor. *The County of Ross*. Madison, WI: S. A. Brant, 1902.

Bering, John A. *History of the 48th Ohio Veteran Volunteer Infantry*. Hillsboro, OH: Highland News Office, 1880.

Bertera, Martin, and Ken Oberholtzer. *The 4th Michigan Volunteer Infantry at Gettysburg: The Battle for the Wheatfield*. Dayton, OH: Morningside, 1997.

Beyer, W. F., and O. F. Keydel, editors. *Deeds of Valor*. Detroit: Perrien-Keydel, 1906.

Bigger, David D. *Ohio's Silver-Tongued Orator: Life and Speeches of General William H. Gibson*. Dayton, OH: United Brethren Publishing, 1901.

Biographical and Historical Catalogue of Washington and Jefferson College. Cincinnati: Elm Street Printing, 1889.

Biographical and Historical Memoirs of Mississippi. Chicago: Goodspeed Publishing, 1891.

Biographical Catalog of the Matriculates of Haverford College, 1833–1922. Philadelphia: Printed for the Alumni Association, 1922.

Biographical Catalogue of Phillips Academy, Andover, MA, 1778–1830. Andover, MA: Andover Press, 1903.

Biographical Cyclopedia and Portrait Gallery with an Historical Sketch of the State of Ohio. 6 vol. Cincinnati: Western Biographical Publishing, 1883–95.

Biographical Encyclopedia of Ohio of the Nineteenth Century. Cincinnati: Galaxy Publishing, 1876.

A Biographical History of Darke County, OH. Chicago: Lewis Publishing, 1900.

Biographical History of Eminent and Self-Made Men of the State of Indiana. Cincinnati: Western Biographical Publishing, 1880.

Biographical History of Genesee County, MI. Indianapolis: B. F. Bowen, 1908.

The Biographical Record of Knox County, OH. Chicago: Lewis Publishing, 1902.

Blackburn, Theodore W. *Letters from the Front: A Union "Preacher" Regiment (74th Ohio) in the Civil War*. Dayton, OH: Morningside, 1981.

Blake, Francis E., compiler. *Increase Blake of Boston: His Ancestors and Descendants*. Boston: David Clapp, 1898.

Blazier, George J. *Marietta College: Biographical Record of the Officers and Alumni*. Marietta, OH: The College, 1928.

Blount, Jim, compiler. *Greenwood Biographies*. Hamilton, OH: Greenwood Cemetery Association, 1990.

Bogan, Dallas R. *Warren County's Involvement in the Civil War*. Springboro, OH: D. R. Bogan, 1991.

Bowling, Noland (Hubbard). *Meet Your Ancestors: Some Descendants of Edward Philpott (1597?–1678), William Barton (1605?–1674), Francis Posey (1600–1654), William Smoote (ca 1597–1673), Moses Hobart (1709–1780), and Moses Hubbard (1774–1856)*. Utica, KY: McDowell, 1985.

Bowman, Mary L. *Civil War Veterans of Athens County, OH: Biographical Sketches*. Athens, OH: Athens County Historical Society & Museum, 1989.

Boyd, L., compiler. *The Irvines and Their Kin*. Chicago: R. R. Donnelley, 1908.

Brennan, J. Fletcher, editor. *Biographical Cyclopedia and Portrait Gallery with an Historical Sketch of the State of Ohio*. Cincinnati: John C. Yorston, 1879.

Brewer, James D. *Tom Worthington's Civil War: Shiloh, Sherman, and the Search for Vindication*. Jefferson, NC: McFarland, 2001.

Brigham, W. I. Tyler. *The History of the Brigham Family*. New York: Grafton Press, 1907.

Broadstone, Michael A., editor. *History of Greene County, Ohio: Its People, Industries and Institutions*. Indianapolis: B. F. Bowen, 1918.

Brode, Patrick T. D. "Colonel Rankin's Canadian Lancers in the American Civil War," *Detroit in Perspective: A Journal of Regional History*. Vol. 4, No. 3 (Spring 1980).

Brown, Charles G., editor. *The Sherman Brigade Marches South: The Civil War Memoirs of Colonel Robert Carson Brown*. Washington, DC: Charles G. Brown, 1995.

Brown, Genevieve. *A History of the Sixth Regiment West Virginia Infantry Volunteers*. Morgantown: West Virginia University, 1936.

Brown, J. Willard. *The Signal Corps, U.S.A., in the War of the Rebellion*. Boston: U.S. Veteran Signal Corps Association, 1896.

Brown, William B. *Family History of Jeremiah Fenton (1764–1841) of Adams County, OH, and His Descendants*. Des Moines, IA, 1910.

Bush, Bryan. "Col. Samuel N. Yeoman, 90th Ohio Volunteer Infantry," *North South Trader's Civil War*. Vol. 27, No. 4 (July-August 2000).

Byrne, Frank L., and Jean Powers Soman, editors. *Your True Marcus: The Civil War Letters of a Jewish Colonel*. Kent, OH: Kent State University Press, 1985.

Caldwell, John A. *History of Belmont and Jefferson Counties, OH.* Wheeling, WV: Historical Publishing, 1880.

Campbell, James E. *Military Record of Samuel Campbell and His Descendants.* N.p., 1919.

Candage, Charles S. *Crockett Genealogy, 1610–1988.* Camden, ME: Picton, 1989.

Canfield, Silas S. *History of the 21st Regiment Ohio Volunteer Infantry in the War of the Rebellion.* Toledo, OH: Vrooman, Anderson & Bateman, 1893.

Cantwell, Edward N., compiler. *The Generation of the Upright.* Lyons, IA: W. B. Farver, 1911.

Carroon, Robert G., editor. *From Freeman's Ford to Bentonville: The 61st Ohio Volunteer Infantry.* Shippensburg, PA: Burd Street, 1998.

Case, Nelson, editor. *History of Labette County, KS, and Its Representative Citizens.* Chicago: Biographical Publishing, 1901.

Case, Theodore S., editor. *History of Kansas City, MO.* Syracuse, NY: D. Mason, 1888.

Castel, Albert. *Tom Taylor's Civil War.* Lawrence: University Press of Kansas, 2000.

Catalogue of the Lambda Iota Society of the University of Vermont, 1836–1903. N.p., N.d.

A Centennial Biographical History of Crawford County, OH. Chicago: Lewis Publishing, 1902.

Centennial Biographical History of Hancock County, OH. New York: Lewis Publishing, 1903.

Centennial Biographical History of the City of Columbus and Franklin County, OH. Chicago: Lewis Publishing, 1901.

Chamberlin, William H. *History of the 81st Regiment Ohio Infantry Volunteers During the War of the Rebellion.* Cincinnati: Gazette Steam Printing House, 1865.

Chapin, Gilbert W., compiler. *The Chapin Book of Genealogical Data.* Hartford, CT: Chapin Family Association, 1924.

Chapin, Orange, compiler. *The Chapin Genealogy, Containing a Very Large Proportion of the Descendants of Deacon Samuel Chapin.* Northampton, MA: Metcalf, 1862.

Child, Elias. *Genealogy of the Child, Childs and Childe Families.* Utica, NY: Curtiss & Childs, 1881.

Christen, William, Gary Pritchard, David Curtis, Timothy Pack, and Gregory Kolasa. *Stonewall Regiment: A History of the 17th Michigan Volunteer Infantry Regiment.* Detroit: 17th Michigan Volunteer Infantry Regiment, 1986.

Clark, Charles T. *Opdycke Tigers, 125th O. V. I., A History of the Regiment.* Columbus, OH: Spahr & Glenn, 1895.

Close, Lewis R. *Lewis Gile Close: Ancestors and Descendants.* N.p.: Lewis R. Close, 1955.

Clowes, Walter F. *The Detroit Light Guard.* Detroit: John F. Eby, 1900.

Coggeshall, William T. *The Poets and Poetry of the West.* New York: Follett, Foster, 1864.

Col. Isaac N. Ross: In Memoriam. Worcester, MA: C. F. Lawrence, 1881.

Combination Atlas Map of Howard County, IN. Chicago: Kingman Brothers, 1877.

Comley, W. J., and W. D'Eggville. *Ohio: The Future Great State. Her Manufacturers.* Cincinnati: Comley Brothers, 1875.

Commemorative Biographical Record of the Counties of Harrison and Carroll, OH. Chicago: J. H. Beers, 1891.

Conard, Howard L., editor. *Encyclopedia of the History of Missouri.* 6 vol. New York: Southern History, 1901.

Cone, Stephen D. *Biographical and Historical Sketches, A Narrative of Hamilton and Its Residents.* Hamilton, OH: Republican Publishing, 1896.

Conley, Avlyn D. *The Darnall, Darnell Family.* Baltimore: Gateway, 1979.

Connelly, Thomas W. *History of the 70th Ohio Regiment.* Cincinnati: Peak Brothers, 1902.

Conover, Charlotte Reeve. *The Story of Dayton.* Dayton, OH: Otterbein Press, 1917.

Conover, Frank. *Centennial Portrait and Biographical Record of the City of Dayton and of Montgomery County, OH.* N.p.: A. W. Bowen, 1897.

Cooley, John C. *Rathbone Genealogy.* Syracuse, NY: Courier Job Print, 1898.

Cooley, Mortimer E. *The Cooley Genealogy: The Descendants of Ensign Benjamin Cooley.* Rutland, VT: Tuttle Publishing, 1941.

Coolidge, Orville W., editor. *A Twentieth Century History of Berrien County, MI.* Chicago: Lewis Publishing, 1906.

Cooper, W. *Sketches of the Senators and Representatives in the Fifty-fourth General Assembly of the State of Ohio.* Columbus, OH, 1861.

Cope, Alexis. *The 15th Ohio Volunteers and Its Campaigns, War of 1861–65.* Columbus, OH: Edward T. Miller, 1916.

Corbet, Margaret B. *Larned Cemetery.* Larned, KS: M. B. Corbet, 1990.

Core, Earl L. *The Monongalia Story.* Parsons, WV: McClain, 1979.

Coyle, William, editor. *Ohio Authors and Their Books.* Cleveland: World Publishing, 1962.

Crabb, W. Darwin. *Biographical Sketches of the State Officers and of the Members of the Sixtieth General Assembly of the State of Ohio.* Columbus: Ohio State Journal Book and Job Rooms, 1872.

Cranmer, Gibson L. *History of the Upper Ohio Valley.* Madison, WI: Brant & Fuller, 1891.

Crawford, Kim. *The 16th Michigan Infantry.* Dayton, OH: Morningside, 2002.

Crofts, Thomas. *History of the Service of the 3rd Ohio Veteran Volunteer Cavalry in the War for the Preservation of the Union from 1861–65.* Toledo, OH: Stoneman Press, 1910.

Cullum, George W. *Biographical Register of the Officers and Graduates of the U.S. Military Academy.* 3d ed. Boston: Houghton, Mifflin, 1891.

Culp, Edward C. *The 25th Ohio Veteran Volunteer Infantry in the War for the Union.* Topeka, KS: George W. Crane, 1885.

Curfman, Margaret B. *Doubleday Families of America*. Wichita, KS: McCormick-Armstrong, 1972.

Curry, William L. *History of Jerome Township, Union County, Ohio*. Columbus, OH: Edward T. Miller, 1913.

_____, compiler. *Four Years in the Saddle: History of the 1st Regiment Ohio Volunteer Cavalry*. Columbus, OH: Champlin Printing, 1898.

Cutcheon, Byron M., compiler. *The Story of the 20th Michigan Infantry*. Lansing, MI: Robert Smith Printing, 1904.

Cuthbertson, William C. *The Genesis of Girard*. Girard, KS: W. C. Cuthbertson, 1984.

Cutright, W. B. *History of Upshur County, WV*. Buckhannon, WV: W. B. Cutright, 1907.

Cyclopedia of Michigan: Historical and Biographical. New York: Western Publishing and Engraving, 1890.

Danner, John, editor. *Old Landmarks of Canton and Stark County, OH*. Logansport, IN: B. F. Bowen, 1904.

Davidson, Henry M. *History of Battery A, 1st Regiment Ohio Volunteer Light Artillery*. Milwaukee: Daily Wisconsin Printing House, 1865.

Day, Lewis W. *Story of the One Hundred and First Ohio Infantry, A Memorial Volume*. Cleveland: W. M. Bayne Printing, 1894.

Dedication of the New York Auxiliary State Monument on the Battlefield of Gettysburg. Albany, NY: J. B. Lyon, 1926.

Demmon, Isaac N., editor. *General Catalogue of Officers and Students University of Michigan, 1837–1911*. Ann Arbor, MI: Ann Arbor Press, 1912.

Develling, Charles T. *History of the 17th Regiment Ohio Veteran Volunteer Infantry*. Zanesville, OH: E. R. Sullivan, 1889.

Dickinson, Jack L. *Wayne County, West Virginia in the Civil War*. Huntington, WV: J. L. Dickinson, 2003.

Dictionary of Canadian Biography. Vol. 12, 1891–1900. Toronto: University of Toronto Press, 1990.

Dills, R. S. *History of Fayette County: Together with Historic Notes on the Northwest and the State of Ohio*. Dayton, OH: Odell & Mayer, 1881.

Dodge, William Sumner. *History of the Old Second Division, Army of the Cumberland*. Chicago: Church & Goodman, 1864.

Doubleday, Charles W. *Reminiscences of the Filibuster War in Nicaragua*. New York: G. P. Putnam's Sons, 1886.

Douglas, Ben. *History of the Lawyers of Wayne County*. Wooster, OH: Clapper Printing, 1900.

Drury, Augustus W. *History of the City of Dayton and Montgomery County, OH*. Chicago: S. J. Clarke Publishing, 1909.

Duke, John K. *History of the 53rd Regiment Ohio Volunteer Infantry During the War of the Rebellion*. Portsmouth, OH: Blade Printing, 1900.

Durant, Samuel W. *History of Oakland County, MI*. Philadelphia: L. H. Everts, 1877.

_____, compiler. *History of Kalamazoo County, MI*. Philadelphia: Everts & Abbott, 1880.

Dwight, Benjamin W. *History of the Descendants of Elder John Strong*. Albany, NY: J. Munsell, 1871.

_____. *History of the Descendants of John Dwight of Dedham, MA*. New York: John F. Trow, 1874.

Dwight, Melatiah Everett. *The Kirbys of New England*. New York: Trow Print, 1898.

Frederick H. Dyer. *A Compendium of the War of the Rebellion*. Des Moines, IA: Dyer Publishing, 1908.

Easton, Augustus B., editor. *History of the St. Croix Valley*. Chicago: C. F. Cooper, 1909.

Ebright, Homer K. *The History of Baker University*. Baldwin, KS, 1951.

Ecelbarger, Gary L. *Frederick W. Lander: The Great Natural American Soldier*. Baton Rouge: Louisiana State University Press, 2000.

Edgar, John F. *Pioneer Life in Dayton and Vicinity, 1796–1840*. Dayton, OH: W. J. Shuey, 1896.

Eicher, Genevieve. *Henry County, OH*. Napoleon, OH: Henry County Historical Society, 1979.

Eighteenth Annual Reunion of the Association of the Graduates of the United States Military Academy. East Saginaw, MI: Evening News Printing and Binding House, 1887.

Eldredge, Robert F. *Past and Present of Macomb County, MI*. Chicago: S. J. Clarke Publishing, 1905.

Eleventh Annual Reunion of the Association of the Graduates of the United States Military Academy. East Saginaw, MI: E. W. Lyon, 1880.

Ellis, Franklin. *History of Berrien and Van Buren Counties, MI*. Philadelphia: D. W. Ensign, 1880.

_____. *History of Genesee County, MI*. Philadelphia: Everts & Abbott, 1879.

_____. *History of Shiawassee and Clinton Counties, MI*. Philadelphia: D. W. Ensign, 1880.

Ellis, William A., editor. *History of Norwich University, 1819–1911, Her History, Her Graduates, Her Roll of Honor*. Montpelier, VT: Capital City Press, 1911.

Ely, William. *The Big Sandy Valley: A History of the People and Country from the Earliest Settlement to the Present Time*. Catlettsburg, KY: Central Methodist, 1887.

English, Emory H. "Thomas Drummond," *Annals of Iowa*. Third Series, Vol. 30, No. 5 (July 1950).

Estes, David F. *The History of Holden, MA*. Worcester, MA: C. F. Lawrence, 1894.

Evans, Lyle S., editor. *A Standard History of Ross County, Ohio*. Chicago: Lewis Publishing, 1917.

Evans, Nelson W. *A History of Scioto County with Pioneer Record of Southern Ohio*. Portsmouth, OH, 1903.

Everett, Franklin. *Memorials of the Grand River Valley*. Chicago: Chicago Legal News, 1878.

Felter, Harvey W. *History of the Eclectic Medical Institute, Cincinnati, Ohio*. Cincinnati: Alumnal Association of the Eclectic Medical Institute, 1902.

Fifteenth Annual Reunion of the Association of the Graduates of the United States Military Academy. East Saginaw, MI: Courier Printing, 1884.

Fifty-Fifth Annual Report of the Association of the Graduates of the United States Military Academy. Saginaw, MI: Seemann & Peters, 1924.

Finney, David Dorsey, Jr. *Colonel Norman Jonathon Hall of the 7th Michigan Infantry, 1837–1867: A Biographical Sketch.* Howell, MI: NaBeDa Press, 2001.

Fisher, Ernest B., editor. *Grand Rapids and Kent County, MI.* Chicago: Robert O. Law, 1918.

Fisher, Philip A. *The Fisher Genealogy.* Everett, MA: Massachusetts Publishing, 1898.

Fitch, John. *Annals of the Army of the Cumberland.* Philadelphia: J. B. Lippincott, 1864.

Flandrau, Charles E. *Encyclopedia of Biography of Minnesota.* Chicago: Century Publishing and Engraving, 1900.

Fluharty, Linda Cunningham. *Major George C. Trimble, 11th West Virginia Infantry, A Soldier's Life Revisited.* Baton Rouge, LA: Linda C. Fluharty, 2006.

Foote, Abram W. *Foote Family, Comprising the Genealogy and History of Nathaniel Foote of Wethersfield, CT, and His Descendants.* Rutland, VT: Marble City Press, Tuttle, 1907.

Ford, Henry A., and Mrs. Kate B. Ford, compilers. *History of Cincinnati, OH.* Cleveland: L. A. Williams, 1881.

Franklin College Register: Biographical and Historical. Wheeling, WV: West Virginia Printing, 1908.

Frost, Josephine C. *The Frost Genealogy.* New York: Frederick H. Hitchcock, 1912.

Fry, Charles "Bud." *The Generals of Belmont County, OH.* St. Clairsville, OH: R & M's Home Office, 1995.

Fryer, David F. *History of the 80th Ohio Veteran Volunteer Infantry.* Newcomerstown, OH, 1904.

Fuller, John W. "Our Kirby Smith," *Sketches of War History.* Vol. 2, Ohio MOLLUS. Cincinnati: Robert Clarke, 1888.

Gano, John A., et al. *Old Woodward Memorial.* Cincinnati: Robert Clarke, 1884.

Gardiner, Allen. *The Lewton Family.* Topeka, KS: Topeka Genealogical Society, 1974.

Genealogical and Biographical Record of Miami County, OH. Chicago: Lewis Publishing, 1900.

General Catalogue of the Graduates and Former Students of Miami University During Its First Century, 1809–1909. Oxford, OH, 1909.

Gibney, John Michael. "A Shadow Passing: The Tragic Story of Norval Welch and the Sixteenth Michigan at Gettysburg and Beyond," *The Gettysburg Magazine.* No. 6. (January 1992).

Gilbert, Henry C. *The Civil War Letters and Diaries of Henry C. Gilbert.* Transcribed and published by Alcetta Gilbert Campbell. Corvallis, OR: Alcetta G. Campbell, 1991.

Gleason, William J. *Historical Sketch of the 150th Regiment Ohio Volunteer Infantry.* Cleveland, OH, 1899.

Golden Jubilee, Transactions Grand Lodge F&AM Michigan. N.p., 1895.

Goodspeed, Weston A., and Charles Blanchard, editors. *County of Williams, Ohio, Historical and Biographical.* Chicago: F. A. Battey, 1882.

Goss, Charles F. *Cincinnati: The Queen City, 1788–1912.* Chicago: S. J. Clarke Publishing, 1912.

Goss, Dwight. "The Bench and Bar of Kent County," *Historical Collections: Collections and Researches Made by the Michigan Pioneer and Historical Society.* Vol. 35. Lansing: Michigan Historical Commission, 1907.

_____. *History of Grand Rapids and Its Industries.* Chicago: C. F. Cooper, 1906.

Gracie, Archibald. *The Truth About Chickamauga.* Boston: Houghton Mifflin, 1911.

Graf, Leroy P., and Ralph W. Haskins, editors. *The Papers of Andrew Johnson.* Vol. 6, 1862–64. Knoxville: University of Tennessee Press, 1983.

Graham, Albert A. *History of Fairfield and Perry Counties, OH.* Chicago: W. H. Beers, 1883.

_____, compiler. *History of Richland County, OH: Its Past and Present.* Mansfield, OH: A. A. Graham, 1880.

Grant, Arthur H. *The Grant Family.* Poughkeepsie, NY: A. V. Haight, 1898.

Grebner, Constantin. *"We Were the Ninth," A History of the Ninth Regiment, Ohio Volunteer Infantry.* Translated and edited by Frederic Trautmann. Kent, OH: Kent State University Press, 1987.

Guinn, James M. *A History of California and an Extended History of Los Angeles and Environs.* Los Angeles: Historic Record, 1915.

Hake, Amy L., compiler. *The Lemert Family in America: The Story of Lewis Lemert and His Descendants.* Schenectady, NY: A. L. Hake, 1968.

Halstead, William L. *The Story of the Halsteads of the U.S.* Ann Arbor, MI: W. L. Halstead, 1934.

Hamilton, William D. *Recollections of a Cavalryman of the Civil War After Fifty Years.* Columbus, OH: F. J. Heer Printing, 1915.

Hanna, William. *History of Greene County, PA.* N.p., 1882.

Hannaford, Ebenezer. *The Story of a Regiment.* Cincinnati: E. Hannaford, 1868.

Hannibal, Edna A., compiler. *Clement Briggs of Plymouth Colony and His Descendants, 1621–1965.* Palo Alto, CA: E. A. Hannibal, 1969.

Harden, Henry O. *History of the 90th Ohio Volunteer Infantry in the War of the Great Rebellion.* Stoutsville, OH: Fairfield-Pickaway News, 1902.

Harris, Edward Doubleday. *A Genealogical Record of Thomas Bascom and His Descendants.* Boston: William Parsons Lunt, 1870.

Harrison, James L., compiler. *Biographical Directory of the American Congress, 1774–1949.* Washington, DC: Government Printing Office, 1950.

Havens, Barrington S. *Some Descendants of Nicolas Groesbeck.* N.p.: B. S. Havens, 1979.

Havighurst, Walter. *Men of Old Miami, 1809–1873.* New York: G. P. Putnam's Sons, 1974.

Hays, Ebenezer Z., editor. *History of the 32nd Ohio*

Veteran Volunteer Infantry. Columbus, OH: Cott & Evans, 1896.

Hazen, William B. *A Narrative of Military Service.* Boston: Ticknor, 1885.

Heitman, Francis B. *Historical Register and Dictionary of the United States Army.* Washington, DC: Government Printing Office, 1903.

Helm, Thomas B. *History of Wabash County, IN.* Chicago: John Morris, 1884.

Henry, Guy V. *Military Record of Civilian Appointments in the United States Army.* New York: Carleton, 1869.

Henry, Reginald B. *Genealogies of the Families of the Presidents.* Rutland, VT: Tuttle, 1935.

Hewes, Fletcher W. *History of the 10th Regiment Michigan Volunteer Infantry.* Detroit: John Slater's Book Printing Establishment, 1864.

Hewitt, William. *History of the Twelfth West Virginia Volunteer Infantry, The Part It Took in the War of the Rebellion, 1861–1865.* Steubenville, OH: H. C. Cook, 1892.

Higgins, Katharine C. *Richard Higgins and His Descendants.* Worcester, MA: K. C. Higgins, 1918.

Hill, Colonel Edward, and Mrs. Edward Hill. *Proceedings of the Third Brigade Association, First Division, Fifth Army Corps, Army of the Potomac, 1894–1896–1897–1898.* Record No. III. New York: Francis E. Fitch, 1899.

Hill, Norman N., compiler. *History of Coshocton County, OH: Its Past and Present.* Newark, OH: A. A. Graham, 1881.

_____, compiler. *History of Knox County, OH, Its Past and Present.* Mount Vernon, OH: A. A. Graham, 1881.

Hinman, Wilbur F. *The Story of the Sherman Brigade.* Alliance, OH: W. F. Hinman, 1897.

History of Caldwell and Livingston Counties, MO. St. Louis: National Historical, 1886.

History of Champaign County, OH. Chicago: W. H. Beers, 1881.

History of Cincinnati and Hamilton County, OH. Cincinnati: S. B. Nelson, 1894.

History of Clermont County, OH. Philadelphia: L. H. Everts, 1880.

History of Columbiana County, OH. Philadelphia: D. W. Ensign, 1879.

History of Crawford and Richland Counties, WI. Springfield, IL: Union Publishing, 1884.

History of Darke County, OH. Chicago: W. H. Beers, 1880.

History of Dayton, OH. Dayton, OH: United Brethren Publishing, 1889.

History of Defiance County, OH. Chicago: Warner, Beers, 1883.

History of Delaware County, OH. Chicago: O. L. Baskin, 1880.

History of Greene and Sullivan Counties, IN. Chicago: Goodspeed Brothers, 1884.

History of Hancock County, OH. Chicago: Warner, Beers, 1886.

History of Hocking Valley, OH. Chicago: Inter-State Publishing, 1883.

History of Jackson County, MI. Chicago: Inter-State Publishing, 1881.

History of Kent County, MI. Chicago: Charles C. Chapman, 1881.

History of Logan County, OH. Chicago: O. L. Baskin, 1880.

History of the Lower Scioto Valley, OH. Chicago: Inter-State Publishing, 1884.

History of Miami County, OH. Chicago: W. H. Beers, 1880.

History of Montgomery County, OH. Chicago: W. H. Beers, 1882.

History of Morrow County and Ohio. Chicago: O. L. Baskin, 1880.

History of Noble County, OH. Chicago: L. H. Watkins, 1887.

History of Pettis County, MO. N.p.: F. A. North, 1882.

History of Saginaw County, MI. Chicago: Charles C. Chapman, 1881.

History of the City of Denver, Arapahoe County, and Colorado. Chicago: O. L. Baskin, 1880.

History of the Upper Peninsula of Michigan. Chicago: Western Historical, 1883.

History of Trumbull and Mahoning Counties, OH. Cleveland: H. Z. Williams & Brother, 1882.

History of Union County, OH. Chicago: W. H. Beers, 1883.

History of Warrick, Spencer and Perry Counties, IN. Chicago: Goodspeed Brothers, 1885.

History of Washington County, OH. Cleveland: H. Z. Williams & Brother, 1881.

History of Washtenaw County, MI. Chicago: Charles C. Chapman, 1881.

History of Wyandot County, OH. Chicago: Leggett, Conaway, 1884.

Hitchcock, A.B.C. *History of Shelby County, OH, and Representative Citizens.* Chicago: Richmond-Arnold Publishing, 1913.

Hoffman, Mark. *"My Brave Mechanics," The First Michigan Engineers and Their Civil War.* Detroit: Wayne State University Press, 2007.

Hopkins, Timothy. *The Kelloggs in the Old World and the New.* San Francisco: Sunset Press and Photo Engraving, 1903.

Hopper, George C. "The Battle of Groveton; or, Second Bull Run," *War Papers Michigan MOLLUS,* Vol. 1. Detroit: Winn & Hammond, 1893.

Horton, Joshua H., and Solomon Teverbaugh. *A History of the 11th Regiment Ohio Volunteer Infantry.* Dayton, OH: W. J. Shuey, 1866.

Hover, John C., et al., editors. *Memoirs of the Miami Valley.* Chicago: Robert O. Law, 1919.

Hubbell, John T., editor. "Stand By the Colors: The Civil War Letters of Leander Stem," *Register of the Kentucky Historical Society.* Vol. 73, No. 2–4 (April, July, October 1975).

Hurst, Samuel H. *Journal-History of the 73rd Ohio*

Volunteer Infantry. Chillicothe, OH: S. H. Hurst, 1866.

Hyde, C. W. G., and William Stoddard, editors. *History of the Great Northwest and Its Men of Progress.* Minneapolis: Minneapolis Journal, 1901.

Illustrated History of Southern California, Embracing the Counties of San Diego, San Bernardino, Los Angeles and Orange. Chicago: Lewis Publishing, 1890.

In Memoriam, Founders and Makers of Michigan; a Memorial History of the State's Honored Men and Women. Detroit: S. J. Clarke Publishing, 1933.

In Memoriam Samuel S. Fisher. Cincinnati: Robert Clarke, 1874.

In Memory of Toland Jones, the Beloved Physician and the Honored Soldier. London, OH: London Democrat Print, 1894.

Jameson, Ephraim O. *The Choates in America, 1643–1896: John Choate and his Descendants.* Boston: Alfred Mudge & Son, 1896.

Jenkins, Kirk C. *The Battle Rages Higher: The Union's 15th Kentucky Infantry.* Lexington: University Press of Kentucky, 2003.

Joblin, Maurice. *Cleveland, Past and Present; Its Representative Men.* Cleveland: Maurice Joblin, 1869.

_____. *Cincinnati Past and Present; or, Its Industrial History as Exhibited in the Life-Labors of Its Leading Men.* Cincinnati: Elm Street Printing, 1872.

Johns, Lizzie H., compiler. *Records of the Eckley Family in America.* Alhambra, CA: L. H. Johns, 1962.

Johnson, Allen, and Dumas Malone, editors. *Dictionary of American Biography.* Volumes 2, 6, and 9. New York: Charles Scribner's Sons, 1964.

Johnson, Mark W. *That Body of Brave Men: The U.S. Regular Infantry and the Civil War in the West.* Cambridge, MA: Da Capo, 2003.

Jones, Adolphus E., editor. *In Memoriam, Cincinnati 1881, Containing Proceedings of the Memorial Association.* Cincinnati: A. E. Jones, 1881.

Jones, Robert H. *Guarding the Overland Trails: The 11th Ohio Cavalry in the Civil War.* Spokane, WA: Arthur H. Clark, 2005.

Jordan, John W., and James Hadden, editors. *Genealogical and Personal History of Fayette County, PA.* New York: Lewis Historical Publishing, 1912.

Kaufmann, Wilhelm. *The Germans in the American Civil War.* Translated by Steven Rowan and edited by Don Heinrich Tolzmann with Werner D. Mueller and Robert E. Ward. Carlisle, PA: John Kallmann, 1999.

Kelly, Howard A. *Cyclopedia of American Medical Biography.* Philadelphia: W. B. Saunders, 1912.

Kennett, John. "History of the First Cavalry Division from November 1, 1862, to January 1, 1863," *GAR War Papers, Papers Read Before Fred C. Jones Post, No. 401, Department of Ohio, GAR.* Cincinnati: Elm Street Printing, 1891.

Kepler, William. *History of the Three Months' and Three Years' Service of the 4th Regiment Ohio Volunteer Infantry in the War for the Union.* Cleveland: Leader Printing, 1886.

Kerr, Winfield S. *John Sherman, His Life and Public Services.* Boston: Sherman, French, 1908.

Kimmell, J. A. *Twentieth Century History of Findlay and Hancock County, OH.* Chicago: Richmond-Arnold Publishing, 1910.

Kirkman, Grace Goodyear. *Genealogy of the Goodyear Family.* San Francisco: Cubery, 1899.

Klement, Frank L., editor. "Edwin B. Bigelow, A Michigan Sergeant in the Civil War," *Michigan History.* Vol. 38, No. 3 (Sept. 1954).

Knapp, John I., and Richard I. Bonner. *Illustrated History and Biographical Record of Lenawee County, MI.* Adrian, MI: Times Printing, 1903.

Kowalis, Jeffrey J., and Loree L. Kowalis *Died At Gettysburg!* Hightstown, NJ: Longstreet House, 1998.

Kraynek, Sharon L. D. *Medina County Gazette Newspaper Abstracts, 1854–1898.* Apollo, PA: Closson Press, 1997.

Lambert, D. Warren. *When the Ripe Pears Fell: The Battle of Richmond, Kentucky.* Richmond, KY: Madison County Historical Society, 1995.

Lambert, Lois J. *Heroes of the Western Theater: 33rd Ohio Veteran Volunteer Infantry.* Milford, OH: Little Miami Publishing, 2008.

Lamborn, Samuel, compiler. *The Genealogy of the Lamborn Family.* Philadelphia: M. L. Marion, 1894.

Lane, Samuel A. *Fifty Years and Over of Akron and Summit County.* Akron, OH: Beacon Job Department, 1892.

Lang, George, Raymond L. Collins, and Gerard F. White, compilers. *Medal of Honor Recipients, 1863–1994.* New York: Facts on File, 1995.

Lang, Theodore F. *Loyal West Virginia from 1861 to 1865.* Baltimore: Deutsch Publishing, 1895.

Langworthy, William F., compiler. *The Langworthy Family.* Hamilton, NY: W. F. and O. S. Langworthy, 1940.

Lanman, Charles. *The Red Book of Michigan; A Civil, Military and Biographical History.* Detroit: E. B. Smith, 1871.

_____, editor. *Journal of Alfred Ely.* New York: D. Appleton, 1862.

Lee, William O., compiler. *Personal and Historical Sketches and Facial History of and by Members of the 7th Regiment Michigan Volunteer Cavalry.* Detroit: Ralston-Stroup Printing, 1901.

Leeke, Jim, editor. *A Hundred Days to Richmond.* Bloomington: Indiana University Press, 1999.

Leeson, Michael A. *History of Macomb County, MI.* Chicago: M. A. Leeson, 1882.

Leib, Charles. *Nine Months in the Quartermaster's Department; or The Chances for Making a Million.* Cincinnati: Moore, Wilstach, Keys, 1862.

Leonard, John W., editor. *Who's Who in America, 1899–1900.* Chicago: A. N. Marquis, 1899.

Lewis, George W. *The Campaigns of the 124th Regiment Ohio Volunteer Infantry.* Akron, OH: Werner, 1894.

Logan, Andy. *The Man Who Robbed the Robber Barons.* New York: W. W. Norton, 1965.

Longacre, Edward G. *Custer and His Wolverines: The Michigan Cavalry Brigade, 1861–1865*. Conshohocken, PA: Combined Publishing, 1997.

Loop, Myron B. *The Long Road Home: Ten Thousand Miles Through the Confederacy with the 68th Ohio*. Edited by Richard A. Baumgartner. Huntington, WV: Blue Acorn Press, 2006.

Lounsberry, Clement A. *North Dakota History and People: Outlines of American History*. Chicago: S. J. Clarke Publishing, 1917.

Loveland, John B., and George Loveland. *Genealogy of the Loveland Family in the United States of America from 1635 to 1895*. Fremont, OH: I. M. Keeler, 1895.

Loveridge, Jessie Moore. "I am an American," *Michigan and the Civil War: An Anthology*. Lansing, MI: Michigan Historical Center, 1999.

Lowry, Terry. *The Battle of Scary Creek: Military Operations in the Kanawha Valley, April–July 1861*. Charleston, WV: Pictorial Histories Publishing, 1982.

Lowry, Thomas P. *Tarnished Eagles: The Courts-Martial of Fifty Union Colonels and Lieutenant Colonels*. Mechanicsburg, PA: Stackpole, 1997.

Lowther, Minnie K. *History of Ritchie County*. Wheeling, WV: Wheeling News Litho, 1911.

_____. *Ritchie County in History and Romance*. Parsons, WV: McClain Printing, 1990.

Lytle, James R., editor. *Twentieth Century History of Delaware County, OH*. Chicago: Biographical Publishing, 1908.

Manion, Richard L., and Nan Card. *Sandusky County, Ohio, Civil War Soldiers*. Fremont, OH: Sandusky County Kin Hunters, 1992.

Mason, Edna W. *Descendants of Capt. Hugh Mason in America*. New Haven, CT: Tuttle, Morehouse & Taylor, 1937.

Mason, Frank H. *The Forty-second Ohio Infantry, a History of the Organization of That Regiment in the War of the Rebellion*. Cleveland: Cobb, Andrews, 1876.

Mason, Mary E. *The Family of Hugh Mason, William Mason and Allied Families*. Parkersburg, WV: Baptist Banner Publishing, 1930.

Masters, Daniel A. *No Greater Glory: The 144th Ohio Volunteer Infantry in the Civil War*. CD-ROM. Maumee, OH, 2002.

Matheny, Herman E. *Major General Thomas Maley Harris ... and Roster of the 10th West Virginia Volunteer Infantry Regiment, 1861–1865*. Parsons, WV: McClain Printing, 1963.

_____. *Wood County, WV, in Civil War Times*. Parkersburg, WV: Trans-Allegheny, 1987.

Mathews, Alfred. *History of Cass County, MI*. Chicago: Waterman, Watkins, 1882.

McAdams, Francis M. *Every-Day Soldier Life, or A History of the 113th Ohio Volunteer Infantry*. Columbus, OH: Charles M. Cott, 1884.

McBride, James. *Pioneer Biography: Sketches of the Lives of Some of the Early Settlers of Butler County, Ohio*. Cincinnati: Robert Clarke, 1869.

McClurg, Alexander C. "An American Soldier, Minor Millikin," *Military Essays and Recollections: Papers Read Before the Commandery of the State of Illinois, MOLLUS*. Vol. 2. Chicago: A. C. McClurg, 1894.

McCord, William B., editor. *History of Columbiana County, OH*. Chicago: Biographical Publishing, 1905.

McCormick, Robert W. "Challenge of Command: Worthington vs Sherman," *Timeline: A Publication of the Ohio Historical Society*. Vol. 8, No. 3 (June-July, 1991).

McCourt, Martha F. *Descendants of Thomas Bruff*. Astoria, OR: M. F. McCourt, 1973.

_____, and Thomas R. Luce. *The American Descendants of Henry Luce of Martha's Vineyard, 1640–1985*. Vancouver, WA: M. F. McCourt, 1985.

McCray, Kevin B. *A Shouting of Orders: A History of the 99th Ohio Volunteer Infantry Regiment*. Westerville, OH: K. B. McCray, 2003.

McCreery, William B. "My Experience as a Prisoner of War, and Escape from Libby Prison," *War Papers Michigan MOLLUS*, Vol. 1. Detroit: Winn & Hammond, 1893.

McDavitt, Fred. "The 51st Ohio Volunteer Infantry: A Regimental History," *Civil War: The Magazine of the Civil War Society*. Vol. 12 (March 1988).

McDonough, James L. "The Last Day at Stone's River — Experiences of a Yank and a Reb," *Tennessee Historical Quarterly*. Vol. 40, No. 1 (Spring 1981).

McDougal, Henry Clay. *Recollections, 1844–1909*. Kansas City, MO: Franklin Hudson Publishing, 1910.

Memorial of Colonel Charles Whittlesey, Late President of the Western Reserve Historical Society. Cleveland: Williams' Book Publishing, 1887.

Memorial Record of Butler County, OH. Chicago: Record Publishing, 1894.

Memorial Record of the Counties of Delaware, Union, and Morrow, OH. Chicago: Lewis Publishing, 1895.

Memorial Record of Western Kentucky. Chicago: Lewis Publishing, 1904.

Memorial Volume of Denison University, 1831–1906. Granville, OH: Published by the University, 1907.

Men of Progress: Embracing Biographical Sketches of Representative Michigan Men. Detroit: Evening News Association, 1900.

Meyer, Steve. *Iowans Called to Valor*. Garrison, IA: Meyer, 1993.

Michigan Biographies. Lansing, MI: Michigan Historical Commission, 1924.

Michigan Pioneer Experiences, 1710–1880, with Genealogical Data and Anecdotes. N.p.: Michigan Daughters of the American Revolution, 1933.

Miller, Rex. *Croxton's Raid*. Fort Collins, CO: Old Army Press, 1979.

Mills, James C. *History of Saginaw County, MI: Historical, Commercial, Biographical*. Saginaw, MI: Seemann & Peters, 1918.

Mollohan, Marie. *By the Banks of the Holly: Notes and Letters from the Desk of Bernard Mollohan*. New York: iUniverse, 2005.

Monfort, Elias R., Henry B. Furness, and Frederick H. Alms, editors. *GAR War Papers, Papers Read Before Fred C. Jones Post, No. 401, Department of Ohio, GAR*. Cincinnati: Elm Street Printing, 1891.

Moon, Robert C. *The Morris Family of Philadelphia*. Philadelphia: R. C. Moon, 1898.

Moore, Horace L. *Andrew Moore and His Descendants*. Lawrence, KS: Journal Publishing, 1903.

Morrison, Leonard A. *History of the Alison or Allison Family in Europe and America*. Boston: Damrell & Upham, 1893.

Morrow, Josiah. *History of Warren County, OH*. Chicago: W. H. Beers, 1882.

Mushkat, Jerome, editor. *A Citizen-Soldier's Civil War: The Letters of Brevet Major General Alvin C. Voris*. DeKalb: Northern Illinois University Press, 2002.

Myers, Robert C. "The Worst Colonel I Ever Saw," *Michigan History*. Vol. 80, No. 1 (Jan.-Feb. 1996).

National Cyclopedia of American Biography. Volumes 4, 5, 11, 13, and 19. New York: James T. White, 1898–1926.

Neff, William B. *The Bench and Bar of Northern Ohio*. Cleveland: Historical Publishing, 1921.

Neibling, Robert C. *The Neibling Family History*. Montgomery, AL: R. C. Neibling, 1972.

Norvell, John E. *History of the Norvell and Related Families*. 3d ed. Canandaigua, NY: J. E. Norvell, 2006.

Nye, R. Glen. *A Genealogy of the Nye Family: Nyes of German Origin*. N.p.: Nye Family of America, 1965.

Obituary Record of Graduates of Yale University Deceased During the Academical Year Ending in June 1903. New Haven, CT: Tuttle, Morehouse & Taylor, 1903.

Official Army Register of the Volunteer Force of the United States Army for the Years 1861, '62, '63, '64, '65. Washington, DC: Government Printing Office, 1865–1867.

The Ohio Legislature: Biographical Notices of the Members of the Fifty-fifth General Assembly of the State of Ohio. Columbus, OH: John Wallace, 1862.

Osborn, Hartwell, and Others. *Trials and Triumphs: The Record of the 55th Ohio Volunteer Infantry*. Chicago: A. C. McClurg, 1904.

Our Memorial Chapel Dedicated Tuesday, May 30th, 1876 with the Life and Services of Col. Lewis P. Buckley and a History of Buckley Post No. 12, GAR. Akron, OH: Beacon Publishing, 1876.

Owen, Charles W. *The First Michigan Infantry, Three Months and Three Years*. Quincy, MI: Quincy Herald Print, 1903.

Palmer, Lyman L. *History of Napa and Lake Counties, CA*. San Francisco: Slocum, Bowen, 1881.

Pape-Findley, Nancy. *The Invincibles: The Story of the 4th Ohio Veteran Volunteer Cavalry*. Tecumseh, MI: Blood Road, 2002.

Park, W. J. *Biographical Sketch of the Park Family of Washington County, PA*. Covington, KY: J. J. Vance, 1880.

Parsons, Henry. *Parsons Family: Descendants of Cornet Joseph Parsons, Springfield, 1636 – Northampton, 1655*. New York: Frank Allaben Genealogical, 1912.

Penn, William A. *Rattling Spurs and Broad-Brimmed Hats: The Civil War in Cynthiana and Harrison County, KY*. Midway, KY: Battle Grove Press, 1995.

Perkins, George. *A Summer in Maryland and Virginia; or Campaigning with the 149th Ohio Volunteer Infantry*. Chillicothe, OH: Scholl Printing, 1911.

Perrin, William H. *History of Crawford County and Ohio*. Chicago: Baskin & Battey, 1881.

_____, editor. *History of Effingham County, IL*. Chicago: O. L. Baskin, 1883.

_____, editor. *History of Stark County, OH*. Chicago: Baskin & Battey, 1881.

Peskin, Allan. "The Civil War: Crucible of Change," *Timeline: A Publication of the Ohio Historical Society*. Vol. 3, No. 3 (June-July 1986).

Phillips, Stanley S. *Civil War Corps Badges and Other Related Awards, Badges, Medals of the Period*. Lanham, MD: S. S. Phillips and Associates, 1982.

Pierson, Enos, compiler. *Proceedings of Eleven Reunions, Held by the 16th Regiment, O.V.I.* Millersburg, OH: Republican Steam Press, 1887.

Pinney, Nelson A. *History of the 104th Regiment Ohio Volunteer Infantry, 1862 to 1865*. Akron, OH: Werner & Lohmann, 1886.

Pioneer Collections: Report of the Pioneer Society of the State of Michigan. Vol. 3. Lansing: Pioneer Society of the State of Michigan, 1881.

Pond, Daniel S. *A Genealogical Record of Samuel Pond and His Descendants*. New London, OH: Record Office, 1875.

Portrait and Biographical Album of Ingham and Livingston Counties, MI. Chicago: Chapman Brothers, 1891.

Portrait and Biographical Album of Jackson County, MI. Chicago: Chapman Brothers, 1890.

Portrait and Biographical Album of Lancaster County, NE. Chicago: Chapman Brothers, 1888.

Portrait and Biographical Album of Lenawee County, MI. Chicago: Chapman Brothers, 1888.

Portrait and Biographical Album of Oakland County, MI. Chicago: Chapman Brothers, 1891.

Portrait and Biographical Album of Polk County, IA. Chicago: Lake City Publishing, 1890.

Portrait and Biographical Album of Sedgwick County, KS. Chicago: Chapman Brothers, 1888.

Portrait and Biographical Record of Fayette, Pickaway, and Madison Counties, OH. Chicago: Chapman Brothers, 1892.

Portrait and Biographical Record of Kalamazoo, Allegan and Van Buren Counties, MI. Chicago: Chapman Brothers, 1892.

Portrait and Biographical Record of Leavenworth, Douglas and Franklin Counties, KS. Chicago: Chapman Publishing, 1899.

Portrait and Biographical Record of Saginaw and Bay

Counties, MI. Chicago: Biographical Publishing, 1892.
Portrait and Biographical Record of Southeastern Kansas. Chicago: Biographical Publishing, 1894.
Portrait and Biographical Record of the Scioto Valley, OH. Chicago: Lewis Publishing, 1894.
Powell, William H. *Records of Living Officers of the United States Army.* Philadelphia: L. R. Hamersly, 1890.
_____, editor. *Officers of the Army and Navy (Volunteer) Who Served in the Civil War.* Philadelphia: L. R. Hamersly, 1893.
_____, and Edward Shippen, editors. *Officers of the Army and Navy (Regular) Who Served in the Civil War.* Philadelphia: L. R. Hamersly, 1892.
Powers, Robert B. *A Record of My Paternal Ancestors.* Delaware, OH: R. B. Powers, 1967.
Price, George F. *Across the Continent with the Fifth Cavalry.* New York: D. Van Nostrand, 1883.
"Question and Answer OCWGJ 2007–20: 5th OVI, Col. Dunning and Owl Symbol," *Ohio Civil War Genealogy Journal.* Vol. 12, No. 1 (2008).
Raus, Edmund J., Jr. *A Generation on the March: The Union Army at Gettysburg.* Gettysburg, PA: Thomas, 1996.
Rawling, Charles J. *History of the First Regiment Virginia Infantry.* Philadelphia: J. B. Lippincott, 1887.
Reader, Frank S. *History of the 5th West Virginia Cavalry.* New Brighton, PA: Daily News, 1890.
Reavis, Logan U. *St. Louis: The Future Great City of the World.* Centennial Edition. St. Louis: C. R. Barns, 1876.
Record of Service of Michigan Volunteers in the Civil War, 1861–1865. Vol. 2 (Second Michigan Infantry). Kalamazoo, MI: Ihling Brothers & Everard, 1905.
Record of the 94th Regiment Ohio Volunteer Infantry in the War of the Rebellion. Cincinnati: Ohio Valley Press, N.d.
Reed, George I., editor. *Bench and Bar of Michigan.* Chicago: Century Publishing and Engraving, 1897.
Reed, Louis. "Colonel Rathbone of Burning Springs," *West Virginia History.* Vol. 23, No. 3 (April 1962).
Reid, Whitelaw. *Ohio in the War: Her Statesmen Generals and Soldiers.* Cincinnati: Moore, Wilstach & Baldwin, 1868.
Reminiscences of the Cleveland Light Artillery. Cleveland: Cleveland Printing, 1906.
Report of the Proceedings of the Society of the Army of the Tennessee at the Eighth Annual Meeting. Cincinnati: F. W. Freeman, 1877.
Report of the Proceedings of the Society of the Army of the Tennessee at the Eleventh Annual Meeting. Cincinnati: F. W. Freeman, 1885.
Report of the Proceedings of the Society of the Army of the Tennessee at the Sixteenth Meeting. Cincinnati: F. W. Freeman, 1885.
Report of the Proceedings of the Society of the Army of the Tennessee at the Twenty-Fourth Meeting. Cincinnati: F. W. Freeman, 1893.
Report of the Proceedings of the Society of the Army of the Tennessee at the Twenty-Ninth Meeting. Cincinnati: F. W. Freeman, 1898.
Rhoades, Rendall. "The Celebrated Haines' Patent Fruit Jar," *Hayes Historical Journal.* Vol. 7, No. 4 (Summer 1988).
Rhodes, Edwin S. *The First Centennial Atlas of Tuscarawas County, OH.* New Philadelphia, OH: E. S. Rhodes, 1908.
Richmond, Joshua B. *The Richmond Family, 1594–1896.* Boston: J. B. Richmond, 1897.
Ridlon, Gideon T. *Saco Valley Settlements and Families.* Portland, ME: G. T. Ridlon, 1895.
Ritter, Charles F., and Jon L. Wakelyn. *American Legislative Leaders, 1850–1910.* Westport, CT: Greenwood, 1989.
Robertson, John, compiler. *Michigan in the War.* Lansing, MI: W. S. George, 1882.
Roe, George M., editor. *Our Police, A History of the Cincinnati Police Force.* Cincinnati, OH, 1890.
Ross, Robert B. *The Early Bench and Bar of Detroit.* Detroit: Richard P. Joy and Clarence M. Burton, 1907.
Roster Chace Mac-acheek Piatt Zouaves, 34th Regiment Ohio Veteran Volunteer Infantry. N.p., 1906.
Roster 11th Ohio Infantry Association, Proceedings 25th Reunion 1897, Proceedings 26th Reunion 1898. Dayton, OH: Reformed Church Publishing, 1898.
Roster 11th Ohio Infantry Association, Proceedings 29th Reunion 1901, Proceedings 30th Reunion 1902. Dayton, OH: Reformed Church Publishing, 1902.
Roster of the 147th Regiment Ohio Volunteer Infantry. West Milton, OH: Radabaugh Brothers, 1913.
Sarchet, Cyrus P. B. *History of Guernsey County, OH.* Indianapolis: B. F. Bowen, 1911.
Sargent, Edwin E. *Sargent Record.* St. Johnsbury, VT: Caledonian, 1899.
Saunier, Joseph A., editor. *A History of the 47th Regiment Ohio Veteran Volunteer Infantry.* Hillsboro, OH: Lyle Printing, 1903.
Sawyer, Franklin. *A Military History of the 8th Regiment Ohio Volunteer Infantry.* Cleveland: Fairbanks, 1881.
Scharf, J. Thomas. *History of St. Louis City and County.* Philadelphia: L. H. Everts, 1883.
Schenck, John S. *History of Ionia and Montcalm Counties, MI.* Philadelphia: D. W. Ensign, 1881.
Schneider, Frederick. *Incidental History of the Flags and Color Guard of the Second Michigan Veteran Volunteer Infantry.* Lansing, MI: Winfield S. Sly, 1905.
Scott, William F. *Philander P. Lane, Colonel of Volunteers in the Civil War, Eleventh Ohio Infantry.* New York: Privately Printed, 1920.
_____. *The Story of a Cavalry Regiment, the Career of the 4th Iowa Veteran Volunteers, from Kansas to Georgia.* New York: G. P. Putnam's Sons, 1893.
Scribner, Harvey, editor. *Memoirs of Lucas County and the City of Toledo.* Madison, WI: Western Historical Association, 1910.
SeCheverell, John H. *Journal History of the 29th Ohio*

Veteran Volunteers, 1861–65. Its Victories and Its Reverses. Cleveland, OH, 1883.

Seeley, Thaddeus D., editor. *History of Oakland County, MI.* Chicago: Lewis Publishing, 1912.

Shea, John Gilmary, editor. *The Fallen Brave: A Biographical Memorial of the American Officers Who Have Given Their Lives for the Preservation of the Union.* New York: C. B. Richardson, 1861.

Shepherd, Rebecca A., Charles W. Calhoun, Elizabeth Shanahan-Shoemaker, and Alan F. January, editors. *A Biographical Directory of the Indiana General Assembly.* Vol. 1, 1816–1899. Indianapolis: Indiana Historical Bureau, 1980.

Sherman, John. *John Sherman's Recollections of Forty Years in the House, Senate and Cabinet: An Autobiography.* Chicago: Werner, 1895.

Sherman, Sylvester M. *History of the 133rd Ohio Volunteer Infantry and Incidents Connected with Its Service During the War of the Rebellion.* Columbus, OH: Champlin Printing, 1896.

Shoemaker, Michael. "War Sketch by Col. Shoemaker. Narrative of the Capture of Colonel Michael Shoemaker of the Thirteenth Regiment of Michigan Volunteer Infantry, Near Tyree Springs, in Tennessee; His Journey to Richmond, Virginia; His Confinement and Experience in Libby Prison; His Exchange and Return by the Way of Fortress Monroe and Annapolis," *Pioneer Collections: Report of the Pioneer Society of the State of Michigan.* Vol. 3. Lansing, MI: Pioneer Society of the State of Michigan, 1881.

Simon, John Y., editor. *The Papers of Ulysses S. Grant.* Vol. 5: April 1-August 31, 1862. Carbondale: Southern Illinois University Press, 1973.

Simonhoff, Harry. *Jewish Participants in the Civil War.* New York: Arco Publishing, 1963.

Slease, William Davis. *The Fourteenth Pennsylvania Cavalry in the Civil War.* Pittsburgh: Art Engraving and Printing, 1915.

Sligh, Charles R. *History of the Services of the First Regiment Michigan Engineers and Mechanics During the Civil War 1861–1865.* Grand Rapids, MI: White Printing, 1921.

Smith, Charles H. *History of Fuller's Ohio Brigade.* Cleveland: A. J. Watt, 1909.

Smith, Denison B. "Memorial of Gen. Charles B. Phillips," *Addresses, Memorials, and Sketches.* Published by The Maumee Valley Pioneer Association. Toledo, OH: Vrooman & Anderson, 1900.

Smith, Jacob. *Camps and Campaigns of the 107th Regiment Ohio Volunteer Infantry.* N.p., 1910.

Smith, William E., and Ophia D. Smith, editors. *Colonel A. W. Gilbert, Citizen-Soldier of Cincinnati.* Cincinnati: Historical and Philosophical Society of Ohio, 1934.

Snook, John H. "Governor Wisner and the Twenty-Second Michigan Volunteer Infantry," *Michigan History.* Vol. 31, No. 1 (March 1947).

Society of the Army of the Cumberland. Twentieth Reunion, Chattanooga, TN, 1889. Cincinnati: Robert Clarke, 1890.

Society of the Army of the Cumberland. Twenty-first Reunion, Toledo, OH, 1890. Cincinnati: Robert Clarke, 1891.

Society of the Army of the Cumberland. Twenty-fifth Reunion, Chattanooga, TN, 1895. Cincinnati: Robert Clarke, 1896.

Society of the Army of the Cumberland. Twenty-seventh Reunion, Columbus, Ohio, 1897. Cincinnati: Robert Clarke, 1898.

Society of the Army of the Cumberland. Twenty-eighth Reunion, Detroit, MI, Sept. 26 and 27, 1899. Cincinnati: Robert Clarke, 1900.

Society of the Army of the Cumberland. Thirty-second Reunion, Indianapolis, IN, Sept. 20, 21, 1904. Cincinnati: Robert Clarke, 1905.

Society of the Army of the Cumberland, Thirty-ninth Reunion, Chattanooga, TN, October 18,19, 1911. Chattanooga, TN: MacGowan-Cooke Printing, 1912.

Spring, Agnes Wright. *Caspar Collins, the Life and Exploits of an Indian Fighter of the Sixties.* New York: Columbia University Press, 1927.

Staats, Richard J. *A Grassroots History of the American Civil War, Volume III: Captain Cotter's Battery.* Bowie, MD: Heritage, 2002.

_____. *The History of the 6th Ohio Volunteer Cavalry, 1861–65: A Journal of Patriotism, Duty and Bravery.* Westminster, MD: Heritage, 2006.

Sterling, Wilson, editor. *Quarter-Centennial History of the University of Kansas, 1866–1891.* Topeka, KS: George W. Crane, 1891.

Stevenson, Thomas M. *History of the 78th Regiment Ohio Veteran Volunteer Infantry.* Zanesville, OH: Hugh Dunne, 1865.

Stewart, Nixon B. *Dan McCook's Regiment, 52nd Ohio Volunteer Infantry.* Alliance, OH: N. B. Stewart, 1900.

Stipp, Joseph A. *The History and Service of the 154th Ohio Volunteer Infantry.* Toledo, OH: Hadley & Fullagar, 1896.

Stockton, Thomas C. *The Stockton Family of New Jersey and Other Stocktons.* Washington, DC: Carnahan Foundation, 1911.

Street, Henry A., and Mary A. Street *The Street Genealogy.* Exeter, NH: News-Letter Press, 1895.

Sullivan, David M. *The United States Marine Corps in the Civil War—The First Year.* Shippensburg, PA: White Mane Publishing, 1997.

Sutton, Joseph J. *History of the Second Regiment West Virginia Cavalry Volunteers During the War of the Rebellion.* Portsmouth, OH, 1892.

Swanson, Clifford L. *The Sixth United States Infantry Regiment, 1855 to Reconstruction.* Jefferson, NC: McFarland, 2001.

Teall, Mrs. Sarah Sumner. "Onondaga's Part in the Civil War," *Annual Volume of the Onondaga Historical Association.* Syracuse, NY: Dehler Press, 1915.

Teetor, Paul R. *A Matter of Hours: Treason at Harper's Ferry.* Rutherford, NJ: Fairleigh Dickinson University Press, 1982.

Templeman, Eleanor Lee. *Arlington Heritage: Vignettes of a Virginia County.* New York: Avenel, 1959.

Tenney, Luman H. *War Diary of Luman Harris Tenney, 1861–1865.* Cleveland: Evangelical Publishing, 1914.

Thackery, David T. *A Light and Uncertain Hold: A History of the 66th Ohio Volunteer Infantry.* Kent, OH: Kent State University Press, 1999.

Thatcher, Marshall P. *A Hundred Battles in the West, St. Louis to Atlanta, 1861–65, the Second Michigan Cavalry, with the Armies of the Mississippi, Ohio, Kentucky and Cumberland.* Detroit: M. P. Thatcher, 1884.

Thoburn, Thomas C. *My Experiences During the Civil War.* Compiled and edited by Lyle Thoburn. Cleveland, OH, 1963.

Thornton, Leland W. *When Gallantry was Commonplace: The History of the Michigan Eleventh Volunteer Infantry, 1861–64.* New York: Peter Lang, 1991.

Thrapp, Dan L. *Encyclopedia of Frontier Biography.* Glendale, CA: Arthur H. Clark, 1988.

Tolles, William M., and Alyce J. Morow. *Tolles in America.* Baltimore: Gateway, 1997.

Tourgee, Albion W. *The Story of a Thousand: Being a History of the Service of the 105th Ohio Volunteer Infantry.* Buffalo: S. McGerald, 1896.

Towne, Edwin E. *The Descendants of William Towne.* Newtonville, MA, 1901.

Townshend, David G. *The Seventh Michigan Volunteer Infantry.* Fort Lauderdale, FL: Southeast, 1993.

Travis, Benjamin F. *The Story of the Twenty-fifth Michigan.* Kalamazoo, MI: Kalamazoo Publishing, 1897.

Trimble, John F. *Trimble Families of America.* Parsons, WV: McClain Printing, 1973.

Trowbridge, Francis B. *The Champion Genealogy: A History of the Descendants of Henry Champion of Saybrook and Lyme, CT.* New Haven, CT: Tuttle, Morehouse & Taylor, 1891.

Trowbridge, Luther S. *A Brief History of the 10th Michigan Cavalry.* Detroit: Friesema Brothers Printing, 1905.

Trudeau, Noah A. "Fields Without Honor: Two Affairs in Tennessee," *Civil War Times Illustrated.* Vol. 31, No. 3 (July-August 1992).

Tucker, Willard D. *Gratiot County, Michigan. Historical, Biographical, Statistical.* Saginaw, MI: Seemann & Peters, 1913.

Twelfth Annual Report of the Descendants of the French Creek Pioneers. Buckhannon, WV: Buckhannon Record, 1960.

Twenty-Second Annual Reunion of the Association of the Graduates of the United States Military Academy. Saginaw, MI: Seemann & Peters, 1891.

The Union Army. 8 vol. Madison, WI: Federal Publishing, 1908.

The United States Biographical Dictionary. Kansas volume. Chicago: S. Lewis, 1879.

The United States Biographical Dictionary and Portrait Gallery of Eminent and Self-Made Men. Minnesota volume. New York: American Biographical Publishing, 1879.

The United States Biographical Dictionary and Portrait Gallery of Eminent and Self-Made Men. Missouri volume. New York: United States Biographical Publishing, 1878.

University of Michigan: General Catalogue of Officers and Students, 1837–1890. Ann Arbor, MI: Published by the University, 1891.

Upham, Warren, and Mrs. Rose Barteau Dunlap, compilers. *Minnesota Biographies, 1655–1912. Minnesota Historical Society Collections, Vol. 14.* St. Paul: Published by the Society, 1912.

Upton, Harriet Taylor, and Harry Gardner Cutler. *History of the Western Reserve.* Chicago: Lewis Publishing, 1910.

Van Brunt, Walter, editor. *Duluth and St. Louis County, MN.* Chicago: American Historical Society, 1921.

Van Horne, William E. "Lewis D. Campbell and the Know-Nothing Party in Ohio," *Ohio History.* Vol. 76, No. 4 (Autumn 1967).

Van Tassel, David D., and John J. Grabowski, editors. *Dictionary of Cleveland Biography.* Bloomington: Indiana University Press, 1996.

_____, and _____, editors. *The Encyclopedia of Cleveland History.* Bloomington: Indiana University Press, 1987.

Vinton, John A. *The Symmes Memorial.* Boston: David Clapp, 1873.

_____. *The Upton Memorial.* Bath, ME: E. Upton, 1874.

Vital Statistics, Early Clark County, Ohio, Families. Vol. 1. Springfield, OH: Friends of the Library Genealogical Research Group, 1985.

Waggoner, Clark, editor. *History of the City of Toledo and Lucas County.* New York: Munsell, 1888.

The War of the Rebellion: A Compilation of the Official Records of the Union and Confederate Armies. Washington, DC: Government Printing Office, 1880–1901.

Weaver, Bryan P., with H. Lee Fenner. *Sacrifice at Chickamauga: A History of the 89th Ohio Volunteer Infantry Regiment.* Palos Verdes Peninsula, CA: Moyweave, 2003.

Whitford, Noble E. *History of the Canal System of the State of New York.* Albany, NY: Brandow Printing, 1906.

Whitney, Carrie Westlake. *Kansas City, Missouri, Its History and Its People, 1808–1908.* Chicago: S. J. Clarke, 1908.

Whitney, William A., and Richard I. Bonner. *History and Biographical Record of Lenawee County, MI.* Adrian, MI: W. Stearns, 1879.

Whittlesey, Charles B. *Genealogy of the Whittlesey-Whittlesey Family.* New York: Whittlesey House, 1941.

Whittlesey, Charles. *War Memoranda. Cheat River to the Tennessee, 1861–62.* Cleveland: W. W. Williams, 1884.

Wickham, Gertrude V. R. *The Pioneer Families of Cleveland, 1796–1840.* Cleveland, OH: Evangelical Publishing, 1914.

Wildes, Thomas F. *Record of the 116th Regiment Ohio Infantry Volunteers in the War of the Rebellion.* Sandusky, OH: I. F. Mack & Brother, 1884.

Wiley, Samuel T. *History of Monongalia County, WV, from Its First Settlement to the Present Time.* Kingwood, WV: Preston Publishing, 1883.

Willard, Eugene B., supervising editor. *A Standard History of the Hanging Rock Iron Region of Ohio.* Chicago: Lewis Publishing, 1916.

Williams, George E. *A Genealogy of the Descendants of Joseph Bolles of Wells, ME.* West Hartford, CT: G. E. Williams, 1970.

Williams, Thomas J. *An Historical Sketch of the 56th Ohio Volunteer Infantry During the Great Civil War.* Columbus, OH: Lawrence Press, 1899.

Williamson, Charles W. *History of Western Ohio and Auglaize County.* Columbus, OH: W. M. Linn, 1905.

Willison, Charles A. *A Boy's Service with the 76th Ohio.* Huntington, WV: Blue Acorn Press, 1995.

Wilson, Harrison. *Memoirs of the Civil War.* N.p., 1923.

Wilson, Lawrence, editor. *Itinerary of the 7th Ohio Volunteer Infantry, 1861-64.* New York: Neale Publishing, 1907.

Wing, Talcott E., editor. *History of Monroe County, MI.* New York: Munsell, 1890.

Winter, Nevin O. *A History of Northwest Ohio.* Chicago: Lewis Publishing, 1917.

Wisner, G. Franklin. *The Wisners in America and Their Kindred.* Baltimore, MD: G. F. Wisner, 1918.

Wood, Charles R. *The Klunk (Clunk) Family.* Coatesville, PA: C. R. Wood, 1976.

Wood, George L. *The Seventh Regiment: A Record.* New York: James Miller, 1865.

Woodbridge, Dwight E., and J. S. Pardee, editors. *History of Duluth and St. Louis County, Past and Present.* Chicago: C. F. Cooper, 1910.

Woodford, Frank B. *Father Abraham's Children: Michigan Episodes in the Civil War.* Detroit: Wayne State University Press, 1961.

Woods, Joseph T. *Services of the 96th Ohio Volunteers.* Toledo, OH: Blade Printing & Paper, 1874.

Woolson, Alvin M. *First Ohio Volunteer Heavy Artillery, Company M.* Toledo, OH: A. M. Woolson, 1914.

Worthington, Thomas. *Brief History of the 46th Ohio Volunteers.* Washington, DC, 1880.

Wulsin, Lucien. *The Story of the 4th Regiment Ohio Veteran Volunteer Cavalry.* Cincinnati, OH, 1912.

Young, J. A. *Fall Creek Township, Henry County, Indiana, in the War of the Rebellion and the War with Mexico.* New Castle, IN: J. A. Young, 1887.

Zucker, Adolf E., editor. *The Forty-Eighters: Political Refugees of the German Revolution of 1848.* New York: Columbia University Press, 1950.

Manuscript Sources

Bentley Historical Library, University of Michigan, Ann Arbor, MI.
    Eli Augustus Griffin Collection.
    George Lockley Papers.
    Orlando H. Moore Papers.
Center for Archival Collections, Bowling Green (OH) State University
    Arnold McMahan Papers.
    Brigham Family Papers.
Military Order of the Loyal Legion of the United States (MOLLUS)
    Obituary Circulars of various State Commanderies.
National Archives
    Court-martial Case Files, 1809-1894 (Record Group 153).
    Dispatches from U.S. Consuls in San Jose, Costa Rica (Record Group 59).
    Letters Received, Adjutant General's Office (Record Group 94).
    Letters Received, Appointment, Commission and Personal Branch, Adjutant General's Office (Record Group 94).
    Letters Received, Commission Branch, Adjutant General's Office (Record Group 94).
    Letters Received, Volunteer Service Branch, Adjutant General's Office (Record Group 94).
    Military Service Files (Record Group 94).
    Pension Files (Record Group 15).
    Records of General Courts-Martial and Courts of Inquiry of the Navy Department, 1799-1867 (Record Group 125).
    U.S. Census records (Record Group 29).
    U.S. Military Academy Cadet Application Papers (Record Group 94).
Ohio Historical Society
    Civil War Papers of Orris A. Lawson.
    Correspondence to the Governor and Adjutant General of Ohio, 1861-66.
Schaffer Library, Union College, Schenectady, NY
    Special Collections.
U.S. Military Academy Library
    Cullum Files.
William L. Clements Library, University of Michigan, Ann Arbor, MI.
    Henry C. Gilbert Papers, 1826-64.

Internet Sources

S.E. Williams. "Col. Job Reeder Parker," *http://www.48ovvi.org/oh48parker.html.*

Schoonover Mastertree, Part 1, compiled by Roger Schoonover and revised by Mary Schoonover, *http://www.geocities.com/mfs53211/mastertree1.html.*

http://www.illustratedredlands.com/Individuals/TollesWR.htm.

http://sanduskyhistory.blogspot.com/2009/11/colonel-arthur-t-wilcox.html.

http://www.friendsofsilverbrook.org/site3/obituaries.html.

http://www.online-isp.com/~maggie/macomb/farrar1.htm.

http://www.arlingtoncemetery.net/calounsberry.htm.

http://www.lumbardgenealogy.com/gendata/p14.htm.

http://thirdmichigan.blogspot.com/2009/09/daniel-mcconnell.html.

Newspaper Sources

Adrian (MI) Daily Times and Expositor
Akron (OH) Beacon Journal
Akron (OH) City Times
Akron (OH) Daily Beacon
Alexandria (VA) Gazette
Alliance (OH) Daily Review
Army and Navy Journal
Athens (OH) Messenger
Bangor (MI) Advance
Batavia (NY) Republican Advocate
Bellefontaine (OH) Republican
The Bismarck (ND) Tribune
Boston (MA) Evening Transcript
Brooklyn (NY) Daily Eagle
Brown County (OH) News
Bryan (OH) Press
Bucyrus (OH) Evening Telegraph
Butler County (OH) Democrat
Cadiz (OH) Republican
Cambridge (OH) Jeffersonian
Canton (OH) Repository
Carroll (OH) Chronicle
The Central Methodist (KY)
Chambersburg (PA) Valley Spirit
Chicago (IL) Daily Tribune
Chicago (IL) Times-Herald
Chillicothe (OH) Advertiser
Cincinnati (OH) Commercial Gazette
Cincinnati (OH) Commercial Tribune
Cincinnati (OH) Daily Commercial
Cincinnati (OH) Daily Gazette
Cincinnati (OH) Enquirer
Cincinnati (OH) Freie Presse
Cincinnati (OH) Volksfreund
Circleville (OH) Democrat and Watchman
Clarksburg (WV) Telegram
Cleveland (OH) Leader
Cleveland (OH) Plain Dealer
Cleveland (OH) Press
Coshocton (OH) Age
Coshocton (OH) Democrat
Coshocton (OH) Morning Tribune
Daily Kansas Tribune
Davenport (IA) Weekly Leader
Dayton (OH) Daily Journal
Dayton (OH) Evening Herald
Delaware (OH) Daily Journal Herald
Delaware (OH) Gazette
Delaware (OH) Semi-Weekly Gazette
Detroit (MI) Advertiser and Tribune
Detroit (MI) Evening News
Detroit (MI) Free Press
Duluth (MN) Tribune
Dunn County (WI) News
East Liverpool (OH) Tribune
Eaton (OH) Register
Findlay (OH) Weekly Jeffersonian
Fremont (OH) Daily News
Fremont (OH) Weekly Journal
Fulton County (OH) Tribune
Geauga (OH) Republican
Grand Rapids (MI) Daily Democrat
Grand Rapids (MI) Herald
Gratiot County (MI) Herald
Hamilton (OH) Daily Democrat
Hancock (OH) Courier
Hillsboro (OH) Gazette
Hillsdale (MI) Standard
Holmes County (OH) Republican
The Humming Bird (Richmond, IN)
Iowa State Register
Jonesville (MI) Independent
Kalamazoo (MI) Daily Telegraph
Kansas City (MO) Star
Kenton (OH) News-Republican
Kokomo (IN) Daily Tribune
Lancaster (OH) Gazette
Lansing (MI) State Journal
Larned (KS) Chronoscope
Larned (KS) Tiller and Toiler
Leavenworth (KS) Times
Lebanon (OH) Western Star
Lexington (KY) Daily Leader
Lexington (KY) Herald
Lima (OH) Times-Democrat
Lincoln (NE) Evening State Journal
Linn County (KS) Republic
London (England) Times
Los Angeles (CA) Times
Louisville (KY) Courier-Journal
Madison County (OH) Democrat
Mahoning (OH) Dispatch
Mansfield (OH) Daily Shield
Mansfield (OH) Herald
The Mansfield (OH) News
Mansfield (OH) News Journal
Marietta (OH) Daily Times
Marietta (OH) Register
Marietta (OH) Republican
Marietta (OH) Semi-Weekly Register
Marshall (MI) Statesman
Marysville (OH) Evening Tribune
Meigs County (OH) Telegraph
Miami (OH) Union
Middletown (CT) Tribune
Minneapolis (MN) Morning Tribune
Monroe (MI) Democrat
Morgantown (WV) Evening Post
Morgantown (WV) New Dominion
Mount Clemens (MI) Monitor
Mount Gilead (OH) Union Register
Mount Vernon (OH) Democratic Banner
Muskegon (MI) News and Reporter
Napoleon (OH) North-West
Newark (NJ) Daily Advertiser

New Hampton (IA) Tribune
New Lexington (OH) Tribune
New York (NY) Herald
New York (NY) Times
New York (NY) Tribune
Niles (MI) Daily Star
Niles (MI) Republican
Norwalk (OH) Daily Reflector
Ogden (UT) Standard
Ohio Democrat and Times
Ohio State Journal
Orange (NJ) Chronicle
Ottawa (KS) Herald
Owosso (MI) Weekly Press
Painesville (OH) Telegraph
Parkersburg (WV) Daily State Journal
Parkersburg (WV) News
The People's Journal (Greenwich, NY)
Perrysburg (OH) Journal
Petersburg (VA) Daily Index-Appeal
Philadelphia (PA) Inquirer
Philadelphia (PA) Public Ledger
Pittsburgh (PA) Dispatch
Pontiac (MI) Gazette
Pontiac (MI) Republican
Portage County (OH) Democrat
Port Huron (MI) Press
Portsmouth (OH) Times
Ravenna (OH) Democratic Press
Richland Center (WI) Republican Observer
Richland (OH) Shield and Banner
Ritchie (WV) Gazette
Rocky Mountain (CO) News
Rutland (VT) Herald
Saginaw (MI) Courier-Herald
Saginaw (MI) Daily Courier
Saginaw (MI) Evening News
St. Clair (MI) Republican
St. Clairsville (OH) Gazette
St. Louis (MO) Globe-Democrat
St. Louis (MO) Post-Dispatch
St. Paul (MN) Pioneer Press
Salem (OH) Daily Herald
Salem (OH) Era
Salt Lake (UT) Tribune
San Bernardino (CA) Weekly Times-Index
San Diego (CA) Sun
San Diego (CA) Union
San Francisco (CA) Chronicle
San Francisco (CA) Examiner
Santa Cruz (CA) Surf
Santa Fe (NM) Daily New Mexican
Santa Rosa (CA) Republican
Schenectady (NY) Evening Star
Scioto (OH) Gazette
Seattle (WA) Post-Intelligencer
Sidney (OH) Daily News
Sidney (OH) Journal
Silver Cliff (CO) Rustler
Steubenville (OH) Daily Gazette
Steubenville (OH) Daily Herald
Stevens Point (WI) Daily Journal
Summit County (OH) Beacon
Tacoma (WA) Daily Ledger
Toledo (OH) Blade
Tulare (CA) Evening Register
Tuscarawas (OH) Advocate
Urbana (OH) Citizen and Gazette
Ventura (CA) Free Press
Wabash (IN) Plain Dealer
Washington Court House (OH) Cyclone and Fayette Republican
Washington Evening (DC) Star
Washington (DC) National Tribune
Washington (DC) Post
Weekly Michigan Argus
Wellington (OH) Enterprise
Weston (WV) Republican
Wheeling (WV) Daily Intelligencer
Wheeling (WV) Daily Register
Worcester (MA) Daily Spy
Wyandot (OH) Chief
Wyandot County (OH) Republican
Xenia (OH) Democrat-News
Yazoo City (MS) Herald
Yazoo (MS) Sentinel
Zanesville (OH) Daily Courier

Index of Names

*Page references in **bold italics** indicate pages with images.*

Abbott, Ira C. 138
Acker, George S. 137
Adams, Robert N. 12
Adams, Wesley Rowe 18, 19
Alger, Russell A. 137
Allen, William 113
Allison, Charles William Brandon 12, *20*
Ames, Adelbert 88
Ammen, Jacob 7
Anderson, Allen L. 20
Anderson, Charles 13, *20*
Anderson, David 140, *141*
Anderson, Nicholas L. 5, 20
Anderson, Robert 20
Andrews, Ebenezer Baldwin 8, *21*
Andrews, George W. 6, *21*
Andrews, Lorin 5, *22*
Anisansel, Henry 182, 184
Appler, Jesse Josiah 10, 22
Armstrong, James Boydston 16, 22, *23*
Ashwill, Henry C. 16, 23
Askew, Frank 6
Asper, Joel Funk 18, *23*

Bacon, Edward 138, 141, *142*, 145
Bailey, Joseph 141
Ball, Ephraim 17, 24
Ball, William H. 15
Banks, Nathaniel P. 116
Banning, Henry B. 13, 15, 19
Barnard, John G. 157
Barnett, James 4
Bartilson, Mathias H. 12, *24*, 104
Bartlett, Joseph Ridgeway 9, 24, *25*
Bassford, Stephen Allen 13, *25*
Bausenwein, Valentine 10, 25, *26*
Bayard, George D. 98
Beach, Samuel Elmore 139, *142*
Beatty, John 5, 45, 84, 114
Beatty, Samuel 7
Becker, Godfried 8, 26
Belton, Francis S. 117
Blair, Austin 169
Blair, Frank P., Jr. 64
Blake, Harrison Gray Otis 17, 26, *27*
Bliss, Lester *94*
Blunt, James G. 108
Bolles, William Mather 182, *184*

Bond, John R. 14
Boone, Thomas Chalkley 15, 26, *27*
Boreman, Arthur I. 190
Bosley, William K. 5, 27
Bowman, Daniel 13, 27
Bradley, Edwin D. 9, 27, *28*
Briggs, Edward 12, *28*
Briggs, George Gooding 137, *143*
Brigham, Joseph Henry 11, 28, *29*
Brodhead, Thornton F. 137
Brown, Allison L. 16, *29*
Brown, Charles E. 11
Brown, Robert Carson 11, 29, *30*
Brown, Simeon B. 138
Brown, William R. 183
Bruff, Joseph 15, *30*
Buckland, Ralph P. 11
Buckley, Lewis P. 8, *31*
Bukey, Van H. 183
Burke, Joseph W. 6
Burns, Barnabas 13, *31*
Burnside, Ambrose E. 45
Burstenbinder, Otto 11, 32
Butler, Benjamin F. 147
Butler, Lewis 18, *32*
Butterfield, Francis W. 19, *32*

Campbell, Archibald P. 137, *143*
Campbell, Lewis Davis 11, *33*, *34*, 109
Candy, Charles 11
Cantwell, James 12, 33, *34*
Capehart, Henry 182
Carlton, Caleb Henry 13, *34*, *35*
Carpenter, John C. 35
Carpenter, Leonard Willard 5, *35*
Carroll, Samuel S. 5, 33
Casement, John S. 14
Cass, Lewis 177
Cassilly, William Biddle 11, 35
Champlin, Stephen G. 138
Chandler, Zachariah Morris 12, 36
Chapin, Marshall Wright 140, *144*
Childs, Jonathan Webster 139, *144*
Choate, William Alden 9, *36*
Churchill, Mendal 8
Clancy, Charles W. 10, 36, *37*
Clark, Stephen Russell 4, *37*
Clark, Thomas Scott 138, *145*
Clarke, Charles Edward 138, *146*
Clarke, Melvin 8, 37, *38*

Close, James Titus 184, *185*
Coates, Benjamin F. 13
Cockerill, Armstead Thompson Mason 8, *38*
Cockerill, Joseph R. 11, 38
Coleman, Augustus Henry 6, 38, *39*
Collins, William Oliver 4, *39*
Comly, James M. S. 7
Commager, Henry S. 18
Connell, John MacNeill 7, 39, *40*
Constable, Robert Allen 12, 40
Cooper, William Craig 16, *40*
Copeland, Joseph T. 137, 168
Core, Andrew S. 183, *185*
Corse, John M. 125
Cotter, Charles S. 4, *41*
Cowen, Benjamin R. 193
Cox, Jacob D. 191
Cradlebaugh, John 15, *42*
Craig, William *43*
Crampton, Harvey 16, 43
Cranor, Jonathan 9
Creighton, William R. 5, 43, *44*
Crockett, Le Roy 11, 44
Crook, George 8, 90, 120
Crowell, Elijah Henry 146
Croxton, John T. 160
Culver, Joshua B. 139, 146, *147*
Cummins, John E. 18
Curtenius, Frederick William 138, *147*
Curtis, William B. 183
Cutcheon, Byron M. 140, 141

Darnall, Morgan Alexander 183, *186*
David, James Ira 137, *148*
Dawson, Andrew R. Z. 19
Day, Charles H. 184, 186
Dayton, James H. 183, 186, *187*
DeCourcy, John Fitz Roy 6, 44, *45*
DeLand, Charles V. 138
Dennison, William 84, 102, 108
DePuy, Harmon G. 5, 45
DeVilliers, Charles A. 6, 45, *46*, 75
Devol, Hiram F. 8
Dickey, Moses Riley 6, *46*
Doan, Azariah W. 12
Doolittle, Charles C. 140
Doubleday, Charles William 3, *47*
Drummond, Thomas 4, *47*
Duffie, Alfred 53

Index of Names

Duffield, William Ward 139, 148, *149*
Dunning, Samuel H. 5, 48
Dunphy, William Henry 139, 149
Duval, Isaac H. 183
Dwight, William 141

Eaton, Charles G. 11
Eaton, Willard G. 139, *149*
Eckley, Ephraim Ralph 12, *48*
Eggleston, Beroth B. 3
Eith, Bernhard 3, 49
Elliott, Lyman S. 9, *49*
Ely, Ralph 139
Enochs, William H. 183
Este, George P. 6
Evans, James 183, *187*
Ewing, Hugh 8

Farrar, Judson Smith 140, 149, *150*
Fearing, Benjamin D. 13
Fenton, William Matthew 139, *150, 151*, 167
Ferguson, John 11, 18, 49, *50*
Findley, Robert Pressly 12, *50*
Fisher, Samuel Sparks 16, 50, *51*
Fitch, William T. 8, *51*
Fitzgerald, William Pitt Nelson 10, 51
Floto, William 3, 51
Foote, Thaddeus 138, *151*
Force, Manning F. 7
Ford, Thomas H. 8, *52*
Forsyth, James W. 11
Fox, Dorus Morton 141, 151, *152*
Franklin, Freeman E. 8, *52*
French, Daniel 15, *53*
Frizell, Joseph W. 13
Frost, Daniel 183, 187, *188*, 191
Fry, John Christian 7, *53, 54*, 131
Fuller, John W. 8, 129
Fyffe, Edward P. 8
Fyffe, James Perry 10, *54*

Gambee, Charles B. 10, *55*
Garfield, James A. 9
Garis, Conrad 17, *55*
Garland, John 175
Garrard, Israel 4
Gibson, Horatio G. 4
Gibson, William H. 9
Gilbert, Alfred West 9, 55, *56*
Gilbert, Henry Clarke 140, *152*
Gilbert, Samuel A. 9
Gilmore, William Edward 7, *56*
Gilruth, Isaac Newton 8, *57*
Given, Josiah 12
Given, William 14
Godman, James H. 5
Good, Joseph 14, *57*
Gould, Ebenezer 137, *153*
Granger, Gordon 137
Grant, Claudius Buchanan 140, *153*
Grant, Ulysses S. 84, 134
Graves, Frank 139, *154*
Graves, Phineas *155*
Graves, William Henry 139, *154, 155*
Gray, George 137, *155*

Grending, Augustus 79
Griffin, Charles 144
Griffin, Eli Augustus 140, *156*
Groesbeck, John Brown 9, *58*
Groom, John C. 14, 58
Grosvenor, Charles H. 7
Grosvenor, Ira Rufus 139, *156, 157*

Haffner, Theodore 3, 58
Haines, Joel 16, *59*
Hall, Albert S. 14, *59, 60*
Hall, Jairus W. 139
Hall, Norman Jonathan 139, *157, 158*
Halleck, Henry W. 22, 25
Halstead, Benton 19, *60*
Halstead, Murat 60
Hamilton, William D. 4
Harker, Charles G. 11
Harris, Andrew L. 12
Harris, Leonard A. 4, 16, 60, *61*
Harris, Thomas M. 183
Harrison, Anna Tuthill 123
Harrison, Benjamin 61
Harrison, James Findlay 6, 61, *62*, 123
Harrison, William Henry 61, 123
Hart, James H. 11
Hastings, Smith Hugh 137, 157, *158, 159*
Hatch, John P. 148
Hatfield, Joseph D. 13, 61
Haughton, Nathaniel 8
Hawkins, Joseph G. 6, *62*
Hawley, Chauncey Gillett 4, 62, *63*
Hayes, Edwin L. 14
Hayes, Philip C. 14
Hayes, Rutherford B. 7
Haynes, Nathaniel 18, *63*
Hayward, William Henry 17, *63*
Hazen, William B. 9
Heath, Thomas T. 3
Hewes, David T. 182, 188
Hibbets, Jefferson Jackson 8, *64*
Higgins, David Jordan 8, 64, *65*
Hildebrand, Jesse 12, *65*
Hill, Charles W. 15
Hinson, Joseph 8, 65, *66*
Hitchcock, Peter M. *54*
Hoge, George W. 18
Holloway, Ephraim S. 9
Holt, Joseph 134, 141
Hooker, Joseph 58
Horner, John Wesley 140, 158, *159*
Houghton, Moses B. 138
Howard, Oliver O. 80
Howland, Horace N. 3
Hudson, John E. 18, *66*
Humphrey, John H. 9, 66, *67*
Humphrey, William 138
Hunt, Samuel Henry 16, 66
Hunter, David 47, 84
Hurd, John R. 18
Hurlbut, Stephen A. 122
Hurst, Samuel H. 11
Hutchinson, Frederick S. 140

Innes, William P. 138

Innis, Gustavus Swan 16, *67*
Irvine, James 6, 67, *68*
Irwin, William Smith 16, *68*

Jackson, Lyman J. 17, 69
Jarvis, Dwight 6
Jaynes, Anderson D. 16, 69, *70*
Jeffords, Harrison H. 139, *159, 160*
John, Howard Daniel 15, 69
Johnson, Andrew 175
Johnson, Daniel Dye 183, *188*
Johnson, Richard W. 24, 108
Johnston, Thomas W. 137, *160*
Jones, Frederick Charles 7, 69, *70*
Jones, Henry Ewing 10, 69, *70*
Jones, James Andres 8, *71*, 129
Jones, John S. 18
Jones, Theodore 8
Jones, Toland 14, 71, *72*
Jones, Wells S. 10
Jones, William Graham 8, *72*
Judah, Henry M. 94

Kaemmerling, Gustav 5, *73*
Kautz, August V. 3
Keegan, Patrick H. 139, 160, *161*
Keifer, Joseph W. 14
Kell, John 5, 73, *74*
Kelley, Benjamin F. 182
Kellogg, Francis William 137, *161*
Kelly, John H. 15
Kennedy, Robert P. 19
Kennett, Henry G. 12, 74
Kennett, John 3, *74*
Kidd, James H. 137
Kimberly, Robert L. 19
King, John H. 131
Kingsbury, Henry D. 19
Kinney, Peter 10, 74, *75*
Kirby, Isaac M. 14
Kirkup, Robert 5, 75, *76*
Klunk, John B. 183, 189

Lane, John Q. 13
Lane, Philander Parmele 6, 75, *76*
Langworthy, Albert 13, 75
LaPointe, George Washington 139, 161, *162*
Latham, George R. 182
Lawrence, Walter E. 76
Lawrence, William 12, *77*
Lawson, Orris A. 5, *77*
Lee, Fitzhugh 98
Lee, John C. 10, 17
LeFavour, Heber 140
Legg, Andrew 16, *78*
Leggett, Mortimer D. 12
Lemert, Wilson Cooper 13, *78*
Lewton, Lewis Law 18, 79
Lightburn, Joseph A. J. 183, 192
Limberg, George T. 14, 79
Lippincott, Sara Jane (Clarke) 146
Litchfield, Allyne C. 137
Lloyd, William R. 4, *79*
Lockley, George 138, *162*
Logan, John A. 54
Long, Eli 3, 98
Long, Richard, Jr. 11, *80, 81*
Longstreet, James 175

Index of Names

Longstreet, Maria Louise (Garland) 175
Loomis, Cyrus O. 138
Loudon, DeWitt Clinton 11, 80, *81*
Lounsberry, Clement Augustus 140, *163*
Loveland, Frank Clarence 4, *81*
Lowe, John Gilbert 16, 82
Lowe, John Williamson 6, *82*
Luce, Constant 140, 163
Lucy, Jackson A. 15, 82, *83*
Lum, Charles Matthew 139, *164*
Lumbard, George Washington 139, 164, *165*
Lytle, William H. 6, 61

Manderson, Charles F. 7
Mann, William d'Alton 137, *165*
Marble, John Miner Carey 17, 83
March, Edwin Johnson 138, 165, *166*
Marker, Caleb 17, *83*
Marrow, Isaac Harrison 5, 83
Marsh, Lucius P. 84
Marshall, John Grant 13, 84
Mason, Edwin C. 18, 84
Mason, John S. 5
Mason, Rodney 11, 84
Mason, William Bion 12, *85*
Matthews, Stanley 10, 85, *86*
Maxwell, Obadiah C. 19
May, Dwight 139, *155*
May, William J. 139, 166
Mayer, Frederick John 3, 85
McCaslin, Maxwell 184, *189*
McClain, Richard William 10, *86*
McConnell, Daniel 138, *166*
McConnell, Henry K. 11
McCook, Alexander McD. 4, 41, 87, 100, 121
McCook, Anson G. 5, 19
McCook, Daniel 10, 87
McCook, Edwin S. 87
McCook, George Wythe 17, 86, *87*
McCook, Robert L. 5, 58, 87
McCoy, Daniel W. 18
McCreery, William Barker 140, 150, *167*
McGee, John Lowry 182, 189, *190*
McGroarty, Stephen J. 10, 12
McIlvain, Alexander 11, *87*
McLean, Nathaniel C. 12, 106
McMahan, Arnold 7, 87, *88*
McMillen, William L. 13
Merritt, Wesley *72*
Metham, Pren 12, *88*
Meyer, Edward S. 89
Meyer, Seraphim 14, 88, *89*
Miller, Hiram 17, 89, *90*
Millikin, Minor 3, 89, *91*, 108
Milroy, Robert H. 189
Minty, Robert H. G. 137
Mitchell, John G. 14
Mitchell, John Thomas 11, 90
Mix, Elisha 137
Mizner, Henry R. 140
Mizner, John K. 137
Moody, Granville 12
Moor, August 8, 26
Moore, Alpheus S. 4, 90

Moore, Frederick W. 12
Moore, Marshall F. 11
Moore, Orlando Hurley 140, *167*
Moore, Oscar Fitzallen 8, *91*
Moore, Thomas 17, *92*
Moore, Thomas Watson 16, *92*
Morris, Thomas Clarkson 12, 92, *93*
Morrow, Henry A. 140, 154
Morton, Thomas 7, 12, *93*
Moss, John William 182, *190*
Mott, Samuel R. (57 OH) 10, 94
Mott, Samuel R. (118 OH) 15, *94*
Munford, Thomas T. 123
Mungen, William 10, 94, *95*

Nash, James Madison 7, 95, *96*
Neff, George W. 13
Neibling, James McCleery 7, 95, *96*
Nettleton, Alvred B. 3
Nolan, Michael P. 14, 95, *97*
Norton, Jesse Smith 7, *97*
Norvell, Freeman 137, *168*
Noyes, Edward F. 9

O'Dowd, John 18
Oley, John H. 182
Oliver, John M. 140
Opdycke, Emerson 15, 30
Osterhaus, Peter J. 25
Owens, Wesley 4, *98*

Palmer, John M. 110
Paramore, James Wallace 3, *98*
Park, Horace 9, 99, *100*
Parker, Job Reeder 9, 99, *100*
Parkhurst, John G. 139
Parrott, Edwin Augustus 4, 99, *101*
Parry, Augustus C. 9
Partridge, Benjamin F. 140
Patrick, John Halliday 5, *101*
Patton, George S. 97
Paxton, John C. 182, 190, *191*
Payne, Oliver H. 15
Pearce, John S. 13
Perkins, George Tod 14, 101, *102*
Phelps, Edward Herrick 9, *102*, *103*
Phillips, Charles B. 15, 102, *103*
Philpott, James Elliott 12, *103*
Piatt, Abram S. 6, 8
Pickands, James 15, *104*
Pierce, Byron R. 138
Poe, Orlando M. 138
Pond, Francis Bates 10, 104, *105*
Poorman, Christian L. 13, 105, *106*
Porter, Andrew 72
Poschner, Frederick Anton 9, 105
Potts, Benjamin F. 8
Powell, Eugene 19
Powell, William H. 182
Powers, Edwin H. 10, *106*, *107*
Pulford, John 139
Purington, George Augustus 3, 106, *107*
Putman, David 17, *107*

Quinn, Francis 139, 169

Rankin, Arthur 138, *169*
Ransom, Owen Perkins 3, 108

Rathbone, John Castelli 183, 188, *191*
Ratliff, Robert W. 4
Raynor, William H. 10
Reasoner, Cyrus 17, 108
Redfield, Alexander H. 168
Reid, William Pitt 15, 108
Reilly, James W. 14
Reily, James 109
Reily, Robert 12, 33, *109*
Rice, Americus V. 10
Richardson, Israel B. 138
Richardson, William P. 8
Richmond, Nathaniel Pendleton 182, *192*
Rippey, Charles Hendee 13, *109*
Roberts, Horace Smith 138, *170*
Robie, Oliver P. 3, *110*, *111*
Robinson, Aaron Black 15, 110, *111*
Robinson, James S. 12
Robinson, John C. 138
Rosecrans, William S. 7, 192
Ross, Isaac Newton 13, *111*
Rosson, Benjamin F. 16, *112*
Runkle, Benjamin P. 9
Ryan, Michael Clarkson 112

Sage, Harley H. 17, 18, 112
Sanderson, Thomas W. 4
Sargent, Charles Henry 113
Saunders, Miles J. 18, 113
Saviers, Lemuel 140, 170, *171*
Saylor, Thomas 141, 170, *171*
Scammon, Eliakim P. 7, 190, 195
Schenck, Robert C. 80, 195
Schleich, Newton 10, *113*
Schneider, Frederick 138, 171, *172*
Schoonover, Jonas 8, *114*
Scott, A. R. 79
Scott, Robert K. 11
Seidel, Charles B. 3, *114*
Seward, Dudley 3, *115*
Shackelford, James M. 45
Sheldon, Lionel A. 9
Sheridan, Philip H. 137
Sherman, John *115*
Sherman, William T. 22, 116
Sherwood, Isaac R. 14
Shoemaker, Michael 139, 172, *173*
Siber, Edward 9, 116
Sill, Joshua W. 8
Simpson, James H. 130
Sinclair, Robert P. 140, *173*
Skinner, Leonard 183, 192
Slack, James R. 71
Slevin, Patrick S. 14
Smith, Benjamin F. 4, 15
Smith, Charles C. 4, 116
Smith, Edmund Kirby 117
Smith, Israel C. 138
Smith, Joseph Lee Kirby 9, *116*, *117*
Smith, Orland 11
Smith, Orlow 11
Smith, Thomas C. H. 3
Smith, Thomas Kilby 10
Smith, William Sooy 6
Snider, Joseph 182, 183, 192, *193*
Sowers, Edgar 15
Spaulding, Oliver L. 140

Index of Names

Spiegel, Marcus M. 15, *117*
Sprague, John W. 11
Sprague, Thomas S. 151
Stafford, Joab A. 18
Stagg, Peter 137
Stanley, Timothy R. 7, 36
Stedman, William 4
Steedman, James B. 6, 41, 118
Steedman, Samuel Harris 11, 117
Stem, Leander 14, *118*
Sterl, Oscar William 14, 118, *119*
Stevens, Ambrose A. 140
Stevens, William Edward 12, 119, *120*
Stevenson, Robert 17, 119, *120*
Stewart, William E. *155*
Stockton, John 137, *174*
Stockton, Thomas Baylis Whitmarsh 140, *174*, *175*
Stough, Israel 17, 119
Stoughton, William L. 139
Street, Ogden 6, *120*
Strickland, Silas A. 10
Strong, Hiram 13, *121*
Strother, David H. 182
Stuart, Charles Edward 139, *175*
Sullivan, Jeremiah C. 122
Sullivan, Peter J. 9
Sumner, Edwin V. 72
Swaine, Peter Tyrer 13, 121, *122*
Swayne, Wager 9, 112
Swift, Frederick W. 140

Taylor, Jacob E. 9, 19
Taylor, Jonah R. 10, 121
Taylor, Oliver Perry 17, *122*
Taylor, Thomas T. 9
Taylor, William Henry Harrison 3, 61, 122, *123*
Terry, Henry D. 139
Thoburn, Joseph 182, 193, *194*
Thomas, George H. 76
Thompson, Francis W. 182, 193, *194*
Throop, William A. 138

Thruston, Gates P. 82
Tiffin, Edward 57
Tod, David 76, 84, 102, 104, 118
Toland, John T. 8, *123*
Tolles, William Ransom 14, *124*
Tomlinson, Abia Allen 183, *194*
Town, Charles H. 137, *176*
Trimble, Allen 125
Trimble, George C. 191
Trimble, William Henry 10, *125*
Trowbridge, Luther S. 138
Turley, John A. 13
Tyler, Erastus B. 5

Upton, Edward Nathan 9, *125*

Vallandigham, Clement L. 45
Van Derveer, Ferdinand 8
Van Vorhes, Nelson Holmes 13, *126*
Vance, Joseph W. 13, *127*
Vodrey, William H. 16, 127, *128*
Von Schrader, Alexander 12
Von Steinwehr, Adolph 106
Voris, Alvin C. 11

Waite, Charles 141
Walcutt, Charles C. 9, 125
Walker, Moses B. 8
Wallace, Frank 74
Wallace, William 6, 127, *128*
Ward, Durbin 7
Warner, Darius B. 14
Warner, Willard 18
Washburn, James 15, *128*
Way, William B. 137, *176*, *177*
Weber, Daniel 9, 128, *129*
Webster, George Penny 13, 71, *129*
Welch, Norval E. 140, 176, *177*
Welles, George E. 11, 102
Wells, Henry H. 140
Wells, Milton 184
West, Henry R. 11
Wheeler, William White 141, 177, *178*

White, Carr B. 6
Whittelsey, Franklin Ward 138, *178*
Whittlesey, Charles 7, *130*
Wilcox, Arthur Tappan 18, *130*
Wilcox, James A. 14
Wildes, Thomas F. 18
Wiles, Greenberry F. 12
Wiley, Aquila 9
Wilkinson, Nathan 183, 194, *195*
Willcox, Orlando B. 138
Williams, Adolphus W. 140
Williams, Thomas 141
Wilson, Harrison 7, 54, *131*
Wilson, Lewis 4, 131
Wilson, Robert B. 16, *132*
Wilson, William T. 15
Wiltsee, John Fox 3, *132*
Wisner, Moses 140, 178, *179*
Wisner, Reuben P. 179
Wistar, Isaac J. 72
Withington, William H. 140
Wolff, Samuel M. 11, *133*
Wood, Charles H. 10, *133*
Wood, Oliver 7
Wood, Thomas J. 24
Woodbury, Dwight Avery 139, *179*
Woods, Charles R. 12
Woods, William B. 12
Wormer, Grover S. 141
Worthington, Thomas 9, *134*
Worthington, Thomas (Ohio Governor) 134
Wright, Crafts James 7, 134, *135*
Wright, George Bohan 14, *135*
Wright, Horatio G. 154
Wright, William B. 141, *180*

Yates, John Barentse 138, *180*
Yeoman, Samuel Nye 13, *136*
Yeoman, Stephen B. 136
Young, Thomas L. 15, *94*

Zahm, Lewis 3
Zeigler, John L. 183, 195

www.ingramcontent.com/pod-product-compliance
Lightning Source LLC
Chambersburg PA
CBHW081554300426
44116CB00015B/2875